The Decline

by Thomas Molnar

of the

Intellectual

Meridian Books   M128 $2.25

THE DECLINE OF THE INTELLECTUAL

Thomas Molnar

The
Decline
of the
Intellectual

Meridian Books

THE WORLD PUBLISHING COMPANY

Cleveland and New York

A MERIDIAN BOOK
Published by The World Publishing Company
2231 West 110th Street, Cleveland, Ohio 44102
First Meridian printing December 1961
Second printing June 1965
Library of Congress Catalog Card Number: 61-15749
Printed in the United States of America   2FD665

To the memory of my Mother

CONTENTS

ONE
The Emergence of the Intellectual 1

TWO
The Shaping of Ideologies 40

THREE
The Intellectual as a Marxist 72

FOUR
The Intellectual as a Progressive 116

FIVE
The Intellectual as a Reactionary 157

SIX
From Ideology to Social Engineering 199

SEVEN
Planetary Coexistence 223

EIGHT
Planetary Ideology 241

NINE
The American Intellectual 260

TEN
The European Intellectual 289

ELEVEN
Intellectual and Philosopher 319

Notes 351

Index 359

THE DECLINE OF THE INTELLECTUAL

1

The Emergence of the Intellectual

It is a hard task to put labels on historical periods, and even more risky to put into a meaningful formula the essence of the *Zeitgeist*. The longer the period to be embraced the less adequate is any brief description of it, since so many trends, factors, currents, and exceptions must be taken into consideration. When we come to the problem of defining a stretch of history like the Middle Ages or modern times, the difficulty of the historian or of the historian of culture is truly enormous. In fact, a somewhat acceptable solution may be offered only if we remain within the territory of generalities; yet these generalities are not so vague if we discover the underlying aspirations of peoples, nations, social classes, and elites—for then it will seem to us that history consists of a number of great *élans* toward the realization of certain goals, and that the distance or nearness of these goals at any particular time, as well as the impetus of the *élan*, give us a sufficiently good reading of the period in question.

Let me explain my meaning. What is the most significant feature of modern times, a feature already present in the late Middle Ages and grown truly overwhelming during the first half of the twentieth century? The answer to this question may be anything from the decline of the religious world view to the rise of science or the conquest of technology. Yet all three answers—and many other plausible ones—must be regarded, rather, as symptoms or instruments of change, not as the underlying, basic human substance. I propose, therefore, to identify this "human substance" as the immemorial aspiration of mankind, but suddenly given new and concrete forms, toward the triple aim of Peace, Unity, and Prosperity, and to *distinguish this age from any previous age by the fact that these goals had come within the sphere of possible achievement.* One might find, perhaps, other phenomena, embedded even deeper in the history of man, and which may be, for this reason, more explanatory of this stretch of history: for example, demographic or climatic changes, widespread epidemics, or the movements and migrations of masses. But on these issues our knowledge is fragmentary; besides, they are situated somewhere outside history (in the sense that they are outside human consciousness); we know that their influence is decisive, but we cannot reduce them to human dimensions.

On the contrary, what is so intriguing about these fundamental aspirations of mankind—whether of individuals or of societies—is that we know that they are always with us, in the minds and working hands of people, in the decisions of governments, the rebellions of masses, etc. This knowledge does not authorize us to expect history to be a so-called constructive enterprise, one impatient thrust in the direction of clearly envisaged goals; even if man did not carry the burden of original sin and thus cause good and evil with the same turn of the hand, mankind would still be faced with the diversity of views as to the best approach and the means to reach the end. What I find so fascinating, however, is that since the late Middle Ages the triple aspiration I have mentioned has received, for the first time in history, such concrete forms that the destiny of men has taken, as a result, a sharp turn toward rationality, predictability, and conscious planning. Only since that historical moment (which we call the Renaissance) have Peace, Unity, and Prosperity become not happy hazards, coincidences of favorable circumstances, fruits of conquest, or gifts of the gods, as in the past, but goals within the grasp of human minds and hands. Mastery over nature, the power of science, and large-scale organization for improvements of all sorts sprang then into existence, not, of course, as a *deus ex machina,* but nevertheless, in their totality, as a mighty transformation under the very eyes of the contemporaries.

The post-medieval world saw, then, the first conscious, purposeful, and efficient attempt to carry out the dreams of men in the direction indicated. Before examining at some length the conceptual world and the thinking of the representative minds of this period (from the fourteenth century to the end of the eighteenth), we may ask why it happened at that particular time and not earlier. One could, of course, answer this question by referring to the history of important inventions and their practical application at that moment: the invention of the harness, of linen, of gunpowder, of the magnetic needle, of printing, etc. Or one could mention the development of continental commerce, of market places, towns, and maritime leagues. But I prefer to formulate the question in a different way: what was the new factor that redirected the endeavors of men and began to pull together, like an invisible but immensely powerful hand, their manifold activities in view of the above-mentioned goals?

If we examine these goals, we find that all three are complex and partially overlapping notions, the respective elements of which fall under the categories of politics, economics, science, morals, law, religion, etc. For example, *peace* may be domestic or international; it raises problems dealt with by morals, natural and positive law, the churches, and ideologies—or interests determined, in their turn, by geography, history, the progress of military science, etc. And the same is true of the other concepts, *unity* and *prosperity.*

Now, politics, law, economics, and religion are as old as mankind, and they form a heritage common to us all, because the conceptual formulation and enrichment of each has been the work of individuals and communities, philosophers and rulers, sometimes known to us, sometimes anonymous, but at any rate, spread over the whole surface of the globe. No matter how many trends of thought have entered into these formulations and definitions, the important fact is that in their *public existence,* and therefore as history-shaping ideas, the concrete problems of peace, unity, and prosperity were decision-material only for rulers, governing classes, elites, clergy, and so on.

It is not my task to attempt a detailed analysis of why peace, unity, and prosperity do not seem to have been given more concrete and satisfactory forms during so much of history. Many theories have made an intellectual fortune for themselves by trying to explain the constant wars, fragmentation and enmity, and near-universal misery of most historical periods: Marxism; the British and French schools of political economists of the eighteenth century; the ideas of historians like Toynbee and Spengler; and, naturally, those of philosophers, churchmen, and statesmen. What interests me here is that such *was* the case, that much of political theory, philosophy, and literature (folk literature and other) has been a long cry of despair over the condition of man, the incurable ills of his private and public existence—or more concretely, over the interminable and cruel *wars,* the exactions of marauding troops, the general *insecurity* of peasants, merchants, artisans, and travelers, the *poverty* of pariahs, slaves, serfs, journeymen, and proletarians.

These problems—and these themes—are, of course, still with us; in fact, in the twentieth century they have received a new emphasis through the general preoccupation with the so-called underdeveloped countries, with widespread misery, persecution, deportation and displacement, genocide and ideological tyranny. Nor is it likely that these problems will ever disappear: on the contrary, they will reappear again and again, only under new and unexpected forms, generated by the new turns of progress. What was, however, peculiar to pre-Renaissance times was that these problems were present under their immemorial, ancestral aspects: the poverty of a medieval serf or the insecurity of a late-Roman farmer were of the same nature and degree as men have known practically since prehistoric times. And what was worse, there was no reliable sign on the horizon that conditions would ever change, except, at all times, for the talented or lucky individual.

The mentality that this situation created is reflected, as I have said, in literature and art and the various political theories, especially those that were more directly inspired by popular views. It is also reflected in religions and world views: the general and always latent dissatisfaction sought escape in the past, in a mythical state of happiness characterized mainly by the more down-to-earth forms of plenty. This does not mean to say that men do not have, at all times, reason to believe in an ideal existence; but it is worthy of note that so much of popular literature, like the medieval fabliaux, for example (whose line of descent is extremely long and can be traced to India), is obsessed by hunger, self-defense against the mighty, and the need to outsmart others because of lack of communal feeling and solidarity. What explains this obsession if not the basic aspiration for prosperity, peace, and unity?

Even when the escape is not in the direction of a mythical past, that is, in the case of a well-established and strong institution, a nation, for example, or the Church itself, we see merely a different way of conceiving an ideal age—in the past. The medieval Church and Empire, from Charlemagne to Pope Boniface VIII and the Habsburgs, looked to the unity of the Roman Empire, the *auctoritas* of the emperors, and to the universalism inherent in the Pax Romana as models of organization for the body politic. The same backward glance was cast by the French Revolution, by the Russian czars (who maintained that Muscovy was the "Third Rome"), and for that matter, by the Marxists themselves in their desire to prove the historical existence of a primitive communist society.

Thus, if not the reality, certainly the *ideal* of a world peaceful, prosperous, and united (that is, secure) existed, no doubt, throughout history, but especially since Roman-Christian times, when the public philosophy (Stoicism) and religion, for the first time emancipated from the tutelage of the body politic, lifted, so to speak, the three notions to a higher level, accessible if not to the ordinary mortal, at least to his consciousness. By recognizing in each human being the *person*, Christian religion and Greek philosophy made implicit the duty of every ruler to extend, henceforward, the concept of the common good to all his subjects, and conversely, they made it clear to these subjects that their freely given collaboration for the common good is one of its essential conditions. Thus the double concept of political duty and responsibility was born.

Now, the immense significance of the post-Renaissance age in this respect is that for the first time, gradually and systematically, science, economic science, and finally, politics—later religion and morals too—were taken out of the hands of the privileged classes and put into the hands of a wider body, consisting of the bourgeois, the scientists, the lay administrators, civil servants, the scholars and experts. I will indicate on the following pages some of the important landmarks of this new development (the origin of which goes back to the appearance of the first *legists* —experts of Roman law versus ecclesiastical law—of the French kings, and of the University of Bologna), but its tremendous importance may be measured here in a few words.

With the Renaissance, peace, unity, and prosperity ceased to be mere symbols of a never-never land; they became imperative material preconditions of the bourgeois organization of production, transportation, commerce— and hence of public safety, rule of law, guarantees of international exchange. In this task the role of scientists, scholars, career servants, etc., is easy to sketch. If we call them by one collective name, *intellectuals,* we come closer to understanding the nature of their function and importance, and also the nature of their alliance with the merchant, the speculator, the shipowner, the entrepreneur; with some, perhaps excusable, generalization—to be elaborated upon later—we may say then that the intellectual appeared as the man possessing the knowledge, the culture, and the special terminology indispensable for the middle classes in their revolutionary breakthrough of the walls of traditional society and world view. In different domains, both intellectuals and the bourgeois class were working for the enlargement of the political, economic, and intellectual horizon, and against the restrictive authority of feudal society and the Church.

What then was the decisive transformation around 1500, the new factor that redirected the endeavor of men? Again, briefly: the *redistribution of power* among the members of a class larger than ever before, the *application of scientific thinking* and *organizational skill* to problems that had seemed insoluble or subject to empirical methods only, and to the possibility, based on rational foresight and calculation, of bringing the great dreams of mankind within the scope of history.

But this was not all; there was another important requirement, implicit in the other three, which was seen and understood by the best minds: it is true, as we have said, that peace, unity, and prosperity had never materialized in any part of the world except for short periods, when they benefited only a minority and were, in general, threatened from all sides. Yet, as ideals, they were extraordinarily powerful, and, as ideals, they were built into every social, political, philosophical, and religious system. They were part of the cement that held together any edifice consisting of human beings.

It was thus understood by the post-Renaissance man, indeed by those who had helped prepare the Renaissance, that in the coming world—and world view—the centrifugal forces would, eventually, put such a stress on society, the body politic, the Church, that the traditional and imperfect unity, security, and peace might give way, without anything to replace them. Thus we see the division of the modern mind—and a fascinating division it is!—between *optimism* in building the free community of emancipated individuals, and the *concern* that something new—and better—should be found in lieu of the traditional order; a new cohesion, a new unity, morality, religion, among men. Since this concern was inherited from the Church (its more antique sources were Plato and the Roman Empire), it never managed to get rid of its religious undertone; thus the post-Renaissance—and contemporary—ideologies that are expressions, in their own different ways, of this ultimate concern with the peace, unity, and prosperity of mankind carry in themselves the seeds of the religious preoccupation.

I shall now try to give a working definition of the "intellectual." As the term itself is hardly a century old, we must begin by some contemporary comments. André Malraux defines the intellectual as a man whose life is guided by devotion to an idea; Peter Viereck holds that he is a "full-time servant of the Word, or of the word," that is, a kind of priest either of a lofty ideal, or of literary, artistic, philosophical, pursuits. On the other hand, during the Dreyfus case in France, the right-wing nationalist Maurice Barrès referred with contempt to the "intellectuals," meaning pen pushers and leftist ideologues, in the camp of Dreyfus's partisans. In 1927, again in France, Julien Benda reproached his fellow *clercs* for taking a part in the commotions of the political community, thus betraying their vocation as guardians of culture. Twenty years later, Jean-Paul Sartre, on the contrary, wanted to involve them in the struggles of politics and the building of a new society. And, finally, Russell Kirk, the philosopher of American neoconservatism, rejects the term "intellectual" as alien to the spirit of the English language (when used as a noun) and to American political tradition, and as having an uncomfortable, ideological connotation.

Among so many authoritative but contradictory interpretations of the meaning and role of the intellectual, we must nevertheless decide in what sense we are going to use the term on these pages.

Is the Socratic demand regarding the necessity of the "examined life" sufficient to characterize the intellectual? If this were the case, the intellectual would simply be the *philosopher*, the lover of wisdom, in the pursuit of which he acquires distinction. Also in this sense, it would be difficult to separate the intellectual from the *scholar*, the *scientist*, the *researcher*. Yet one feels that the intellectual, while he may well be a philosopher, a scientist, or a scholar, or for that matter, a diplomat, a writer, an artist, is not exactly any of these. Rather, it is clear that he puts his mental ability, education, articulateness, and experience to some political or social use, that he is not satisfied, ultimately, with *interpreting* the events—of economic, social, political nature—around himself, but is trying to *influence* and *transform* them. He thus combines theory and praxis, and is likely to formulate an ideology or to adhere to one.

During the Middle Ages there was no scarcity of "intellectuals." From Abélard to Roger Bacon, men of powerful mind set out by themselves, seeking not only new approaches to the truths held by the Church but also roads that led in directions not approved by her. It is not an exaggeration to say that a definite growth in independent thinking—and consequent clashes with orthodoxy—took place when, from about 1350 on, the Church began to freeze in an attitude of intolerance before the threat of the growing power of the cities and of the merchant class. After the fourteenth century the Church had no men to serve her greatness and glory who could compare with a Saint Bernard, a Saint Dominic, a Thomas Aquinas. William of Occam belongs practically to a later age, and the heretics and would-be reformers, the Wycliffs and the Husses are forerunners of forces—social and national— for which the Church had no room in her system.

Yet these men and others like them can be called intellectuals only if we put this term between quotation marks. An intellectual cannot be measured by his mental powers, insights, and creativity alone. It is, rather, the social milieu of which he is a part, and the nature of his relationship to this milieu, that determine his role and status as an intellectual. In order to speak of "intellectuals," therefore, those who belong to this category must possess some degree of common consciousness of their role, their place in society, their relationship to those who are in power and to those who seek it. In short, the intellectuals form a *class* not by virtue of their organization, but to the extent that they have similar aspirations and influence, and a chance to be heard.

Now, in order for the intellectuals to constitute such a "class," they must live in a society that is itself divided into classes. If social cohesion in any given community far outweighs in importance the forces of division, or if society constitutes one monolithic block held together by an all-powerful cadre of leaders regarded as quasi-divine, either the intellectual must vegetate on the fringes of the social body, or else he is compelled to lend his services to the ruling elite.

It is thus evident that unless we risk getting lost semantically in a number of possible meanings, we must define the social significance of the intellectual in terms of his freedom of expression, influence on various segments of society, participation in social change, and the resulting prestige for himself and for the values he holds.

For this reason we may not speak of "intellectuals" in the early Middle Ages (until the twelfth century), and can hardly speak of them in any previous age. As a matter of fact, it is best to restrict the use of the term to about six centuries, that is, from the 1300's until the middle of the present century. It is between these two approximate dates that we may situate the intellectuals as a class constantly gaining in power and influence; before 1300 medieval society was not only strictly organized under the discipline of faith and hierarchy, but—more important still—it was believed to reproduce in the sublunar sphere the eternal order of the universe.• While peasant uprisings, bloody *Jacqueries,* and fierce battles between city proletariat and city fathers were common occurrences, opposition to the established order did not assume philosophical dimensions. Although popular fables and anonymous satires do testify to the deep discontent of the lower classes, only few questioned the very bases of the social order, and even fewer proposed a new one to take its place.••

But if the social order was not questioned as such, fundamental changes were prepared on the level of theoretical politics, grown out of the medieval controversy between papacy and Empire. The conflict itself interests us here only as an issue in consideration of which various political and philosophical concepts received articulate formulation.

The heart of the issue, beyond the dispute over investiture, was the concept of Christian unity. This involved, first of all, the problem of papal supremacy versus condominium with the Emperor as the foremost secular ruler (the doctrine of the two swords); the origin of the latter's authority; the divided allegiance of men as Christians and citizens (vassals); the double function of those who were secular lords and holders of ecclesiastical offices at the same time, etc. Beyond these questions, which were concrete enough to preoccupy medieval public opinion for several centuries, there loomed the momentous issue of the *Respublica Christiana.*

Medieval man was profoundly attached to the idea of unity and believed that it was inscribed in the very nature of things. The commonwealth could function only if its

---

• "As a whole and in each of its parts the world was the portrait of God; that is, the rank and excellence of every created being was determined by the degree to which it bore within itself the stamp of God's Image. A vast hierarchy of being—the non-living, the plants and the animals—was formed by the inter-relations of the many things found in these realms of essence." Romano Guardni, *The End of the Modern World* (New York: Sheed & Ward, 1956), p. 29.

•• Most of the criticism is not original but goes back for ideas to antiquity. What may be considered medieval contribution is a matter of form: allegory, as in the case of the second part of the *Roman de la Rose,* by Jean de Meung.

normal diversity was pulled together by a unifying principle, on the model of the human body, whose various functions are controlled by the head.[1] The theme of the human body recurs in the writings of almost all theologians and philosophers when they concern themselves with the political community, the common good, the just distribution of social activities, and the hierarchical structure of society. Thus it was not indifferent whether the Christian nations were fragmented to the point of constant hostility, whether they were united with regard to faith and morals, and consequently, whether they recognized the supreme authority of the Pope or the *political* and eventually *moral* independence of the Emperor and kings.

Let us repeat once more: the controversy was relevant to the whole sphere of medieval life because it raised the question of who should organize the *Civitas Terrana* in all its aspects; and whether the latter was an entity in its own right or a preparation for the *Civitas Dei*. If Jesus Christ entrusted Peter with the keys of the Heavenly Kingdom, did this mean also that, since all Christians aspire to enter there, Peter's descendants, the popes, had implicitly the right to judge and depose rulers who endangered their subjects' salvation? Or did Peter's authority stop at the gates of heaven, and was it the ruler's prerogative, inherited from Saul and David, to receive his power directly from God?• But then: did Jesus not add that whatever the Prince of the Apostles joined together or set apart shall be joined together or set apart in heaven also? Did this power or did it not include the temporal sphere too?

In addition to references to Old and New Testament, the heritage of the Roman Empire also complicated the problem. In both theory and practice the Christian teaching accommodated itself quite well to the existence of "two powers," because it was beyond dispute that ultimately both the ecclesiastical and the secular power agreed on the same goal, namely, that of authority established for the

• In the judgment of the Pope's partisans, the Pope possessed both swords, and only the fallen nature of man was incarnated in the imperium (imperial authority). The Emperor's power, they argued, was thus derived from the sacerdotium (papal authority).

rule of morality. This point was made clear as early as 800. Furthermore, it also followed from Catholic doctrine that secular rule, like the existence of the human body, is not an evil (as it is according to Manichaeism) but a reality in its own right, created and blessed by God. Already the Christians of the first centuries "asserted that while the Church must remain entirely distinct from all temporal institutions, its members were obliged to submit to secular [in their case, pagan] authority because it was established by God and was, although unknown to itself, in His service." [2] The fact that the secular authority of the time we are discussing was itself Christian certainly complicated matters, because now the ruler himself was no longer pagan but a Christian, subordinated in his conscience to the Pope's moral authority. Yet the Church's attitude toward secular power *in se* remained that of acceptance. Even Gregory VII, who was most tempted to crush the Emperor's power, limited himself to saying that "the imperial or royal function is very difficult to fulfill . . . [that] it leads naturally to guilty ambitions . . . [and that] kings often forget the principle . . . according to which the goal of temporal power is to serve the Christian cause." •

Now the intervention of legal concepts, inherited from Roman law, had as a clear-cut consequence the upsetting of the medieval Christian political equilibrium. The legists themselves were in the employ of kings, especially of the kings of France, and became instruments of royal policy. Their significance may be stated in a few words: they introduced, or rather, reintroduced, the concept of the Roman *auctoritas*, which, with a series of other titles that Augustus had already assumed—tribune, pontifex maximus, imperator, etc.—guaranteed its holder an absolute

---

• Marcel Pacaut, *La Théocratie* (Aubier, 1957), pp. 86-7.

It was Saint Thomas who finally settled Church teaching in this matter; the moral order, Thomas maintained, is a human order and can be brought about by the free co-operation of men. The State is not an evil (as Augustine was inclined to hold), and is not merely an institution appointed by God as a remedy for human sinfulness. It originates in the social instinct of man and must be regarded as an instrument for building an order of right and justice.

rule, certainly in the political, but also in the quasi-religious sphere.

The revolutionary innovation of the King's lawyers contributed decisively to a development that had been on the way for some time, that is, the recognition of the imperial (secular) power as depending on God alone, without the intermediary of the Pope. This much was stated already at the end of the twelfth century, by Simon de Bisignano. From then on, Christian unity, in theory and in practice, may be considered as mortally wounded; first, because the Emperor was finally recognized as equal to the Pope, if not in the "essence and dignity" of his office, at least in the autonomy of his power; second, because the imperial power itself declined amidst dynastic troubles in Germany, and the papacy, also considerably weakened by the captivity at Avignon, was now facing the rise of vigorous, and from a religious point of view, quasi-independent nation-states.

This, however, did not take place in one day. The traditional world view was strong enough to resist within the soul and the conceptual universe of the very men who now attacked it. Thus the fourteenth and fifteenth centuries were to be the stage of a conflict more decisive and critical than the struggle of the investiture, which had been fought, after all, within the same mental framework and with identical verbal weapons. Now not only was the intellectual background of the participants wider—it was clearly the Renaissance—but the external circumstances too were in a state of growing fermentation. The outstanding men who devoted themselves to the theoretical disquisition of the political problem were accordingly divided in their minds. They were sufficiently "medieval" to advocate that the unity of the human race imposes the need of one government over it; they considered the conflict between Church and State an anomaly, and refused, as Otto Gierke points out, to accept the dualism as final. On the other hand, a Marsilius of Padua and a William of Occam were "modern" thinkers insofar as many of their ideas foreshadowed not only the Reformation, but even the English and French revolutions.

This is, of course, not quite so paradoxical as it seems. These thinkers, while they drew the necessary conclusions from the events and transformations that took place under their eyes, while they even contributed to these transformations, nevertheless bemoaned the lost unity of Christendom from a religious, moral, and political point of view. Only, there was this difference between them (in the fourteenth century) and the eleventh- and twelfth-century school of thought known as the "Gregorian"; they were quite willing to interpret God's command that there be a universal monarchy as a justification of the secular power in the form of a universal imperial authority. In other words, hardly was the idea of a *Respublica Christiana*, in its papacy-dominated form, irretrievably lost, than these men sought to re-establish it with its gravitational center shifted from the theocratic model to the secular-monarchical one.

Italians were in the forefront of this movement, since they had firsthand experience of the Pope's temporal rule and saw in it the source of the peninsula's political fragmentation. Dante's monarchical preferences are well known, and the already mentioned Simon de Bisignano did not hesitate to proclaim that in the temporal order the Emperor is greater than the Pope. But the most audacious thinker of this period of transition was certainly Marsilius of Padua, in the first half of the fourteenth century. His political treatise, the *Defensor Pacis*, aimed at establishing more than the independence of the State from ecclesiastical rule; it clearly enunciated the State's superiority and even its monopoly of power. Marsilius no longer mentions the moral nature of the State as it had been maintained for centuries; the State comes into existence because people need each other, and on account of the diversity of their interests, they need an arbitrator. Hence not God, but the people is the source of the power exercised by the ruler.

What about religion and spiritual life? Here too, the State has an important role to play, but not as a guide to moral life. Marsilius rejects the concept, drawn from the history of the Jewish kingdom, according to which the monarch is appointed by God to enforce the nation's respect for divine law; in Marsilius's quite modern interpretation, religion is the citizen's private affair, and the State intervenes merely to guarantee public tranquility within which the individual may be free to worship.

But the State must be, after all, more active than that,

for it does not find, facing it, a Church with a divinely constituted hierarchy. The Church, indeed, is only an assembly of the faithful, proposing candidates to priesthood, but accepting that the State should actually induct them into office. Since the Pope has no more authority than any other priest, logically all matters affecting the Church are initiated and discussed by a council. At this point, however, Marsilius realized that if not the papacy, then the council may rise as a dangerous competitor for the State; in order to secure the latter's complete domination, he placed the council too under the control of the State, which would decide its convocation and would execute its decisions.

A number of theories that were to make their fortunes later find in the *Defensor Pacis* their first articulation in Christendom. While the doctrine of conciliar supremacy—so important in the early part of the fifteenth century—found a serious advocate in Marsilius of Padua, the basic ideas of the Reformation, the contract theory of society, royal absolutism, and even the kind of totalitarian democracy we know today are also broached in the book. It is interesting to note that a generation earlier Dante had opposed the temporal ambition of the Popes on the ground (as we read in the *Purgatorio*) that if the two powers are combined, "one no longer fears the other": the healthy dualism of the commonwealth still represented, for Dante, a system we would call today one of "checks and balances." It was different with the fourteenth-century scholar: he was ready, like the later reformers, to deprive the Church not only of temporal power but of any organizational independence as well. But by limiting the religious sphere to the individual conscience, he had to allow the State to invade the domain of public philosophy and even to rule there absolutely. The anticlericals and secularists of later centuries could contribute no really original argument to what Marsilius of Padua had so carefully put forward.

If the political ideas of William of Occam were even more influential, it is because he was, in addition, a great and respected philosopher. Otherwise, he only completed the edifice raised by the Italian. His own popularity may be explained by his insistence on the authority of councils and by the corresponding view that the ecclesiastical hierarchy, including the Pope, is merely the council's executive organ. All this, within the framework of the Empire—the ruler of which is elected by the hereditary princes—that is, in the view of the age, democratically.

We see, then, that in the arguments expressed by these late-medieval political theories, with every diminution of papal and conciliar power, that of the temporal ruler was growing. The *Pope's* authority was found to be fictitious, usurpatory, or exaggerated; it was left undecided whether the *council* itself should consist of the princes of the Church or include—like a popular assembly—all the faithful on some representational basis; at any rate, its activities would be controlled from the moment of convocation to that when its decisions were applied, by State officials; at the same time, the supremacy of the *temporal ruler* was not only recognized but also found to be rooted in popular will and democratic election. Thus, politically, the Middle Ages came to an end because, as Cassirer put it, "in spite of its great ethical task, the State could never be regarded [in the Middle Ages] as an absolute good." [3]

Is it then surprising that the next step was relatively easy to take? When Machiavelli declared that the Prince is independent not only of the Pope but for the sake of the State's interest, of the rule of Christian morals as well, the last remnant of the medieval equilibrium was shoved aside. "During the Middle Ages," writes Otto Gierke, "we can hardly detect even the beginnings of that opinion which would free the Sovereign (whenever he is acting in the interest of the public weal) from the bonds of the Moral Law and therefore from the bonds of the Law of Nature. Therefore when Machiavelli based his lesson for princes upon the freedom from restraint, this seemed to the men of his time an unheard of innovation and also a monstrous crime." [4]

The significance of Machiavelli's "innovation" (we have seen its first timid roots in Marsilius) was more than what is obvious, namely, the elevation of the *raison d'état* to the pedestal of a jealous, intolerant governing principle. Machiavellism was also the most definitive expression (for the Middle Ages) of the trend toward weakening and abolishing the intermediate bodies between the individual citizen and the ruler of the State. The two models that helped the medieval theorists visualize society and the body politic were the human body and the macrocosm, that is, the total order of the universe. In a society constructed according to these models all parts are equally necessary, as was demonstrated by the Roman legend of Menenius Agrippa, who persuaded the rebellious plebs to return to Rome. The feudal system itself was a political expression of this concept, the wisdom of which, among other things, consisted in setting up innumerable buffer zones between individual and State power, and between smaller power-focuses. Already in medieval theory there was a trend, however, that, according to Gierke, stressed the "concentration of right and power in the highest group, on the one hand, and in the individual man, on the other, at the cost of all intermediate groups. The Sovereignty of the State and the sovereignty of the Individual . . . [became] the two central axioms." [5]

It is evident that Machiavelli's doctrine was hostile to the medieval theory of communities because such a theory would only obstruct the ruler's policies. On the other hand, the spirit of the late *quattrocento*, which permeates the Florentine's writings, reflected an extraordinarily individualistic, asocial age, partly because age-old institutions exploded under the pressure of religious innovations, geographical discoveries, new techniques, etc. The State emerged as the only power strong enough to afford a costly, artillery-equipped, permanent army, to organize the growing overseas trade, and to enforce religious unity, a condition of loyal citizenship.

In this way, Marsilius of Padua, William of Occam, and Machiavelli were forerunners of a new spirit, and also the heralds of new conditions and a new world view. They were aware, perhaps only dimly, that man's place in the universe was changing, and that this change in the order of realities would necessitate a transformation in the order of values as well. It was, for instance, characteristic of this feeling that in *The Discourses* Machiavelli took it for granted that religion should be subordinated to the purposes of the State, and in order to give this requirement an unequivocal emphasis, recommended that this religion be chosen not for its supernatural validity but for its power as a myth and for its value as a cohesive force.•

In fact, from the very beginning of modern times, this—the formulation of a new political myth and unifying doctrine—became increasingly important, without, however, assuming the urgency and dynamism of later ideologies. Ernst Cassirer remarks that, as in the Middle Ages, so in the early part of modern times there was a correspondence between theories of cosmology and of politics, the order of the universe and the order of human existence as conceived by theologians, astrologers, philosophers. The medieval version of this thought came to an end with the beginnings of modern astronomical science, prefigured in the teaching of a Giordano Bruno, for example. But Galileo could be more explicit: in his *Dialogues Concerning Two New Sciences* it is stated that he had discovered new aspects of a "very ancient subject," and "new properties which had not been either observed or demonstrated." The same thing was true in the field of political theory, and Machiavelli applied "Galilean" principles to the study of political movements. But, as I have noted before, although he was no enemy of religion, the Florentine diplomat preferred to adopt, for his State, the religion that was most likely to promote civic virtues. Christianity, with its dual allegiance to God and Caesar, was obviously inadequate; on the contrary, pagan, or rather, the Roman religion served the purpose much better since it glorified the virtue of great commanders and statesmen and was useful in all matters in which the State had to prove its strength in action, deliberation, and maintenance of order.

Machiavelli's exposé of the most efficient methods of

• "It is the duty of princes and heads of republics to uphold the foundations of the religion of their countries, for then it is easy to keep their people religious, and consequently well conducted and united. And therefore everything that tends to favor religion (even though it were believed to be false) should be received and availed of to strengthen it; and this should be done the more, the wiser the rulers are, and the better they understand the natural course of things. Such was, in fact, the practice observed by sagacious men; which has given rise to the belief in the miracles that are celebrated in religions, however false they may be." N. Machiavelli, *The Prince, and The Discourses* (New York: Modern Library, 1940), p. 150.

statecraft was explosive and shocking. But, after all, he only put on paper what had always been, to a greater or lesser extent, the practice of rulers and governments, and his originality consisted, perhaps, in his neglecting, for the first time in Christendom, to affirm the ultimately moral nature of the political phenomenon. But the rapport among nations, people, and institutions did not change with the same speed and irreversibility as the data of physical and astronomical sciences. The Machiavellian revolution did not seem so overwhelming as the Galilean discoveries. The great receptacle within which political and social life was unrolling itself, the State, remained essentially the same, and its constituent bodies, institutions, and the routine of its administrators and citizens were, as is always the case, powerful obstacles in the way of radical change. Even after Machiavelli almost nobody questioned the intimate bond between the Christian religion (religions) and the State, and if, as Cassirer says, "in his [Machiavelli's] theory all the previous theocratic ideas are eradicated root and branch," [6] it is nonetheless true that the absolute monarchs of the seventeenth century were to give new vigor to these ideas.

Thus the post-Renaissance political edifice, that is, the nation-state, inherited most of its concepts from earlier times, and there was no evident and immediate need for a new "public philosophy" to take the place of Christian notions and standards of behavior. This is not to say that such a new public philosophy was not in the making in the minds of certain individuals, political theorists and others, standing at the crossroads of change. But we must wait until social pressure, under the impact of economic realities and humanist-inspired emancipation, fills the just-analyzed political theories with content and supplies them with concrete issues; only then will ideological forces be set into motion and the crisis of modern times appear in its true dimensions.

Inasmuch as we begin the history of modern times with the conventionally accepted triple date of Renaissance, Reformation, and the Voyages of Discovery, we meet, for the first time in the annals of Europe, men whose ideas and ideals could no longer be contained in the traditional receptacles of ecclesiastic and feudal institutions. The man of ideas found all of a sudden that powerful social and economic forces set themselves up outside and in opposition to the Church and the society it had organized; as a result, previously hidden thoughts were beginning to appear and to be carried by the waves of popularity. It is true that only a few meant to profit by the developing freedom in order to bring down the social order and destroy the religious unity of Europe. Some of the best minds, among them the prince of the humanists, Erasmus, refused to make common cause with the Reformation, much less with free thinking.• But it was impossible for them—the humanists, the printers, the itinerant scholars and students, the political commentators, etc.—not to see that in the future their speculations might have widespread, in fact, incalculable, *social consequences,* and that a new social class was emerging which was interested in, and vitally concerned with, the ideas they propounded.

The intellectuals, then, are products of the Renaissance period. They became a *type* when the bourgeoisie as a class got ready to enter political life actively, and when, conjointly, science became a serious organizing factor of progress. The moment of the intellectuals' appearance thus coincided with the initial stages of the transformation of Utopia into reality; in accomplishing this transformation, their role was as decisive as that of the middle classes themselves.

Only when medieval society began to disintegrate, and the nobility to receive the first blows as the result of a serious dip in land values and of the shift from rural to money economy, do we see a corresponding increase in the importance of the intellectual class.

"Classes," Professor Georges Gurvitch explains, "are

• This is how Huizinga characterizes Erasmus and his fellow humanists living in this critical period: "As an intellectual type Erasmus was one of a rather small group: the absolute idealists who, at the same time, are thoroughly moderate. They cannot bear the world's imperfections; they feel constrained to oppose. But extremes are uncongenial to them; they shrink back from action, because they know it pulls down as much as it erects, and so they withdraw themselves and keep calling that everything should be different; but when the crisis comes, they reluctantly side with tradition and conservatism." *Erasmus of Rotterdam* (New York: Phaidon Publishers, 1952), p. 190.

particular groups of vast dimension. . . . Their resistance
to penetration by the rest of society, their mutual incompatibility with other classes, and their highly developed
structuralization imply a collective consciousness and specific cultural achievements." [7] This description of a social
class indicates two important features: first, that classes
are powerful particularistic groups, existing as parts of the
global society, yet in many respects independent of it;
and second, that the ideology they develop is a partial
truth, a subjective interpretation, or, as Professor Gurvitch
writes, "an essentially political way of apprehending
reality, the most partisan of any type of knowledge." •

The appearance of strongly organized classes—and the
phenomenal growth of one of them, the bourgeoisie—
represented nothing less than a scandal in the midst of
the *Respublica Christiana*. For one thing, the Church's
long-standing suspicion of the commercial-industrial classes,
its repeated warnings against profit and usury, received a
dramatic justification in retrospect. For another thing, the
concept according to which the new spirit intended to
organize society was in deep contradiction with the Platonic ideal of social justice, expressed in *The Republic*,
and accepted by Catholic philosophy. No matter what the
real situation had been, was medieval society not conceived,
in theory and in essence, as a family, or, as we have seen,
as the human body in which all parts, equally dear in the
eyes of God, labored for His glory as the hands, the feet,
and the head of a corporate being?

This situation, and the feeling of unity it had produced,
was now vanishing. Many writers date the so-called atomization of society from the Renaissance: the isolation of the
individual from the smaller groups of which he may be
an active member, and his sudden facing of the terrifying
countenance of the State machine, with which he has no
existential bond, but which dominates him nevertheless.
Also, to use Romano Guardini's expressions, from a "servant of Creation"—as medieval man used to be—he be-

---

• "An ideology is not a scientific theory. . . . It is the expression
of hopes, wishes, fears, ideals, not a hypothesis about events."
James Burnham, *Managerial Revolution*, p. 25. "Une idéologie
est une croyance populaire orientée vers un idéal socio-poli-
tique." Jean Furstenberg, *Dialectique du vingtième siècle*.

came, with every new discovery and invention, a "master of nature," yet divided between the exaltation that surged up in him before the increasing awareness of his power, and his anguish before the abyss of infinity that this same power made suddenly visible. Moreover, both Protestantism and post-Tridentine Catholicism distorted to some extent man's original view of himself in relationship to God, because they made him conscious of the burden of faith. Did not even the greatest religious genius of the "Catholic" century (the seventeenth) propose a wager on God's existence as a sort of last argument to accept this burden?

One may say that for three centuries, between the Reformation and the French Revolution, the most important thinkers sought to solve the problems opened by the *spiritual and social fragmentation* of Christendom. It began to dawn upon the best of them that there was a rapport between the two, that, first, the individual is not an entirely self-sustaining and self-protecting unit, but needs organization and protection; and second, that society and the body politic must be more than a meeting point of interests if membership in them is to have a meaning.• These issues were brought into evidence by the fact that there were now two focuses of power, no longer the Pope and the Emperor, but the *monarch* and the *middle class*, that is, the representative of the principle of State and the representatives of the principle of individualism. Their struggle filled the history of three centuries, and since it was such a protracted one and fought in broad daylight, it was believed by almost everybody that the victory of the middle class—complete victory or some compromise—would solve the deeper issues mentioned above. Did the bourgeoisie not have the interests of the individual, that is, of the ultimate human reality, at heart?

An additional factor must be mentioned, one that further sharpened the opposition between king and bourgeoisie, or at least, the most dynamic elements of the latter. The

• This was, of course, the pivotal point of Plato's theory of the State too, namely, that private and public life cannot develop separately, and that the ethical life of men is dependent on the right political order. The latter constitutes the "soul" of the State, its basic principle, which cannot be left to chance but must be sought through rational thinking.

Reformation, which in Germany contributed to strengthen the local power of kings and princes, in France resulted in a bitter civil war foreshadowing the Thirty Years' War fought on German soil. The French Protestants, alienated from their king, began to look at royal power as usurpatory, and to proclaim that sovereignty belonged to the people (Languet and Duplessis-Mornay, *Vindiciae contra tyrannos*). However, as a result of national reconciliation effected by Henry IV, these early democratic ideas had no further sequels in France. But, as G. P. Gooch pointed out in his well-known study, in England—imported via the Netherlands, where the Huguenots had spread them— they were at the origin of such parties as the Levellers, the Communists, and other utopians. The members of all these sects insisted, in one form or another, on refuting the monarchical doctrine and on placing the government "under Christ," that is, in their interpretation, under the democratic rule of all believers. As one of them, Rutherford, wrote in *Lex Rex*, all jurisdiction of man over man is artificial; the king is merely party to a contract and remains subordinated to the people.

What was the ambition of the bourgeoisie, and in what situation did it find itself at the beginning of modern times? The nobility as a powerful and influential class was irreversibly declining. In their financial and political transactions the kings were dealing with the bourgeois, thereby allowing the latter to enter the life of the State through a back door. The bourgeoisie, however, except for such short periods as the Cromwellian Protectorate, did not aspire to political rule; it was too busy expanding its commerce, securing its trade routes, accumulating and investing its capital. It expected the monarch to rule, to organize justice and the police, to hold in check the still voracious appetites of feudal lords, but otherwise not to interfere with business activity. Thus the new class and its economic interests exerted a powerful pressure in favor of modifying the whole concept of the State, of legislation, and of the respective positions of king and subjects. In the second half of the sixteenth century Jean Bodin conceived of royal power as almost tyrannical when dealing with legislation abolishing the medieval obstacles rooted in tradition, privileges, and custom, but severely circum-

scribed and controlled by law when the issue was interference with the rights of private property.

In the next two centuries this trend gained immense
momentum, until it transformed, from within, the conceptual framework of society and the very meaning of the
body politic. The arena of political life was slowly evacu-
ated, until only the two champions, king and middle class,
remained face to face. "There was no middle ground
between humanity as a sandheap of separate organisms and
the State as an outside power holding them precariously
together. . . . All the rich variety of associations disappeared." [8] The par excellence philosopher of this "sandheap of separate organisms" was Hobbes. It has been
pointed out by various scholars that in order to understand the *Leviathan* correctly one must read it backwards,
so to speak: although Hobbes begins with a philosophical-
psychological description of man, and pretends to deduce
from it the nature of the State, in reality it is the latter
that interested him, and he characterized the individual
so as to fit his political analysis.

What these individuals, natural enemies of each other,
seek is a state of security. They find it under the absolute
power of the State: "If a covenant be made wherein neither
of the parties perform presently, but trust one another, in
the condition of mere nature . . . it is void; but if there
be a common power set over them both with right and
force sufficient to compel performance, it is not void." [9]
That this "compelling" State is tyrannical, Hobbes did not
deny, for he equated tyranny with sovereignty.

Hannah Arendt has called Hobbes the "true philosopher
of the bourgeoisie," who understood that "the acquisition
of wealth [which defines that class] conceived as a never-
ending process can be guaranteed only by the seizure of
political power." [10] In this, Hobbes proved to be more
farseeing than the members of the bourgeoisie who, until
the eighteenth century, were far more interested in the
pursuit of private enrichment than in laying their hands
on the mechanism of the State. In fact, this individualism,
raised to the level of a virtue, contrasted well with the coercive machine of the State and the collectively voiced
complaints of the nobles over their loss of privileges. It
became the paramount feature of the ideal man as painted

by the seventeenth-century moralists and by the eighteenth-century *philosophes*.

The situation mirrored and dramatized in the *Leviathan* represented a kind of equilibrium, expressed, for example, in the English Restoration, in the French "classical age," in the Cartesian spirit, in Jesuit influence. It came to a crashing end with the death of Louis XIV, in 1715, which opened the door wide to bourgeois ambitions, this time in their unlimited form. The truth is that the absolutism of monarchical administration (which was a centralizing trend under bourgeois pressure and royal interest) was only acceptable to the middle class until its own economic power became unassailable. Around 1700 the philosophers and other spokesmen of the bourgeoisie denounced the equilibrium between royal power and commercial interest as precarious; later in the century Turgot, one of Louis XVI's finance ministers in the period of crisis, treated as an "illusion" the view that it was possible to protect simultaneously the country's economic interests and the cause of the monarchy.

It is thus the middle class that first abandoned the traditional alliance with the king. Threatened from all sides, the French administration attempted to introduce, at the middle of the eighteenth century, a general direct taxation. But the middle class understood that this desperate, although completely fair and logical, measure would enable the State to tax property and capital; rather than contribute its share, the bourgeoisie as a class "managed to divert the blow by directing it against the clergy." 11

That this diversionary move was successful, and that it paralyzed financial reform until it was too late, was, no doubt, due to the tremendous economic power accumulated in the hands of manufacturers, shipowners, and landed proprietors. But the fact that it was so easy to point at the clergy as the scapegoat, and thereby to block any step in the right direction, was the work of the intellectuals. For decades, then, Voltaire had been attacking the Church and the principle of ecclesiastical ownership not only by showing, through historical references, the invalidity of donations that had benefited the Church, but also by questioning the dogmas themselves. Voltaire's writings, Charles Morazé remarks, "represent the battle of a class." There is no doubt that these writings contributed to the crystallization of public opinion, which saw the confiscation of church property as a salutary measure because it would safeguard the property of the bourgeoisie.

From the middle of the eighteenth century the intellectuals supported the middle class without any reservations and in proportion to the prestige and influence they gained by their heavy artillery attacks on the monarchy, the Church, and the totality of the traditional institutions. This prestige was such that the court, the ministers, the police, and the censors were collectively powerless against it, against the international reputation and support enjoyed by the Voltaires, the Rousseaus, the Diderots. As a matter of fact, not only did the latter have friends and protectors among the most highly placed at court, but the government itself, half agreeing with its relentless critics, encouraged the writers by suggesting ways of eluding censorship. Their works were thus printed on the other side of the border, mainly in tolerant Holland, and were then smuggled in, practically with the connivance of the French authorities. Although there was very little risk involved in these operations, the writers and philosophers easily acquired the popularity of martyrs and the glory bestowed by the opinion-shaping salons. When, for example, in 1759 the sophisticated society of Paris was excitedly watching the quarrel that set Rousseau against Diderot, the Marquis de Castries indignantly remarked: "It is incredible. People do not talk of anything but of those fellows. Persons without an establishment, who do not have a house, who are lodged in a garret. One just cannot get used to all that."

Indeed, it seems that everything favored the development and flowering of the middle classes. Science in the first place. The discoveries of Kepler, Galileo, Newton, the mathematical calculations that assisted engineering, had, of course, their primary, scientific, importance. But two remarks must be made about their political and social significance in general.

The first is that the scientists themselves, like the humanists, their predecessors, possessed an exalted notion of their activity as helping the deeper penetration of nature and thereby of the secret of creation and of God.

For the medieval mind, the study of nature had been "the repetition of the sin of Adam, a compact with the devil";[12] in the seventeenth century, Sir Thomas Browne calls nature a second Scripture: "There are two Books," he says, "from whence I collect my Divinity: that written by God, and another of His servant Nature." This religious commitment of the scientist and the scholar made them the equals of clerics, and it must be added that God's special blessing seemed to render their explorations more successful, influential, and prestige laden than the rather stagnant speculations of contemporary theology.

The second remark concerns the socially symbolic value that science acquired in the seventeenth century. As the scientist and the philosopher were knocking at doors that would open the secrets of the universe, very soon it became obvious that amidst protestations of their orthodoxy, they were nevertheless elaborating an entirely new world image, in opposition to the one the Church had claimed the exclusive right to carve for Christians. Behind this scientific world view the outlines of a new society were clearly visible. The issue was not lost on either the Church or her antagonists; when Galileo's conflict with the Jesuits became a long-drawn-out process, one of the old physicist's friends, the monk Campanella, joyously exclaimed in a letter that he saw "a new world" arising, and a new society. He understood that his own ideas, recorded in his utopian novel, *Civitas Solis* ("City of the Sun"), had no chance of materializing without science first blazing the way for experimentation, in the laboratory as well as in society.•

In the eighteenth century, the alliance between science and the ideals of a new society reached a hitherto unimaginable solidity. The expansion of the middle class flowed in two main channels: industry and commerce. With the decline of the Netherlands, two huge empires, Britain and France, remained the contestants for the

---

• The so-called utopian literature was itself perhaps a more complex phenomenon than has been realized. Some scholars think that Sir Thomas More's *Utopia* presents a caricature of the "ideal" society, not an advocacy of it; on the other hand, Campanella is so exuberantly naïve as to foresee that his Solarians would be exempt of "gout, rheumatism, colds, sciatica, and colic."

domination of the oceans and overseas trade. Both placed their military might and diplomatic skill at the disposal of their industrialists, investors, stockholders, and colonizers. In England especially, but also in France, the nobleman stood shoulder to shoulder with the commoner, nay, with his own lackey, waiting anxiously for news of successfully accomplished commercial ventures on the seven seas, ventures in which they all had invested, some a fortune, others a few bank notes earned, perhaps, on a previous speculation.

Science and technical inventions aroused the greatest enthusiasm everywhere. They were now the guarantees of economic expansion and prosperity. The scientist himself became more and more interested in the application of his knowledge, which he saw rapidly harnessed to the needs of industry. The most significant literary venture of the century, the French *Encyclopédie*, proudly advertised in its title that it summarized everything that man knew, but at the same time conformed to the spirit of the age by devoting to theology and religion an infinitesimal place in comparison with the space taken up by the subjects of positive knowledge. "Divine Science," remarks Professor A. M. Wilson, "bulked just about as large spatially as 'The Manufacture and Uses of Iron' "; and he adds: "Such were the *Encyclopédie*'s unacknowledged ways of waging psychological warfare." [13]

Diderot, D'Alembert, Voltaire, Helvétius, Turgot, were in the forefront of this warfare, psychological, political, and philosophical all in one. Professor Wilson has this to say about the over-all significance and impact of the *Encyclopédie*, and his remarks are valid for a very large part of the eighteenth-century enlightened literature: "The *Encyclopédie* was a great reference book, a great repository of knowledge. But it was more than that, by far. The *Encyclopédie* conveyed to its readers a stimulus that was frequently as much emotional as it was intellectual. . . . It was a detergent, a tool with a cutting edge, a window opener. It was something that one could learn to use for the performance of tasks one was insufficiently equipped to do before." [14]

Almost all eighteenth-century political thinkers may be called controversial. It is a commonplace to say that it was a transition period, the beginning of which was described by Paul Hazard as the "crisis of European consciousness." This crisis was real and deep; it can be detected in the personalities, the lives, the thinking, of the French *philosophes,* all of whom were innerly divided between old and new, and who, therefore, may be quoted alternately as favoring tradition or progress, monarchy or republic, religion or atheism.

The term *"philosophe"* itself is intellectually uncomfortable because it is imprecise, vague, having all sorts of connotations. Seventeenth- and eighteenth-century scholars, especially scientists like Galileo and Newton, called themselves philosophers (from natural philosophy); this indicates that philosophy was considered as the knowledge of exact phenomena, but also as reflection upon these phenomena. On the other hand, philosophy also meant a certain way of looking at the world and the destiny of men, as is demonstrated in the "philosophical tales" of Voltaire. Finally, the *philosophe* was also the man who tried to make use of all existing knowledge for changing things in the spirit of the truth thus discovered. Voltaire and Condorcet, for example, displayed impatience with Montesquieu, who studied the causes of historical and sociological phenomena instead of seeking what *ought to be.* This will to change the world, more often than not of a utopian nature, is what justifies Carl Becker when he speaks of the "heavenly city" of the eighteenth-century philosophers.

Behind the activity of the *philosophes* there was the optimism of the age, an optimism fed, first of all, by what they took to be the near-final shape of the new, scientific world view. Even the cautious Montesquieu expressed faith in the triumph of universal science; in his eyes, writes his biographer, Jean Starobinski, "universal science appears possible and near. The quasi-total exploration of nature was a matter of a very short period: the time to establish the law of universal gravitation of which only the details remained to be studied. Since Galileo and Newton, the spectacle of the universe became all of a sudden visible." [15] Montesquieu had indeed compared nature to a maiden who had for a long time reserved her virginity and who yielded all of a sudden.

The author of *L'Esprit des lois* was the point of intersection of too many traditions, French and foreign (among the latter, Hobbes, Grotius, Locke), to be a representative *philosophe*. He was certainly an individualist in the bourgeois sense, and favored a happy equilibrium among the interests, the institutions, and the classes of society so as to guarantee the security of individuals. The latter would thus be free to look after their own private interests; the difference with Hobbes is, however, that the authority above them will not be tyrannical: the Versailles court and the *douceur de vivre* it spread in French society had, by then, created a sufficiently civilized atmosphere for a tolerant public morality, and Montesquieu was able to trust the spirit of the age to preach an intellectual, moral, and commercial laissez-faire philosophy.

But Montesquieu did not have the *philosophes'* naïve faith in man's goodness, and while hoping to free the individual from his worry about the commonweal, he also counseled vigilance against any return of abuses and violence. The true children of the age of Enlightenment were differently inclined: for a Rousseau, liberty as conceived by Montesquieu was far from sufficient because it made no place for the passionate commitment following from the vision of *good man* versus *evil society*.

We come here to a pivotal concept, around which the whole history of modern times may be said to have turned. Indeed, from Marsilius and Machiavelli the tendency had been to shift away from the religious-moral orientation of the State to at least an adumbration of the contract theory of society, already suggested by the *Defensor Pacis*, and to the concept according to which the Prince may govern without needing the Christian precepts of good and evil. We have seen how the economic pressure of the bourgeoisie forced upon the ruler an increasing authority, which he was supposed to use—according to Machiavelli and Hobbes—in a despotic way if the *raison d'état* so dictated. But it was fatal that this authority should, as often as not, be used against the bourgeoisie itself. Thus the latent conflict between the two depositories of power and wealth became sharper as their power and wealth increased. The result was that royal absolutism and bourgeois individualism did not long remain in equilibrium; finally, the eighteenth century understood that the State could not contain these two antagonistic forces, although the very men who contributed most to the weakening of the monarchical institution and its auxiliaries were also and simultaneously trying to bolster the King's position and work out a compromise formula.• Hence the great admiration of the *philosophes* for the so-called enlightened despots, who seemed to embody their ideal, hence also their dislike of England, where, as Holbach said, any beneficial reform may be blocked by the dissent of one party. Voltaire himself, although he envied his British confreres—Swift, Pope, Newton, Bolingbroke, etc.—for their freedom of discussing the tenets of skeptical philosophy, disliked the climate of political liberty as leading to anarchy.

Once royal power had to yield, on what foundations were the new State, the new society, to be erected? This was the basic question asked by the Enlightenment philosophers, many of whom were economists, statesmen, bankers, or civil servants, in other words, informed about political realities. The question implied the admission that the traditional Christian principles no longer sufficed, that a new consensus, a new public philosophy, had to be secured, and that this public philosophy was to take into consideration two modern phenomena: science and democracy.

This was not yet enough. The motor power of these reflections was supplied by certain ideological tenets, elaborated with passion and reminiscent of various heresies from Church history. Their best expression can, of course, be found in Rousseau, but his thoughts on the matter were by no means exceptional: he only lent the subject passion, a peculiar eloquence, and a deep understanding of his contemporaries' sensibility.••

• "They were sufficiently pessimistic about human nature to doubt the feasibility of popular self-government, and tried to compromise between their rational values and their traditional faith in aristocracy by recommending some form of enlightened despotism or constitutional monarchy." E. Barber, *Bourgeoisie in Eighteenth Century France* (Princeton: Princeton University Press, 1955), pp. 69-70.
•• "There is little in Rousseau that was not in Locke," remarks G. P. Gooch in his *English Democratic Ideas in the Seventeenth Century* (New York: Cambridge University Press, 1954; third edition), p. 302. Harold Laski, who edited the second edition,

The constituting elements of this sensibility were the following: belief in man's goodness when in a state of natural freedom; the indictment of society, its institutions and magistrates, for all the evil that ever befell mankind;• the conviction that, although one cannot return to the primeval perfection, a compromise may be found in view of establishing a free, well-governed society based on popular sovereignty.••

As I have said before, the *philosophes* were equivocal, confused thinkers. They were representatives of bourgeois interests and progress, yet they condemned excessive freedom, luxury, and artificiality in society. Like the Bolshevik intellectuals of the mid-twentieth century, they were at once revolutionary and puritanical. Their peculiar em-

---

finds this statement "too strong"; "the organic State of Rousseau," he writes, "is essential to his thesis, and it is not in Locke."

• "Is there any vicious habit, any crime . . . whose origin cannot be traced back to the legislation, the institutions, the prejudices?" Condorcet, *Sketch for a Historical Picture of the Progress of the Human Mind* (New York: The Noonday Press, 1955), p. 193.

•• These ideas were, at least partly, reintroduced from England, where, around 1648, various utopian systems enjoyed a great popularity. For example, the *Light Shining in Buckinghamshire* (1648) emphasizes that by the grant of God all men are free and no individual was intended to rule over his fellow men. "But man, following his sensuality, became an encloser, so that all the land was enclosed in a few mercenary hands and all the rest made their slaves." Of these robbers the most desperate was made king, in order to protect the misdoings of the rest. (See Gooch, op. cit., p. 181.) As Gooch remarks, the events of 1648-59 were hardly noticed at the time in France. "But the Revolution of 1688 met a very different temper. The bitter memories of the Revocation of the Edict of Nantes were still fresh in the minds of French Huguenots; and the victory of William III inspired them to hope that he might prove their savior." (Appendix C, p. 312.) Books and pamphlets appearing in France attacked the despotism of Louis XIV and pointed to English freedom as a model worthy of imitation. "It is not unfair to say," concludes Gooch, "that the [English] Revolution persuaded the French Huguenots to recover the contract theory of the State which had been their mainstay in the civil wars of the sixteenth century." Let us bear in mind that Rousseau was a Calvinist, born in Geneva.

phasis on *virtue,* a combination of humanitarianism and Roman sternness, was best expressed in what was the substratum of their entire political thought: unanimity. Professor Talmon, who also calls attention to this all-encompassing feature of the eighteenth-century dream, paraphrases "unanimity" by saying that Rousseau and his confreres found a common substance in man, called by him "citizenry," which each individual would attain if he were stripped of his particular interests.

Now this unanimity is not that of Hobbes, that is, the fear of being devoured by "one wolf or another." In a little-known essay, "L'Etat de guerre," Rousseau attacked the author of the *Leviathan:* "A certain superficial philosopher," he wrote, "observes people who have been a hundred times reshaped and remolded in the melting pot of society, and then he declares to have observed man." For Rousseau, the units of the social consensus, of unanimity, were not beastly but, on the contrary, virtuous men. "Primitive man," he wrote in the *Discours sur l'origine de l'inégalité parmi les hommes* (1754), "has a natural piety; but once he becomes sophisticated [*réfléchi*], he turns selfish." This same denial of the Hobbesian view is forcefully put forward by Chastellus (in *De la Félicité publique*), who based his social optimism on the hope of discovering *man* as he had been "before history," that is, before the "series of abuses and crimes" that history was. Incidentally, we may now explain the *philosophes'* predilection for the *savages,* who were the only human specimens, at least according to the *philosophes'* poor knowledge of ethnology, of man as he was supposed to have been "before history." •

A religion, as a dynamic movement, always asserts itself against a rival creed. For the thinkers of the Enlightenment this rival was, of course, Christianity. Hence, the first requirement in the process of disengaging man as he is *in naturam* from the sediments of history and civilization had to be the fight against the clergy. This was expected to be a long fight because, as Grimm wrote in one of his

• "The savages enabled people to say so much foolishness and became the constant reference for J. J. Rousseau, one of the most dangerous sophists of the century . . . who took them for the primitive men." Joseph de Maistre, *Les Soirées de Saint-Petersbourg* (Librairie Garnier), p. 59.

34

letters, "it took centuries to subdue the human race to the tyrannical yoke of the priests."[16] The subsequent stages of this emancipation were described by Condorcet in his *Sketch for a Historical Picture of the Progress of the Human Mind,* written as an outline for a larger work during the Revolution, shortly before the author died in prison.•

The religion of progress Condorcet presented had its prophet in Rousseau. From the age of fourteen the boy from Geneva had conceived the project of investigating "what is the nature of the government which would form the most virtuous, enlightened, wise and best citizens." [17] As I have shown, in the concept (or rather, the emotion-ridden ideal) of unanimity, Rousseau found a substitute for the Divine Will of Christian political philosophy, a substitute from which everything else could be deduced. As he wrote in the *Contrat social* (Chapter vi), he wanted "to find a form of association which would defend and protect with all its common strength the person and the goods of each member, and by which each member, joining the others, might, nevertheless, obey only himself, remaining as free as before." The General Will thus constituted must, of course, be guaranteed against any encroachment by partial interests; "whoever refuses to obey the General Will, shall be compelled to do so by the whole body; this only means that he will be compelled to be free" (Chapter vii).••

It is a commonplace to state today that Rousseau is the father of the contemporary totalitarian movements and, in Professor Talmon's words, of "totalitarian democracy" as well. But in the eighteenth century, mass movements and mobs, the indispensable material and instrument of totalitarianism, were nonexistent, and the philosophy of the General Will served the interests of the bourgeoisie. First, by creating, or rather, consecrating, the climate of enthusiastic fervor that accompanies all movements seeking a

---

• We do not have to devote space here to Condorcet's book; we shall consider it later (in Chapter Two), when we appraise his influence on nineteenth-century thought.

•• "It is said that terrorism is the resort of despotic government. Is our government then like despotism? . . . The government of the Revolution is the despotism of liberty against tyranny." Robespierre to the National Convention, Feb. 5, 1794.

place under the sun; second, by preaching distrust of the magistrates of the Old Regime, issuing from a hypothetical usurpation of power and perpetuating its abuses;• and third, by guaranteeing that the unified will of the nation (*peuple*) ultimately becomes fundamental law and that the executive magistrates use their power strictly according to the intentions of the citizens. The second and third points, taken from the *Discours* of 1754, read like a program of the bourgeoisie, and, indeed, many *cahiers des doléances* drawn up in 1788 for presentation before the States-General seem mere elaborations of the themes supplied by Rousseau's text.

The same cross-influence is evident between Rousseau and the *philosophes* on the one hand, and Rousseau and the middle classes on the other. In their enthusiasm to bring the "people" as close as possible to the "ruler," that is, in fact, to melt the two into one, the *philosophes* completely ignored the intermediate bodies of society, which at all times formed the shield of individuals against despotism. In their view, the laws that the citizenry would unanimously enact would be so perfect that, as Condorcet wrote, "the identification of the interests of each with the interests of all" would naturally follow. Hence, in the language of the National Assembly during the French Revolution, "the abolition of every kind of corporation formed among citizens of the same State is a fundamental basis of the French constitution. . . . The National Assembly abolishes irrevocably all institutions which have been injurious to liberty and equality of rights. . . . There are no longer any guilds, or corporations of professions, of arts, or of trades. . . . The law will no longer recognize monastic vows," and so on.

The French Revolution was the combined work of the bourgeoisie and the intellectuals. In spite of the wisdom of some moderate elements on all sides—the monarchy, the nobility, the clergy, and the third estate—there could be no question of reconciliation of interests. The middle class was aware of its own power and of the winds of history blowing in its direction. The Abbé Sieyès, one of the

• "Any institution that does not lay down as a premise the goodness of the people and the corruptibility of the magistrates, is vicious." Robespierre, *Lettre à ses commettants*, 1793.

motor forces of the Revolution, warned his more moderate colleagues not to accept any compromise offer by the first two estates. The nobility and the clergy, said Sieyès, assessing the forces of the parties concerned, will now be willing to pay a high price for peace, for the maintenance of the status quo as much as is possible. But there can be no reconciliation between oppressor and oppressed, no bargaining between classes with contrary interests.

The Revolution brought to France what the Industrial Revolution, reinforced ideologically by the philosophy of Locke, had brought to England, namely, the liberal view of the State as guardian of moneyed interests and protector against foreign economic competition. The successive regimes, constitutions, and bourgeois political philosophies assert, in various ways, the importance of noninterference by the State with the private domain, which included, naturally, the economic interests of the propertied classes. The prevailing concept was, from Turgot to John Stuart Mill, that the State must concern itself with public safety, and should be called out—in the form of its armed forces —only to restrain the disorderly and crush the rebellious.

What was the gain of the intellectuals? In a way it can be said that the intellectuals had joined the middle-class camp at the beginning of modern times because that was the camp of progress, to which their own cause too could be meaningfully and profitably attached. Yet, almost from the beginning, the intellectual also realized that unless a new principle of cohesion could be found, the world prepared by the bourgeoisie would be an anarchical one in which man would fight man. One may say that for three centuries the existence of classes, based not so much on hierarchical differences as, increasingly, on financial ones, was considered by many thinkers an anomaly. They were trying to find ways of terminating it, if not through a restoration of a purely Christian political philosophy, then by means of new and ingenious systems and Utopias, by contractual agreements, or by the absolute power of the sovereign. In their different ways, Hobbes and Rousseau made the same attempt: to bring back the unity of the Greek *polis* and the virtue of the Roman *civitas*—Hobbes by appealing to the fear of the social atomization he saw coming, which nothing less than a tyrant would be able to check; Rousseau in the name of the State as the expression of the General Will, tolerating no particularistic groups within it and demanding total consent from each citizen.• However, because of their bias, and their infatuation with antique examples, both ignored the contribution of Christian thinking to political philosophy: Saint Paul, Saint Augustine, the medieval thinkers, and above all, Saint Thomas.

In this way we witness an interesting phenomenon. Philosophers whose ambition is to re-create a unified society not torn by political and social strife, assist, by the very criticism they level against existing conditions, that class which is primarily responsible for the disintegration of the previous social unity. The same thing will reoccur in the nineteenth century, only this time to the advantage not of the bourgeoisie but of the proletariat. While Hegel recognizes the role of conflicts in history and the permanence of alienation in the human condition, Marx's chief ambition is to re-establish the lost unity of the individual and society (lost, allegedly, through the economic exploitation of class by class) by the abolition of the capitalist system. The last class, the proletariat, will thus rise up not for selfish reasons, not to impose its own rule on newly subjected groups of men, but in order to bring forth the universal society and the brotherhood of all.••

At the outbreak of the French Revolution, the intellectuals could look back to the distance covered and say proudly with Condorcet: "The philosopher feels delight that he has done some lasting good which fate can never destroy by calling back the reign of slavery and prejudice." "The path of virtue will no longer be arduous." [18] On the road to Unity, Prosperity, and Peace much lasting good had indeed been achieved, and in this work the contribu-

---

• It is interesting to see Rousseau use the analogy of the human body: "The sovereign [that is, the General Will] . . . cannot have contrary interests to those of private citizens. . . . It is impossible that the body would want to harm its limbs. . . . The sovereign, by the mere fact that it exists, is always what it must be." *Contrat social* (Paris: La Renaissance du Livre), Chap. vii.
•• This will be discussed in Chapter Three.

tions of the middle class and the intellectuals were inextricably intermingled. But we are here at the beginning phases of a great misunderstanding. The intellectuals of the seventeenth and eighteenth centuries were of middle-class origin, and through their scientific accomplishments, historical researches, and political analyses they spearheaded the bourgeois movement, which needed this ideological foundation to bring down the mighty medieval edifice. But the middle class itself was more sensitive to economic obstacles and social humiliations than to the battles between theology and profane philosophy; it was interested in liberalizing production and trade, in doing away with such anomalies as taxing merchandise some thirty times on its way down the Rhine; it was bent upon freeing itself from the surviving and now anachronistic fetters of feudal exactions, and upon acquiring political rights that would put an end to an inequality no longer corresponding to the actual power relationship between itself and the nobility.•

At a superficial glance one may say that the intellectuals were suffering from similar evils. As we have seen, their prestige and actual influence was considerable; yet this only poured oil on the fire of their pride and sensitivity: after all, their books were subject to the censorship of clumsy officials and the whim of courtiers, even to burning by the executioner; their travels were curtailed, their persons threatened with exile, their outspokenness punished with jail (as in the case of Diderot), or with the rod (Voltaire's famous *bastonnade* by the Duc de Rohan's men). The abuse of authority weighed on mind and conscience, vexing the intellectuals' love of free expression. Under these circumstances it was difficult to see at the time that intellectual freedom might not be commensurate with the enjoyment of the material and psychological advantages after which the bourgeoisie was yearning.

These misgivings, if envisaged at all, were not voiced. On the contrary, the century ended on a note of optimism, which, incidentally, measured the distance between the quasi-clandestine character of the seventeenth-century

---

• Even as late as 1781, the nontitled bourgeois (*roturier*) in France was barred from obtaining a commission in the army and was unofficially excluded from high ecclesiastical offices.

libertines (a socially and scientifically explosive lot), or Descartes's extreme prudence,• and the celebrating ideologues: "In the new society," Benjamin Constant, novelist, political writer, and statesman, harangued his friends in 1797, "in the new society where the prestige of rank is destroyed, we, thinkers, writers and philosophers should be honored as the first among all citizens."

• See Descartes's letter to Père Mersenne: "Je ne suis point si amoureux de mes pensées que de me vouloir servir de telles exceptions [reference to the fact that Rome had not formally condemned Galileo as a heretic and that the latter was thus exceptionally treated] pour avoir moyen de les maintenir; et le désir que j'ai de vivre au repos et de continuer la vie que j'ai commencée en prenant pour ma devise 'bene vixit qui bene latuit' fait que je suis plus aise d'être délivré de la crainte que j'avais d'acquérir plus de connaissances que je ne désire, par le moyen de mon écrit, que je ne suis fâché d'avoir perdu le temps et la peine que j'ai employée à le composer." Jan. 10, 1634.

2

The Shaping of Ideologies

Philosophically speaking, the origin of the nineteenth-century bourgeois domination is shrouded in mystery, and its fundamental principle carries, imbedded in it, a contradiction. This is a difficult heritage.

The mystery is implied in Rousseau's theory of the social contract: there are many statements in Rousseau's texts concerning the hypothetical, nonhistorical character of this contract, and just as significantly, concerning the hypothetical, nonhistorical character of the "state of nature," Rousseau's basic assumption, upon which he built the contract theory. According to his own admission (in the *Discours sur l'origine de l'inégalité*), Rousseau started the search for the state of nature with the help of "hypothetical and conditional reasonings, which were more proper to cast light on the nature of things than to show their real origin." "O man," he exclaims, "here is your history such as I thought I read it not in books . . . which are lying, but in nature which never lies. All that comes from it [nature] is true." He then admits that what he found through his search is extremely uncertain: "It is not an easy enterprise to extricate what is originally in man's nature and what is artificial, and to grasp a state [of nature] which no longer exists, which might have never existed, which, probably will never exist." When, further on, he studies, still with the highly questionable instrument of his mere insight, the evolution (Rousseau means degeneration) of man from the "state of nature" to civil society, he again abandons the road of rational investigation: "as the events I have to describe might have happened in several different ways, I can make a choice by conjectures only."

Founded on such unstable bases, the social contract may not be binding; he must justify it with an assumption: "The clauses of this contract . . . although they may never have been formally proclaimed . . . are, nevertheless, taken for granted everywhere" (*Contrat social*, Chap. vi). This instability may be the reason that, as we have seen, enforcement must be carried out through compulsion if necessary, and why *unanimity* is assumed to go very deep in the contractants, deeper even than they themselves know. Still, there is a passage in the book (Chapter iii, Section 18) where the possibility of breaking the pact is envisaged: "If all citizens were to assemble to break this contract with a common accord, one cannot doubt that it would be very legitimately broken."

This is a very important passage, consistent with the spirit of the whole theory, because it expresses the fundamentally apolitical nature of society (and the asocial nature of man) as conceived by Rousseau and his intellectual descendants.• However, assuming with Rousseau that the basis of human coexistence is such a contract—and not man's social nature, as Aristotle taught—a people (nation) may indeed break it in two cases: when they are dissatisfied with the ruler, or when the objectives for which the citizens had bound themselves together in the first place have been achieved, or, in the language of Rousseau, an equivalent to the state of nature has been established.

The conditions for the first case are hard to prove. As Lord Percy of Newcastle writes about the modern "total societies," in which he, like many others, sees the embodiment of Rousseau's ideas, their leaders can always say

---

• And of his intellectual forebears as well, as this passage in La Boétie's *Contre-un* shows: "If, by chance, some new people were born nowadays who are not accustomed to being subjected to rule, and if they were presented with the choice of being subjects or living in freedom, what would they choose?"

that the original stipulations of the contract have not, so far, been fulfilled because perfect unanimity has not yet been accomplished. In the case of the Communist leaders of Soviet Russia, Lord Percy writes, "until the purge [of the last opposing minority] is completed, a true people does not exist and the people's will is radically corrupt." [1] This, of course, may go on ad infinitum.

The second case, although it is even more difficult to prove, constitutes, partly for this reason, a permanent temptation for those who have Rousseau's mentality. For them, as for their chief inspirer, the State is fundamentally evil because *politics,* the State's main function, consists of the arbitration of conflicts among individuals, groups, and classes,• defense against other States, enforcement of law, and so on. The existence of the State is thus a reminder that conflicts have not disappeared, that politics still rules the world (within a nation and among nations), and that man's goodness is not yet allowed to have its full scope. Confusing the cause with the effect, believing, that is, that the State and its institutions have corrupted man, not that man, corrupted by the original sin, or otherwise fallible, generates imperfect institutions, the utopian mentality comes to the conclusion that if man-to-man relationships were to replace institutional and political relationships, humanity would no longer need the State; its individual members would have so perfectly assimilated the commands of the common interest that a kind of "social science" could be substituted for politics, and the State, yielding to a sort of over-all administration of "social goods," would wither away.

The eighteenth-century philosophy of the Enlightenment had laid the foundation stone of the "total" State, and at the same time, the theoretical bases of its abolition. The political philosophy against which it had asserted itself, that is, the one inspired by Catholic thought, maintains that political life is coeval with the existence of mankind, that is, as long as man will toil under the burden of the original sin (and this will be until the Day of Judgment, which is, by definition, an extrahistorical occurrence, the

---

• "Political power is nothing but the official sum of the antagonisms obtaining in bourgeois society." Marx, in his polemics against Proudhon.

fulfillment of time, when history comes to an end), the same problems, under various aspects, will present themselves; thus politics, that is, the life of institutions and of the State, while its forms change, will provide the necessary expressions, channels, and arbitrating functions of communal life. Since the philosophy inspired by Rousseau does not recognize this, since it expects, ultimately, that all conflicts will be resolved and absorbed by an educated, peace-loving, united, and prosperous mankind, the place and role of institutions and primarily of the State have become confused in the nineteenth, and critical in the twentieth, century.

I have said, at the beginning of this chapter, that the bourgeois domination in the nineteenth century carried in itself a contradiction. What I meant now becomes clearer: as the State and its institutions, in fact, as all of history, were now taken to be mere instruments toward an extra-historical achievement—the happy society, Utopia—it became more and more difficult to know what use one might make of them, where their functions started or stopped, what part (class) of society they were supposed to protect or discipline. Was the State to protect property as Locke had suggested, or was it to regulate working conditions in factories, mines, and shops? Was it to carry out the bourgeois philosophy of laissez faire, or to allow workingmen's associations? Was it to favor production by all means, or to acknowledge the right to strike? These problems were, of course, not mere outgrowths of the confused ideology that eighteenth-century optimism and enthusiasm applied in their approach to the State; they were equally the products of other factors and events—the industrial revolution itself, the need for markets and raw material. The fact is, however, that the vacuum left by the old political systems and concepts was now filled, with an alarming speed and thoughtless urgency, by hybrid ideological products, part philosophical, part mystical, part economic. Some of them were to become quasi religions over large surfaces of the globe: the doctrine of the General Will, the Supreme Being of Robespierre, Hegel's Divine State, idolatrous nationalism like the Pan-Slav aspirations of Danilevsky, Marx's economic determinism, the dialectical materialism elaborated by Lenin.

In a sense, all these doctrines were reactions to bourgeois-engineered dislocations of society and the body politic. The essentially novel element in them is the *scientific ambition* to comprehend what society, the State, and history are about, and in this respect, these doctrines were again the creations of intellectuals. But this contribution of the intellectuals to the shaping of the nineteenth century was quite different from that which the intellectuals had made in the eighteenth. The French Revolution appears to us now as a watershed in this respect too: *before,* the intellectuals and *philosophes* saw no farther than the bourgeois world; even when they spoke the universalist language of utopianism, their terms were inspired by middle-class aspirations, or at least, were so interpreted by the spirit of the age; *after* the Revolution, the nineteenth-century intellectuals—mostly social thinkers—alarmed by economic misery and social disruption, yet unable and unwilling to "turn back the clock," began to formulate ideologies both to *extend* the fruits of the bourgeois-industrial age and to *remedy* its broken equilibrium.

The pre-eminent role of the intellectuals was—according to appearances—not what it had been in the previous century, when their prestige eclipsed that of noblemen and rulers, when a Frederick the Great was prouder of being a "poet" than a king. But their real power and influence was even greater, as Benjamin Constant had predicted. Already Condorcet had stated that in the moral and political sciences, the philosophers "have carried the progress of enlightenment" much farther than the level of public opinion, whereas "those who direct public affairs," that is, the government and its magistrates, "are very far from rising to the level of public opinion; they follow its advance, without ever overtaking it, and are always many years behind it and therefore ignorant of many of the truths that it had learned." [2] In other words, Condorcet noticed the dawning of the age of technicians, specialists who were to influence both "public opinion" • and governments. A few years later, this same distinction was made by Saint-Simon when he spoke of an "essentially industrial nation" and an "essentially feudal government." The bour-

---

• "Public opinion" was defined by Condorcet as "the body of beliefs held in common by the average man of education."

geois impatience with a government that was still, in spite of the Revolution, inspired by traditional ideas and methods is evident from these quotations.

The similarity of Condorcet's and Saint-Simon's views, and of the views of the latter and those of the entire socialist movement of the nineteenth century, is manifest. The influence of Condorcet, who, with many others, transmitted the basic ideas of the Enlightenment to the age of the bourgeoisie, may be summarized as follows: in accordance with a rational scheme, the scientific organization of all departments of human life is possible. This sentence expresses, but in more modern terms, the same view that Montesquieu, at the beginning of another new era, harbored concerning the adequate explanation science offered of the world. I have quoted Montesquieu's triumphant statement regarding nature, which now yielded, like a forced virgin, all her secrets. His optimism went even farther: "the sciences are now linked with one another," he wrote, ". . . and the entire corpus of sciences is linked to the belles-lettres." His commentator, Jean Starobinski, adds that the Cartesian views and the elegant rhetorics of the age united for the advancement of knowledge. Montesquieu claimed "the possibility of describing the world in a unique language, but one that is nontechnical, nonquantitative, nonmathematicized—in the reasonable language of the gentlemen [*honnêtes gens*]."

Now, Condorcet was inspired by the same faith, only, encouraged by the steady progress of science *and* technology, he was more hopeful that mankind would use its increasing knowledge for "truth, happiness and virtue." In his way, he was even more impatient than the dignified Montesquieu: "Philosophy," he wrote, "has nothing more to guess, no more hypothetical surmises to make; it is enough to assemble and order the facts and to show the useful truths that can be derived from their connections and from their totality." [3] Although he was a mathematician, he meant by "philosophy" not the "natural philosophy" of the thinkers of the century and a half from Bacon to Montesquieu, but the hoped-for and already envisaged social calculus and moral science. "Just as mathematical and physical sciences tend to improve the arts that we use to satisfy our simplest needs, is it not also part of the necessary order of nature that the moral and political sciences should exercise a similar influence upon the motives that direct our feelings and our actions?" [4]

Not only Condorcet, but D'Alembert, Turgot, Quesnay, and of course, Saint-Simon and Comte felt that the double key of nature—power and freedom—had finally been delivered to mankind, and that the world was now ready to receive the beneficial onslaught of a new race. The idea that mankind was progressing from barbarism to reason and enlightenment became a commonplace. As always when such feelings are prevalent, people needed summaries and generalized pictures of what had been accomplished and what lay ahead. Intellectual inventories were drawn up: such was Diderot's *Encyclopédie*, Voltaire's *Dictionnaire philosophique*, Turgot's *Tableau philosophique successif de l'esprit humain*, Condorcet's *Historical Picture of the Progress of the Human Mind*, and Comte's theory of the three phases. One may even say that Goethe's *Faust*, this *Divine Comedy* in reverse, was also a kind of summing up, and, at the end of Part II, an anticipation of the transformed world.

What were the phases of this grand transformation as they were reflected in the writings of the nineteenth-century intellectuals? We may conveniently begin with the sociopolitical aspect of the problem, especially since we have seen the *philosophes'* and intellectuals' attacks on the concepts of State and politics.

Generally speaking, with the rise of the middle class, with the evidence of its industrial and technological efficiency, the need for a tighter organization of society also became manifest.• This was a problem with two aspects: (1) while maintaining the myth of economic liberalism and the policy of noninterference by the State, the manufacturers themselves began to demand increasingly that the government intervene and protect them against strikes and workingmen's associations;•• but, naturally, the greater

• Thus proving that the combination of the liberal concept of freedom with unlimited industrialization was not a durable marriage but a short honeymoon.

•• "In the capitalists' propensity [toward monopoly] . . . they have succeeded in enlisting the support of an ever increasing number of other groups and, with their help, in obtaining the support of the State. . . . [The monopolists] have gained this

the demand for government intervention, the more important the State became through the various services it was called upon to render; hence, (2) the conflicting forces—capital, labor, and the accompanying ideologies and parties—with which economic and philosophical liberalism was unable to cope dealt each other such blows that the end result had to be either a complete breakdown of civilized coexistence, or the elimination of all major conflicts.

Both aspects of the problem were intelligently grasped by Saint-Simon and his school; in his periodical, *Industrie Littéraire et Scientifique*, Saint-Simon wrote this: "As the whole of mankind has a common purpose and comon interests, each man ought to regard himself in his social relations as engaged in a company of workers" (1817). In this way, the problems of production (according to Saint-Simon, the only reasonable and positive end that human society can fix for itself) may be solved, and also all other problems pertaining to social relationships, since in the society of the future the control of these relationships will be entrusted to the men "who are most capable of exercising them in conformity with the general aims of the community." That this community will be uniform in its goals and aspirations, the Count and his followers did not doubt: "the industrial system is the one toward which mankind has always been moving," we read in the eighteenth volume of Saint-Simon's collected works; "this will be the final system; all other political systems that have existed should be considered as merely preparatory." • In their exposition of their master's doctrine (1829-30), his disciples taught equally that the final destiny of mankind was a state in which all antagonisms between men would have

---

support . . . frequently by persuading [these groups] that the formation of monopolies was in the public interest." F. A. Hayek, *The Road to Serfdom* (Chicago: University of Chicago Press, 1944), pp. 195-6.

• "The French Revolution is the first attempt of mankind to take its destinies in its own hands. . . . One may say, with Robert Owen, that all that preceded it was the irrational period of human existence, and that one day this period will count in the history of mankind . . . only as a strange preface." E. Renan, *L'Avenir de la science* (written in 1848, published in 1890, Calmann-Lévy), p. 747.

disappeared; society would be characterized by the joint action of its members upon nature, and the discipline imposed by co-operative action would render cohesive associations increasingly imperative.•

Saint-Simon's was the first systematic exposition of the new science of society based on the enormous production possibilities that he foresaw. Two aspects of his thought stand out with particular force. The first is his insistence that the whole history of mankind had been a preparation for the present quasi-final stage; he gave added emphasis to this idea when he said that men would do, henceforward, *consciously* what they had *previously* been doing unconsciously.•• In this way he registered the insight that he shared with his confreres that the earlier idées-force, which I have identified as peace, unity, and prosperity, had become active elements in the destiny of humankind, indeed more forces than mere ideas. The second notable aspect of Saint-Simon's thought was held in common with the physiocrats,••• only Saint-Simon extended it to build a far-reaching program and a more complete system. It was contained in his idea of general harmony, in the interest of which all obstacles (including national sovereignty) must be overcome. The "industrial regime," which he contrasted, as we have seen, with the "feudal government," must be universal, for otherwise it might suffer shipwreck on the opposition of any nation. No such accident can be allowed to happen in Saint-Simon's view; the accumulated produce of society and the very mechanisms, industrial and social, of production, should not be endangered by the struggle of exploiters and exploited, or for that matter, by the intervention of the government, which is a "source of injury to industry . . . even where it tries to encourage it."

• See on the subject Professor Hayek's study in the *Counter-revolution of Science* (Glencoe, Ill.: The Free Press, 1952).
•• "We want men henceforth to do consciously, by direct effort and with more fruitful results, what they have hitherto been doing, as it were, unintentionally, slowly, indecisively, and with little success." *Oeuvres choisies* (Bruxelles: 1859), XVIII, 166.
••• The physiocrats wanted to abolish existing institutions and privileges and to bring about economic equality through laissez faire. They were little interested in the political aspects of liberty.

Thus we see again the identification of government with a parasitic, impatiently endured organism whose role, inasmuch as it is useful, could be taken over by other functions, growing directly out of "industrial relationships." •
In fact, Saint-Simon declared as early as 1816 that politics is the science of production, and he predicted the complete absorption of politics by economics. There are many statements in the writings of Comte, Guizot, the whole school of the utopian socialists, and of course, in Engels and Lenin, about the absorption of political matters by the educated citizenry so as to concentrate on industrial relationships. The supposed peacefulness of such relationships and the rationality inherent in industrial production impressed in an exaggerated manner these observers of the early stages of the industrial revolution. They were right and wrong at the same time.

First, why were they wrong? As has been said earlier in this chapter, the bourgeois regime had an ambiguous attitude toward the State: it wanted to use *and* restrict it at the same time. While with regard to work legislation the capitalists took the well-known view of hands-off for the State, the question of industrial and commercial expansion was considered an enterprise worthy of State support. Imperialism, which is a case in point, "was born," as Hannah Arendt writes, "when the ruling class in capitalist production came up against national limitation to its economic expansion. The bourgeoisie turned to politics out of economic necessity . . . [in order] to proclaim expansion to be an ultimate political goal of foreign policy." [5]

Another reason they were wrong was the discovery, made by the second generation of utopian socialists (in some instances, by the founding generation itself), that the societies and co-operatives constituted in the spirit of Saint-Simon, Fourier, Cabet, and Owen became themselves capitalist enterprises, in which the founding members were the entrepreneurs and the late-joiners the workers. Martin Buber quotes from a letter by an ex-member of Cabet's

---

• There is a famous text in Saint-Simon's *Parabole* (1819) where he claims that the disappearance of King, ministers, high political personnel, etc., would not substantially affect life in France, whereas the disappearance of France's fifty best chemists, physiologists, bankers, agriculturists, steel producers, etc., would ruin it.

Icaria: "We had a furious will to succeed but . . . the Old Adam in us, or the beast, inadequately suppressed, made a violent appearance." And from another letter: "We were so few and so like people outside, that it was not worth the effort to live in the community." Did Rousseau not say that "whoever dares undertake to give institutions to a people must feel able to change, so to speak, human nature"? (*Contrat social*, ii, 7).

Thus, barring the possibility of changing human nature, what the Saint-Simonians and others failed to understand was that an "industrial regime" will experience the same power struggles as any other regime, particularly if it spreads, as Saint-Simon preconized, over a large territory, in fact, over the entire globe. For in that case the system, no matter how unified in principle and in the minds of its planners, will become sufficiently differentiated to reproduce, on a different scale, the usual problems of any society. In other words, workers and entrepreneurs are not bees and queens, fixed once and for all in their respective functions, but human beings who may regroup themselves, who seek better conditions, develop new ambitions and desires.

Now, in what respect were these early nineteenth-century intellectuals right in proposing a new society—and a new morality—founded on industrial rapports?

Although Saint-Simon seemed to be naïve when he called upon the workers to accept the entrepreneurs as leaders of society, he did not quite misjudge the sensibility of the age. The very suggestion implied that the workers had become socially important, and this meant that sooner or later they would have to be associated with political power, or with whatever else would take its place in Saint-Simon's mind. At any rate, Saint-Simon was right in assuming that a *modus vivendi* would be found between the two partners of the industrial society, and that despite the violence of the conflicts with which the century was to resound, neither the proletariat nor the capitalist system would disappear in the predictable future. On the contrary, both would be, in a sense, disciplined.

In this foresight Saint-Simon was not alone. The apostles of liberalism and socialism, Spencer and Marx, had predicted this development, namely, that the numerous frictions created by class struggle will necessarily slow down, and finally eliminate, antagonism among groups. Society will then pass from its barbarous, militant phase into an industrial phase, writes Spencer in the *Principles of Sociology;* the resulting state of consolidation will be characterized by stable, harmonious relationships, ending in the "establishment of the greatest perfection and the most complete happiness." The *élan* that drives mankind in this direction cannot be stopped; it eliminates the waste it produces and trains the surviving "fit ones" in the mechanisms of co-operation.

The conclusions of Marx are not different, except that he modeled his system after the discipline of *history,* not, as Spencer, after the science of *biology.* Accordingly, in Marx's teaching, the "unfit," the human waste, is not the pauper, the economically powerless, but the bourgeois capitalist, because he is in a hopeless disagreement with the indications of history. Otherwise, the necessity of the process is the same: from conflict between classes to that leveled, co-operating community which is the precondition of economic prosperity and universal brotherhood.

However, before that stage would be reached, there were important reasons for the slowly emerging attitude of co-operation, or at least, coexistence, between capital and labor. As John Strachey remarked in *Contemporary Capitalism,* Marx's analysis of capitalism's economic concentration (and subsequent mass pauperization) would have proved correct if the pressure of the Marxist syndicates and later, political parties had not forced capitalism into concessions. Strachey himself regrets it, but he is forced to state that as a result of this pressure, capitalism has survived.

On the other hand, capitalism itself has contributed to the strengthening of the working class. The authors of the Communist Manifesto registered this fact and chalked it up in favor of their belief in the inevitable triumph of the proletariat: "The bourgeoisie itself supplies the proletariat with its own elements of political and general education, in other words, it furnishes the proletariat with weapons for fighting the bourgeoisie."

The conflict that dominated the century, that is, the successive emancipation of all lower classes, cannot be described simply as one between capital and labor. The picture is complicated by other idées-force—nationalism,

political radicalism, colonialism—which developed along
other lines. Class struggle itself took several forms: the
bourgeoisie fought its rear-guard actions against the still
surviving political and social privileges of the nobility;
at the same time, it was also engaged in suppressing certain
forms of Jacobinism and other anarcho-utopistic tendencies that were directed more radically against property
than Marxism itself was to be. Yet all significant trends
and movements were converging toward some form or
other of popular emancipation: whether Prussian nationalism awakened by Napoleonic occupation, imperialism,
and the problem of colonial masses, or industrialization itself, which brought in its wake the fateful problem of the
proletariat.

The most important European nations and the United
States had completed this process (or at least, its "take-
off phase," to use Professor W. W. Rostow's expression)
by 1870. Until then they had had to solve a variety of
problems, from national unity (Germany, Italy, the United
States) to the final defeat of old privileges. Generally
speaking, by setting up a democratic-liberal State-machin-
ery, the victorious middle class was preparing for the rest
of the population an instrument with which to achieve economic and political equality. Once admitted to the ballot
box, the lower classes, this time from within the nominally
still bourgeois citadel, made further contributions to the
elasticity of the parliamentary system. In England the
process was relatively peaceful, and it was accomplished
in the lifetime of two generations (1832-85); in France
it took three revolutions and repeated changes of regime.
In the end, however, political and economic democracy
proved their worth by eliminating the major causes of discontent, and more important still, by creating an atmosphere and a machinery favorable to the continuation of
the process.

The emerging and basically reformed societies understood the necessity of maintaining and increasing the level
of production as the condition of prosperity. The immediate result was spectacular: from the middle of the century, economic reports and statistical graphs outcrowd in
number and importance the war bulletins in the life of

nations.• The more distant result was even more significant: the emphasis on production as the national goal was bound to strengthen social cohesion between all groups, between producers, distributors, and consumers. The respective functions of these fundamental groups corresponded now less and less to the functions of the three classes of medieval Europe: the peasant and artisan, the merchant, and the nobility. The relationship that began to obtain among them was also different from traditional class-relationships: each group began to share and perform the others' functions. The stake of each in the order and welfare resulting from this interplay became equally large.

From the early nineteenth century on, the combined forces of political rights and economic opportunities (with the resulting occupational instability) have brought about a most important change in the life of Western communities: a virtual abolition of *status,* and its replacement by *functions.* Traditional society had been based on the axiom of rather strictly defined status in life, an even more significant distinction than the rough division into classes. In the Middle Ages, for example, different systems of justice applied to knights, laborers, tradesmen, and their relationship to one another was also strictly regulated by tradition and by law. Later, even well into the modern age, family ties, landed property, inherited privileges, were still very important factors in the classification of individuals, and hence, in obtaining advancement and in making a career. The new society of the nineteenth century opened a free career for individual talent and competence; it acknowledged no activity that could not be learned and performed by anyone. This view was one of the consequences of economic liberalism; money economy, remarked Georg Simmel, depersonalizes the traditional man-to-man relationships and substitutes functions for persons. Thus

• In fact, from the end of the sixteenth century, there was an increasing interest in such economic data, not merely the volume but also the rate of production of goods and the rate of increase in the circulation of merchandise, etc. The novelty of this phenomenon in the late sixteenth and early seventeenth century is exposed in Professor John U. Nef's book, *Cultural Foundations of Industrial Civilization* (New York: Cambridge University Press, 1958).

a man can choose among functions in a society where he depends on the unknown many instead of a known few. This increasing dependence on functions, that is, on society, correlates with the decreasing dependence on any one person.

The consequence is that functions become all important and persons interchangeable, especially since perfected techniques facilitate the performance of most functions. Thus the depersonalization (or "alienation") of the individual has appeared together with the establishment of huge bureaucratic machines, rationalized working conditions, anonymous business companies, and a ubiquitous administration.

The phenomenon of social atomization was thus the critical experience of the nineteenth century. To what extent was it noticed by the contemporaries and what remedies were suggested by those who were alarmed by it?

The intellectuals of the early part of the century already showed the cleavage; it was to become wider as the features of the contemporary world became more accentuated. There were those intellectuals whose main preoccupation was nationalism and industrial growth. These two do not necessarily go hand in hand, yet, as Professor Rostow noted, intense nationalism, accompanied by xenophobia, etc., may often give the decisive impulse to industrialization. Whatever the relationship between them, nationalism and the industrial revolution were mass phenomena, and their advocates were more interested in the organization of armies and of production than in the organization of society and the political community as such. The two aims, a strong army and a productive mass of workers, were considered primary in the building of the nineteenth-century nation-states. Let us note also that these two aims had a common cause outside the national frontiers too: imperialistic ventures were begun by the factory owner but were carried out, at the start, by semimilitary adventurers in whose person commercial interests and military glory coalesced, and later, by regular armies and colonial garrisons.

Both organizations, the modern army and modern industry, were based on the concept of discipline. Here, too, there were similarities between them: the masses that supplied both were of peasant or recent-peasant origin, that is, they were recruited from a stratum of the population that from time immemorial *had served* in some capacity and had developed the characteristic features of obedience and fatalism. In this respect the army was favored, being an incomparably older institution than industry, with a long tradition, an unbroken hierarchy, and exalting career-prospects. Also, its leaders were either the same men who had ruled over the peasant-soldier as landowners and lords, or the popular generals of the democratic armies (the armies of the French Revolution and of Napoleon, or the liberation armies of Garibaldi, Kossuth, etc.), which carried on their banners the sacred word, "freedom." These factors further strengthened discipline.

The situation in the industrial field was, no doubt, different, yet there, too, worker-discipline was the natural outgrowth of ancestral serf-obedience. Not everywhere in the same measure. In England a large part of the workers had been *dépaysé* since the sixteenth and seventeenth century as a result of land closure; by the nineteenth century the workers were certainly better adapted to the conditions that industrialization had created in the previous century. The United States (after 1870) formed a special case with its immigrant workers, who, for one thing, were grateful for the opportunity of exchanging their earlier peasant condition for a new and more prestigious urban existence, and for another thing, considered "Americanization" more important than an immediate change of economic status. Americanization *was* for them an improvement of social status.

On the Continent, the workers were still dazed by the industrial-urban conditions, although this state of mind was somewhat relieved by the nearness of their village existence, in time and in space. In many cases they managed to combine the industrial and the agricultural way of life, and even returned to their native places after decades spent in workshops. The ideal, as nineteenth-century novels make clear, was to earn enough money in the city to obtain a higher status in the village, which was still "home." To the same extent, which was, of course, diminishing, the industrial masses were not yet "atomized," that is, rootless and exposed to the winds of ideologies. This may be observed also by looking at their leaders: of peasant stock and themselves peasants or small artisans, these leaders

still had a traditional frame of mind, considered industrialization an alien, bourgeois phenomenon, and preferred to
work for social justice through persuasion and through
reference to human brotherhood.

The problem of industrial discipline was, thus, generally not noticed, since it was not yet a universal problem
and since the traditional forms of society were still strong
enough to impose on the working classes. Much less were
other problems, the *political* consequences of social atomization, noticed, since they were even more deeply hidden
in the womb of time, except to the most perspicacious observers. The first half of the nineteenth century inherited
the fervor of Rousseau and Robespierre for unanimity; it
became the principal virtue of the age, the par excellence
civic virtue supposed to permeate society, or what was
called "the people." Up until the year of enthusiasm, 1848,
in speeches and writings, the people was acclaimed in the
most exalted terms, and it was believed, in the words of
George Sand, for example, that once the predicted better
world had arrived, mankind would greet Truth with a
unanimous voice. "The soon-to-come universal man," she
wrote, "will be as wise and noble as the ancient sage."
And even more significantly, in a letter dated April 23,
1848: "the ideal expression of the sovereignty of all is not
majority but unanimity. The day will come when Reason
will get rid of its blinders, and the conscience of liberated
people of all hesitation. Not one voice will be raised in
the Council of Humanity against Truth."

The ideologues of progress, Michelet and Quinet, for
example, believed that the day had come for the extension
of Christian moral sense, aristocratic taste, Greco-Roman
humanistic values, from a privileged minority to the totality
of the citizens. The accomplishments of spiritual and intellectual culture, it was held, would now be shared by
all; a soon-to-come democratic community would be so
much richer than any previous society as all men would
participate in the progress of sentiments, humaneness, private and public virtues.

The basic mistake of these men was to assume that the
pillars on which traditional society had rested would also
form the support of the new society. But not everybody
was so optimistic, or, in any event, the prevalent optimism
was of a different nature and direction. The early socialists

and social thinkers trusted that industrialization would create a unanimity stamped with its own brand, and that this unanimity—or better, industrial co-operation—would be the future basis for happiness and virtue.

Saint-Simon himself, the first and in many respects the most farsighted among the social thinkers, was of the opinion that the philosophers of the future would have to inculcate into the population the necessity to "subject all children to the study of the same code of secular morality, since a community of positive moral ideas is the only link that can unite men in society." [6] It is not quite clear whether Saint-Simon meant that for the industrial society to succeed a new morality must be created, or that the latter would be a by-product of the industrialization process. Renan's statement, in *L'Avenir de la science* (1848), is equally ambiguous, although it refers not to industry but to its precondition, science: "By every way open to us we begin to proclaim the right of human reason to reform society by means of rational science. We can state without exaggeration that science holds the future of humanity. Science alone can explain human destiny and teach the way of attaining it. The scientific organization of mankind is the final word of modern science, its bold but legitimate pretension" (p. 757). Like Saint-Simon, Renan predicted a secular-scientific morality for mankind. Life, he once explained to the young Romain Rolland, is good, and an industrious mankind may look forward to infinite progress in every direction, including community life; for while moral conscience is declining, the rules of duty will remain the basis of any society made up of human beings. The public philosophy, he added, is turning into a scientific philosophy; if other beliefs and thoughts are needed, they will be personal and private to each individual.•

What Renan meant by science was not only the exact and detailed work going on in laboratories but also the ideology that scientism was spreading in the minds of men, leaders,

---

• Romain Rolland, an exceptionally sensitive man, was seized with alarm before this dreary prospect, and asked the master what, in his opinion, the weaker souls would do once they were deprived of religion. Renan replied: "So much the worse for them! They are weak and overwhelmed by science! Why did they have to search for truth in the first place?"

and nations. His ideal may not have been a technological society, as was the ideal of Saint-Simon and the other socialists, but nevertheless it was a society centrally organized, disciplined, and scientific minded, in which, as the geographer Letronne had put it in 1824, "reforms changing the whole social structure can be put through in the twinkling of an eye." Let us not forget, in this respect, that up until 1848 French socialism, which owes so much to the Napoleonic ideal of centralization and to the mentality originating in the *Ecole Polytechnique,*• was inspired by science to a larger degree than contemporary German socialism. The latter became "scientific" (and antidemocratic) with its discovery of the doctrines of Lassalle and Marx; but French socialism had a longer authoritarian and antidemocratic tradition. Saint-Simon himself threatened to treat his recalcitrant opponents "as cattle."

The basic assumptions and predictions concerning a new social morality and discipline, growing out of or accompanying industrialization were similar in the nonsocialist quarters; but, naturally, the tone was not that of optimism but that of alarm, or at least, caution. Already Chateaubriand remarked in the epilogue to his *Mémoires d'outre-tombe:* "The folly of the age is to achieve the unity of the peoples, while turning the whole species into a single unit. Granted; but while we are acquiring these general faculties, is not a whole chain of private feelings in danger of perishing?" ••

Chateaubriand was the first French romantic, if we do not count Rousseau himself. But it is not difficult to show that romanticism, all over the Continent, was a reaction against increasing industrialization and bourgeois pragmatism. Although for us the similarity of interests between the military and the industrialist is evident, for the romantics the celebration of war, the rough medieval life,

---

• See F. A. Hayek, *The Counterrevolution of Science,* for a detailed discussion of the influence of this institution.

•• "What we are wont to regard as moral progress is the domestication of individuality brought about (a) by the versatility and wealth of culture, and (b) by the vast increase in the power of the State over the individual, which may lead to the complete abdication of the individual." J. Burckhardt, *Force and Freedom* (New York: Pantheon Books, 1943), p. 149.

and the knightly adventures meant an escape into the picturesque past from a present the drabness of which was already apparent to the sensitive temperaments of poets, painters, and musicians. In Germany, England, and France, Goethe, Schiller, Sir Walter Scott, Byron, Victor Hugo, and Vigny attempted to reawaken their compatriots with the memory of bygone brilliance, the style of old chronicles, the legends and loves sung by minstrels and troubadours, the miracles and colors of cathedrals and crusades. The romantic poets, especially in France, even had a political role to play; as Professor René Rémond writes: "the young romantic poets were the hope of the Royalist party. . . . Literary currents and political thought thus went in the same direction. . . . Royalists and Romantics had common sensibilities, common aversions, a common nostalgia." [7]

The opposition of the romantics was ephemeral and dictated by impulse, not by reasoned insight. But there were others who detected not only the flaws in the optimists' reasoning and the vacuity of their slogans but also the dreariness of the picture they painted through pleasantly colored glasses. The too-little-known Antoine Augustin Cournot had summarized quite early (1840) the arguments that the deafening sound of progress was to suppress for another half a century, but that were to reappear with the twentieth. In fact, Cournot agreed with Saint-Simon and his followers that industrialization would be more than the organization of production, that it would impose, in every field of human endeavor, certain forms of rationalization, and that it would lead to a kind of "universal utilitarianism." But the range of his vision was wider than Saint-Simon's. "We wish merely to light the way for the necessary course of things and to remove obstacles," the latter wrote. But precisely: what some consider obstacles others may see as salutary checks to the ambitions of power-thirsty men; what for one is a roadblock in progress for another is the guarantee that private sentiments will not be discarded as so much rubbish.

At any rate, Cournot became convinced that the triumph of *intelligence,* that is, rational organization, over *life* and the forms it creates will result in a gradual abolition of moral distinctions, traditions, and even of the variety of human societies. Perfected administrative techniques will undermine spontaneity and will supplant history. Did Condorcet not demand that history should cease to be a record of individual facts and become instead the systematic observation of masses, in order, as he insisted, that we might establish "the laws of society and predict its future"?

Thus history and civilization were to become epiphenomena of industrial production, at the same time as personal freedom was expected to coalesce with civic virtues. The picture that the early nineteenth century had of its future is thus before us: an industrious mankind would be rationally organized by technicians; progressively, all nonindustrial activities and interests, too, would come under the organizational competence of experts; the unity of society (later, of mankind) would be secured by the identity of all the organizational patterns (used in every field of activity), the model being industrial organization and the discipline it demands and develops. With the help of a constantly entertained enthusiasm and unanimity, it would be then easy to erase even the memory of traditional and Christian virtues and to equate the new virtue with work-discipline and with total (not even mere majority) vote for Truth.

This picture may seem to be overdrawn, but only because the blueprints it reproduces in a summary fashon are never fully translated into reality. It would be a mistake to underestimate the importance of this utopian trend, although it was certainly ahead of its time. This was, among other things, due to the fact that, generally speaking, the intellectuals of the first half of the century were preoccupied not only with the problem of discipline and social cohesion, but also with its counterpart, authority and its justification under new conditions. One of the dividing lines between the intellectuals of the age was whether the new discipline and morality would be rooted in the Christian tradition or would be a new, scientific-democratic morality. The conflict was somewhat obscured by the fact that most intellectuals, including the utopians and the socialists, were still steeped in the religious tradition, but the religious tradition itself was sufficiently diluted by the ideological struggles since the Renaissance to allow a considerable latitude of interpretation.•

Whether we look at it from the angle of social discipline or of social authority, the central problem was to secure the loyalty of the masses. Generally speaking, two schools of thought were competing to give meaning and scope to the loyalty of modern man: we may call the first the "polytechnic mind," which relies on science and on the scientific organization of society, giving shape to mankind's generous dreams about progress; the second is the "conservative mind," which is aware that if the old forms of society are blown away, then the old forms of culture, civic responsibility and traditional virtues are also condemned to disappear.•• Needless to say, the age favored the polytechnic mind and the radical schools of thought that it engendered or supplied with ideas. Russell Kirk distinguishes, in his book *The Conservative Mind,* five schools of radical thought, all influential in the course of the century: the

• This general problem was in the center of Tocqueville's and Gobineau's preoccupations, and fills the pages of their famous correspondence. Tocqueville, whose main purpose was "to find and show what is there really new and divorced from Christianity in the modern moral systems," had entrusted his younger friend with research and documentation. Tocqueville was, of course, moderately optimistic because he thought that "Christianity is the great source of modern morality," and because he hoped that the new age would not produce a morality other than one rooted in Christianity. Gobineau, however, was frankly pessimistic: he saw in the modern democratic State a new social entity emerging which would break with Christianity. "Private charity is on the decline," he wrote Tocqueville, "the State assumes more and more responsibility." Correspondence of 1843. See Tocqueville, *The European Revolution and Correspondence with Gobineau,* edited by John A. Lukacs (Garden City, N.Y.: Doubleday Anchor Books, 1959).

•• In a way, the two mentalities were joined in the mind of the old Renan. In his preface (1890) to his youthful work (*L'Avenir de la science,* 1848), which he disavows, we see his doubts as they appeared forty years later: "What is serious is that we see in the future . . . no means of giving mankind a catechism that would be acceptable from now on. . . . I say in all frankness that I do not see how the bases of a noble and happy life will be established without the old dreams." Op. cit., p. 726.

rationalism of Enlightenment (Hume and the *philosophes*), Rousseau's romantic emancipation, the utilitarianism of Bentham, Comtian positivism, and finally, the collectivistic materialism of Marx. Such a list could be made up about conservative thought too, as Kirk so well demonstrates in his book; but when we study the influence of the respective groups, we see that the conservatives found no echo except in scattered areas, and were repulsed at once by the working classes, to which they preached moderation, and the middle classes, which saw them as defenders of feudal privileges.

We must now carefully explain the phenomenal success of the radical schools of thought. The following factors should be considered: the political, scientific, and industrial advances of the age began to bring proof, if any were needed, that the human being is subject to change and improvement, provided the environment is suitably manipulated. The large industrial masses, which were, after all, slowly climbing out of their misery, the masses of immigrants to the United States, adjusting with relative ease to their new conditions, were convincing data that the ideal society, conceived by Saint-Simon, Fourier, Owen, or later, by Marx, was no sheer Utopia. It was found that over and beyond the outstanding individual who had been supposed to shape history as his personal material, there stood something far more powerful, even if perhaps blind, like Hegel's Spirit of History, whose instruments may be collectivities, masses, movements and revolutions, or for that matter, forces of production and the spirit of nationalism.

History thus came to be conceived not as a normal reflection of the human condition on an enlarged scale, and, like individual destiny, under the supervision of God, but as a drama with superhuman and nonhuman protagonists, and nearing its climax. It was believed that the individual would finally destroy the artificial frames forced upon him by blind forces and those who conspired with them, and would establish the universal society of nonalienated men.• These hopes had been engraved in the most signifi-

• This was true in the United States no less than in Europe; as Emerson wrote Carlyle in 1840, "everybody here is carrying in his pocket a blueprint for a new society."

cant doctrines since the Renaissance. First, they exalted the individual as the foundation stone of society, a doctrine whose sinister but logical consequences only Hobbes had the courage to describe; second, they put forward the idea that man is virtuous, which meant, according to the typical logic of the Enlightenment, that reconstructed society would also be virtuous; third, if the individual is *first* in the political order (the imaginary signatories of the social contract) and *virtuous* in the moral order, then he does not need the *State* as an institution arbitrating the conflicting interests of other institutions, but rather a *society*, being a loose framework for human relationships.

But we may locate the reasons for the triumph of radical philosophies in other domains as well. The principal secret of this triumph is that radicalism, in the hundred years from the *Encyclopédie* to the revolutions of 1848, was an equivocal doctrine, favoring both the bourgeoisie and the proletariat. This point, incidentally, explains why this same period may be considered the high noon of the Western intellectuals' influence: their own position being itself ambiguous, their leadership was sought by both contending classes.

Why was radicalism adopted, for one historic moment, by the middle class as well as by the workers and their representatives? The simplest reason, I think, is that it was the philosophy of industrialization at its initial phases: it helped the bourgeoisie destroy the old order in its economic and spiritual foundations, and it helped the proletariat develop a consciousness and a discipline of their own.•

• This overlapping, for some time, of bourgeois and proletarian interests and movements is mentioned by Engels in *Socialism: Utopian and Scientific:* "Upon the whole, the bourgeoisie, in their struggle with the nobility, could claim to represent at the same time the interests of the different working classes of that period [from the Reformation to the French Revolution]. Yet, in every great bourgeois movement there were independent outbursts of that class which was the forerunner, more or less developed, of the modern proletariat. For example, at the time of the German Reformation and the Peasant War, the Anabaptists and Thomas Münzer; in the great English Revolution the Levellers; in the Great French Revolution, Babeuf." (New York: International Publishers, 1935), p. 33.

On doctrinal as well as practical issues middle class and working class could see eye to eye in the light of radicalism. Take, for example, the obsessing ideal of the vanishing State and of vanishing history as explained above. Before Rousseau had tackled this problem so disturbingly, the ideal of the vanishing State was a product of the evangelical movements of the Reformation period, thus popular in origin rather than burgher. In its nineteenth-century form, however, it seemed to be a bourgeois invention. "Society needs less and less governing," Guizot optimistically declared around the mid-century, and Saint-Simon's ex-secretary, Comte, explained that in the future the administration of goods will increasingly replace the commanding of persons. But what did the bourgeoisie mean by these statements? It meant that while some functions of the State would be rendered superfluous, others would be handled according to business methods and business interests. Thus, if not the State, at least politics would be absorbed by man-to-man relationships, which, in the minds of the bourgeoisie, meant primarily commercial relationships within the framework and under the protection of the liberal State.

In the interpretation of the proletarian leaders the great but ambiguous• radical doctrine of the vanishing State took another form. For the utopian socialists, the total social change was to take place outside the State. This was, of course, authentic radicalism, as was also the materialization of their plans whenever they managed to establish socialist settlements, based on "relationships of production and distribution" alone. For the Marxists, the future relationship of the emancipated (nonalienated) workers, while the doctrine of the "withering State" had not yet been explicitly advanced,•• was to have as a background a society that would be entirely unrecognizable to us, with its legal system and other institutions shaped by extra-historical forces for which we have no precedent.••• Thus the theorists of the working class agreed, under the wide,

• Let us point out again that this ambiguity was inherent in Rousseau's theory.
•• This concept was suggested by Engels, and developed by Lenin. But it is, naturally, contained in Marx's system.
••• This point, together with other aspects of Marxism, will be discussed in Chapter Three.

accommodating dome of nineteenth-century radicalism, with the bourgeoisie in their opposition to the nature and requirements of politics.•

The same apparent agreement (agreement as to the way, but not as to the goals) existed also in regard to the bourgeois and socialist approaches to the intermediary bodies of society. We have seen that the French Revolution itself was sparked by the accumulated bitterness of the capitalist class over restrictions due to medieval grants, privileges, incoherent system of taxation, excessive burdens on production and transportation. The Revolution, inspired by the Jacobin spirit, abolished with a veritable fury the political bodies like local Parliaments, which were able to obstruct the free flow of the General Will. Had Rousseau not declared that "in order to grasp the nature of the General Will, no partial societies should be allowed to exist in the State, and each citizen should only express his own opinion"? [8]

In bourgeois interpretation this distrust and hatred of intermediate bodies could be used for the prohibition of workers' associations; the assumption—a basically Protestant-Jacobin one—was that all individuals are self-sustaining units, and that it would be unfair if the individual factory-owner had to face the workers' collective demands. The fallacy of this reasoning is, of course, evident; as Harold Laski wrote, the premise of "capitalist democracy . . . is that because the main modern States are built upon universal suffrage, each citizen, in fact, counts for one and not more than one in the making of political decisions." [9] In England, the workers' demand to organize was first positively answered in 1824; on the Continent it took a longer time, and, naturally, not without attempts by the State—for example, Bismarck's—to secure a controlling hand in the organization.

• Hans Morgenthau sums up this fatal turning-away from politics in the Western world: "Of politics nothing is left but the struggle of individuals and groups for access to the levers of power, in terms either of majority or oligarchic rule, crying out again either for expert management, or else for utopian reform, oblivious of the distinction of what is desirable and what is possible and of the ineluctability of power itself." *Dilemmas of Politics,* Introduction (Chicago: University of Chicago Press, 1958), p. 3.

For reasons already exposed, the socialist-proletarian movements were also opposed to intermediate bodies, although, while their own struggle for recognition lasted, it was their natural interest to set up precisely such bodies and to strengthen, in the same manner, whatever allies they had. Because of their position, they had to project their own image of a unanimous society into the future, as the utopian socialists, utopian communists, and Marx did; the latter maintained from the beginning, taking up in this respect too a point made by Hegel, that particular groups are responsible for lies as phenomena of moral life, because they posit their own particular existence as an absolute good. In theory and in practice, from Saint-Simon to Marx, and from Marx to the present-day Soviet regime, there was no question ever of allowing either political or economic opposition, even of recognizing that such opposition may have a *raison d'être*. Not only political parties, other than the Bolshevik, may not exist under Soviet rule, but the labor unions themselves, so free and vigorous in the West, are but pseudo-organizations that represent the interest of the State and its production policy vis-à-vis the workers.•

The just-examined problems are the political manifestations of radical philosophy. But the latter was much more than a political movement; I have said repeatedly that since the Renaissance, science was one of its main auxiliary forces, whether astronomy, physics, natural philosophy, or paleontology. In the nineteenth century the main scientific support of radicalism was the theory of evolution. Without going into the fascinating details of the Darwinian controversy, let us bear in mind that both capitalistic and socialistic interests could claim that the evolutionary theory proved their own respective points.

For the bourgeois capitalists, the "struggle for life" and the "survival of the fittest" were welcome slogans. They appealed especially to the Calvinistic mentality, and therefore, the evolutionary theory had its greatest popu-

---

• In the true spirit of Rousseau, Vichinsky once told General Catroux, then ambassador to Soviet Russia, that according to Soviet State philosophy not the citizen, but the State, is in need of protection.

larity in Anglo-Saxon countries, vanguards of capitalism. Herbert Spencer was, of course, the great sociological interpreter of Darwin's ideas. "The ultimate development of the ideal man is logically certain," he wrote. "Progress, therefore, is not an accident but a necessity. Instead of civilization being artificial, it is a part of nature; all of a piece with the development of the embryo or the unfolding of a flower." [10] It was easy to build on such a premise a justification of free enterprise. In the United States, W. G. Sumner drew the inevitable conclusions: "The millionaires are a product of natural selection. . . . It is because they are thus selected that wealth . . . aggregates under their hands. . . . They may fairly be regarded as the naturally selected agents of society for certain work. . . . There is the intensest competition for their place and occupation." [11] As for those who fail, they fail as a result of natural selection: "Poverty belongs to the struggle for existence, and we are all born into that struggle." [12]

The proletarian doctrinaires could also turn to their own advantage the theory of evolution. To them "Darwinism" was valid in the moral sphere too, and the law of natural selection applied to the moral history of mankind. *Evil* was the weaker element in the struggle, and *good* was obviously the fittest, which would survive. Moreover, the connection between the Darwinian theory and Hegelian dialectics was evident: in this respect the socialist form of society was superior to the capitalist form. Evolution was not blind: it had a direction, and as we have seen earlier in the present chapter, this favored the proletarian over the entrepreneur.

The essential philosophical agreement of the bourgeoisie and the working classes under the aegis of radicalism was, of course, of a short duration. While radicalism and its various forms contributed to the atomization of belief and behavior—the pillars of society—the bourgeoisie, by its very dynamism, was creating a climate of progress and conflict in which the individuals were set against one another. This was a centrifugal motion. But, curiously enough, the same conditions brought about a centripetal motion as well: the universalism that the middle class inherited from the generous ideals of the French Revolution acted among the atomized individuals as a catalyst, awakening them to the *consciousness of their isolation,* and hence, to their solidarity.

The result is the *modern political party.* It may be defined as the political concretization (in terms of action) of ideologies, that is, of philosophical systems, which had proliferated since the Renaissance. If they—the parties— became such an explosive force, it is, given their intellectual origin, because they were the sacralization of non-Christian goals, and as such, were destined to replace religion in the hearts of men.

Political parties came into being wherever the interests of the landowning nobility and the entrepreneurial class clashed. It was only later that working-class parties also appeared and gave an altogether new turn to events by becoming, naturally, mass-parties, mass-movements. With the increase of democracy, it was inevitable that the parties of the working class occupy an ever larger sector of political life and that they become the main protagonists of the political situation as it unrolled with the advance of the century. This crystallization of political life, the tacit awareness that the "economic issue" dominated the stage, rearranged class loyalties and class alliances, and rearranged also the commitments of intellectuals. Toward the end of the century only two classes subsisted: upper and lower, and everybody was conscious of where he belonged and what interests he defended. The intellectuals alone remained with a divided loyalty, depending on how they interpreted the realities of the age: the movement of emancipation, the struggle to dominate the State, the various and partly hidden sources of power, the explosive forces of socialism and nationalism.

At the turn of the century the choice facing the intellectuals was a difficult one. Although on the surface everything seemed to indicate a classic era to become in the eyes of posterity "the good old times," in reality everything was in ferment, waiting to erupt. The Einsteinian revolution in physics, the works of Russell and Whitehead in logic, the new language of poetry (Mallarmé, Valéry), Nietzsche's obsession with the Superman, Freudian psychoanalysis, the Fauves and the Cubists, were some of the explosive forces bent on shaping the twentieth century in the scientific, philosophical, and artistic order. In politics,

Marxism, the syndicalism of Sorel, the Dreyfus case, the Fabian Society, the doctrine of Maurras occupied the center of interest. The State, in Western societies, although still a bourgeois stronghold, began its career as an agent of general welfare and, at the same time, as a centralized power, jealous of competitors. Yet, it also became a plaything of parties and thus of conflicting ideologies, which, in turn, were bound to give contradictory directions to the State machinery.

The ambiguity of the role of the State was, in fact, the crisis to which I have alluded in the first paragraph of this chapter. After the passage on the stage of European history of Rousseau and Condorcet, of Owen and Fourier, of the British Chartist movement and Bismarck's state socialism, of Marx, Mill, and Maurras, the nature of the crisis could be expressed in one simple question: "To whom did the State belong?" Other, related questions could of course be asked: should the State be the supreme arbitrator? or the guide to the good life? Should it be abolished and thus, presumably, allow mankind to rise to a higher level of its destiny? Should it consider itself a shortcut to Utopia? Should it be more centralized? and if so, in whose interest?

That these questions had a very real meaning may be seen from two examples, chosen at random. Tocqueville's is the first. The leitmotiv of his somewhat ill-humored answers to Gobineau is, as we have seen, that the new, democratic State is an expression of the old Christian moral doctrine. "Christianity made charity a personal virtue," he wrote in September, 1843. "Everyday now we are making a social duty, a political obligation, a public virtue of it. And the growing number of those who must be supported, the variety of needs which we are growing accustomed to provide for . . . now make every eye turn to the State. Governments now are compelled to redress certain inequalities, to mollify certain hardships, to offer support to all the luckless and helpless. Thus a new kind of social and political morality is being established, a kind which the antique peoples hardly knew but which is, in reality, a combination of some of their political ideas [reference to the closely knit structure and civic life of the *polis*] with the moral principles of Christianity." [13]

Yet, it is characteristic of the prevailing confusion that

the same Tocqueville foresaw the centralizing tendency of modern democracy, and feared it not a little. This is what he noted in his *European Revolution* (Book Five, Chapter Three): "The pendular motion of our revolutions is illusory. It will not withstand close examination. In the beginning [there is] always a movement toward centralization. . . . To sum up, the last word always rests with centralization which grows deeper even when it seems less apparent on the surface, since the social movement, the atomization, and the isolation of social elements always continues during such times."

The second example consists of a brief quotation. Its author is Casimir Périer, leading statesman of the July Monarchy, in the 1830's. This was a time when workingmen's associations were not authorized by law; the fear of the proletariat, the fear that insurrections like at Lyons might be repeated, had created a climate hostile to working-class revendications. It is in this climate that Périer declared: "The only hope of the working class is in the resignation to its fate."

The intellectual himself was loaded down with the burden of his past. He had done a great deal, yet nothing seemed to be finished. It looked, however, as if the plans sketched by earlier thinkers needed only a last fillip to become realities. If we look at Marxism and, generally, at the worker movements of this period, we find them in a millennial state of mind that explains why so many intellectuals espoused their cause. *Socialism* carried in itself charisma, and not even Christians could avoid its attraction. Did Christianity not teach the two principles, which now socialism seemed to embody even better: the equal rights of every man to the goods of this world, and the duty of those who have more to help those who have less?

A second choice was liberalism, or, as it was to be known later, especially in the United States, *progressivism*. Its philosophy was not socialistic in inspiration; it had in common with socialism only that both had been developing from one main stem, radicalism. But while socialism had a charismatic focus and a concrete, human testing ground, progressivism was belief in science, the infinite perfectibility of man, and elimination of evil. Socialism, concerned with man, was revolutionary; progressivism, concerned with ideas, was theoretical. Socialism, with nihilism and Messianism grafted on it, became the religion of backward nations; progressivism, never quite rid of western Christian ways, became the ideology of industrialized, democratic societies.•

The third choice was *reaction*. The word itself has an uncomfortable ring, and therefore "conservatism" is sometimes used in its stead. At times it may even be revolutionary, as socialism and progressivism become orthodoxies, empty of inspiration and significance. Conservatism has been updated the moment that intellectuals have found themselves in a dead-end street where their ideologies had propelled them, and had to yield the black fruits of their travails for the social engineers to reap. The conservative (or reactionary)•• was then able and justified in claiming the squandered inheritance of Western civilization, Christendom, individual freedom, and high culture.

These choices are not the only ones, but I find them to be the most representative; those who made them have become types, and as such, they—the Marxists, the progressives, and the conservative intellectuals—have entered political life, literature, journalism, and even the philosophical vocabulary of our time. They are figures of transition between the early-nineteenth-century intellectual and the social engineer, the modern, ideologically sophisticated (or cynical) bureaucrat, the party official. Incarnating the genuine choices of a historical moment, they teach the philosopher by the example of their errors.

• We shall see in Chapter Four, "The Intellectual as a Progressive," how this theoretical stand had to yield to socialist action, and how the progressive became a straggler of Marxism.
•• Bernanos called himself a "reactionary," that is, one who resists the trend of actions he finds harmful.

3

The Intellectual as a Marxist

The confusion about the function of the State and of politics, a confusion entertained throughout the nineteenth century, was a symptom and a result of growing ideological impatience: when so many remedies were offered for the improvement of society, when the whole of human condition could finally be envisaged from a scientific point of view, that is, subject to infinite manipulation and transformation, then emphasis on the traditional rules of coexistence appeared like a will to sabotage the future. In the optimistic view of the century, when thinkers like Burke and Tocqueville were ignored and buried under the "rubbish-heap of history," the radical attitude was natural to man, and the basis of this attitude was the rejection of and contempt for the State as the necessary framework of society. Not only did contemporary *ethnography* misjudge the civilizations of primitive peoples, thereby supporting the view that the State may be replaced either by a restored communism or by some other form of unanimity, blessed by nature; *economic experience* also suggested that the modes of production, of labor relations, and of distribution of products determine the *political* superstructure, and that, therefore, rational economic behavior is the key to what always appeared to be the fundamental irrationality of power relations.

A strong line of thinking thus became absolutely hostile to the State; it considered this most important of all political phenomena either as infinitely elastic and compressible (J. S. Mill), altogether dispensable (Marx and Engels), or the supreme obstacle to total happiness (Bakunin). Thus Liberals, Socialists, and Anarchists were largely in agreement that the State must somehow be suppressed before the *homo oeconomicus* may come into his own. Naturally, they conceived the process of suppression differently, and they disagreed also on the order of the historical stages it will follow. The liberals, listening with one ear to the political tradition of Christianity and to the concrete examples of history (especially of English history), believed in an orderly, gradual transformation, liberating mankind from the last vestiges of un-freedom, but preserving, at the same time, enough of State power to insure general orderliness and tolerance. The socialists were, of course, much more violent: in their eyes, the proletarian dictatorship was *ipso facto* the act of abolition (of the State), even if the leaders of the proletariat would be obliged, during this period of transition, to run the inherited State machinery. The anarchists went much further still: the socialists admitted, at least, that if the State itself comes to an end, *authority* as such can never be dispensed with; "how would these people [the anarchists] propose to run a factory, operate a railway, or steer a ship without a will that decides in the last resort?" asked Engels, scandalized by the lack of realism of Bakunin's partisans.[1] The latter, indeed, maintained that the chief evil is the State, for guaranteeing the capitalist his accumulation and manipulation of fortunes, and other social privileges, while Marx and Engels thought that preventing the concentration of capital in a few hands would ring the death knell of the State itself.●

● A few characteristic remarks of Bakunin on the State, in his *Federalism, Socialism, Antitheologism:* The State must become again simply "society," it must "dissolve itself into society, freely, in accordance with justice" (p. 56). "The State is the most flagrant, the most cynical negation of mankind" (p. 150). "We conclude that it is absolutely necessary to destroy the State" (p. 155). Bakunin advocated the foundation of a League for Peace and Freedom, "leaving no basis other than the interests, the needs and the natural affinities of the populations" (p. 16).

But the disappearance of the State was, in itself, not sufficient to liberate man from the evils under which he had always suffered. Prosperity and Peace had, as an essential condition, the Unity of the globe under a system that, naturally, nobody could or even dared to define, but which was believed to be apolitical, a sort of Paradise for non-religious souls. Already Saint-Simon had suggested that the "industrial regime" would have to be universal, for otherwise it would be opposed by those nations that decided to remain outside it. The socialists wholeheartedly approved this view, only they added that the capitalist system would be unable to achieve this universality because it depended on the differentiation between exploiters and exploited in the international order too. The various utopian theories and movements of the nineteenth and twentieth centuries share in this universalism (or "one-worldism," to use the modern expression), only, as it is usual with them, they stress peace and freedom as opposed to the socialist insistence on efficiency. Thus Martin Buber hopes for the establishment of a "depoliticized society" over the earth, and recommends that, in order to avoid a gigantic centralization, we must "not hand the work of planetary management over to the political principle." [2]

Instead of elaborating new social theories, Buber prefers to point to the concrete examples of the *kibbutzim*. But he has undivided praise only for the ideas of Landauer, which he summarizes with enthusiastic approval. The State, Landauer thought, is the form of expression of a certain way in which individuals live together; should they enter into other relationships, the State would be different too. If "voluntary order" could be established, the State, while not eliminated, would be sidestepped. For this to happen, however, that is, for such extra-Statual organizations to exist, there must be a basic inspiration, a communal spirit. Otherwise, Landauer and Buber admit, they would re-create the State.

I have mentioned this example as fairly characteristic of modern utopian thinking; all such theories seem to have one critical issue to face: the guaranteeing of a common faith and common will by which the State may be, first, unhinged, second, prevented from re-creating itself. All utopian movements are directed against the State and against politics and are hostile to power, which is a factor of differentiation and thus contrary to the universalist spirit, which would cover the globe equally and uniformly like a blanket. But the distinguishing trait of modern utopianism is that Utopia, if one may say so, has entered the realm of possibility: the aspiration for Unity, Peace, and Prosperity has assumed concrete forms, while the other necessary ingredient—a communal spirit—may be generated, spread, and enforced through communication media and propaganda, thus creating the impression that it is spontaneous, unanimous, and enthusiastically upheld.

The ideologies I am going to discuss in the following chapters have derived their influence and success either from this *assumed imminence* of the utopian goal or from the equally urgent will to combat it. The fact that these ideologies (and the reactions to them) have appeared as political parties strengthened them immensely; since by definition they have been disruptive of the State, they could claim its inheritance: power thus flowed in their direction; since they, *de facto,* participated in the life of the State (and of the government), they profited by the power-equipment, organizational channels, and bureaucratic methods characteristic of the modern State.

Thus parties and party ideologies have been one of the localization centers of power in the modern world. Whether we look at the socialist, communist, or fascist variety, we are struck by an *organizational* character, by which, in fact, they re-create the State they combat, and in which they make use of the political principle they deny. The second aspect of the parties that strikes their student is the ideological content, which endeavors to encompass the whole range of human vision and action. But the core of these ideologies is the conviction that the conditions of vision and action can and should be changed because their supreme ideal is, precisely, *reality become value.*•

• "It is superficial to think that utopianism is characterized by an exaggerated thirst for values, linked to an idealistic contempt for reality. Let us rather say that the utopian mind is fascinated by the idol of a reality which would be 'all value,' corresponding to the concept of a perfection-value incarnating automatically all valid values, including the possibility of a complete materialization." A. Kolnai, "La Mentalité utopienne," *La Table Ronde,* Sept., 1960, p. 65.

In the following, I will concentrate mainly on one aspect of Marxism, namely, the face it has shown to the intellectuals whom it attracted, fascinated, repelled, but whom it did not leave indifferent. I hope it is clear from the foregoing that the intellectual agitation subsequent to the French Revolution and Western industrialization had decisively shaken the intellectuals' attachment to the traditional forms of the community, confused their understanding of political realities, and provoked their nostalgia for a society in which their own, and everyone else's, *alienation* may once and for all be ended. Only such fervent hopes—to understand history, to re-establish unity in their own thinking, and to change the world so that the cognitive faculty might again be applicable to it—can explain the extraordinary magnetic power that ideologies had for the intellectuals. Hannah Arendt is right when she defines ideology as "the logic of an idea," by which we obtain not "a body of statements about something that *is*, but the unfolding of a [historical] process. . . . Ideologies pretend to know the mysteries of the whole historical process —the secrets of the past, the intricacies of the present, the uncertainties of the future—because of the logic inherent in their respective ideas." [3]

Marxism, then, should be studied here for two reasons: one is that it illustrates an intellectual choice, logically following from the utopian aspiration for the total, unanimous, peaceful, and prosperous society; the second is the historical development of this ideology under the concrete pressure of actual occurrences (Bolshevik seizure of power, Soviet State, Stalinism, World War, conquest of satellites, competition with the United States), which obliged the (Marxist) intellectuals to make further choices, adapt themselves, constantly reinterpret new events—that is, to live, not only intellectually, but actually, with Communism as a historical-institutional-political phenomenon. This interest in the Marxist intellectual type under this double aspect allows us to divide the rest of this chapter into two parts: the first will discuss the philosophical premises and doctrines of Marxism, the second will be devoted to the process of intellectual adjustments necessitated by the historical development of Communism and the Soviet State.

(1) In order to understand the intellectuals' deep fasci-

nation with Marxist thought, one must keep in mind that this thought has a never-quite-defined but intriguing ambition: to be absorbed ultimately by the *real world of praxis,* and that it announces its propositions with a claim on *scientific accuracy.* From our discussion of the main ideological content of modern times, the hope that unity, peace, and prosperity may now materialize, we could conclude that, at least from the middle of the eighteenth century (the *Encyclopédie* began its publication in 1751) the intellectuals were intent upon finding the bridge relating theory and practice, an actual outlet for the scientific-technical inventions accumulated, so to speak, in the minds of the savants. For the prerevolutionists of the Enlightenment the *feudal state* represented the main obstacle preventing the healthy burst of scientific discoveries and their application; in the eyes of their nineteenth-century successors, *capitalism* and the *capitalist state* remained the reactionary force standing arrogantly between the work of the mind (science) and the transformation of the world for the benefit of all people. With the disappearance of this form of production and distribution, with the disappearance also of the bourgeois State serving as a framework for a corrupt "superstructure," not only would the happiness of all be guaranteed, but philosophy itself would turn into action. Long before Marx enunciated his famous eleventh thesis on Feuerbach ("the task of philosophy is no longer to interpret the world, but to change it"), the thinkers of the nineteenth century tried to get rid of what they considerèd the "limited" scope of speculation.

A philosophy which, by some mysterious alchemy, would turn into concrete reality, and even into action, is, when the mystery is stripped away, science. We have seen that at the threshold of each significant step in the history of modern consciousness there was an optimistic profession of faith in science, whether by Bacon, by Montesquieu, or by Condorcet. Half the success of Marxism must be explained by its early self-identification with the scientific world view. The cocky sureness of Condorcet was matched by the matter-of-factness of Engels when he spoke of the achievements of science in contradistinction to Kantian philosophy, which was guarding jealously an unknowable *Ding an sich.* "One after the other these ungraspable things have been grasped, analyzed, and, what is more,

78

reproduced by the giant progress of science; and what we can produce we certainly cannot consider as unknowable. . . . There is no reason why we should not . . . arrive at the knowledge of . . . producing artificial albumen . . . and of organic life." [4]

Now Marx did not express the same unlimited faith in science, or at least, he (and most of the time Engels too) drew the line at its applicability: "the material transformation of the economic conditions of production. . . can be determined with the precision of natural science," he wrote in the Preface to A Contribution to the Critique of Political Economy, but not so the "legal, political, religious, esthetic, or philosophic—in short, ideological—forms in which men became conscious of [politico-economic] conflicts and fight them out."

Marx was an economist, whereas most of the Marxist intellectuals have been of humanistic formation, and at any rate, poor on economics. They are more interested in the "superstructure" than in its economic underpinnings; this is, perhaps, the main reason that contemporary Marxist thought had retreated imperceptibly to Hegelianism, thus reversing Marx's historic act of "putting the Hegelian system on its feet." Hegel has provided them with more material for strictly philosophical speculation; it must also be recognized that Marx's youthful writings, that is, the Marx still under Hegelian influence, were discovered only in the 1920's and gave then a new impetus to Hegelian studies. The result was that the modern Marxists, particularly in the Western world, have been studying—scientifically and with prophetic ambitions—the superstructure with which they feel more akin.• This in itself would be a sufficient reason to turn to Hegel first in dealing with the typology of Marxist intellectuals.

The basic difference between Hegel and Marx is in their concepts of *alienation*. For the first, the inevitable destiny of human conscience is to objectify (reify) itself in its rapport with surrounding nature as well as with other people, with the State, even with God. The "misery of consciousness" is thus inscribed in the human condition. Yet, on the plane of history and of the evolution of the

• Hegelian studies were restored in France—the center of Marxist thought in the West—in the mid-thirties.

concept of State, Hegel did find a kind of reconciliation: inasmuch as the discrepancy between private and public life is also a source of alienation, the ancient *polis* and the modern (Prussian) State do offer a synthesis: in the former, the private and public existence of the citizen coincided; in the latter, the individual may preserve his subjective freedom, while he also participates in the general will. The modern State is again strong enough to bring unity out of multiplicity.

Thus Hegel proposed two elements, both of which were destined for a glamorous intellectual career in the Marxist system: the reification of consciousness and the reconciliation of the alienated individual within the framework of the State. The powerful intellect of Marx proceeded, however, to transform both ideas.

Marx followed Hegel's lead in asserting that man alienates his freedom in many ways, but his own great discovery was that the key to all of them is alienation through *work*, that is, through that (privileged) activity by which man acts on and transforms his environment, nature. To be sure, Hegel mentioned first that the work of man transcends him; but it was Marx who hit upon the idea that work means working conditions, hence a system of production, expected fruit of one's labor, and a system of distribution and profit. Thus work may be the instrument of damnation (in the capitalist system, based on exploitation), or of salvation (in the socialist, classless society where the abundant produce will be distributed to all according to their needs).•

• Let us note at this point that this dichotomy between capitalist and socialist production, a dichotomy to which Marx and his successors to the present day have been thoroughly committed, is imaginary because it does not take account of the slow transformation of capitalism. But, as Bertram Wolfe remarks, by 1844 Marx had reached the general conclusion of his law: the cracking up of industrial society. The later accumulated documentation which would refute his conclusions because they show that the workers were actually improving their condition under the capitalist system were not taken into consideration by Marx. The State simply did not follow Marx's prophecies, writes Wolfe. "Supposed to be the 'executive committee' of a numerically dwindling bourgeoisie, its democratization has made it ever more subject to the labor vote, farm vote, and the

History, from the point of view of the working man, was, then, an understandable process with a culminating point, and no longer the puzzle of the philosophers, the Sphynxlike *Weltgeist* of Hegel, or the human condition writ large of religions. "Communism has solved the enigma of history," wrote Marx triumphantly. Hence, his thought was to be defined as a philosophy of action, which would reach its climax in the abolition of alienation, that is, of history. But what is characteristic in this thought is that it tends towards its own annihilation, or as the Marxists put it, its "dialectical negation"; to be sure, philosophy has a service to render, it must show man to himself and teach him the modalities of criticizing the conditions among which he lives (and which are responsible for his alienation). The ultimate goal, however, is different. Philosophy will have accomplished its task when it finally negates itself, that is, transcends itself in action, and yields its function to practical energy. "In order to materialize," writes Henri Lefèbvre, prominent Marxist philosopher and Marxist theoretician, "philosophy must deny itself, because, if it is sincere, then it wills its own transformation into something else. . . . Criticism in itself, no matter how radical, changes man's real chains of oppression into ideal chains, and destroys them in theory only." [5]

With Marx, the world witnessed the first thinker who stepped out of the category of thought• and set out to establish an original link between it and the world of matter and of men. Many of these links proved to be, of course, extremely tenuous and woven of artificial threads.

---

vote of the intermediate classes. Out of labor's influence on government, and out of the general, quite classless pressure of society as a whole, there have come state regulation of economic life, legal limitation of hours, minimum wages, protection of health and conditions of labor, legalization of the right to organize, institutionalization of collective bargaining, and the whole sweep of the security legislation." "The Prophet and his Prophecies," *Problems of Communism*, Nov.-Dec., 1958.

• In fact, this is as impossible as stepping out of one's shadow. No matter how intimately we espouse the real world with our thinking, we still *think* about it and do not actually *grasp, qua* thinkers, concrete reality. This critique was developed brilliantly by Julien Benda in his attacks on Bergson's metaphysics and theory of the *durée*.

There are, in Marx's thought, many altogether unwarranted assumptions, such as the identification of the proletariat with its function, that is, work, which allows Marx to say that "philosophy finds in the proletariat its material weapons, while the proletariat finds in philosophy its spiritual weapon." But while such statements could not stand up under genuine philosophical scrutiny, their symbolic value, or, better said, their intellectual exchange value is considerable, because they point from philosophy to history, both being, in the Hegelian-Marxist system, categories of the same science, namely dialectics. For Marx, *substance* and *conscience* are mere metaphysical, that is, unreal, terms, expressing an artificial separation of *nature* and *man.* The two are joined in praxis, that is, in the existence and function of the working class. In this way, the fate of philosophy as a cognitive instrument is attached to the vicissitudes of historical classes and their conflicts, and ultimately to the proletariat, which is called upon to terminate history and, with it, philosophy too. Thus Lefèbvre is justified when he speaks interchangeably of "communism" and of "philosophy": "Communism is defined as a movement and consciousness of movement advancing towards the highest conceivable form of social organization. It puts an end to the quarrel among men, and between him and nature, between existence and essence, reification and self-affirmation, freedom and necessity, individual and species. It solves, in theory and practice, all these contradictions . . . and it is aware that it solves them. . . . Thus philosophy becomes actualized by suppressing itself, and by suppressing its problems as well as the terms of these problems. . . . Philosophy turns into the world of reality. . . . It ceases to exist." [6]

Texts like this proliferate in the writings of Marx and Engels. After having explained Hegel's dialectic method, Marx noted in *Das Kapital:* "[in my method] the ideal is nothing else than the material world reflected by the human mind and translated into forms of thought." This is true of (philosophical) materialism also, which disappears not because it is false as materialism, but because it is useless as a philosophy. Materialism itself is reabsorbed, as Lefèbvre states, in an anthropology, "that is, in an *ensemble* of human sciences. . . . Total man and total society are closely linked concepts because they have the same content: total praxis." The philosopher himself becomes then the "sociologist" (or "communist") who no longer has to consult his own mental image of reality, but reality itself. As Marx wrote against Proudhon in the *Misery of Philosophy*, "as the economists are the scientific representatives of bourgeois society, so the socialists and communists are the theoreticians of the proletariat. . . . To the extent that history marches forward and the struggle of workers is more clearly outlined, they need not seek science in their minds, but only realize what goes on before their eyes."

In his last years, Marx lived in a millennial state of mind, expecting the great revolution to take place in the foreseeable future. The progress in revolutionary will and technique that he studied and observed from 1789 through 1830 and 1848, to the Commune of Paris, convinced him that the working class was learning from its defeats and would put these lessons to good use. By no means less optimistic in the long run, Engels, who outlived his great companion by a sufficient number of years to witness the entrance of the socialist parties into parliamentary-democratic life, was disposed to make more cautious statements. With him and with the Western branch of communist thinkers, Marxism became a *philosophy* once again, as it was only natural in view of the fact that a rather long period was now again envisaged before *action* could replace speculation. The militant phase once more became a necessity, since the bourgeoisie, as George Lukács explained, was now ready to counterattack and develop a sort of smokescreen of irrational philosophies from Nietzsche and Bergson to phenomenology and (later) existentialism.[7] This obliged the Marxist avant-garde to forge the speculative weapons of class war and to begin the always hard task of interpreting Marx himself so as to explain the unexpected delays and the various phases of development.

The Marxist intellectuals thus put themselves in the comfortable position of prolonging an activity that was natural to them, that is, philosophizing, and, at the same time, of repudiating this activity in the name of an assumed total reconciliation of theory and practice. I say that this position was comfortable because it allowed the use of arguments on several levels, as when the victory at Stalingrad was interpreted as a proof of Stalin's philosophical correctness, or when the French Communist Edgar Morin declared that the "Red Army is philosophy on the march." Marxist philosophy thus became many things to many people, and not even the ideological orthodoxy enforced in the Stalin era could prevent the party philosophers from elaborating their own speculative systems.

By examining these systems in an orderly fashion, and then relating them to the political reality within which they found expression, we may grasp the typical features of the Marxist philosopher and of the Marxist intellectual as distinct from the philosopher, yet sharing his basic beliefs and accepting his premises.

In the *German Ideology* Marx and Engels had refuted Stirner's contention that communism demands an absolute morality. No, they replied, communism would merely liberate the virtualities of man, suppressed by class domination and deformed by class struggle. By owning the means of production, the capitalist class interposes itself between nature and the worker (and men in general), deforms and falsifies their relationship, and robs the worker not only of the fruits of his labor, but also of his full humanity. As through a badly refracting mirror, the worker sees himself, nature, and society in a false light; he is "mystified" by the whole civilizational structure constructed for his enslavement (alienation). The unbelievable naïvety of Marx and Engels is well illustrated in this passage from the *German Ideology:* "As soon as labor is distributed, each man has a particular, exclusive sphere of activity . . . from which he cannot escape. He is a hunter, a fisherman, a shepherd, or a critic, and must remain so . . . while in a communist society . . . each can become accomplished in any branch he wishes. Society regulates the general production, and thus it makes it possible for me to hunt in the morning, fish in the afternoon, rear cattle in the evening, criticise after dinner . . . without ever becoming hunter, fisher, etc."

Man's potentialities are liberated in other ways as well. "Marx announced the end and the accomplishment of philosophy," writes Henri Lefèbvre. "Since Liberty, Justice, and Truth were to materialize, there was no need of a specific activity to defend and illustrate Truth, Liberty, and Justice. The cause of philosophy was to enter the current of practical life in a manner which was both unexpected and scandalous for the philosophers: by the detour of proletarian revolution. The proletariat . . . was supposed to assume the supreme philosophical mission, the carrying-out of the goals and interests of philosophy." [8] This does not mean, wrote Lefèbvre in an earlier work, *La Conscience mystifiée,* that socialism solves all the problems of mankind; but "it inaugurates an age in which man may formulate in true terms (without mixing social prejudices with them) the human problems of knowledge, love, and death."

Now there was some justification on the part of earlier Marxist thinkers to paint such a rosy picture of socialist emancipation. The Marxian analysis established with excellent insight what were the effects of accelerated industrialization on the life and mentality of workers, and Marx, at least, cannot be accused, like our contemporary Communist intellectuals, of wilfully ignoring that under a socialist regime the same effects—and far worse—have been experienced by the workers. Generally, Marx argued that the capitalist system cripples the workers' human faculties by "taking more out of them" than they would produce under normal conditions. First, collectively organized work reaches a high average output through the division of labor, which ties the worker to his specialized skill. This is what Marx called "a life-long annexation of the laborer to a partial operation." Second, the immediate result is that the worker remains dependent on the capitalist system since his specialty has no use except in the framework of a factory. Third, the more efficient the worker becomes in his "partial operation," the more his mental faculties become mechanized and his intelligence warped.

These considerations led Marx to have an excessively optimistic notion of the human condition under socialism when, by definition, the workingmen would become the masters of the machines and of the whole system of production, and therefore masters of their own destiny. "Alienation," writes Henri Lefèbvre, "is a function of ownership and of the historically inevitable perversion of appropriating the world *as* property." [9] The remedy is evident: "The proletariat seizes power," writes Engels in *Socialism: Utopian and Scientific,* "and turns the means of production into state property. But in doing this, it abolishes itself as

proletariat, abolishes all class distinctions and class antagonisms, abolishes also the State as State. . . . When at
last it [the State] becomes the real representative of the
whole of society, it renders itself unnecessary. . . . State
interference in social relations becomes, in one domain
after another, superfluous, and then dies out of itself; the
government of persons is replaced by the administration of
things." This process is not quite smooth; in the *Critique
of the Gotha Program,* Marx predicted a "period of revolutionary transformation . . . in which the State can be
nothing but the revolutionary dictatorship of the proletariat"; but afterward, "in a higher phase of communist
society, once the enslaving subordination of the individual
to the division of labor, and therewith also the antithesis
between mental and physical labor have vanished," society
and the individuals will coincide without the obstacle of
the various forms—State, institutions, law, religion—that
alienation has assumed.

Marx, Engels, and Lenin devoted considerable attention to the "period of revolutionary transformation" supposed to take place between capitalist and communist
societies. None of them could very well describe what
actual Communist society would be like, and in this respect
their writings are disappointingly primitive. But a practical
revolutionist like Lenin was understandably preoccupied
with the transitional period he intended to organize after
the revolution he sought to bring about. Thus, while in
the works of Marx and Engels we see few and stereotyped
remarks concerning the postrevolutionary phases of society,
in those of Lenin we note the increasing concern with the
State, with the shocktroops and the dictatorship of the
proletariat, the tasks and programs of the new society.•

• As has been noted by various writers, Lenin, not satisfied
with the workers' revolutionary zeal and will to change the
structure of their lives, proceeded to make of the Communist
Party a revolutionary elite that would seek power and impose
its aims on the working-class movement. He outlined this conspiratorial scheme in the pamphlet *What is to be done?* (1902).
We witness here too an irruption into utopian theory of unanimity and collective will of the political element. It is true, on the
other hand, that in this procedure Lenin had the support of
various passages of Marx and Engels, who had foreseen the
necessity of minority action in destroying the State and assuring
the transitional dictatorship.

Marx based his predictions not so much on theory as on his own observations. These predictions were therefore limited and timid. Marx was a genuine revolutionist, more interested in the mechanism of socioeconomic contradictions and the actual work of the revolution itself than in the subsequent stages. Also, his sense of the concrete impelled him to draw all the possible conclusions from events he witnessed. The Paris Commune was, in this respect, an important field of observation. In order to prevent the State and its organs from becoming masters of society, he wrote in *The Civil War in France,* "the Commune made use of two infallible means. In the first place, it filled all posts—administrative, judicial, and educational—by election on the basis of universal suffrage of all concerned, subject to the right of recall at any time by the same electors. And, in the second place, all officials, high or low, were paid only the wages received by other workers. The highest salary paid by the Commune to anyone was six thousand francs. In this way an effective barrier to place hunting and careerism was set up." And, in another passage, concerning economic production: "If limited cooperative societies are to regulate national production upon a common plan, thus taking it under their own control and putting an end to the constant anarchy and periodical convulsions which are the fatality of capitalist production, what else would it be but communism?"

The organization of the communist society appeared to Marx—as it did to other nineteenth-century social thinkers—as an easy enterprise. Individual good will and collective interest, reinforcing each other, were supposed to do miracles. Once the State and its heavy machinery—army, bureaucracy, police, etc.—disappear, what used to be grave issues would be light with enthusiasm and cooperation. Already in the "transitional society" "the general costs of administration not belonging to production will be very considerably restricted in comparison with present-day society, and it diminishes in proportion as the new society develops" (*Critique of the Gotha Program*). For Lenin this was evidence itself. It is at once comic and tragic (in view of the subsequent evolution) to read his declarations about the simplicity of running the socialist State which, of course, will be no State at all. The State "will inevitably perish with the disappearance of classes,"

Engels had written in *The Origin of the Family, Private Property and the State.* "The society that will organize production on the basis of a free and equal association of the producers will put the whole machinery of State where it will then belong: into the museum of antiquities, by the side of the spinning wheel and the bronze ax." Lenin was, in this respect, a conscientious disciple: for him too, "the State is the product and the manifestation of the irreconcilability of class antagonisms," although, until the higher phase of communism arrives, the workers will have to make use of the State machinery as the defeated bourgeoisie will have left it, "to control the amount of labor and the amount of consumption." But while the bourgeois State was strictly and exclusively a mechanism of control, thus a huge bureaucratic apparatus, "the establishment of workers' control over the capitalists must not be carried out by a State of bureaucrats, but by a State of armed workers." And then this incredible statement: "This accounting and control . . . will be the extraordinarily simple operations of checking, recording and issuing receipts which anyone who can read and write and who knows the first four rules of arithmetics can perform." •

The philosophy of communism, then, is not meant, like traditional philosophy, to be a perpetual search for the meaning of human destiny, nor a permanent reflection on the condition of man, but, first, an instrument of victory for the proletariat (and for the classless society), and, second, a historical record of the existence and of the abolition of alienation, of the State, and of philosophy

• Against those critics of the Bolsheviks who contended that the new, revolutionary regime would never be able to master the machinery of State, Lenin maintained that the question is not to get possession of the old machine and use it for new aims; that is reactionary Utopia, he said! After seizing the power, Trotsky reports the views of Lenin as they were expressed in *The State and Revolution* also, our task is not to re-educate the old machine, but to shatter it to fragments. And with what replace it? With the soviets. From being leaders of the revolutionary masses, instruments of education, the soviets will become organs of the new State order. Trotsky, *The Russian Revolution* (Garden City, N.Y.: Doubleday Anchor Books), p. 263.

itself. The critic of communist philosophy is thus entitled to say that insofar as it is considered an instrument, it is not philosophy but *ideology*, that is, as Engels defined ideologies in a letter to Mehring, a "false consciousness." Insofar as it is an ephemeral activity, coincident with certain stages of economic development but not with other stages, and insofar as it yields to "class-consciousness," • communist philosophy denies itself and abolishes its own universe of discourse.

This, however, is not the last word about it. Even if philosophically one may not, strictly speaking, make any statement about Marxist philosophy, one must discuss it for two reasons: one is that the conditions have not yet been established, even in Soviet Russia and even in the admission of its leaders, when philosophy would let itself be "absorbed" by the "total consciousness" of the communist society; in other words, its career is still that of *any* philosophy in general. The second reason is that Marxist philosophy is at the center of the Marxist intellectual's approach to the world, it is his deepest inspiration. In this respect, too, the fate of Marxist philosophy seems to be that of any philosophical speculation: no matter how often and how many Marxist thinkers conclude that the end of philosophy is praxis, they never make the last, decisive step, namely, abandoning their own philosophical activity.

Among the intellectual and political acrobatics to which the world has been treated by Soviet Russia and communist ideology since 1917 (in fact, even before, considering the internecine struggle of Bolsheviks and Mensheviks, Lenin and Plekhanov, etc.), the philosophical-intellectual *salti mortali* have been the most dazzling. It is true that the Stalin-Hitler pact of 1939 was, perhaps, the least expected about-face that this century has witnessed in the field of politics, but after all, national interests are the hardest facts of life and they often command brusque swerves according to the curves of the road. But more amazing than the 1939 pact itself was its ideological justification, as is, in general, the ideological justification for all those

• According to G. Lukács, the disappearance of philosophy is marked by the emergence of class-consciousness, which takes its place and function.

turns that the Communist Party has taken and imposed on its members, whether diplomats, economists, simple militants, or intellectuals.

The latter are in the most difficult position of all as if they were in need of being reminded—through a series of incredible humiliations—that intellectual independence is a major sin when the existence of philosophy itself is a hardly tolerated, almost anachronistic survival. This is how Communism tries to solve this contradiction: "It denies the existence of philosophy as such, and refuses to acknowledge the philosopher's independence. It maintains that philosophy has already coalesced with science, on the one hand, and with the practical politics of the Party, on the other. . . . It has adopted the thesis that there are no longer any autonomous philosophers, inside or outside the Party, but that each militant is a philosopher." [10]

Let us be clear about it: the plight of the Marxist intellectual is not so much that he is attached to the Party (and through the Party to the political existence of Soviet Russia) as a public crier is attached to the circus whose offerings he must vaunt; this link, this dependence, is a voluntary one, for after all, outside the Soviets and the satellites the philosopher's life and safety are guaranteed when he leaves the Party and denounces its enforced dogmatism. The real plight of the Marxist intellectual may be expressed in the form of an intellectual dilemma: either he preserves his status as a philosopher and thus, by Party definition, he has ceased to be a Marxist and has joined the enemy; or he remains in the Party, and then he is dutybound to consider it as the incarnation of philosophy and the key of all knowledge, and himself as a mere chip from the block of "total consciousness," that is, not a philosopher at all.•

He may always leave the Party and yet remain a Marxist—the partisans of a third choice will argue. But this argument omits the fact that the Marxist is attached to the ideals that Marxism writes on its flag, ideals that are

---

• "If the Party is a philosophy, one must begin by adhering to it in order to reach [*accéder*] this philosophy, the very key of knowledge." Henri Lefèbvre, *La Somme et le reste* (Paris: La Nef de Paris, 1959), II, 688-9.

the realization of the total society of non-alienated men; the road to this society, not merely the shortest, but the *only* road, leads through Marxist critique and the establishment of socialism. Unless the Marxist intellectual breaks with his ideals—his vision of the world, his concept of man and society—he must remain within the framework of the communist movement as it defines itself at any one time, and allow it to carry him in its wake.•

What then is the communist *ideal* which commands the Marxist's loyalty and devotion?

"The task of history," Marx wrote in 1844 (*Toward the Critique of Hegel's Philosophy of Right*), "once the world beyond truth [religion] has disappeared, is to establish the truth of this world. The immediate task of philosophy which is at the service of history, once the saintly form of human self-alienation [religion, Church] has been unmasked, is to unmask self-alienation in its unholy forms. Thus the criticism of heaven turns into the criticism of the earth, the criticism of religion into the criticism of right, and the criticism of theology into the criticism of politics."

Hence the task of the communist philosopher-intellectual stands clearly before him: he must engage in a sort of rearguard action against the enemies of the classless society who, not being able to block history in its inexorable march forward, wish to delay its inevitable conclusion. This delaying maneuver, which is the sole meaning and content of bourgeois strategy, expresses itself under various forms, but it must first be combatted (unmasked) on the plane of philosophy, that is, on the plane chosen by the bourgeois themselves, who always like to claim autonomy for their theoretical disciplines. I have mentioned, in this connection, that G. Lukács, in several of his works,[11] has made one of his principal Marxist duties to accomplish the work of unmasking the socio-economic and political realities under the systems of "bourgeois" philosophy. He reproached

• This is evident if we consider the claim to theoretical but also practical infallibility of the Party. Communist policy, wrote Pierre Hervé shortly after the war, "is the day-by-day elaboration of a strategy and a tactics, adjusted to the diverse conditions of time, place, situation, etc., subordinated to the basic law which is to watch over the permanent interests of the workers." *Action*, Feb. 15, 1946.

Bergson for "attacking the objectivity and the scientific character of knowledge that natural sciences now guarantee," and for "inventing a vision of the world which, behind the fascinating appearances of life constantly in motion, safeguards a conservative and reactionary statism." With regard to post-World War II existentialist philosophies, Lukács concluded that "the most important element of these irrationalist ideologies is to make believe that man's condition under imperialistic capitalism is, in reality, the universal human condition in general." All irrational philosophies, Lukács says, are symptomatic of bourgeois reluctance before progress; and since the tools of progress are reason and science, the philosophies inspired by the bourgeoisie "deprecate and glorify intuition," reject the concept of progress in history, and mystify their adherents and their (class-) enemies by creating myths.

But philosophy, as we have seen, is only one of the weapons of the classless society with which history is now pregnant. The other weapon is the proletariat itself, that is, the force whose mission is to transform history. If traditional *philosophy* has been a rightly suspected exercise in collective mystification, then *science* must take its place as the only reliable mode of cognition, and must be put in the hands of the proletariat, which is eminently qualified to handle its truths since both the workingman and science are in immediate contact with the only reality: nature, the material world. Hence, parallel to the effort of Marxist philosophers to refute bourgeois affirmations concerning the *Ding an sich* and other metaphysical and axiological entities, we see the ambition of Marxist thinkers to establish the absolute validity of the scientific view of the world. "The products of the human brain," wrote Engels in *Anti-Dühring*, "being in the last analysis products of nature [and "material translated in the human head"], do not contradict the rest of nature but correspond to it." Lenin's purpose in *Materialism and Empirio-Criticism* is, of course, the same, that is, to prove that the outside world is exactly reproduced in the human mind (reflection theory), and that, consequently, science, the system of measurement of the outside world, makes valid judgments concerning the only existing (material) reality.

Equipped with an understanding of *history* and with the formidable instrument of *science,* the proletariat (and

the communist militant in general) may now set out to
change the world with the help of philosophy which, in
their hands, turns into the very instrument of transformation. How do the Marxist intellectuals and militants themselves receive this sudden revelation, this unexpected
power?

They have accepted, in the words of Henri Lefèbvre,
"to contribute to a history which was to unravel according
to their own norms, goals and ideals. For them history, as
seen [and foreseen] by reason and history [as a succession
of events] must coincide." They knew, of course, that
there would be minor discrepancies and unforeseen inci-
dents, but which would not alter, only delay, the final
result. "Stalinism did not fit this optimistic perspective;
but Fascism, at least, seemed to be liquidated, and victory
over it deserved through the sacrifice of the dead fallen
in the war. War and liberation were again gigantic forces
of history, clearing the way. History was to continue and
the intellectuals, supplied with a dose of easy rationalism
and another dose of moralism, trusted it." [12]

It goes without saying that the repeated disappointments, deceptions, and failures that the Marxist intellectuals suffered in the last forty years, have not shattered
their conviction that history *was* working for them, for
the accomplishments predicted by Marx. As the hard core
of Nazis does not doubt to this day that Hitler's goals
were correct, and that he was only prevented from
carrying them out, so the Communist intellectual may
accuse even Stalin of deviation, yet he does not question
the validity of communist theory, historical analysis, and
social ideal. Even in the eyes of ex-Communists (unless
they renounced the philosophical premises of their earlier
views), the "Left," whether democracy, socialism, or
progressivism, has only one historical task: to work out
new modalities for the passage from their present system
to the communist system (undefiled by Stalinism, Bolshevik brutality, etc.); as Lefèbvre puts it, "the divergences
[within the Left] are not about long-range objectives
. . . but [only] about the rhythm and the mode of the
transition [to communism]." [13]

What would communism mean, philosophically and historically? The end of necessity, of coercion, that is, in

Marxist terminology, the end of politics and of the State. In the words of Engels, the withering away of the State would be the "leap of humanity from the realm of necessity into the realm of freedom." "Politics will be abolished," Marx wrote in his polemics against Proudhon, "with the disappearance of class rule . . . because political power is nothing but the official sum of the antagonisms obtaining in bourgeois society."

What would replace the State, and how would the rapport among men develop in a society without politics? In a letter to Bebel (1875), Engels wrote this: "As long as the proletariat still needs the State, it needs it not in the interest of freedom, but for the purpose of crushing its antagonists; and as soon as it becomes possible to speak of freedom, then the State, as such, ceases to exist."

Thus the communist society would be classless and would not know the humiliating division of labor; as Marx declared in his *Critique of the Gotha Program*, everybody would work according to his needs; the "superstructure," that is, morality, law, religion, art, philosophy, would no longer be superimposed on the population in the form of mystifications, ideologies, and other "opiates," but would become the very expression of man, his life, his possession, his work. As soon as the communist mode of production spreads over the earth, man will achieve perfect domination over nature and, through the just system of distribution, a perfect harmony with his fellows. Man will thus coincide with himself and with humanity: religion and philosophy, having no functions to fulfill, will perish with the State.

What about morality, law, politics? Since they express certain modalities of rapports between men, they are linked to the fundamental rapport: the mode of production. If the latter changes, if man-to-man relationships become simple, brotherly, and free, law, that is, the network of penalties imposed by the exploiters on the exploited, simply disappears.• The same is true of morality: in the pre-com-

---

• No wonder that law and sociology officially do not exist in the Soviet Union. Law is taught at the Police Academy, and sociology is smuggled in, unofficially, in the anthropology departments of the universities.

94

munist societies the label of "sin" was applied to such deeds
that were in the interest of the upper classes to discourage.•

Politics would, of course, similarly vanish, according to
Marx's statement, quoted above. In the writings of Marxist
intellectuals the function of government is consistently
disparaged because the act of governing implies, in their
estimation, a symptom of inequality, oppression and, above
all, economic exploitation. The greater the difference between economic levels, and consequently, the wider the
gap between classes, the Marxists seem to argue, the more
dangerous is the situation for the governing class and the
more overwhelming the necessity to govern, that is, to op-
press. "Less government," wrote Harold Laski, "only means
more liberty in a society about the foundations of which
men are agreed, and in which adequate economic security
is general; in a society where there is grave divergence of
view about those foundations, and where there is the
economic insecurity exemplified by mass-unemployment, it
means liberty only for those who control the sources of
economic power." [14] It is then obvious that when classes
as such disappear, when society becomes level, the need
for *politics*, in the Marxian sense, no longer exists. Its place
is taken by *social technique:* "Only in Marxism does politics
actually become what its name implies, namely an art in
the Greek sense of the word: competent and adequate
action on the evolution of social and state existence: social
technique." [15]

(2) The great, the unspeakable tragedy of the Marxist intellectual in the post-1917 period has been that he became
once again, an *alienated man,* together, of course, with the
citizens of the Soviet State and the members of communist
parties all over the world. What is more, his alienation
assumes extremely brutal forms and reproduces the same
features on the basis of which Marx had made the diag-

• "No human being is born with a conscience; a conscience is
developed as a matter of natural community, group, and family
experience; and when this body of ethical experience derives
from man's age-old struggle against oppression, slavery and
injustice, it is humanistic, wedded to life and mercy and justice,
and pledged to ever broadening horizons of human freedom."
Howard Fast, *Prospectives,* Nov., 1957.

nosis of bourgeois-capitalistic society: mystification; slogans; exploitation; huge political, propagandistic, and bureaucratic apparatuses; not to mention the physical deprivations, persecutions, tortures, and enslavement. In the light of the known facts within the Communist empire and within each communist party and cell, it is really tragic, and at the same time absurd to speak, as the French Marxist, Pierre Naville, does, of communist "society [which] will be founded on joy [*jouissance*] . . . which becomes a primary consideration as the purpose of social and economic organization." [16] And this will be, according to Naville, only "the first phase of communism," when philosophy terminates and "philosophical thought yields to the quantitative science of concrete reality" !

The new alienation of the Communist intellectual could be more or less justified as long as the Soviet State was surrounded by hostile capitalist lands threatening its social experiments and economic achievements. But, as Lord Percy of Newcastle writes in an earlier-quoted passage, societies like the one that the Bolsheviks created, that is, based on ideology and assumed unanimity, will always have a cheap excuse for the use of coercion and terror; it is forever easy to evoke the monstrous image of the "enemy" lurking within or without, a menace to the total society and a cause for preserving indefinitely the state of siege. Thus the existence of a hostile outside world, capitalist, Fascist, "antiprogressive," or of any other label, may always be safely assumed; this state of affairs would end only with the total conquest of the globe and the absolute enforcement of Communism, theory and practice.•

It is important to understand that the feeling of alienation of the Communist intellectual is not derived from the open advocacy of world conquest and consequent total society. It is precisely his main ideological and psychological motivation for joining the Marxist movement that society should finally be united, without distinctions, and joyous. In Marxism and in the coercive methods of Bolshe-

---

• At the 18th Communist Party Congress (March, 1939), the question arose why had the State not vanished after exploitation and the exploiting classes had been suppressed? Why did the State maintain its power? Stalin's reply was that socialism had triumphed in one country only; and that the State was not to disappear before capitalist encirclement itself would crumble.

vism, he finds the technique by which this goal may materialize, a goal well worth certain sacrifices, particularly if what is sacrificed are only the illusory and despicable forms of bourgeois-democratic freedom. From the communist society he expects a Utopia, that is, the end of politics; "the question facing us today," writes H. Lefèbvre, after recalling a long series of disappointments with Stalinism and with the French Communist Party, "is whether the Marxian élan and hope . . . may be rediscovered, in spite of the deceptions; . . . whether the State will finally wither away, politics disappear, freedom reach new heights, and partial liberties multiply." [17]

The real alienation of the Communist intellectual—and the all-important consciousness of his failure—has other sources. He does not condemn, far from it, the goals and ideals of Marxism; he indicts, very timidly and hesitantly, the Communist leaders for not having achieved them; then, in the meditation over this failure he is eventually led —not in every instance—to discover the error and utopianism of Marxism itself. Accordingly, we must distinguish the types of Marxist intellectuals at mid-century: the unreconstructed ones who see in the vicissitudes of Soviet history the deviation from pure Marxism, and the penitent ones who realize the unrealistic nature of Marxist aspirations. There is a third type too: those ex-Communists who have reached the understanding that the Marxist ideal is not only unrealistic, but, indeed, evil, and not an "ideal" at all. But the latter can no longer be called Communists or Marxists, and thus remain outside our discussion.

However, as long as the Marxist intellectual accepts his partisanship and openly militates in the ranks of Communism, those differences are negligible. The only distinction one should not underestimate is between the intellectuals who are citizens of Soviet Russia, China, or the satellite countries, and those who live and work in the countries outside the Soviet orbit, even though they may be members of the Communist Party and frequent visitors to Russia. I believe that the acts and words of the latter reveal more of the Marxist mentality and its undiminished utopianism; while the former, about whose real feelings, aspirations, and deep commitments we have only occasional hints—like in the Pasternak case—are today much closer to the type that I will discuss in the chapter on social engineers.

It seems to me, then, rather obvious that the Marxist intellectual in the West has not given up his "bourgeois" mentality completely. Even according to his own premises this would have been impossible since the society in which he lives has not yet made "the leap into freedom," has not yet established the socioeconomic conditions that would "reflect" in his own mind. As a result of his rootedness in the Western tradition, the Marxist intellectual obstinately believes in the inner man, whose change he expects and predicts, although this is in contradiction to his Marxist faith. Again we may quote Rousseau, whom these intellectuals follow perhaps as often as they follow Marx: "For a society in its initial stages to be able to adopt the right political precepts and to follow the fundamental rules of the common good, the effect ought to become the cause: instead of the communal spirit being the achievement of the new institutions, it would be more desirable that it might inform them; [in other words, it would be better] if men were what they ought to be *before* the laws are instituted, rather than become what they ought to be *through* these laws." [18]

This is why I said, at the beginning of this chapter, that the Marxist intellectual of the West has tended to return to Hegel from the moment the *utopian* promises of the Soviet State and communist society appeared, for the first time, to be broken. As long as Soviet society and leadership could be looked upon under the aura created by the Revolution and the Red Army, as long as economically and socially it seemed like a grandiose experiment of bold pioneers, the Marxist intellectuals saw Utopia materialize under their eyes. Lenin's definition of the new society, "the soviets plus electrification," was an exhilarating program for these men who had had enough of their own "bourgeois style" nationalism and traditionalism. The feeling that Utopia had arrived was further emphasized by the 1929 capitalistic "krach," subsequent misery, unemployment, rise of fascist parties; in comparison, the constructive-sounding Five-Year Plans and the transformation of the muzhik into an enlightened industrial worker "owning the means of production" and therefore the State, represented the victory of Good over Evil.

The disappointment came with the purges, liquidations, the bestial extermination of Ukrainian peasants. These were, of course, rumors rather than verified facts at the time, and as a result, relatively few people revised their pro-Communist attitude. But they were sufficient to elicit the first critical examinations (for example, André Gide's *Retour de l'URSS*) and, significantly, for the beginning of the rehabilitation of Hegel (1936-9). It was in 1936 also that appeared *La Conscience malheureuse* (taking its title from a phrase of Hegel) of Benjamin Fondane, one of the first to call attention to existentialism (Heidegger, Kierkegaard, Shestov) and to analyze, in the terms of contemporary problems, the forever tragic discrepancy between thought and action, intellect and insight, science and metaphysics. These problems were, of course, not new; but what Fondane understood was that they left in the contemporary consciousness the deep mark of dissatisfaction with the duality of man, and pointed to the incurable *"déchirement"* of the self (another term for "alienation").

If Marxism had been examined with a merciless intellectual integrity, it would have been found incapable of welding together the alienated man. But with doses of Hegelianism added to Marxism, the latter became more palatable, and the resulting confusion and contradiction were overlooked as far as Stalinist-Communist dogma, then in elaboration, was concerned.• The Marxists in the West continued to be intellectual acrobats, riding two horses, as it were, utopianism and Soviet Bolshevism, constantly in danger of being pulled apart or falling between the two.

The *utopian* pull manifests itself in the will and hope to change man. Edgar Morin, a French Communist who recently recanted, declared in an interview[19] that the real moral problem is to transform man into a human being, a task that only the "revolutionary Left" has understood and tried to carry out. If it has failed, it is because an

---

• For quite a long time, until the mid-twenties, Marx's early writings were imperfectly known. They were unknown to a Lenin, for example. When they were first presented, the reaction was more than cool; young Marx was still a Hegelian, whereas official Communist philosophy was based on the writings of the mature and old Marx.

"intellectual atrophy" had taken hold of it, a "regression towards the deification of order, that is, the inruption of reactionary tradition." In other words, the revolutionary Left, that is, Communism, exists somewhere among the eternal realities, but it has been evinced by a reactionary mode of thinking (which is, presumably, also such a reality). The teaching of dialectics itself is thus conveniently cast aside: it is not possible, in Morin's assumption, that the "revolutionary Left" was carrying in itself a reactionary potential, simply because the revolutionary leftists are human beings, subject to failure, abuse, and intellectual rigor mortis; the truth must be that "reaction," like microbes from the outside, have attacked an essentially healthy body.

This type of thinking, so characteristic of Marxists, reveals the same mentality observable in all movements of utopian scope, that is, small and cohesive groups ambitioning to revolutionize the world through the complete transformation of human beings. In G. P. Gooch's description of the sects of seventeenth-century England many of the traits of twentieth-century Communism may be studied. The Levellers and other splinter sects considered themselves perfect, or at least transformable into saints by the enforcement of a certain orthodoxy. They usually proposed sharing of property, as a result of which "there would be no need of government, for there would be no thieves or criminals." [20] Instead, the citizens of these reconstructed societies were supposed to be "true Christians," placing themselves "under the government of God and Christ." [21] The same is true of the hard core of Jacobins during the Terror of Robespierre; the latter proudly bore the name of "Incorruptible," while his colleague, Saint-Just, was known as "the pure" man (*le pur*) of the Revolution.

The utopian conviction of the Marxist intellectuals is shown in its clearest light when they begin to investigate the causes of mid-century Communist failure. The core of this failure was expressed not by a Marxist, but by a "progressive" intellectual, Albert Camus, with his accustomed lucidity. The other works on the same theme are more or less illustrations of Camus's diagnosis.• The well-

---

• Two of Camus's works must be mentioned in this respect: *L'Homme révolté,* and a short essay, *Remarque sur la Révolte.*

known thesis of Camus is a distinction between "revolt" and "revolution." The first is a spontaneous act, the direct effect of suffering and just indignation, which, however, cannot remain localized in the individual as an isolated gesture. "I suffer, therefore we are" (*Je souffre, donc nous sommes*) is briefly, according to Camus, the story of each revolution in its first stages: the realization that others share his fate leads the rebel to the enlarged consciousness of his own plight, but also to the hope of solidarity with others. The revolution, however, is necessarily a collective and organized enterprise, demanding leadership, obedience, hierarchy, structure: new forms of alienation. In the evolving revolutionary machine, dogma, terror, persecution of heresy, secret police, leadership cult, and bureaucracy make their inevitable appearance. The individual and his rebellion are absorbed in the collectivity and its new conformism.

At the time of its publication, in 1951, *The Rebel* (*L'Homme révolté*) provoked a storm of denunciations by Communist intellectuals and sympathizers. The book was also the cause for the break between its author and Jean-Paul Sartre, subsequent to an exchange of letters between the two (and the latter's lieutenant, Francis Jeanson) on the pages of *Les Temps Modernes*. Since then, however, and increasingly since the suppression of the Budapest insurrection, other similar theses have seen the light of day, authored by Communist intellectuals expelled from the party or having broken with it. That none of them is able to transcend the magic circle of ultimate utopian commitment (and therefore of Marxist loyalty and even of hopeful considerations about Russia), is symptomatic of their basic inspiration. Let us take, for example, the well-known French Marxist author, Daniel Guérin's new book, *Jeunesse du socialisme libertaire*.[22] Like others of its kind, this book draws certain conclusions from the Stalinist-Communist deviation and attempts to renew the tradition of a socialism informed by the spirit of freedom. Guérin too seeks the secret of the corruption of revolutions and explores the possible guarantees against the historical fate that threatens them. In other words, he tries to find underneath the "strong revolutionary organization" the initial act of revolt, the unspoiled spontaneity. He too, however, is obliged to select as his ideal models pre- or extrarevolutionary ephemeral groups—like the direct democracy of 1793-4 with its popular societies, and the first Commune of Paris—whose chief characteristic is precisely that they were ineffectual and were soon absorbed by the larger movement, organized, unafraid of power and its ruthless use. They were so absorbed—and had been destroyed even before the absorption—because, as Guérin must admit, they were fast subverted by minorities in some cases, by skillful tribunes in others. Without a strong leadership supervising doctrine and behavior, but also drowning out the group's initial idealism and freedom, they proved to be easy prey to political adventurism.

Guérin's attempt at rehabilitating Marxism is not essentially different from other recent attempts by his countryman, Pierre Hervé (*La Révolution et les fétiches*), by Howard Fast in the United States, by Djilas in Yugoslavia. Their case must be carefully distinguished from that of Koestler, Chambers, even of Silone, all of whom had turned their backs on Marxism as a result of having changed their philosophy. But Hervé, Djilas, Guérin, Fast, et al., are still driven by the original inspiration and are still hoping that by some miracle the utopian element will win out over the other lines of force that constitute the present dynamism of Soviet Communism. Indeed, many of these men, unshaken by the revelations of the last twenty years and by the philosophical, historical, and socioeconomic studies of revolutions and the totalitarian regimes they engender, continue putting their faith into the Soviet regime itself as it stands. Jean-Marie Domenach, editor of the leftist Catholic *Esprit*, maintained, in a conversation with me, that Soviet Russia is still the only hope of world socialism, the latter being, in his judgment, the necessary and desirable superior stage of history. In the October, 1959, issue of his magazine, in connection with Khrushchev's visit to the United States, he wrote the following: "Even though the Soviet leaders have become so technical-minded at the expense of their Marxism, they continue to be bearers of an idea and their political actions continue to represent a dream: the dream of economic equality, of man's universal victory and conquest of earth and heaven." [23] That the Soviet leaders have proved to be ruthless oppressors, imperialists, and mass-murderers, and that "man's universal victory and conquest"—whether through Sovietization or other means—has remained a meaningless statement in view of the price paid for technologization in terms of freedom lost, does not seem to affect Domenach's trust in some ultimate Paradise.

The same undaunted hope in the utopian future, ushered in by Communism, has been in the center of Sartre's political views. His peregrinations to Communism, then back to simple "progressivism," and then back again, are notorious, and reflect very well the hesitations, sudden *élans*, and hopelessness of the Marxist intellectuals in the West. There was a moment, in 1948, when the messianic expectation sweeping through Saint-Germain-des-Prés crystallized in what was to be Sartre's *Rassemblement Démocratique Révolutionnaire*. The program reflects the Marxist inspiration: "an economic and political structure in which the State shall wither away while the intellectual and manual workers will democratically decide on their destinies." [24] Nothing came of this ambitious program, or for that matter, of the suprapartisan *Rassemblement*. As Mme de Beauvoir explained years later, Sartre finally understood his group's weakness and gave up the idea of a front of the non-Communist Left. Instead, he chose "to ally himself with the real forces," which would succeed where he had failed, that is, with the Communists.• From that moment, Sartre's line of reasoning on the pages of *Les Temps Modernes* became as follows: the Soviet regime is a far cry from the Marxist-Leninist teaching. Nevertheless, the Soviets are more likely to lead mankind toward progress than is the Western world. Therefore, every denunciation of the Soviets, even if based on evidence, weakens the forces of progress and strengthens conservatism and reaction. As long as Soviet Russia exists, the enemies of the working class will have to be on the defensive. With the Soviet Union discredited or defeated, the proletariat would lose its only hope.

Was Soviet Russia discredited, in the eyes of Sartre, by the Hungarian freedom fight of 1956? At the time of these events, many of his fellow intellectuals and writers were dropping their membership in the *Comité National des Ecrivains*, which, under the presidency of fellow-travel-

---

• Compare with Guérin's above analysis of the fate of "idealist" groups caught up in a revolutionary movement.

ing Vercors, had failed to protest against the purges in the satellite countries, the anti-Semitism following the Moscow "doctors' plot," etc. But Sartre, in spite of his denunciation of the Russian behavior in Hungary (article in *L'Express*, November, 1956; preface in *Les Temps Modernes*, January, 1957), cannot help envisaging the future—of Hungary, of France, of the world—as inaugurated by a (renovated) Communist Party. "If various trends of thought within the Party," he wrote in the second article, "are not allowed to express themselves and must become factions, then the party structure should be reconstructed and a new party constitution worked out." In other words, Sartre, in this instance too, eluded the issue. He was ready to find fault with the *organization*, but not with the basic *philosophy* of the Party (from which its despotic organization logically follows). When, in concluding his one-hundred-and-twenty-page preface, Sartre offered his "intellectual resources" for the work of reconstruction, the reader could be sure that the new facts, if any were needed, had not made any impact on his basic commitment.

Once again we must conclude that in the judgment of these Marxist intellectuals: (1) there is no salvation outside the working class, and (2) the working class is truly represented by Communism (Soviet Union) only. When they follow this reasoning, these intellectuals end up with a curious contradiction. First of all, there is no doubt that they consider the proletariat as the Levellers considered themselves: a society of saints, qualitatively different— pure, virtuous, and carrying the hope of mankind—from other classes which, by dint of violence and abuse, prolong their existence in the teeth of history's decree. There are enough texts in Marx, Engels, Trotsky, Lenin, Lukács, etc., to show that the proletariat, the last category of men to be emancipated, possesses the virtues of the sacrificial lamb, of a Christ crucified. Not only that its emancipation puts an end to exploitation of man by man and ushers in the Stateless, classless, apolitical, "truly" human society, but it is also entrusted, like an army of avenging but just angels, with the last struggle against the forces of evil (in the period called the "dictatorship of the proletariat").

Now if the members of the proletariat are not saints (in the sense in which the Levellers, Brownites, and Anabaptists understood this term, that is, a society of elects), then prosperity, economic equality, the normal satisfactions of life that the Marxist intellectuals want to secure for them, would be welcome achievements no matter how obtained. For, in fact, the great scandal for Marx was that the capitalist system produced surplus goods, and yet the producers themselves, the workers, were unable to purchase them, to reap what they had sown. Everything else followed from this initial anomaly and injustice: accumulation of capital, cyclical crises, minimal wages, the workman's alienation.

By a political-economic act of enormous importance, the Western democracies, and particularly the United States, have admitted the working class to the status of consumers which, of course, has a direct bearing on their civic role, civil rights, and individual and collective freedoms. In terms of "alienation" the Western workers have far less to complain about than the average Soviet citizen, and if their prosperity is partly paid for by the inhabitants of underdeveloped areas (through the fluctuation of the world price of raw materials, influenced by the great industrial empires), the Soviet citizen's scant luxury is similarly secured by the Kremlin's slave-labor methods, arbitrary fiscal policy, and imperialistic economic policy toward the satellites.•

But the Marxist intellectual is not interested in the economic welfare of the proletariat (or of the colonial peoples); nor is he interested in it even secondarily. For him a superhuman, perfect society is of far greater import; thus, rooted in his ideological commitment, he will observe American prosperity and Russian or Chinese misery, and conclude that in the dynamic march of history the first is on the decline, the second is on the upgrade. To sustain this conviction, he will believe doctored statistical figures, patently false production rates, and the outward signs of compulsory enthusiasm in the population. The hard core of his belief remains that "Americanization" is the enslave-

• First of all, the industrial production of the satellite countries is subordinated to over-all political aims, directed by the Kremlin. Secondly, commercial exchange between the Soviet Union and any one of the satellites is done according to prices dictated by the former. For example, until the mid-fifties, the lists of world-market prices were not even available to the satellite governments.

ment of the worker, while Sovietization is in the direction of liberation and progress.• This is natural since in his abstract love for the proletariat (and for humanity), he must reject ephemeral prosperity and comfort when, on the other side, he envisages the end of history and the divinization of man. Like Pascal offering his wager, the Marxist intellectual agitates against the acceptance of immediate worldly goods and tries to persuade his fellow men to choose the total salvation that classless society guarantees. "Feuerbach and Marx," Eric Voegelin writes, "interpreted the transcendent God as the projection of what is best in man into a hypostatic beyond; for them, the great turning point of history, therefore, would come when man draws his projection back into himself, when he becomes conscious that he himself is God, when, as a consequence, man is transfigured into superman." [25] This is the ultimate meaning and aspiration of Marxism and of the Marxist intellectual.

Marxism would have remained an ideology, and the Marxist intellectuals' writings a file in utopian literature, had the Revolution not taken place in Russia, and a State, claiming to embody Marx's teachings, not been created. Through this historical act, the revolutionary modernization of Russia, the Marxist intellectuals everywhere in the world have become "the elect," servants, masters, and interpreters of the world-historical spirit, and public figures whose words and acts carry weight, often beyond their measure as individuals and intellectuals. No wonder, then,

---

• There are two reasons for this belief: one is that according to Marx's teaching, it is not the standard of living—high or low—of the working class that determines whether we deal with a capitalist or socialist system, but rather whether everybody lives by his work, or some live on their investment, that is, unproductively. In this respect Western and American societies are capitalistic. The second reason is Stalin's general indictment, in the mid-thirties, of all socialist and social-democratic parties under the label of "social fascism," that is, a policy of coexistence with the Right. According to many observers, the Hitlerist victory in 1933 was due to the policy of non-co-operation of the German Communists vis-à-vis the Socialists, imposed by Stalin. The Popular Front in France was a belated attempt to reverse this policy.

that the existence, the development, the vicissitudes of Soviet Russia as a State and as a revolutionary force (the "workers' fatherland") has been, for the last forty years, one of the most momentous intellectual phenomena, making and breaking careers, bestowing or reviling reputations.

The Marxist intellectuals' experience and reaction during this period has been characterized by the extraordinary tortuous and tortured relationship they have maintained with the Soviet Union. The land of the proletariat was a *fact*, and its interests supreme; loyalty to it had precedence over patriotism, friendship, and family ties, because the expected communist society was itself to be a universal homeland, family, and friend.• The intellectuals were clinging to these idealized features while the Soviet State itself, making use at once of ideological intransigence and Asian-type despotism, was following the way of all political entities, that is, pursuing its own complex interests. The more these interests demanded cunning, ruthlessness, and ideological leaps, the more baffled the intellectuals became, since the discrepancy did not cease widening between hard reality and the utopian image. The leaders of the Kremlin, although they must have been torn also between their ideological commitments and political Machiavellism, must have understood and certainly utilized the state of permanent shock of the western Marxist intellectuals: they knew that the latter—in France, in Germany, in Spain, in the United States—could be counted upon to justify any ideologically inconsistent move of the Soviet political machine and to become more loyal, servile, and uncritical in proportion, precisely, as they were thus humiliated.•• The

• "Western communists," wrote N. Berdyaev, "when they join the Third International, play a humiliating part; they do not understand that in joining the Third International they are joining the Russian people and realizing its messianic vocation." *The Origin of Russian Communism* (Univ. of Michigan Press, 1960; first edition in 1937), p. 144.

•• It is part of the technique of humiliation that the Soviet leaders inflict systematically on fellow-traveling Western intellectuals that they shower abuse upon them, thereby forcing them to progress further on the road of subservience. At a writers' congress in Vienna the Soviet writer Fadeev called Sartre a "capitalist hyena," in spite of his known sympathies.

Kremlin could always claim that it had a better mastery of dialectics and a more perfect seismograph for registering the oscillations of history. The most dramatic mystification and exploitation of the twentieth century was the way the Kremlin mystified and exploited the Marxist intellectual.

Thus the latter, who sought the universal end of alienation, became doubly alienated: from the bourgeois society in which he lived, and from the Soviet State, which obstinately refused to conform to his ideal. This alienation, the process of reaching it and of becoming conscious of it, took various forms. There are those who viewed with increasing alarm the *embourgeoisement* of Soviet society (or parts of it); others objected to its *bureaucratization*, its *timidity* and enforced *conformity* in artistic and literary expression. Then there were those who came slowly to the realization that, as Pierre Fougeyrollas wrote, "there are political and psychological forms of alienation which cannot be abolished by economic mutations" (*Le Marxisme en question*). And finally those, and their case is not the least interesting, who belong to an already Sovietized generation, but who, after defecting to the West, remain forever perplexed by not finding an ideal either under the Soviet system, or in what had appeared to them, by contrast, an absolutely free world.

Their case, however marginal—they are mostly Hungarian and Polish refugee intellectuals—provides the clue to the understanding of the Marxist intellectuals' failure and defeat. The Marxist intellectuals aim at a world that does not and cannot exist. In a conversation I had in London (1958) with a prominent young eastern European refugee intellectual (high position in the Communist Party of his homeland, Stalin Prize for literature, best-seller status for his novels, extensive travels in the Soviet orbit), it became clear to me that after having thoroughly understood the incredible corruption of the Communist system and Communist soul, this man, thirty-eight years old at the time, was equally disappointed with the West for not being as just, as perfect, as free, and as prosperous as he had been convinced, before his escape, it would be. The Marxist mentality is thus a utopian mentality in search of the extrahistorical and extrahuman perfection; in the last forty years the Marxist has been led to believe that this perfection has materialized (the end of philosophy, as Marx announced, the reign of Liberty, Justice, Truth), in the Soviet Union first, then, putting his ideological gears in reverse, in the West. Disappointed in his search he has become a non-Stalinist Marxist (a socialist libertarian, according to Guérin) reserving his vacant loyalty to Mao, to Khrushchev, to Tito, or to a new Popular Front, or a nihilist (like my interlocutor in London), or a religious man.

Let us see now what are the concrete evils that gnaw at the Marxist intellectuals' loyalty to the Soviet Union. Leon Trotsky had denounced Stalinist bureaucracy since 1925, and ten years later, in exile, he warned that the "dictatorship of the proletariat" was replaced by the dictatorship of the bureaucrats (*Worker-State, Thermidor and Bonapartism*). Yet, after years of bitter disappointment, he still believed that "the dictatorship of the proletariat has found a disfigured but unquestionable expression in the dictatorship of a bureaucracy."[26] Trotsky still belonged to the Old Guard of revolutionists; in his eyes no amount of evidence could demonstrate that the Party he had helped to power had simply turned against the Revolution. But younger members tend to conceive of bureaucracy as no mere temporary necessity, nor an accidental cancerous growth on what Lenin had promised would be an administration so easy that housewives could run it, but the symptom of an evil that is, perhaps, inevitable.

Inside Russia, of course, no one dares say that Communism has failed. For one thing, the Russian Communists are, certainly in most cases, Russians first (and in China, Chinese), who cannot ignore that their country has progressed, regardless whether the Marxism dogma is valid or not. In fact, since Russia *has* progressed, *has* become an industrial power on the way to challenging the United States, it may be intellectually comfortable to attribute the new position and power to Communist politics and economics, thereby managing to reconcile, on the surface of one's intellectual commitment, patriotism and membership in the Party.

For another thing, compared to *what* can Communism be said to have failed? Public pronouncements by Soviet intellectuals still claim that their society is advancing toward total communism, and *embourgeoisement* or artistic orthodoxy is denounced only by a few, in the rare intervals known as periods of "thaw," and even then in a cryptic language. The Western Marxist may declare that his own faith in Utopia is the genuine image Marx had fixed on the horizon of history; the Soviet intellectual may never confess to the discrepancy between his Utopia and the actual regime under which he lives.

But in a certain sense the Marxist intellectual, inside and outside Russia, was fooled (mystified) not by the Bolshevik Party, but by the masses whose ambition turned out to have been, all along, more modest than Utopia, and for whose benefit the bureaucrats have reconstructed the State. Marx's revolution, the complete and radical transformation of man's condition, was betrayed not so much by the Party, as by the general development of this age: industrialization, modernization. In this sense, the Revolution proved to be a means toward an economic goal, and the nature of the means followed partly from specific Russian conditions, partly from the totalitarian nature that the ideology and the Revolution had authorized. The Marxist intellectual then faces a society in the process of *embourgeoisement* (the process is far more rapid on the top than at lower levels), a political system for which the *raison d'état* is an absolute standard (not tempered by Western moral tradition), and an intellectual (artistic, literary, philosophical) life that, instead of being subjected to ideological conformity—logically, this is what the Marxist intellectual had asked for—is subjected to the *raison d'état*, that is, to political expediency.

In the understanding of the above, the Soviet intellectuals are incomparably more advanced than their Western Marxist confreres, who have had no grasp of Communist reality but have confidently trod the clouds of Marxist Utopia. Already in the twenties, Mayakovsky saw the temptation and natural bent underneath the revolutionary enthusiasm. I do not know whether he approved of the earthly ambition of the Soviet worker to become a bourgeois, or whether he threw up his hands (and threw away his life) in disgust over the general "betrayal" of the Revolution. At any rate, when his Prisypkin (in *The Bedbug*) intends to marry above his status, and his friends and fellow workers reproach him for it, this is what he answers: "It is none of your business, respectable comrades. What have I been fighting for? I fought for a better life. Now I have it: a wife, a home, education in good manners. . . . If one had fought the war, one has earned the right to rest a bit and sit idly on the riverbank, throwing pebbles in the water. My well-being will, perhaps, raise the level of my whole class." •

Mayakovsky's *The Bedbug* was for a long time prohibited in Soviet Russia. The reason is that Prisypkin's motives are incompatible with the demands of collective enthusiasm. In the case of Zorin's play, *The Guests,* similarly prohibited, the reason is the same, although more than twenty-five years later: Zorin's characters prove that Soviet society is in the process of differentiation like any society in the history of men. The guests, indeed, are the aristocracy of a regime that officially denies that thirst for power may exist under Communism, except, perhaps, as a "survival of bourgeois attitude, encouraged by agents of Western capitalism" (a stereotyped expression, hence my quotation marks). The fact is, of course, that while the Soviet government asserts, for propaganda use, that there will be, under Communism, more production not only of corn and pig iron but also of Newtons and Einsteins, Soviet society

• Not only intellectuals and artists felt crushed and committed suicide in Soviet Russia at the time. Highly placed Party members and members of the revolutionary elite also were swept by the horrible realization of what they had built. On November 6, 1927, A. I. Yoffe killed himself in his Moscow apartment, after having addressed a "political testament" to Trotsky, himself already threatened with exile. Here are passages of his letter: "Human life has a meaning only insofar as it is at the service of an infinity, in our case, of mankind. To work for something else, which is finite, is meaningless. . . . If, however, mankind is also finite, the end must be so far away, that for us mankind represents an absolute end. For me, who has faith in progress, I can imagine that if this planet disappears, mankind will go to inhabit another, younger planet. . . . My death is a gesture of protest against those who have reduced the party to such a condition that it is unable to react against this ignoble act [the exclusion of Trotsky and Zinoviev]. . . . Although I am convinced that the bell of awakening will eventually ring for the party, I cannot believe that it has already rung. I do not doubt that today my death is more useful than the prolongation of my life." Quoted by Victor Serge, *Mémoires d'un révolutionnaire* (Editions du Seuil, 1951), p. 249.

is differentiated according to competence, need, talent—
and, naturally, ideological conformism.

Hence the necessity to hide reality under the cloak of
ideology, which, like the Emperor's cloak, is visible only
to those who *must* see it, either to flatter the powerful or
to persuade themselves. This is what G. F. Hudson wrote
in a recent issue of *Foreign Affairs* about the de-ideologized
Soviet society:

Most recent observers of Russia have remarked on the
waning of old fanaticism, the spread of a mood which is
not discontented with the regime so much as cynically dis-
enchanted with it. Preoccupation with jobs and incomes is
in a truly bourgeois spirit. Khrushchev may talk about
the revival of Leninism and the transition to the higher
stage of the true Communist society, but there is little
sign that the upper and middle strata of the new social
order are yearning for a Utopia of perfect equality and
collective living; they are much more concerned with
climbing the ladder of success under a system of quasi-
capitalist incentives and getting the good things of life for
themselves and their families. Such starry-eyed "idealists"
as there may be are to be found mainly among young
people who take seriously the faith they are officially taught
and who do not see their elders living up to it.[27]

There is a good general evaluation of Soviet society
in terms of economic future and State-Party relationship
in the first volume of François Perroux's *La Coexistence
pacifique*.[28] The French economist's thesis is that an industrial society, even in Russia, opposes a natural resistance
to State pressure. Thus in proportion as production increases, the demand for consumer goods and freedom will
manifest itself, the "abstraction of proletarian unity" will
explode, and Soviet society will become progressively differentiated. Since the first Five-Year Plan, Perroux writes,
the middle class has been strengthened step by step, because the number and importance of specialists, directors
of enterprise, engineers, scientists, and other professionals
is rising. It is they who build the "socialist society," not
the workers and the peasants.

But the Party must, by necessity, clash with the industrial elite it has permitted to emerge. "The Party-State,
engendering both industry and socialism, brings into existence the political agents of centralization and the economic

agents of a relatively decentralized economic command. Doing this . . . it creates rivals for itself because it permits new elites and even the conditions for the existence of a public opinion."[29] In order to fight this new industrial elite (which has its own view of what is good for the nation's economy and what are the ideal conditions of running a factory), the politically reliable Party official is delegated to exercise control over them or is appointed in their place, thereby creating a distance between himself and the Party apparatus. Hence a contradiction, the internal contradiction of the Soviet regime, according to Perroux: "If the Party regroups its elites, it loses contact with the masses; if it attempts to reconstruct a small minority, homogeneous and having the passion of the ideological struggle, it risks destroying, one after the other, successive industrial elites. This danger the Party cannot run in a country where such elites are small in number."[30]

The validity of this diagnosis was borne out by the 1959 reorganization of the Soviet industrial structure, that is, the writing of a new chapter in the history of Party-Industry rapports. "It is the manager," Victor Zorza wrote at the time in the *Manchester Guardian,* "who has to deliver the goods, and he can often frighten into silence the Party secretary who will also be blamed in case of failure to fulfill the plan, into looking through his fingers at the various irregularities to which the manager must sometimes resort to make sure that the plan will be carried out." • To establish a new and expectedly more effective control over managerial freedom, it was decided to set up "special Party control commissions" with wide powers *to influence but not to dictate* to the management. Nevertheless, as Mr. Zorza wrote, "the duties of the control commissions are so wide in scope that friction, if not conflict, will be difficult to avoid." This fluctuation of Soviet economic policy, like the fluctuation of the use of terror by the Kremlin leaders, proves conclusively that the contradic-

---

• *Manchester Guardian Weekly,* July 16, 1959.

It is a well-known practice in satellite industrial plants, punished severely when discovered, that the director saves some extra funds on the production figures with which he bribes foremen and teams of workers who otherwise would sabotage production. Such practices are quite general at any echelon of the production process.

tion of the system, indicated by Perroux, cannot be solved without sacrificing either *planning* (that is, the ideological core) or economic *progress*, condition for Russia to remain a great power. There is little doubt that in the end a nationalistic choice will be made that will be, at the same time, the last defeat of the Marxist intellectuals.

It has been observed that at every critical juncture in the Soviet Union, ideology is subordinated to expediency and realistic considerations. During the Second World War, patriotism, military ranks, discipline and decorations, even religion, were to some extent rehabilitated; in order to catch up with American nuclear armament, the ideologically decried Einsteinian physics was speedily reintroduced in courses and laboratories; the collective tractor stations were unceremoniously disbanded by Khrushchev in order to accelerate agricultural output.

Such defeats, humiliating for Marxist ideology, must be and can be compensated for by issues that are not matters of survival, and on which conformism is in the interest of cohesion and of the controlling role of the Party apparatus. One may thus say that the latitude grudgingly granted to the plant manager is paid for by the strictness enforced on writers, artists, and thinkers. This would be consistent, although in an unexpected sense, with Stalin's statement in *Marxism and the Linguistic Question:* "The superstructure is created by the basis so that the former may serve the latter." In the spirit of this statement, what is called "socialist realism" has been imposed from the early thirties up till now; its definition reflects the utopian position of Marxism in that it anticipates the coming into existence of Communist society, but, at the same time, commands the writer and the artist to contribute to the process of transformation. According to the Statutes of the Union of Soviet Writers, elaborated in 1934, "socialist realism is the fundamental method of soviet literature and literary criticism: it demands of the writer a truthful and historically concrete representation of reality in its revolutionary development. Furthermore, socialist realism must contribute to the ideological transformation and to the education of the workers in the spirit of socialism."

Now what does the imposition of socialist realism mean? In a most interesting article published in *Esprit* (February, 1959), an anonymous Russian author answered this ques-

114

tion in the following manner: "Socialist realism starts from an ideal model to which it compares living reality. Our slogan: 'to represent life in a truthful fashion in its revolutionary development,' actually means that we are called upon to give an ideal interpretation of reality, to paint what ought to be as something that already exists. . . . We represent life as we wish to see it and as it is supposed to become by adjusting ourselves to the logic of Marxism."

Although this unanimity concerning the general goal certainly does not exist, the writer must take it for granted. This is a passage from Stalin Prize-winner V. Ilenkov's novel, *The Highway* (1949), as quoted by the author of the *Esprit* article: "For thousands of years, people have suffered because they did not think alike. We, Soviet men, for the first time, we have understood each other . . . we think in an identical fashion on the principal things of life. We are strong with this ideological unity. This is the source of our superiority over other people who are torn and divided by their pluralism of thought." •

There is then the fruit of utopian thinking by intellectuals and writers who expect of the State, of an ideology, of philosophy, of literature, of art, to bring about their own destruction for the sake of "transforming reality." This can be done only by denying the existence of problems where they exist; in regimes built on such an attitude there are usually more problems than elsewhere, and the larger their number, the more aggressively are they denied. The anonymous author, victim once more of the ideology to which he clings and which he believes was betrayed, sums up unwittingly this attitude when he writes: "So that prisons may forever disappear, we have built new ones. So that frontiers between States may crumble, we have sur-

---

• This text, in its vulgarity and self-satisfied stupidity, reads like an illustration of the following passage from Dwight Macdonald's *Memoirs of a Revolutionist* (Farrar, Straus and Cudahy, 1957; Meridian Books, 1958), p. 227: "The aristocratic culture from which Herzen and Tchaadayev and Pushkin drew their strength has been replaced by 'popular' culture which has no taste, no sense of reason or fair play, but is simply the mediocrity and the 'practical' cynicism of the man-in-the-street raised to complete state power. It is as if the norms of Hollywood were imposed by force on all American artistic and intellectual production."

rounded ourselves with a Chinese Wall. So that work may become in the future a rest and a pleasure, we have introduced forced labor. So that not a drop of blood may ever be shed, we have killed, killed, without respite."

No more eloquent funeral oration could be pronounced over the tomb of an ideology that has failed its believers because they despised the true nature of man.

4

The Intellectual as a Progressive

The difficulty of arriving at a definition of the word "progressive" as applied to ideologies, policies, and intellectuals is truly considerable. The progressives' tents are, indeed, scattered over the entire landscape of the modern world: humanism, radicalism, secularism, life-adjustment education, socialism, latter-day ("ritualistic") liberalism, socialism, Freemasonry, and varieties of libertarian Marxism are all inspired by similar basic beliefs, even if their respective holders do not always see eye to eye on each other's tenets. The term "progressive" is, at the same time, an emotionally charged one because the modern concept of "progress" is the most immediately available term when people want to speak of history as openness on infinite improvement, social emancipation, higher living standards. Therefore, on the level of popular journalism and mass media of communication, the term is endowed with magic qualities that nobody may doubt or contradict; on the level of third-zone intellectuals and idea peddlers the adjective "progressive" is a label under which any blatant nonsense or sentimental trash may pass without inspection. On yet another level, more respectable than the other two, "progressive" means attachment to the historical current of the enlightened and radical ideas, it means a mentality favoring reforms until conditions for mankind might approximate the ideal.

What ideal? Whose ideal? This is the point where the "progressive" first crosses swords with his various adversaries, for this is the point where "progressivism" ceases to be a method and becomes a world view, an ideology, a religion. This, of course, the progressive denies because, in his view, "progress" is, by definition, the ideal of everybody, of history itself, since it is the collective enterprise of mankind; and he thinks of himself as an eclectic and a representative of cultural pluralism who chooses the best that other systems have to offer. Thus, for example, it is impossible to pin him down as an *agnostic,* because another progressive may actually be a believer and a religious man; nor can he be identified as a *political radical,* because many progressives preach understanding and co-operation among classes; and he rejects being called a *philosophical pragmatist* for the simple reason that most progressives believe in "values" and have, in general, a great although vague respect for the humanistic tradition.

And so it goes with every attempt to categorize the progressive intellectual, because he is convinced (this is how he justifies his eclecticism) that to be a *human being* is to stand for *progress;* he rejects with indignation the charge that he is an ideologue, because in his aspiration to be universal he cannot accept being called limited and particularistic in any sense.

Nevertheless, from the point of view that we have adopted in this book, the position of the progressive appears a central one in the history of ideologies. Indeed, the progressive ideology has been a more direct, more organic outgrowth of the trends we have examined: medieval secularism, Reformation-inspired democracy, the philosophical criticism of the Enlightenment, utopianism from Rousseau to Saint-Simon, than either Marxism, or (as we shall see) Fascism. Modern progressivism is heir to nineteenth-century radicalism, while both Marxism and the reactionary ideologies, in spite of the extraordinary and steady success of the first and the spectacular flare-up of the second, have only been branches of the main ideological stem. It has assimilated, however superficially, and in an increasingly impoverished form, the Christian and humanistic traditions, and as a result, it has extended its influence to issues, to thinkers, and to public opinion closed to ideological solicitations that break more radically with these traditions. As to the future, it may be predicted that given the progressive intellectuals' commitment to utopian thinking, progressivism will outlive Marxism itself which, in proportion as Soviet Russia becomes a middle-class State, loses its ideological appeal. Meanwhile, however, the progressive who shares, in essence, his ideals with the Marxist, deplores the failure of Communism to spread these ideals peacefully.

Like other ideologies of modern times, progressivism has a double origin: *philosophically,* it grew out of a certain image of God, the universe, man, and human nature, an image we call secular; *historically,* it has been an attempt to reconstruct the unity—social and political—of mankind after the Renaissance break. Like other ideologies, progressivism adopted the premise that the new unity must be secular because there is no other order in the universe except the *human order;* it followed from this that the unified and perfect society the progressives want to establish does not recognize any divine order, therefore no divine obligation beyond itself. Allegiance is only due to the *Civitas Terrana,* from the laws and rules of which all reference to a transcendental order must be excluded. Thus, while the various radical proponents of the "perfect society" have been willing to tolerate an individual rapport between the individual conscience and his God, they have insisted that the social cohesion be the fruit of a secular morality which, being the only valid one from the point of view of the community, is an end in itself. (This is how a new, secular "metaphysics" has stolen itself into the idea of modern societies.)

If now secular or social morality is actually to be the foundation stone and guarantee of people's coexistence, one must admit that the "social man" who lives up to the standards of his environment is also the "good man." For him to prove himself good he must show his attachment to society, its goals and methods; for society to show *its* goodness, it (its leaders and spokesmen) must demonstrate that people are attached to it and that it fulfills their aspirations. Once the individual's attachment to society is taken for granted (the anticollectivist, the nonconformist, that is, the *private man,* is not a political adversary but a heretic, outside the sphere of unanimity), and once society rewards him by nursing him from cradle to grave, there is no need for *politics,* which is the balancing of conflicts and interests: the dialogue between the good man and the good society is sufficient in itself and makes any other form of association and channel superfluous, even suspect.

The progressive has, of course, the same equivocal attitude when faced with the rapports of the individual and society as Rousseau and his nineteenth-century followers. He maintains that because of man's essential goodness, any society or group, if left alone without outside pressure, finds a way of getting along, of regulating itself; there is in each individual a kind of mirror image of the General Will that guides his deliberating mind and his voting hand. This is, of course, the basic assumption of democracy which, in the interpretation of the progressives, has become the elimination of power from human affairs. "Contemporary democracy," writes John Strachey, "is the diffusion of power throughout the community. And the diffusion of power pushed further and further points in turn towards the elimination of power. For if everyone could have exactly equal power, no one, clearly, would have any power over his fellows. That, of course, is for us a distant ideal; it is the ideal of perfect cooperation in perfect liberty." [1]

Thus freedom is equated with absence of power; but power—that is, power-concentration—is never absent, only, under democratic conditions it is harder to locate. The progressive, however, assumes that freedom, being the absence of power, is a moral good in itself, used only for noble goals and in self-restraint. It never occurs to him that, as Maritain writes, "from transmutation to transmutation, the Rousseauist principle [each is born free and should obey only himself] ends, by way of an almost continuous series, in communist sociolatry, or through a reactive backward movement, in totalitaran statolatry." [2]

This idea is certainly behind the image Americans have of their democratic system, which is supposed to allow complete freedom and self-expression, and which, nevertheless, generates decisions with which all may concur. Hence the American practice of letting groups and associations (television advertisers, labor unions, student bodies) police themselves when crime, abuse, or misbehavior is revealed in their midst. The assumption is that free men are good and honest, and although they will always be tempted to transgress morality, the law, or a set of rules, publicly expressed confidence in their goodness and honesty will bring them back to the honorable path.

Contrariwise, the progressive intellectual is enthusiastically willing to use the coercive political power of the State (bureaucracy and legislature) when he wants to carry out his plans or when he sees them threatened. He becomes very easily a follower of Robespierre in compelling his fellow men to be free. In spite of his constantly affirmed belief in individual freedom, he does not pass up any opportunity for seizing power and settling at the command post. In fact, he seems to say that the real freedom of the individual consists in alienating this freedom for the benefit of the collectivity, which will then guarantee for him security among, and equality with, the others. But quite naturally, he exempts himself from this obligation of alienating his own freedom: once he has colonized the seat of power, he turns it into a source of prophetic wisdom, an oracle, never believing that power continues to be what it had always been: a double-edged political instrument. Thus Johannes Messner, who has studied intensively the British Labour movement in and out of government, shows how concentration of property even in the hands of a democratic State (through nationalization) has created a new autocracy of the bureaucrats which, trying to impose equality, is led to limit or suppress individual freedom. The socialist State weakens private property until the State emerges as the only economic giant among individual pygmies who either succumb resisting it or accept its over-all tutelage.●

● This development was consciously prepared by the Fabians: "We should continue our policy of inocculation," wrote the Webbs in 1895, "of giving to each class, to each person coming under our influence, the exact dose of collectivism that they were prepared to assimilate. And we should continue to improve and enlarge such machinery of government that came into our hands." The Webbs believed in the "inevitable development of an official administrative class in the modern State. A very powerful class, representing the power of the future." Anne Fremantle, *This Little Band of Prophets: The British Fabians* (New York: New American Library, Mentor Books, 1959), pp. 102, 105.

Strachey, Galbraith, and other economists argue that national-

The same process and the same results—to take another example—are observable in the history of progressive education in the United States. The disciples of John Dewey, too, began by claiming to speak in the name of a "progressive," that is, a liberating, ideal, the "emancipation" of children and students from the traditional authority of parents, teachers, and social conventions. They voiced the right of self-expression, of individual search for the inner truth, the free flowering of the personality. The school, the classroom, the home—and finally society—were to turn into the free associations of equals, through the freely given co-operation of autonomous human beings. The teacher—to speak of the academic aspect of progressive education only—was to be at best a kind of discussion leader, someone who might propose the activities of the day, but who was not permitted to impose. From this point on there have been, of course, infinite variations on the same theme, one more absurd than the other. Freedom is the hardest task to assume; but the semblance of freedom is an easy tool because its essence is irresponsibility; this explains the extraordinary amount of nonsense that educational quacks have poured over American society and its

---

ization is made necessary by the concentration of production in the hands of a few giant corporations that adopt monopolistic methods. But as the recent history of corporations shows, no matter how few they are in number, their interests often diverge either under the pressure of the State or of labor unions, etc. Furthermore, in frankly socialistic countries the existence of small business is not merely made extremely difficult, but it is actually extinguished. All told, even a little competition is better than no competition at all; the precarious struggle for survival of small business is still a better condition for it than its brutal suppression by State power and State management. The economic mismanagement, waste, carelessness in Soviet-controlled territory, reports of which reach the Western press daily, is proof of the noncompetence of the State in running a country's economy. "The proof has been made," writes the French socialist politician, André Philip, "that the socialization of the means of production does not suffice to solve the social problem. Even in a nationalized enterprise the worker has the feeling of exploitation and oppression, and the change of ownership does not modify the internal social rapports. . . . Political and industrial power concentrated in a few hands, the leading class would possess a power which would be superior to that ever held by a capitalist class." *Le Socialisme trahi*, p. 51.

schools in the last thirty years. But this was only possible because with the slogans of freedom, spontaneity, personalized teaching, elective courses, democratic education in their mouths and textbooks, progressive educators established, first, the tyranny of their dogmas in individual schools and school boards, and second, an interlocking directorate over most of the educational system of the country. Through their extremely powerful organizations they have gone after educational monopoly, colonizing teachers' colleges, then government bureaus, federal and state, until finally they clamor now for federal support and for the abolition of private schools as "un-democratic."

Now these are only two examples, and besides, the two—British Labour and American progressive educators —may be called exceptions, or not really progressive by those who acknowledge being progressive but decline any similarity between their own and the ideals and practices of Labourites and educators. My task is therefore to analyze the philosophy, mentality, and attitudes of progressive ideologues to show their debt to a certain world view they have in common. In other words, we must now identify the progressive intellectual in some of his protean forms.

Let us bear in mind that progressivism is the ideological formulation of the philosophical belief in Progress as the Enlightenment presented it. In this way it is an older belief than Marxism, which is the joint product of progressivism, radical utopianism, English economic thought, Hegelian philosophy, and the materialism of Feuerbach, Büchner, et al. Marxist thinkers hold the collaborators of the *Encyclopédie*, especially Diderot, in high respect, and acknowledge their debt to the materialist La Mettrie and Condillac. On the other hand, the progressives share the Marxist veneration for history—not as the tale and structure of the human condition, but as an awesome mechanism guiding the ages, and guiding mankind benevolently on the road to betterment. It is true that a materialistic view of the world and of man would be quite incompatible with the, after all, spiritual assumption of a historical force, but this gap is bridged by the doctrine of evolution, which grants matter the faculty (whence developed?—the progressive does not say) of renewing and perfecting itself. At the end of the evolutionary process the progressive envisages the supreme creation of a kind of hazy god—not the initiator but the product of life and evolution—toward which everything tends in a similarly unfathomable way. History, then, is one of the evolutionary forms.

In this respect the French Jesuit Pierre Teilhard de Chardin has done a considerable service to those progressives whom the grosser versions of Darwinism cannot satisfy, for example, the Christian progressives and the spiritualists in general. Father Chardin, indeed, taught that the conditions of the biosphere (that is, the manifestation of life, including human life, on our planet) are now such that they permit the next, perhaps last, step in evolution, the *noosphere*, the manifestation of the pure mind or spirit. The new, spiritual being will experience the world, outside and within (the moral sphere) in an ever-deeper fashion, until he will experience the genesis of God Himself. In the words of Father Chardin, mankind converges to a point Omega at which the noosphere will be intensely unified and will achieve a hyperpersonal organization: this process is the emergence of the divinity (Christogenesis). Thus like Bergson's ideas, but more radical and more radically expressed, Father Chardin's thought concludes not only to the coming of a man biologically and spiritually superior to us, but to the coming of God as the supreme product of the process. "The universe is a god-creating machine," said Bergson; God lies ahead of us, holds the Jesuit anthropologist-theologian.•

Before the end—and the end-product—of evolution is reached, the numerical increase of men and the improvement of communication are supposed to create more mental substance. "Mankind as a whole," comments approvingly Sir Julian Huxley in his introduction to Chardin's *The*

• The conclusion of the Catholic Father Chardin closely resembles that of Ernest Renan who wrote the following, after he had repudiated his Christian faith: "Since the universal labor of all living beings is to make God more perfect, that is, to bring about the definitive resultant which will close the circle of things by unifying them . . . reason will one day take in its hands the super-vision of this great task, and after having organized mankind, it will organize God." *L'Avenir de la science*, p. 757.

124

Phenomenon of Man, "will achieve more intense, more complex, and more integrated mental activity which can guide the human species up the path of progress to higher levels of hominization." • Taking the biological forms of evolution as the units of his thought, Father Chardin believed in a global unification of human awareness as a necessary prerequisite for any future progress of mankind. "To see life properly," he wrote, "we must never lose sight of the unity of the biosphere that lies beyond the plurality and essential rivalry of individual beings." [3] He thus predicts as necessary and good the *associative* stage in the evolution of man, once the *individualistic* stage is completed: a stage of collective awareness in which mankind becomes *one,* as if the human individuals were mere organisms of a unified, superhuman being. Sir Julian Huxley draws just this conclusion: "The incipient development of mankind into a single psychosocial unit, with a single noosystem or common pool of thought, is providing the evolutionary process with the rudiments of a head." [4] He, the nonreligious evolutionary progressive, disagrees with the theses of the Jesuit only insofar as he envisages, as the meaning and achievement of history, not God, but "the higher manifestations of human nature in art and love, in intellectual comprehension and aspiring adoration." •• Huxley believes, in seeming opposition to the Jesuit's profession of faith, in the gradual elimination of the supernatural, and in the establishment of a religion—or, as he phrased it with characteristic lack of precision—"a belief-system, framework of values, ideology, call it what you will"—which is "evolutionary" because everything in this world has similarly evolved, "the earth, the animals and plants, our human selves, mind and soul, brain and body." The end of evolution, Huxley says, is existence organized by knowledge—"the framework of facts and ideas"—which is to replace religion since man will no longer need a "refuge from loneliness" and an "umbrella of divine authority against the responsibility of personal decisons."

• P. 17.

The term "hominization" is Father Chardin's.

•• This and some following quotations are from Sir Julian Huxley's discourse before the centennial Darwin celebration, held in the fall of 1959 at the University of Chicago.

Whether he follows the materialist Huxley or the spiritualist Chardin, the progressive believes in the progress of history, man, society, and, as we have seen, of God Himself who, in his eyes, is not a *person* but a *process,* or a *product.* For the progressive, everything is in motion and has a direction, and although we may only know the platform on which we stand ourselves, we may be certain of the whole movement that envelops us. "At the heart of liberalism," writes Yves Simon, "lies an almost religious belief in a kind of Demiurge, imminent in the stream of contingent events, or, better, identical with the very stream of contingencies. . . . Owing to this benevolent Spirit of Nature, contingency and chance are supposed to result indefectibly in happy achievements." [5]

The vast involvement of the progressive intellectual with the contemporary world makes it necessary to define three categories according to background, aim, and method. We shall, then, divide the rest of this chapter into three parts: the discussion of the progressive intellectual as (1) a *liberal-humanist* who secularizes the values men hold dear and seeks for the conditions of their realization in individual and social existence, (2) a *fellow-traveler of socialism and communism,* for whom these values have coalesced into the primary one of the "perfect society," from which, in turn, these values will obtain a new life, and (3) an *esthete* who finds no rational order in the universe and therefore no relationship between values, and who, as a result, cultivates those—in preference *beauty*—which, although precarious, may be torn away from the general meaninglessness to become the exquisite flower of a day.

(1) At the basis of the progressive world view there is a misunderstanding of human nature. Or we should rather call it a limited concept, one impoverished by five hundred years of Western humanism. *Humanitas* is a Greco-Roman idea, adopted by Renaissance scholars to stress the rationality of man against the supposed irrationality of the Middle Ages. Thus rationality became man's trademark, and, for a while, the symbol and guarantee of his dignity. Denis de Rougemont has termed the Christian

concept of the human person the irreducible essence of Western civilization; but since the Renaissance the non-rational aspirations of the human person have been increasingly ignored and discredited; the seventeenth century's enthusiasm for science further narrowed the concept of man and the scope of his knowledge; and in the eighteenth, the ideal was no longer the divinely inspired, existentially rich human person, but the "machine man" of La Mettrie, and Condillac's living statue constructed through the successive addition of the senses.•

Thus it was taken for granted that with every hurdle of irrationality successfully cleared, man reached higher degrees of humanity. "But even the noblest definition of man that humanism has worked out," writes Heidegger in his *Letter on Humanism,* "falls short of describing him." The series of definitions that humanism, allied, in turn, with science, technology, liberalism, and socialism, has proposed became less and less complete: either they locked up the human being behind the bars of skepticism (from Montaigne to André Gide), or confined his aspirations to political and social forms like "free citizen," "liberal bourgeois," "class-conscious proletar."

These alliances have cost humanism its original *raison d'être.* By the eighteenth century the "humanist" became the "scientist" and the "organizer of the scientific society"; the *Encyclopédie* was, to quote again Professor Arthur Wilson's study, at once a "repository of knowledge," an "intellectual and emotional stimulus," and a "window opener" toward unlimited social vistas. But in the nineteenth and twentieth centuries, science and the scientific society have won out and emancipated themselves, leaving humanism as a mere ideological residue to provide them with emotional-cultural respectability. Humanism appears now as a straggler in all modern movements, a venerable yet embarrassing reminder of the heroic age.

With the eclipse of humanism two things happened: *one* was that science further reduced and diminished the image of man that humanism had deprived of its sacral character

—————

• "The peculiar vice of classical humanisms," writes Jacques Maritain, "concerns not so much what this humanism affirms, as what it neglects, denies and divides. It is what we may call an anthropocentric conception of man and culture." *Scholasticism and Politics,* p. 12.

and left in a mutilated state; this new image displayed human nature without any basic and indestructible psychological and spiritual realities. On the contrary, according to the evolutionary creed, man is not the "crown of creation," that is, a finished product, but only a bio-psychological phase with numerous imperfections to be corrected by the creature representing the next phase. If we ask the progressive toward what forms of perfection does evolution point, he will admit that it is an *ideal form,* a sort of *god-man* (see Chardin and Huxley) whom the human beings he and we know may approximate, but who will be "infinitely superior." He will further admit that the goal will be constantly approached via natural evolution, but that we may give some little encouraging pushes to this process by manipulating the evolutionary factors, such as genes, or, more crudely, by manufacturing supermachines that will do the physical work and brain work of millions in the fraction of a minute. Man, as he is, is, therefore, regarded by the consistently reasoning progressive as a remarkably good mechanism, but far from possessing the excellence of his descendants a million years from now, or the perfection of the mechanism that engineers are now about to construct.

In a book that I reviewed a few years ago, Mr. Jerome Rothstein,[6] an engineer, informed the reader of the unlimited potentiality of cybernetics to bring about (1) a unified world; (2) machines "endowed with values, capable of playing games or seeking goals"; (3) the prospect of "cutting down the infinitude of possible philosophies to the smaller set of possibly valid ones" so as to "solve the problems that really matter"; (4) a "world atmosphere" in which free experimentation with ideas (a contradiction, incidentally, to the demand expressed in number 3!), plus birth control and the outlawing of wars will save billions of man-hours for constructive activities, such as spreading the earth's civilization (if any remains!) to other planets.

These then are the goals of the perfecting process, either through natural or manipulated evolution, or through the construction of super-machines. Not every progressive possesses Mr. Rothstein's silly imagination, but misconceptions about human nature do inevitably lead to misconceptions about the destiny and goals of man. Even a far more cultured and sophisticated progressive than Rothstein, Simone de Beauvoir, preaches, in her *The Second Sex*, the desirability of women becoming like men and of stopping to look at themselves from the point of view of men's sexual attraction. "It is not nature that defines woman," she writes, "it is she who defines herself by dealing with nature on its own account in her emotional life" (p. 65).

The *second* consequence of the eclipse of humanism is the emphasis on *values*. Humanism used to be the "cause of man." But man, whom it implicitly defined as a lonely point in the infinity of space, a drama without a dénouement, was credited, in the absence of God and of absolutes, with the invention of limited platforms on which he might precariously stand while contemplating the abyss underneath. But precisely: when he says "value," the neohumanist does not realize that he means a substitute for truth, that is, a mere subjective valuation, the shadow instead of the substance. In his view man is no longer the "shepherd of Being" (Heidegger), but, as the locus of the valuating act, a self-proclaimed freedom, a self-appointed god.

Yet emptiness surrounds this proud self-affirmation, and pride turns into despair. This is the experience of the absurd as described by Albert Camus who, in his brief life, never managed to answer the central question of the entire modern humanism: "Is man able, alone and without the support of the eternal, to create his own values?" [7] Thus the humanist is forced to maintain that the more "values" he embraces, the deeper he cuts into the stuff of reality and the longer roots he extends into the soil of cultures. If "man is the sum of his acts," as the existentialist humanism of Sartre (and of Malraux) teaches, then more value-creating acts (and of what act may we say, for lack of a philosophically acceptable criterion, that it does *not* create values?) indicate a richer "presence" in the surrounding ocean of absurdity. The result is that the humanist's ideal man becomes the "stranger" of Camus who keeps inventing reasons to stay alive and accumulating "values" to populate the empty universe with phantoms. For he must hold, with Sartre, that "life has no meaning a priori . . . it is up to us to give it a meaning [since] value is nothing else than the meaning we choose." This humanism, however, implies the defense of the inhuman act, too, which is also freely invented: the act of abolishing the other's freedom, of crushing his dignity; the universe of the Marquis de Sade; the concentration camp of Hitler and of Stalin.

How does the humanist escape this dilemma, the dilemma of justifying good as well as evil? How is he to explain his preference for "positive acts," generating "positive values" when nothing in this world links together the "strangers" frozen in their loneliness, the monads so hostile that the existence of one is the hell for the other? And finally: how does he find *meaning* in a world which, in spite of the feverish activity he recommends, remains in his eyes obstinately absurd?

There are two attempts to answer these questions: existentialist humanism and scientific humanism. Both lead to the threshold of inhumanity.

"The first step forward of a man aware that he is a *stranger*," writes Camus, "is to recognize that he shares this experience with all other men. . . . The disturbed feeling of one thus becomes a collective evil." [8] And again: "When I experience the absurd, my suffering is individual. From the moment that I revolt, I know that I share it with others. . . . I revolt, therefore *we* are." [9]

Revolt—which is, by the way, condemned to frustration as it launches its offensives against the human situation[10]—is thus the only moment when people may feel a bond, a solidarity, a common purpose. But is it not precisely Camus who denounced revolutions for leading to a new oppression, a new tyranny, and a new isolation of the beaten, fearful individual? "The total revolution," he wrote, "took for granted the absolute plasticity of human nature, the possibility of reducing it to the state of a historical force. But the seed of revolt in man is his refusal of being treated as a thing and of being reduced to history." [11]

In this way the act of revolt cancels itself out, because its "metaphysical ambition is to build, after the death of God, the community of men finally divinized." [12] But the "insecurity of this new god [incarnated in the totalitarian State] demands that we sacrifice to it everything we have. . . . It interprets all revolt as an automatic choice against the only truth." [13]

The answer of scientific humanism, too, must ultimately

lead to the destruction of the initial inspiration, that is, the defense of man. While existential humanism—with the experience of absurdity at its core—has been a reaction against the totalitarian claims of science and against its neutrality on good and evil, scientific humanism is the heir of the original conviction: science can and must serve man, it can and must strengthen his values by supplying them with a firm foundation.

In a sense, the scientific humanist expects of science the same role Camus expects of revolt: to be the ferment of history, its activating force. But while revolt is a rare occurrence, science is a continuous accumulation process of directed experience and knowledge; and it is a communal process too, which requires co-operation, exchange of views, and agreed standards of measurement and proof. Moreover, it is held extensible from the physical world to the moral and social sphere; the pattern of scientific thinking, Dewey advocated, "may be adopted as a norm in thinking wisely about political and social affairs."

Thus the conquest of the rational man finds its ultimate flowering in the reign of science. But again: while in the system of Camus *absurdity* and *revolt* are two poles of a dialectical situation—the situation of man itself—between which the tension never relaxes, the scientific humanist believes that he can shed the past and consider irrelevant the wisdom of ages. This is a world of change, Sidney Hook asserts, and intelligence alone can master its problems, not a "transmitted cultural tradition." The past witnessed a clash of world views, between "anti-scientific dogmatism" and the "scientific method"; the former was imposed by "the educated classes of hierarchically ordered European societies which sided with church and king and the social status quo"; the latter implies a democratic society and form of government because it means openness to experimentation and it encourages change. For this reason it may never be appropriated by a class or an elite. "If we reject the scientific method," Hook writes, "as the supreme authority in judgment of both fact and value, what can we substitute in its stead? Every alternative involves at some point an institutional authority which, historical evidence shows, lends itself to abuse, which proclaims itself to be above all interests and becomes the expression of a particular interest invested with the symbols of public authority." [14]

In other words, Hook invites us to place our complete trust in *science*, as the existentialist humanist insists that we place it in *revolution*. Both want to break with the past, and both imagine that a world can be built in which abuse disappears because one particular type of spirit—revolutionary or scientific—inspires society and its institutions. Both consider man infinitely malleable and the community all mighty, provided it operates according to the best formula.

Thus, as the neohumanist is unable to escape the embarrassment of justifying any act, he must end up by denying the problem of good and evil. He asserts that they are not part of the structure of man, or, to put it otherwise, that they can be either abolished in their source or else neutralized in their effects: the Revolution establishes the good society, Science elaborates the best social techniques. In other words, man is relieved of the burden of good and evil and of the anguish of having to find a meaning in an absurd existence. It is the collectivity that assumes these burdens: it sets the goals, it elicits the individual's consent through education and indoctrination, and institutionalizes the responses thus guaranteed in advance. In the end, then, the neohumanist delivers the individual to the collectivity, and promises him to solve his problems on the communal level. The *ideal society* thus comes to replace the *ideal man*.

The *political* assumption of progressivism parallels its (secular) humanistic assumptions, from which it has grown out philosophically. This is how Schopenhauer commented on the basic progressive attitude of his time:

Always and everywhere, there has been discontent with governments, laws and institutions: this is because people are inclined to believe that they are responsible for the misery which, in reality, is inseparable from human existence. . . . But never was this inclination so blatantly exploited as by our contemporary demagogues; in opposition to Christianity they profess optimism; in their eyes the world has its *raison d'être* within itself, and it is perfectly organized in view of the happiness of man. They attribute to governments the miseries which contradict their optimism; if the political leaders did their duty, the earth would turn into heaven, which means that everybody could, without any effort, eat his fill, get drunk, make love and then die; this is what they mean when they speak of the infinite progress of mankind.

Naturally, this is a rather simplified and crude description of the progressive program, but only because it speaks of irresponsible agitators and of masses indulging their appetites, instead of the philosophical premises from which the demagoguery and the promise of an earthly Paradise follow. It does not mention the progressive's enamoredness with Reason and his demand that society be rationally organized, that is, scientifically, since it is science that dictates to reason and fills its categories with content. But it points to the basic attitude of the progressive, his contempt for the structure of life, its given situations and hard data; and it evokes the impatience with which he presses for the social, political, economic, international, pattern that his ideology dictates him to favor. This is not necessarily equivalent to a belief in heaven on earth, although the progressive's imagination often goes to this extreme; usually, however, the envisaged and blurred picture of what would be the opposite of life's actual imperfect conditions has a great fascination for him, and he is apt to denounce as cynics those who call him back from the nowhere-never land to reality. Because he insists on the here-and-now materialization of his plan (he is confident that he speaks for evolution and/or history), he develops a habit, well known from Molière's satires of contemporary medical practice, that is, the stereotyped recommendation of the same cure for all diseases: in the case of Molière's physicians, bloodletting; in that of the progressive, the ballot box (since, as said before, the right decision is sure to win out).

Inspired by a sound view of the world, the progressive's opponent also stresses the obligation to strive for a constantly improved state of the world, but he knows, as Maritain says, that "good and evil grow together"; that history and Christ (or the religious ideal) will never be reconciled; that the goal of the individual transcends history, and while he can be saved, history cannot aspire to salvation.

The progressive does not make this distinction; first, because there is nothing outside history, in his eyes, and history itself is not a network of human relationships, a way of describing the condition of man, but a reality, an essence. Secondly, for him the ideal, the utopian perfection, the flawless society, the beloved community, is simply a chapter he is sure to read later in the great book of history, but from which he may snatch entire passages for his present use. Not that he does not believe in peaceful evolution, the guaranteed achievement of mankind's goals; but he has no sense of historical time (he lives in the future), and since he believes that evil (an untoward accumulation of unfavorable circumstances) is constantly receding before good, he is easily scandalized by the stubbornness of facts that contradict him.

Does this mean that he is a bold seeker on the frontiers of possibilities? After all, he is not bound by the unpleasant facts that stare the realist in the face; he does not have to take evil for granted as a forever inevitable ingredient in human affairs. Yet, what we see today is that the progressive, always responsive to abstractions, is easily swayed by historical abstractions, which transform his search into a very limited enterprise, monotonous and orthodox. Indeed, the only difference between the progressive and his eighteenth-century rationalist brother is that the latter used *static* abstractions (liberty, equality, fraternity, universal happiness), while the former is seduced by *dynamic* ones, such as the march of history, the irreversible course of events, evolution, historical necessity, the gradual unfolding of a universal consciousness, and the like.

The relative remoteness of the *end* is, of course, recognized by the progressive deep in his heart. This is why he is willing, in his impatience, to give all his devotion to the means—in this way he may feel the agreeable sensation of immersing in the current of history and of evolution. In the process, the distinction between means and end may altogether disappear: what are but *instruments*, for example "democracy," "progress," or—in the present world-political context—international negotiations, institutions, declarations, are taken by him for realities possessing virtues on which actions, policies, and world-wide projects should be based. The League of Nations, the United Nations, summit conferences, are considered by him more than what they are, that is, highly complex *tools of diplomacy* in view of reaching certain particularistic goals and fighting for national interests, good or bad; they are considered goals, good in themselves, torn-out passages from the last chapter of history, sacred texts from the future when the world will be brotherly and peaceful. This is because in the eyes of the progressive these tools display the features which he believes will be the generalized and permanent features of Utopia. Therefore, he takes it for granted that there is actually, or at least potentially, a unanimous consensus of mankind on these issues. Only this belief permits the progressive to press for "final" solutions in particular instances, like the abolition of all war when there is a concrete nuclear danger, the abolition of poverty when underdeveloped lands face the problem of over-population, or the immediate establishment of a world government when the conflict between two super-powers assumes alarming proportions.

Thus the progressive mentality reveals its inability to deal with political matters. While it elevates the tools of policy-making to the rank of a final good, it commits the fatal error of believing that power, interests, particularisms, and ideologies (other than his own)—that is, the basic facts of human coexistence in this forever imperfect world —are evil, and not only evil, but downright anomalous, irreconcilable with the exalted notions the progressive has formed of the goodness of man and the noble goal of history. In local affairs, where the realities of a situation are so intertwined with his emotional response and point of view that they seem like branches of the same tree, he usually accepts the conflicts of life for what they are, and understands the mixed nature of human affairs both in his own soul and in that of his neighbor. But with regard to remote transactions, he is likely to believe that interests, traditions, loyalties, irrational drives, foreign to his own milieu, are unreal, and that they could easily be reconciled if only all parties chose the ways of reason, made concessions, and let good will prevail.

In the United States, progressive political thought assumes specific forms for two main reasons. One is that the population, steeped in the tradition of local autonomy and the town meeting, labors under the impression that contractual arrangements and *ad hoc* compromises ought to be a planet-wide rule. The "American way" of "talking things out" is thus easily identified with the par excellence instrument of the political order which, in the American mind, informed by the seventeenth-century puritanical-democratic ideologies, is the same as the moral order.• It is forgotten, among other things, that the moral order can never completely displace the natural order, and that the political animal is necessarily the inhabitant of both.

The reason is that although the American revolution for independence was a conservative revolution (for the restoration of political order violated by George III and his government), the Declaration of Independence is clothed in the rationalistic language of the eighteenth century; since its terms are abstractions, they could be later filled with progressive content and thus remade into slogans serving the progressive cause. It is significant, for example, that in the so-called McCarthy era, passages of the text of the Declaration of Independence and of the Preamble to the Constitution, when read without indication of source, were considered subversive, even Communist-inspired. The alarm of progressives (liberals) over this issue was quite justifiable: for a fleeting moment, a segment of American public opinion, alerted by the rightist reaction to contemporary trends, became aware of the progressive nature of the hallowed documents.

When reflecting about political matters, the progressive —in America as elsewhere—tends to discount power. In his imaginary happy planet-wide commonwealth individuals and nations respect only kindness, helpfulness, "togetherness"; power is a nasty child who can be told to remain outside. He thus ignores the fact that power has two faces, that is, that the domestic aims of government

• "If there was ever a people whose intellectual baggage equipped them for a journey into Utopia it was the New England Puritans. In their Bible they had a blueprint for the Good Society; their costly expedition to America gave them a vested interest in believing it possible to build Zion on this earth." D. J. Boorstin, "The Puritan Tradition," *Commentary*, Aug., 1958. The twentieth-century descendants of the New England Puritans conceive now of the whole globe as a potential Zion, built with the help of American good will, idealism, and financial aid.

and nation are not of the same nature as their external aims. The domestic goal is to insure a degree of *unity* in the diversity, through the instrumentality of elections, representation, compromise between central authority and local autonomy. The goal of foreign policy is *security* from attack—military, ideological, economic. The instruments of unity are fair play, concessions, reconciliation of interests; those of security range from diplomatic skill to recourse to war, because the stage for international rapports is, to a large extent, in the state of nature.

But can we not, asks the progressive, modify the factors of international politics so as to bring them to resemble more closely the factors of national politics? In other words, can mankind not set up an international body—government, army, teams of disarmament inspection—that would play the same co-ordinating, pacifying role as government and police play in the lives of societies limited by geography and sovereignty? Or, in the same order of things, can we not promote universal disarmament among nations that should trust each other?

The answer to these and similar questions seems unimaginative to the progressive; politics is the art of the possible, and the domain of the possible is limited because it is the restricted territory of conflicting interests. Such conflicting interests, as Professor Morgenthau points out, have made of the Security Council and the General Assembly of the United Nations a camp split into hostile groups instead of, as it had been intended by gullible statesmen, a nucleus of world government. This can surprise the progressive only, for the realist knows that it is futile to ask either the United States or the Soviet Union to forget their differences, or to allow a police force to patrol them.

It is then evident that the progressive's concept of politics is in reality a headlong rush toward Utopia, and that this Utopia itself is a sketchy thing, a matter of pious inspiration rather than of reflection. This is shown also by the attitude of many progressives with regard to *leaders*—military and political—in whom they recognize not the necessary phenomenon of crystallization and direction of the collective impulse and interest, but essentially *evil men*. I have quoted Schopenhauer, who observed that his century's radical demagogues and masses considered the government, its officials, and institutions as a group of conspirators who hide the key to Paradise. The progressive of our own time hardly thinks in any different way: he, too, believes that leaders are merely ambitious men rising above the heads of others and are ruthless because by their occupancy of positions of command, they must choose, prefer, punish, and decide. To the universalist mentality of the progressive, this is a limitation that contradicts the basic pacifism of the (abstract) man and goes against his conviction that the true progress of history consists exclusively in "constructive" (peaceful, co-operating, humanitarian, sentiment-directed) endeavors. The leader, if nothing else, is a reminder that people have not yet made the hoped-for step of developing the supreme moral consciousness after which each individual would be his own police force and his own judge.

In the meantime, the progressive satisfies himself by proclaiming his pacifism in which he sees, rather than a political choice, a substitute for politics. What he calls pacifism is, of course, the usual verbal tribute to international co-operation and institutions; he forgets that these institutions, as I have said above, are only instruments of diplomacy and that, as such, they can be used and maneuvered by ideological or power groups. But even if he finally realizes this, he maintains that these institutions would be servants of a lasting peace *if* the international or interhuman climate changed, and the moral temperature of mankind rose. He even has his models ready, supposedly the guiding moral lights in the darkness brought about by the prospects of the "nuclear holocaust": they are, with little variation from one progressive-liberal newspaper editorial to the other, such figures as Gandhi, Einstein and Schweitzer, Mrs. Roosevelt, and Bertrand Russell. The common characteristics for which they have been chosen—and this, in some cases, without any real knowledge of these figures, but rather considered endowed with the magic-mythical features of pagan deities—are the blend of qualities deriving from a vague *philanthropy*,• which is itself a general and indiscriminate assent to the goodness and meritoriousness of all human beings.

• Jacques Barzun has written some very sharply critical pages about the shallow manifestations of mid-century philanthropy in *House of Intellect*.

The quintessence of this false and sentimental philanthropism was expressed by a young French leftist of the Catholic variety who believes in a society where "the imbecile is honored." This statement may, of course, be interpreted as the last echo of the impatient cry that the economically underdeveloped should be helped to climb (without having made the necessary effort) in one leap to the level of fully developed nations. Why not then the intellectually underdeveloped too?—the enthusiast inquires. But he disregards two inexorable facts: one is that within a free society the "imbeciles" may only be honored (whatever this would mean in practice) if the intelligent and talented ones are proportionately restrained and dishonored. If society is, on the contrary, so organized as to accommodate the "imbeciles," then, as the young progressive Bazarov (in Turgenyev's *Fathers and Sons*) asserts, "it will make no difference whether a man is stupid or clever, bad or good." What he means is that the collectivity, that is, its manipulators, will have mechanized society to the point where it is safe against the blunders and crimes of its members. If man, Bazarov implies, cannot be made into a machine (that is, predictable, rational, and, hence, always making the right decision), then society should be turned into a machine, so that the individual's recalcitrance and incalculable freedom might be neutralized and made ineffective. There again, the price to pay is freedom and the recognition of talent and originality.

(2) The progressive as a liberal-humanist is still distinguishable by the vague and vacillating tribute he pays to the individual and to the concept of equilibrium between the individual and the community. One might almost say that he is conditioned to react favorably to these words and values. This is why the image he has of the collectivity is tainted at once with repugnance (for fear that it may engulf the individual) and with enthusiasm (since he is a friend of mankind, a "philanthrope"). His usual attitude is therefore ambiguous: he insists on the rights of the individual, yet supports the collectivistic programs that crush individuality.

But it is only fair to say that he suffers from this contradiction, from his inability to reconcile the two sides of his intellectual world. He feels that he needs a steadier doctrine to stiffen his conscience. If the values attached to the individual could be guaranteed by society, and if, in turn, society itself could display these values permanently and, as it were, aggrandized, the world drama between man and society (the Marxist "alienation") could be brought to a satisfactory conclusion.

This is why the progressive confronted with a *system* becomes fascinated with its brutal affirmations, particularly when this system, while projecting itself forward and making prophetic statements about the future, also displays a logical approach and consistency. In such a case the progressive is bound to be seduced by the doctrine that preaches *necessity* (the necessary coming of the perfect society, etc.), and although the means and stages by which this necessity proceeds may offend his more delicate feelings, he trusts that the end will justify them as *short cuts*.

Much has been written about that seemingly strange phenomenon, the flux of the liberal intellectuals to the camp of Marxism; the "fellow-traveler's" psychology, childhood, love affairs, and dramatic encounters with misery and injustice, his solitude in bourgeois society and consequent longing for camarderie, have been probed in order to explain the whys and hows of this mass exodus toward the promised land. There is less reason for astonishment than is generally believed. There seem to be, indeed, two main reasons for the option of progressive intellectuals for socialism in its Marxist forms, for Communism, and for support of Soviet Russia: the first is that Communism is a short cut to Utopia since its central creed, dialectical materialism, pretends to be the scientific systematization of *evolution;* the second is that it brings the progressive intellectual closer to the *history*-making part of society, the "masses," the proletariat. Let us examine these two points in some detail.

(a) As I have shown in Chapter Three, the Marxist intellectual looks at Marxist philosophy as the highway to the communist society of the nonalienated man. For him it is not a short cut, not even a freely chosen road: it is the only one. But it is different with the progressive: he, too, believes in a rationally organized society; he, too, is indignant with the existence of evil in the present one— in fact, more so than the Marxist, who has his master's explanation for it—but on account of his dual allegiance

—to Western humanistic "values," and to the final outcome, the Perfect Society—he prefers evolution and slow
progress to revolution with its brutality. The crucial point
in his intellectual pilgrimage arises when he can no longer
resist the temptation of adopting the Communist short
cut whose advantages he is forced to recognize over his
own pragmatic, trial-and-error methods.

The progressive insists, however, on adopting the Communist short cut only temporarily. It is never quite clear
what he means by this: that after a certain time he will
get rid of the Communist alliance, or that Communism itself will, after the first "aggressive" period, become more
amenable to the "values" of liberalism and humanism.•
Whichever it is, the progressive is sufficiently attached to
these values and sufficiently proud of the material and
cultural achievements of his Western world, to recommend
the Communist methods for the "underdeveloped" areas
of the world, preferring softer ways for the society in
which he lives. However, as "underdeveloped," in his vocabulary, applies to the proletariat in his own society too,
he is willing to accept, if not Marxism, at least Communist
collaboration at home. It is true that he "loves" people
and does not want to expose them to barbarism, but he
trusts that his own example—and vigilance—will mitigate
the effects of the harder techniques of the Communists.
Thus he insists on the necessity of finding a common platform with the Communists who represent, in his eyes, the
dynamic element in the contemporary world and to whom
he looks up because they profess to know the nature of
the historical current and the meaning of history; in short,
because they have an advantage over the groping and
hesitant pragmatist that he is.••

This has been the assumption in every alliance and coalition between progressives and Communists in the last
forty-some years, from the "dual government" of Ke-

• As Professor Morgenthau reminds us, Harold Laski, for example, "tries to prove that Bolshevik totalitarianism is really a
kind of advanced liberalism, disfigured by some blemishes of
which time will take care." *Dilemma of Politics,* p. 349.
•• In comparison with the Calvinist believer, the progressive intellectual of quasi-socialist persuasion seems to hold that if we
are to be saved anyway, why not believe those who can show
us, *en cours de route,* the signs of salvation.

rensky with the Bolshevik Executive Committee between March and October, 1917, through the Spanish and French Popular Fronts in the mid-thirties, to the post-1945 governmental coalitions in Europe and China. And a desire for the same combination—between the Communist Party and the non-Communist Left—is sounded in the France of the Fifth Republic by Mendès-France and his associates, and in Italy between the left wing of the Christian Democrats and the Nenni Socialists.

What seduces the progressive in these alliances is that their partners seem to "know better" and have the will to follow up their knowledge with action. We have seen in Chapter Three that oracular pronouncements with respect to the process and end of history abound in Marxist literature. Every phase of history is neatly explained, classified, predicted; socioeconomic phenomena like depressions, pauperization, monopolistic concentration, imperialistic conflicts are shown to follow each other with the inexorability of logic. No hazard, no flaw of calculation, not even demonstrable failure, can weaken the stern belief in science as it is applied to the study of history and the evolution of mankind. Even after his fall from power, in his exile at Alma-Ata and forced wanderings through three continents, Trotsky showed complete self-assurance as an interpreter of events, equipped as he knew himself to be with the compass of dialectical materialism. "The greatest historical strength [of my] opposition," he wrote, "lies in the fact that it keeps its fingers on the pulse of the world historical process, that it sees the dynamics of the class forces clearly, foresees the coming day and consciously prepares for it." [15]

The progressive intellectual cannot resist the force with which the Marxist grasps their common mirage; he cannot say No to this historical infallibility. A good example for his ultimately inevitable Marxist option is provided by the forms and evolution of a certain trend in social thought in America before and after World War I. The utopian school of Dewey, Herbert Croly, Randolph Bourne, et al., had only vague ideas about "building the Good Community with the methods of science." [16] They agreed that all the ideas that "expert social engineers" may devise should be brought to the service of "social ideals," but it seems that these social ideals were no better defined than the "good life of the personality lived in the environment of the Beloved Community" (R. Bourne). Dewey, of course, echoed Marx, contributing his own sentimental utopianism; he too insisted that philosophy should change from "a device for dealing with the problems of philosophers" into a "method, cultivated by philosophers, for dealing with the problems of men." But this was the precise moment (1917) when the great transformation took place in Russia. In the red light over the Winter Palace Dewey's sentimental vagueness appeared even more insufficient than it would have been otherwise. If not he, his disciples were attracted by a more drastic medicine.

Their inevitable Marxist option is well presented by Professor Morton White, who, by juxtaposing two passages from *The Philosophy of John Dewey* (edited by P. A. Schilpp) constructs a dialogue between the latter and an admirer, Professor J. H. Randall, Jr.[17] The admiring disciple presses the master to give a fuller description of what he means by the "social technique" required in order "to enlist the cooperative support of men in doing what we now know how to do." Your philosophy, he tells Dewey, "should culminate in the earnest consideration of the social techniques for reorganizing beliefs and behavior. . . . It should issue in a social engineering, in an applied science of political education—and not merely in the hope that some day we may develop one." In his answer Dewey recognizes the urgency of such a social technology, but also the fact that he had done "little or nothing in this direction." The conclusion that Mr. White draws is most enlightening and may be applied to the ultimate choice of progressives in general, in the United States and elsewhere. "The puzzling thing about Dewey's views on this subject [that is, the elaboration of a clear-cut technique and program of action] is that sometimes he suggests that the fundamental task of philosophy is to build a political technology, and at others he suggests that even the modest theorizing, generalizing, and fixing of ends which a technology involves would lead us into rigidity and dogmatism. . . . By refusing to formulate ends of social behavior for fear of being saddled with *fixed* ends, Dewey hardly encouraged systematic political engineering. Those of his students who landed on the Left were forced to appeal to the tradition of Marx where they could find more than a methodology of politics. . . . The ambiguity of Dewey about the possibility of setting up a social program without lapsing into dogmatism was one of the chief reasons for the defections from liberalism in the Thirties." [18]

These defectors—a Sidney Hook, a Max Eastman—may have returned since then, for, after all, even if not Dewey's own then the pull of the American pragmatic tradition proved to be stronger in the end, particularly since after a brief possibility in the early thirties, no mass support for Marxist ideas was forthcoming. But, as in the case of Eastman, the Deweyite progressive succumbed, at least temporarily, to the view that Lenin and Trotsky were better instruments of a revolution than the instrumentalism of the master.

From the Marxist self-assurance of a Trotsky, the progressive derives not only a well-defined program, glamorized by science, but also the complete description of the only method that may be used to carry it out. This is what Trotsky writes about revolution as the sole *technique of progress:* "From the point of view of the absolute value of human personality, revolution must be 'condemned,' as well as war, as must also the entire history of mankind taken in the large. Yet the very idea of personality has been developed only as the result of revolutions, a process that is still far from complete. . . . Whether this method is good or bad from the point of view of normative philosophy I do not know and I must confess I am not interested in knowing. But I do know definitely that this is the only way that humanity has found thus far." [19]

Trotsky—and of course, Lenin—displayed this determination and "knowledge" of history when confronted with events the outcome of which was more than doubtful. In his chapter on "The Art of Insurrection," Trotsky describes what they, the most extreme faction of the October insurrectionists, meant by such democratic procedures as popular consultation, majority will, and referendum. "The insurrection was thenceforth able to believe in its success, for it could rely upon a *genuine majority* of the people. This, of course, is not to be understood in a *formal sense.* If a referendum could have been taken on the question of insurrection, it would have given extremely contradictory and uncertain results. An *inner readiness* to support the revolution is far from identical with an ability clearly to formulate the necessity of it. Moreover the answer would have depended to a vast degree upon the manner in which the question was presented, the institution which conducted the referendum—or to put it more simply, the *class which held the power*." [20] In order—Lenin answered his critics who opposed the insurrection since they were unsure of popular support—that the soldiers, peasants, and oppressed nationalities, floundering in the snowstorm of an elective ballot should recognize the Bolsheviks in action, it was necessary that the Bolshevik seize the power.

The force of the true Marxist's conviction acts as a temporary stimulant on the progressive fellow-traveler. That "Stalin foresaw Stalingrad"—the luring of the German army into the depth of Russia and the crushing defeat inflicted upon it—was a major argument in the immediate postwar years for those fellow-traveling intellectuals who were reminded of the forced collectivization in the Ukraine, the purges, the pact with Hitler. With this reasoning it is easy to develop a retrospective view of history and to justify, in the light of the 1943 victory at Stalingrad, the terror of the previous decade as a *short cut*. This is what made a noted French intellectual, the philosopher Merleau-Ponty, a fellow-traveler at the time, write that "Marxism is not just a hypothesis, for which, tomorrow, another may be substituted. It is the simple statement of the conditions without which there will be no mankind in the sense of reciprocal relationships between human beings, nor will there be rationality in history. . . . Beyond Marxism there are only daydreams or adventures." [21]

Confident in the revealed Marxist truth, the fellow-traveler develops the same double standards as the Communist intellectual himself. Dwight Macdonald quotes several examples of this type of thinking, which show that the methods and policies that the "totalitarian liberal" rejects with horror when he listens to the voice of his upbringing—or when he finds them in the opposing camp—he subscribes to with a slavish eagerness when they are part of the Soviet paraphernalia of power. On the question of compulsory labor Mr. Macdonald quotes from *The New Republic* (May 7, 1945) an article by A. Yugow, "Shall German Labor Rebuild Europe?" "Words should not intimidate us," announces the author. "Compulsory labor is not always slave labor. . . . [It] becomes slave labor only when it is used in the interest of enriching private individuals and groups. But compulsory labor at critical moments in the life of a nation, used in the interests of society, is not slavery. . . . In the USSR, where there is no private profit and where all labor is performed in the service of society . . . the compulsory labor of both the soviet citizens and the German workers will be most efficient." [22]

After describing some other instances of progressive-intellectual acrobatics, Mr. Macdonald concludes that according to this way of thinking " 'we' may do things with impunity and even approbation which become crimes against humanity if 'they' do them. Slave labor, demagogy, imperialist domination of small nations smell to heaven in Nazi lands but give off sweet perfume in 'ours.' " [23] In other words, they are justified "in the name of social progress, democratic re-education and world peace." [24]

The belief that Marxism is a short cut to the ideal community is held not by the so-called secularist liberals alone. In Christian intellectual circles too this conviction has taken hold of many minds. Thinkers like Teilhard de Chardin and Paul Tillich, in their different ways, favor progressivism, naturally in a "baptized" form, in the spirit of Christ's example when he took the leper in his arms and knelt before him. We have seen the Jesuit scientist's version of the progressive theme; the Protestant theologian in no less starry-eyed about socialism—and obsessively hostile to capitalism. With a fallacious reasoning we recognized in discussing the Marxist intellectual, Tillich disregards the possibility that socialism had in it the seeds of aggression and of will to power; no, that was the conquest of the capitalist spirit that finally doomed the socialist movement. Original socialism, he writes, had in it a "transcendent element," an "eschatological tension." But the capitalist spirit took it captive so that it began to seek its goals on earth. Only socialism that remained outside the conquest of capitalism—that is, anarchism—remained intact.[25] Tillich's (and the group of young Protestant socialists in Germany around 1920) effort to rehabilitate original socialism is expressed in what he calls "belief-ful realism"; its social projection, he claims, "contains the negation of every kind of romanticism and utopianism, but it includes the hope of a social and economic life in which the spirit of capitalism—the symbol of self-sufficient finitude—has been overcome." [26] Thus socialism is consistently identified with selflessness, work for the common good, even spiritual perfection, yet it displays the fatal impatience when Tillich admits that "socialism had a transcendent goal, it looked forward to a point in time when that which is the negation of all time—the eternal— was to be realized." [27] It may be legitimately asked: was Tillich's socialism made for a human society with ordinary virtues, or for the units of Chardin's and Huxley's "interthinking group" who have reached "point Omega"?

But far more significant than the evangelism of a Tillich or the evolutionism of Teilhard de Chardin is the outspoken Marxism of many worker-priests and progressive Catholics, especially in France. In the writings of Jean Lacroix, of Father Montuclard, or of the group around Jean-Marie Domenach and the review *Esprit*, Marxism appears as a short cut not merely toward the Perfect Society of the secularists, but toward the New Jerusalem announced by Christ. At least this is what the mixed language of Marxist dogma and the Gospels seems to indicate.

The Catholic progressives accept history as a revelation by the same right as they accept that of Moses and Christ. André Mandouze argued a few years ago that "as the spiritual sphere belongs by right to Christianism, so the political sphere belongs to Marxism";[28] and as Catholic action, writes Domenach, is in a state of delay over modern political consciousness (of the workers), it ought to emphasize the political message of Christianity rather than the spiritual message, at least until it re-establishes its authority among the faithful. Jean Lacroix actually goes as far as to suggest that as Marxism is "the imminent philosophy of the proletariat," the Church stand aside until Marxism—that is, the *historical* revelation—accomplishes its task of dealienating the worker. Father Montuclard expresses this thought more aggressively when he writes that Christian apostolate among workers is ineffective in a capitalist society and that revolutionary action should precede evangelization. This was the thesis by and large accepted by the worker-priests and the reason the Vatican finally decided to prohibit their activity.•

As with their openly secularist brethren, it is difficult to see at what moment the Catholic progressives would put an end to their collaboration with the Marxists, and how they envisage such a break. To them the Christ of the Gospels may resume His work of salvation only after the revolutionary message had done its work and established the universal classless society. The working class, writes Father Montuclard, will be Christianized again, but not until it has "reconquered human dignity through the [Marxist] philosophy which guides it." But aside from the difficulty of requesting the Marxists (who have their own ideas about the classless society and of religion) to step aside once the common victory is achieved, how would the Church of Christ resume its task when the admitted goal is a society in which the *individual* would find himself totally coinciding with the *collective?* Indeed, Eric Weil who, although Jewish, may be considered a member of the *Esprit* team and is often a spokesman for their political and historico-philosophical ideas, calls for a political order in which the choice between God and Caesar, between the spiritual and the temporal, should disappear. "The goal of political life," he writes in the classical manner of progressive thinking, "is that nobody should have to choose between the two realms." This is, of course, a

• The following passage, quoted from the Polish émigré author, Czeslav Milosz's *The Captive Mind,* characterizes well the outlook of the *Catholiques de gauche:* "I have known many Christians—Poles, Frenchmen, Spaniards—who were strict Stalinists in the field of politics but who retained certain inner reservations, believing God would make corrections once the bloody sentences of the all-mighties of History were carried out. They pushed their reasoning rather far. They argue that history develops according to immutable laws that exist by the will of God; one of these laws is the class struggle; the twentieth century marks the victory of the proletariat, which is led by the Communist Party; Stalin . . . fulfills the law of history, or in other words acts by the will of God; therefore one must obey him. Mankind can be renewed only on the Russian pattern; that is why no Christian can oppose the one—cruel, it is true— idea which will create a new kind of man over the entire planet." P. 199.

complete misunderstanding of the nature and scope of politics and religion: only the progressives and the Marxists believe that the *political order* represents the final answer and the solution to the problem of man's *spiritual allegiance*. But what is also evident is that the Catholic progressive, perhaps even more brutally than the secularist progressive (who has usually more practical contact with political life), advocates the Marxist short cut, the Marxist *phase*, as an accelerator of the historical process; less than the secularist, the Catholic progressive does not doubt that the ultimate goal is the same. He is convinced that all he does is opt for the more efficient method.

(b) We should never forget the dual nature of the progressive's attraction to Marxism: one element follows from his extreme *rationalism* and dreams of a rationally organized society, the other from his equally extreme *sentimentalism*, which comes into play when he declares his (abstract) love for mankind. In all theoretical systems, however, when "mankind" is mentioned, in reality only a segment of it is meant—the leaven of society, the pioneers of change, the human material easiest to mold. Since the middle of the nineteenth century this select segment has been, of course, the people, the masses which, a little later, acquired a better label and a clearer consciousness as the "proletariat."

For the Russian *narodniki* the muzhik represented the people. To him, as Berdyaev writes, "they wanted to kneel down," in recognition of his martyrdom, his Christlike suffering. For the young Romain Rolland, a student in the late 1880's, the people were all those in an inferior position, and while he did not have the Russians' Christian reverence for them, he had the bad conscience of the bourgeois. "I am ashamed," he writes, "when my mother's maid sees me at the table, with a book in my hand. I am ashamed when I meet a working man paining over some difficult task. I cannot take seriously a role that a civilization of exploiters, an anemic and rotten civilization, wants us to play." [29]

These are perhaps the manifestations of a literary sensibility, but this means that Marxism, with its lack of sentimentalism and with a good dose of organizational realism instead, could easily give it a new, more rigorous direction. "The men of my age," wrote Sartre in February, 1956, "know it very well that the great reality of their lives, more important even than the two world wars, was their encounter with the working class and its ideology. This offered us an inattackable vision of the world and of ourselves." It is noteworthy that in this declaration the encounter with the working class is a relatively insignificant event compared to other, more weighty results as the sudden acquaintance with and immersion in a new vision of the world. This is what the progressive intellectuals valued more highly, this is what started them on the fellow-traveling road. As much as their new direction, it was important for them to abandon the old, drifting course of their native middle class. They gave themselves to the proletariat in proportion as the bourgeoisie had less and less to offer. The masses, or for that matter, the individual worker, represented a goal, the rock-bottom of humanity; the aristocrats and the bourgeois, wrote Merleau-Ponty naïvely but significantly, are, first of all, members of a nation, of a class, of a profession; the proletariat is universally *human* because in him man is reconciled with himself.

The average progressive intellectual knows no more about the worker than did Rousseau of the "noble savage"; yet, the primitive was the tacitly assumed figure around whom his social optimism became crystallized. Similarly, the worker was the almost mythical figure which gave the progressive intellectual a sense of reality and a sense of security too because it meant that through his adherence to the proletarian cause he belonged to the anticipated future of mankind.

Although the progressive never goes quite as far as the genuinely Marxist intellectual-militant, his disillusionments are of the same nature. The Marxists, from Mayakovsky to Milovan Djilas, realize with a feeling of mixed horror and shame that the revolution is "stolen" by the bureaucracy and by a comfort-loving elite; the fellow-traveler, who has no direct experience of life in the Soviet Union and in people's democracies, is similarly disappointed when the Western "masses," instead of storming the bourgeois-capitalist citadels, choose, whenever possible, *embourgeoisement*. It is obvious that this has been the case in most of the Western world after 1945, when the so-called bourgeois parties—conservatives or Catholic democrats—began to emphasize the social question. With the United

States leading, western European nations began to adjust their economic machinery to the satisfaction of the large masses, integrating them—through social, economic, and cultural promotion—into the body of consumers and political participants.

The better standard of living has had the effect of turning away the masses of workers from the socialist and communist parties. The electoral defeats of the Left have had, in some countries, the effect of compelling the nominally still working class parties to reorient their policies, draft new programs, abandon the slogans of many decades. The impact of these events on the Marxists and fellow-travelers has not been identical. The former remain sure of themselves as their program is a long-range one, with the entire history as its field of development. Moreover, they are militants not of a merely "leftist" party, but of a *revolutionary* party, depending on a world power and enjoying its reflected prestige. The Marxists can adapt themselves to the world-movements that Soviet policy encourages; they feel themselves at home among the nationalistic Negro masses of Africa, among the victims of apartheid policy, among the organizers of the Cuban revolution. They are, in other words, the acknowledged technicians of revolutions and can rely on a purposeful Soviet diplomacy to co-ordinate their world-wide efforts.

It is different with the fellow-traveling intellectual whose loyalty to Soviet policy is not flawless, and who, therefore, is not quite so able to accept its vertiginous shifts. He has once and for all accepted the Marxist analysis of class struggle and the Marxist analysis of alienation. For him the *embourgeoisement* of the workers is an absolutely perplexing phenomenon to which he has but one reaction: he denies it. He denies, that is, the gain derived from it, and insists that only the upper layer of the working class, the workers' aristocracy, finds itself in a better position, the rest of the "masses" being now betrayed by their own natural leaders as well. "The proletariat and its cadres," wrote David Rousset in a recent number of *Esprit*,[30] "remain subjected to an economy manipulated by others. . . . They hold on to a broken power. The feeling of incapacity to use the force they know they possess . . . is compensated by the awareness that the professionals of politics betrayed their basic interests." Rousset is unwilling to admit that the gains of the working classes are genuine, because he cannot give up his deep-rooted conviction that the workers will only win if they conquer the political machinery, that is, the State. Rather than accept the phenomenon of *embourgeoisement* as an essentially healthy integration of the workers into the life of nations (a development that contradicts the Marxist analysis and forecast), he prefers to elaborate an unsubstantiated theory according to which the working class is "organically incapable" of organizing its rule even after it has won a decisive victory. The working class, he writes, may triumph in the civil war originated by its social revendications, but it cannot transform this triumph into a political and economic accomplishment. And he concludes that "each time the proletariat was confronted with the necessity of constituting a dominant class, this attempt was a failure" (p. 179).• But from the examples he marshals we see that he does not have only the Soviet experience in mind; he registers the same succession of defeats in Germany, England, France, and Spain. In other words, what he means by victory for the working class is not the gaining of vote, of civil rights, of prosperity, but complete and undivided domination, the dictatorship of the proletariat, or, as he would perhaps term it, total democracy. Anything less than that is bitter disappointment, behind which treason or fatality lurks. The masses must be presumed innocent and full of promise for the future so that the progressive intellectual, making of them his fetish, may feel that he adores the only true god.

(3) The progressive intellectual's natural habitat is Utopia, that is, politics in reverse, antipolitics. Whether as a liberal, situating himself in the humanistic tradition, or a fellow-traveler, exhilarated by the wind blowing from the Marxist camp, he is essentially an optimist who believes

---

• "It seems," writes Jean-Jacques Servan-Schreiber, editor of the progressive weekly, *L'Express,* "that the Left is always 'tricked' [*jouée*] when it comes to power in the framework of the present political structure." *Rencontres—Nenni, Bevan, Mendès-France* (Julliard, 1959), p. 27. We have seen in this and the third chapter that the Left can never believe that its failures are caused by anything but external circumstances: "tricks," conspiracies, the penetration of rightists or of rightist-bourgeois mentality in their movements.

in the uninterrupted progress of mankind, leading the individual to more freedom and society to a state of definitive ideological cohesion.

But, as I have pointed out earlier in this chapter, not all "progressives" have the same notion of progress and the same messianistic outlook. While the majority has been fascinated by the conquests of science and the potentialities of rational organization, there are those who, without abandoning the ritual of scientism, find in mechanization, in the way of life imposed by industry, or simply in the ugliness of modern urban and suburban existence, disturbing signs concerning the price to pay for progress and well-being. They would never dare denounce, for example, the process of modernization in so-called backward areas—the disappearance of villages in their countries, the uniformization of exotic lands in the yellow and black continents—yet they cannot generate in themselves the progressive's undivided enthusiasm for such transformation of natural beauty and character into the flatlands of "improved conditions." In the secret of their hearts a flowery meadow appeals to them more than a steel mill; a peaceful village in a valley more than the dam that will flood it and transform it into a green, underwater ghost town.

Nor are they so absolutely convinced of man's goodness. The contrast between beauty and ugliness is, often, a more concrete eye opener on the realities of life than the contrast between good and evil, so inextricably bound up with interests and compromises. Intimate acquaintance with the human body reveals the inevitable decay as also the hardening of the soul under the still mobile features. The artist and the esthete thus know that science and material progress did not bring any new element to the content, to the essence, of their art and artistic contemplation, but, on the contrary, proved to whomever wants to reflect upon it, that under different costumes and set against different backgrounds the portrait is of the same man.

More than that. The esthete is no mere contemplative or critic. He has feeling for forms other than architectural, plastic or musical, and a demand for the harmony of existence, for a style of life. He appreciates gestures, elegance, wit, the Renaissance heritage of the virtuoso, a type that reappeared with the Romantic pose of a Chateaubriand and a Byron, and again in our days, this time in the revolutionary garb of extremist ideologies. And in all these periods, in ours particularly, the esthetic experience and the style of life have been factors of distinction, a desperate affirmation of at least one value: beauty, in the surrounding crassness of moral nihilism, political anarchy, public clownishness, and industrial drabness.

Beauty is thus the glove thrown into the featureless face of an absurd universe. Let us listen to the most desperate description of this absurdness, from the black soil of which, however, the flower of contemporary estheticism draws its feeble sustenance:

That man is the product of causes which had no prevision of the end they were achieving; that his origin, his growth, his hopes and fears, his loves and his beliefs, are but the outcome of accidental collocations of atoms; that no fire, no heroism, no intensity of thought and feeling, can preserve an individual life beyond the grave; that all the labors of all ages, all the devotion, all the inspiration, all the noonday brightness of human genius, are destined to extinction in the vast death of the solar system, and that the whole temple of Man's achievement must inevitably be buried beneath the debris of a universe in ruins—all these things, if not quite beyond dispute, are yet so nearly certain, that no philosophy which rejects them can hope to stand. Only within the scaffolding of these truths, only on the firm foundation of unyielding despair, can the soul's habitation henceforth be safely built.•

Not since Lucretius has there been so much eloquence spent on proving the validity of "unyielding despair" as

• Bertrand Russell, *Mysticism and Logic,* p. 46.

Russell, in whose ideas much of nineteenth- and twentieth-century science finds its philosophical expression, is in no contradiction with many of the evolutionists. They all partake in a cosmic pessimism. "Asked whether life is going anywhere," wrote Father Chardin of his fellow evolutionists, "at the end of its transformations, nine biologists out of ten will today say No, even passionately. They will say: 'It is abundantly clear . . . that organic matter is in a state of continual metamorphosis. . . . By what right can we say that a mammal, even in the case of man, is more advanced, more perfect than a bee or a rose? . . . They are different solutions—but each equivalent to the next. . . . No one of the lines appears to lead anywhere in particular.'" *The Phenomenon of Man,* p. 141.

the foundation of our "safety." But whatever we think of this text, it is easy to derive from it the bitter attitude of Sisyphus who knows the meaninglessness of his task and who performs it nevertheless (instead of choosing suicide) because of the supposed dignity of the gesture. It is equally easy to derive from it the only remaining program for man—other than absurd action, *acte gratuit*—the *esthetic creation* by which he creates meaning (beauty) in a universe where none pre-exists him and none will survive him. This is, naturally, not the progressive's dream of universal happiness; it is faith in the redeeming nature of art and in beauty taking the place of reason gone berserk as the uniting link of men. "The despair," says Lionel Trilling, "that arises from the knowledge of the material nature of the world validates all rituals and all fictions that make life endurable in the alien universe." These "rituals and fictions" populate the indifferent spaces of Malraux and Camus with the monuments of man's presence; they are "new images which are mighty enough to deny our nothingness," says Malraux;[31] they are works "built on sand with the knowledge that there is no future"; but "the wisdom of Sisyphus is the only wisdom that the philosophy of the absurd authorizes." [32]

The experience of the absurd thus dissolves the will to create except in the lucid individual who has measured the distance between ideal and fulfillment. But such individuals are a minority who accept the existentialist vision of Camus and Malraux. The majority needs the warmth generated by collective enthusiasm and the reassuring promise of uninterrupted progress.

It is against this enthusiasm, fatefully combining itself with political credulity, that the philosopher of the absurd points to *action as an end in itself*, rather than as the tool of limitless ambitions. Not that action is an empty gesture; in fact, it leads to tangible, even though temporary, results; at times the rock reaches the mountaintop, and, as Camus tells us, "we must believe that Sisyphus is happy." But action has no meaning beyond the individual and the moment; it brings satisfaction to the agent, it is not a ritual in the temple of History. Only the solitary artist may understand this, who lives for the exalted hours of creation and wearily turns away from the finished work toward a new challenge.

For the philosopher of an absurd human condition the artist's lonely creation is the only method of turning the chance-adventure of a troublesome race in one corner of the universe into a tolerably meaningful enterprise. As Malraux says in his last semifictional work, if our presence here on earth is not mere non-sense, then it must have a continuity, the continuity of art and civilization, binding man to time if not to eternity. Art is the par excellence activity that links an age to "the vanished forms of past grandeur," and helps shape the image of man.

Yet, the artist's isolation from the progressive attitude of the age is only temporary. It is true that the esthetic point of view is the last refuge of humanism and the only reality on which the progressive intellectual may insist without being accused by his peers of devising an ethical or theological absolute. It is also true that for him the esthetic vision of life is an antidote to the materialism of Lucretius and Russell, the only door through which access may be had to a world not yet engulfed by science and the rational society. But, in fact, it is amazing to see— and it is a cause for alarm—that in proportion as we enter the age of technology and barbarism, art in its multiple forms grows side by side with bureaucracy and machinism as a sort of tranquilizer against both, as a right of the citizen to catch his breath while collective devices slowly crush him.

This sudden importance of art—an importance discovered by ideological movements, by the State, and by the business world—has made of the artist a central figure on the public place. His earlier revolt against society, his marginal role as an entertainer, have of course predestined him to the role of an ally of all progressive movements that promise a universal society, that is, a universal public for his books, poems, paintings and partitions. His shudder before the ugliness of capitalist civilization, his isolation from the masses whose warmth and understanding he genuinely needs, make him an ideal, because uncritical, partner of the progressive ideologues who preach the overthrow of all that he hates. This partnership is well illustrated in the joint "manifesto" published by André Breton, the "Pope of Surrealism," and Leon Trotsky, the "Red Napoleon," when the artist visited the revolutionist in Mexico (1938). "Art today can only be revolutionary, that is, it must aspire at the complete and radical reconstruction of society, even if for no other reason than to emancipate intellectual creation from the chains which obstruct it and to allow all mankind to rise to the heights that only geniuses could reach in the past." [33]

Now it is most instructive to note that while, in the last forty years, the esthete and the artist have scorned metaphysics, have turned their back to moral absolutes, political common sense, and to the image of man, there was one thing they did not give up either in the face of ideological pressure or express Communist Party orders: their esthetic vision and creation. It may be said of the English poets of the 1930's, Auden, Spender, Synge, and of the French Eluard, Aragon, Prévert, and Picasso, that, whether fellow-travelers or Party members, their art was not essentially deflected from their genuine vision, a fact that forced the Party into many compromises.• But if they were adamant on the subject of their artistic creation, they yielded the more abjectly on the political issues, because they linked the cause of art and that of revolution and Utopia. The history of surrealism in France, from 1924 to 1935, was the story of the politization of art and artist, resulting in seriocomical vaticinations and the setting up of warring factions. By the time of Breton's joint declaration with Trotsky, the rifts and clashes within the surrealist movement were consummated, some members having drifted away, some others having joined the Communist Party. Revolutionary brotherhood and action appeared to them, as it did to Malraux, Auden, Brecht, Dos Passos, and Silone, the only way of affirming the solidarity of men in a meaningless universe. It mattered little whether this solidarity manifested itself in art, in humanism, or in political choice: what counted, in the context of their philosophical nihilism, was the exalting contrast between the abyss of the surrounding universe and the heroism of their "engagement"; they were seduced by that "true humanism which is the dizziness, accepted by our mind, before the irreducible strangeness of the human adventure." [34]

• The latest example is Louis Aragon's great novel, *La Semaine sainte*, written neither in content nor in form in conformity to Party taste and "socialist realism," yet defended in an official declaration by Thorez as art acceptable to Communists.

5

The Intellectual as a Reactionary

In devoting a chapter to the third type of intellectual in our *tour d'horizon*, we face a difficulty similar to, if not greater than, the one presented by our discussion of the progressive intellectual. In contradistinction to the Marxist intellectual (whose thinking and actions are severely circumscribed by his loyalty to a group of men, to a particular philosophy, and to a country), we have found the progressive intellectual somewhat hard to localize, and even after we have described him, we still run the risk of being contradicted on each issue by any one of those labeled "progressive."

With the conservative intellectual the problem becomes even more complicated. Whatever the dispassionate dictionary definition of the philosophical, political, and cultural conservative may be, the ideological struggles of the last two hundred years have led to the near-identification of conservatism with backwardness, reluctance to change and to progress, even with "reaction," and, ultimately, with "Fascism." This identification, or at least, generalization, may or may not stand up under scrupulous analysis: the fact is, and one may hardly ignore it, that one cannot discuss the conservative intellectual without examining his relationship, if not his kinship, with the other, above-mentioned, "extremist" types. Such a procedure, however, tends to overlook the differences and is open to all sorts of disclaimers. And, indeed, here we reach the second difficulty of speaking of various types of conservatives under one heading: in the historical current of the last two centuries, the type we call conservative has generally been on the defensive, philosophically as much as politically; and, in every such instance, the writings and other manifestations of conservative intellectuals bear the mark of either bad conscience or desperate violence, or again, of a desire to establish a rapprochement with the opponent. Like the progressive intellectual, torn between his humanistic and esthetic values and his utopian-Marxist attachments, the conservative, too, seeks to speak two languages at the same time: one of tradition, the other of ruthlessness and power; now the language of direct communication with the flow of life, then the language of authority and severe restrictions.

Faithful to his inherent dualism of outlook, the conservative intellectual in the last two centuries has had a relatively easy yet treacherous way of dividing the modern times into two distinct periods; one of two (or sometimes both) lines of division is used: either the French Revolution, which, in the words of some contemporary conservatives is likened to a "typhoid fever" separating the healthy old regime from the age of Jacobinism and democracy;• or, further back, the Reformation, which, particularly with Catholic historians, is represented as the great watershed between health and corruption, true doctrine and heresies, man's integrated outlook and his partial view of the world, the result of ideological blinders.

The main reason for this categorical separation of modern history into "good" and "bad" •• is that, surprisingly but not paradoxically, the conservative intellectual is a latecomer among the ideological types. We have traced the

• As many, if not most, conservatives are religious men (and many are Catholics), they place the pre-1789 history under the sign of the cross, and what followed under the sign of Satan. A good example is given by the French right-wing monarchist Pierre Boutang: "The operations of anti-Christendom, in 1789, then again in 1917, consisted in reversing the order of creation and redemption, in imposing on the world a system by which the Christ is judged by History. This leads to the crucifiction of History." *La Nation Française*, Dec. 16, 1959.

•• The progressive has, of course, the reverse image.

radical ideology back to the Middle Ages, and Marxism itself back to the Levellers and Rousseau; but conservatism as an *ideology* was obviously a reaction to these and other ideologies which, in the view of the conservatives, had come to usurp the natural order of things and to alter the normal vision of the world. Conservatism, therefore, became an ideology—that is, an instrument of combat— the day that institutions and the channels of thinking ceased to be of the traditional kind. Just as the progressives believed in perpetual change, rejuvenation, and improvement, the conservatives emphasized preservation and stability; and when the progressives revealed their intention— that of establishing on earth the reign of Utopia—the conservatives countered by insisting that the destiny of mankind remains toil, division, and suffering.

The core of conservative thought—at least in its immediately obvious, one should say, popular, form—is that there is no *real* change, either in the condition of man or in his historical existence. Hence the preoccupation of so many conservative historians and thinkers since the French Revolution in trying to prove that actually nothing changed as a result of it, or, if the evidence refuting them is overwhelming, that the changes are superficial, reversible, collapsible.

This thought, in turn, determines the conservative approach to the modern world, the conservative *mood*, so to speak. In its first movement this mood is one of brooding: underlying conservative criticism—and parelleling the obligatory enthusiasm of the progressive—there is very often a tone of reproach, which degenerates into sarcasm and vituperations, or on the contrary, despair and resignation. And this is important because, as unhappy love finds more heartrending chords on the lyre of sentiments than does carefree and contented love, so the conservative thinkers have been far more sensitive and eloquent in their observations and denunciations than the progressives in the ritual hurrahs at each new conquest of their ideology.

But conservative thought is, naturally, much more than what a mood, however modulated and refined, may express. Historically, in its early stages, conservatives still possessed the power, not its shadow. The order of the day was consequently the turning back of the tide. The natural impulse of conservatism, when the feverish years of the

Revolution and Napoleonic Empire were over, was to restore the old order: the Congress of Vienna, the Holy Alliance, the Bourbon restoration, were its phases.• Even in the newly founded United States the War of Independence, with its domestic radical excesses, led to the elaboration of a conservative constitution, inspired by an elitist philosophy and distrust of mass rule. Until about the middle of the nineteenth century, in Europe and in America, the conservatives possessed sufficient power and prestige to check the advances of progressive democracy, socialism, and mass culture. For every Victor Hugo who was royalist in his youth and freethinking democrat in his old age, there was a Balzac whose early republican sympathies gave way under the weight of his observation of social disintegration and decay.

Only when this equilibrium was finally broken•• in favor of the progressive forces, did conservatism begin to "accept" the modern world and make the first attempts at enrolling the awakened popular-proletarian forces for the creation of a *new order*. The philosophical bases for such an action were laid in the nineteenth century; but only the twentieth tried to carry it out, proving, incidentally, that in both thought and action the conservatives of the period were usually straggling behind their opponents.

Brooding over and restoration of the old order we must call attitudes rather than programs of action. It is true that they are dictated by sentiment and philosophy that are noble inspirations, but as political and ideological forces they should be discounted. To the first half of the nineteenth century, in what we called a period of equilib-

---

• Not all conservatives believed in the possibility of restoring the old order. No less a figure among them than Joseph de Maistre held it an impossible dream. "Maistre sighs for the dark ages," writes Isaiah Berlin in his essay on Tolstoi, *The Hedgehog and the Fox,* "but no sooner were plans for the undoing of the French Revolution suggested by his fellow emigrés, than he denounced them as childish nonsense—an attempt to behave as if what has occurred and changed us irretrievably, had never been. To try to reverse the Revolution, he wrote, was as if one had been invited to drain the Lake of Geneva by bottling its water in a wine cellar."

•• The historical stages were the revolutions of 1848, Marxian socialism, Darwin's theories, the Age of Jackson, etc.

rium, these attitudes lent a *style*, noticeable in the records of parliamentary debates as well as in novels. The writings of Metternich, the speeches of Donoso Cortes, the noble reflections of De Bonald, the *Mémoires* of Chateaubriand, all show the conservative in the role of Cassandra, made particularly difficult by a twofold preoccupation: refraining the popular masses; and warning the leaders against suicidal policies, that is, against the temptations of demagoguery as well as of reaction.

In art and literature also the climate was one of gloom; I have mentioned in an earlier chapter the royalist sympathies of the French Romantic writers, and the last escape of all European Romantics into the medieval past.• What else was the "romantic agony" described by Mario Praz if not refuge into the morbid, which seemed still saner than the eyesores of the industrial revolution and the drab proletarian masses? Baudelaire saw in the invention of photography the end of all art; and Flaubert immortalized both the death struggle of the artist (in Emma Bovary) and the coming victory of the average man, imbued with vulgar scientism and progressive ideology (Monsieur Homais, Bouvard and Pécuchet). "Nothing is left except the vulgar and stupid mob," he wrote Louise Colet in September, 1853. "All of us are equally mired in mediocrity. Social equality has spread to the mind. Our books, our art, our science, are designed for everybody, like railroads and public shelters. Mankind is frenziedly seeking moral abasement, and I resent being a part of it."

The conservative attitude, whether it manifested itself in a mood or in a conscious desire to avenge the past by bringing it once more to life, becomes understandable in the light of the most fundamental beliefs. namely, that the world and the human condition never really change, and when they do, in a superficial manner, it is due to a *conspiracy*. The conservative looks at life as a web of organic relationships, extending from the farthest origins (in fact, from God) to the ultimate end, interference with which is both impossible and sacrilegious. The philosophical core of this belief may be found in Parmenides's teaching about the One (which is indivisible); the conservative looks at change with a mixed reaction of disbelief and disapproval.

• A late American child of this mood was Henry Adams.

162

As a concession, he allows, with Plato, that even if change exists, it takes place in the inferior sphere of phenomena, while the superior sphere of ideal reality is eternally the same. With Plotinus, he further recognizes a hierarchy of beings and a concatenation among them, but in this image again the emanations closest to the origin, to God, are one and indestructible, and the degree of corruption is proportionate with their distance from it.

For change, for evil, for the accidental, the conservative thinker has, of course, an explanation: as we have just seen, it is the remoteness from the original light, the dejectedness of man, his proclivity for sinning, the fruit of his freedom. But this explanation, which enables the conservative to maintain his serenity before evil, is all too general: it does not account for this or that concrete instance, it does not attempt to investigate the mechanism of such and such a transformation. In other words, the conservative does not invent systems as do a Hegel or a Marx, systems whose ambition is to *comprehend* the general and the particular, *master* them with the usurped thoroughness of science, and *predict* any and all subsequent development. On the contrary, faced with the predicament of an age or of a society, the conservative will refer to the laws of the universe, which include, from all eternity, good as well as evil, the sinful nature of man *and* his redemption—or he will accuse a willed causation, the arrogance and sloth of the human creature.• Briefly, in each particular instance he will tend to see the original sin re-enacted.

This "conspiracy" theory can be detected at the origin of each great conservative-reactionary thought of the nineteenth century. Let us remember, in this respect, the pair Tocqueville-Gobineau, briefly referred to at the end of Chapter Two. The former, a great Catholic thinker, undertook to explore what was really new, that is, divorced

• As Burke put it, the world is either God's design, or it is chaos. Incidentally, Burke himself was inclined to believe that changes unfavorable to his own conservative principles were brought about by "conspiracies." He put the blame for the revolutionary ideas finally culminating in the French Revolution on the *philosophes*, who, out of spite for not being suitably recompensed with social rank and distinction, spread their harmful doctrines.

from Christianity, in the moral systems of his age. The reason why he, a conservative French aristocrat, could finally come to terms with these moral systems was that he found them to be not radical novelties but extensions, new applications of old Christian doctrine.

Not so his younger correspondent. In his long letter of September 8, 1843, Gobineau argues vehemently and convincingly for the thesis that modern sensibility and thinking are altogether detached from the Christian root; he seeks to demonstrate it by reference to new attitudes toward the poor and the prisoner, toward virtue, vice, and suffering, toward the individual and the State. Generally speaking, he attributed the new spirit to a completely secularized morality, indulgent toward passions and even harnessing them for socially useful purposes. But this spirit is definitely no longer Christian; "it becomes a sort of philanthropy, sentimental rather than reasonable, the kind which easily goes astray." [1] It is the spirit of the democratic State that Gobineau outlined in this and other letters, but, in fact, he tried to go deeper and reveal the degeneracy of the human race, especially of that part of it —the Aryan race—which he considered superior to others and which, therefore, had the most to lose.

Gobineau did not accuse anybody of having engineered the mixing of races; he spoke in terms of civilizations and claimed the objectivity of a "doctor who announces the coming of the end." [2] But the eagerness with which, for example, American anti-abolitionist preachers and newspapers seized upon his diagnosis, is indicative of the dramatic potentialities that his theory held. Three quarters of a century later, the National Socialists could make an even more effective use of Gobineau's ideas when, by ascribing the decadence of the West both to the spirit of democracy and to racial impurity, they indicted international Jewry (and the spurious "Protocols of the Elders of Zion") for a gigantic conspiracy against the Aryan race.

The tone of Nietzsche is much more passionate than that of the somewhat cool, ambitious, and career-seeking Frenchman; but on the one hand, he is also much more profound, and on the other, he transcends Gobineau's circle of preoccupations so that it is difficult to see in him merely an exponent of nineteenth-century reactionary thought. Also, the milieu in which he moved and to which

he reacted was quite unlike the one Gobineau knew:
Nietzsche was surrounded by self-satisfied and pietistic
burghers who were profiting by German pre-eminence in
commerce, industry, statecraft, and science, and were
tempted to consider—Hegel had encouraged them in this
—history closed with the achievement of German superiority, a feeling which, yet, managed to be not only arrogant, but pedestrian and philistine as well.

The refuge that, to his delight, the young Nietzsche had
found was the circle of German romantic artists and the
household of Wagner in particular. However, the pleasure
of being in kindred company was not to last long; Wagner
and his circle, in which Nietzsche's own sister and her
husband must also be counted, turned out to illustrate, on
a much higher level, to be sure, the same conceit and self-
admiration that Nietzsche denounced in the *Spiessbürgers*.
Wagner's orations against Semitic influence under which
Germanic values were allegedly softening, filled his young
friend with terror: how could such a great man succumb
to the cheap vituperations popular in certain circles and
journals, when the danger was of a cosmic nature and so
had to be the remedy?

But if Wagner was a typical representative of nineteenth-century "conspiracy" theory• so indeed was Nietzsche himself. He was not tempted by the racial theories
of his friends and was anti-Semitic (or rather, anti-
Hebrew) only insofar as he considered Christianity the
great insurrection against nature and the masculine values.
Like Gobineau before him and many right-wing ideologues

• In all his writings about art and the German nation, Wagner
tried to measure the distance between the "ideal German" and
the real one, so as to explain why his countrymen did not respond to his music as they ought to have responded. "If the
latter is not what he should be, if he is not genuinely 'German,'
the fault must rest with somebody or something. There remains
only to find those responsible: they will be the foreigner, the
press, the Jews, our bad dietetics, and the general decadence.
. . . Then will come the hunt for microbes, for intruders,
forgers, and traitors." M. Boucher, *The Political Concepts of
Richard Wagner* (M & H Publications, 1950), p. 111. These
haphazard ideas, crystallized in a strong anti-Semitism, became
strengthened and more unified after Wagner had read the works
of Gobineau. He developed an immense admiration for the
latter and met him several times after 1880.

after him, Nietzsche presented an ideal form of life, surreptitiously undermined by a "plot." This is the pattern of conservative-reactionary thought, no matter how many variations it displays, no matter who are the "good" and the "evil," the "masters" and the "slaves," the "attackers" or the "defenders." For Nietzsche the origin of "good" is not an altruistic act as weighed on the balance of Judaeo-Christian doctrine, but the arbitrarily designated action of a "strong aristocracy." Thus does he answer the question put in *The Genealogy of Morals:* "Under what conditions did man invent for himself those judgments of values: good and evil, and what intrinsic value do they possess in themselves?" [3] The "master morality," however, is soon overwhelmed by the "slave morality": [4] the weak, the slave, and (historically) the Jews have skillfully reversed this evaluation and designated the poor, the weak, as the good. They even repudiated Jesus (the only true Christian, according to Nietzsche), because he brought them a victory heavy with risk and responsibility; and they built the Church, which was a surer means of undermining and defeating Rome.

Mutatis mutandis, the same conspiracy was afoot in his own time—Nietzsche thought. "The democratic movement is the inheritance of the Christian movement"; the slaves and weaklings of two thousand years ago were now called "teeth-gnashing anarchist dogs," "peacefully industrious democrats," "revolution-ideologues," "socialists"; what united them was "their instinctive hostility to every form of society other than that of the autonomous herd"; what made them one was "their belief in the morality of mutual sympathy" and in the "community as the deliverer." [5]

Against such folly, Nietzsche put his hope in the appearance of "new philosophers," who were to bring out, under "new constraints," what "is still in man." Having measured the "universal degeneracy of mankind—idealized by the socialistic fools who call this state a free society," they are therefore the depositories of a new wisdom, "a new mission." •

• *Beyond Good and Evil* (Modern Library), p. 497.

A phrase in this passage shows Nietzsche's disappointment with Wagner, a "new philosopher" who "miscarried." "There are few pains so grievous as to have seen, divined or experienced how an exceptional man has missed his way and deteriorated."

In these words we may see other things too beside a second important exposition of the conspiracy theory. As the century advanced, the charges against the modern, radical-democratic-secular world view became more precise, and conservatism more conscious of its general doctrine and duties. Gobineau in the basically traditionalist French society could hardly discern the signs of the new spirit; he still had difficulty backing up and systematizing some of his extraordinary insights. But Nietzsche, living in the midst of a society born simultaneously to nationhood and success, was in a better position to identify precisely (a precision made extremely vivid by his prophetic genius) the targets at which latter-day right-wing critics were to aim. Thus it can be seen that what we called the "conspiracy" theory has proved as effective an instrument for probing past and present as the more "serious" deterministic systems, which explained history as a gigantic unfolding of a world spirit or of the inexorable logic of class struggle. And as the century progressed and flowed into a new one, conspiracy theories themselves tended to evolve into systems, retaining, in a greater or lesser extent, their original mood and readiness to cast suspicion on the opposing ideologies.

In the person of Dostoevsky, nineteenth-century conservatism possesses a very powerful support. It is significant that the Russian novelist's most important works, *Crime and Punishment, The Brothers Karamazov, The Possessed,* and *The Idiot,* which are, in reality, stages of a continuous preoccupation, not to say obsession, have a common inspiration in a factual conspiracy by the student Nechaev and his group. These anarchists and nihilists, tied together by their fascination with the strange figure of their young leader, carried out a number of criminal acts (arson, murder, violence) at the latter's order, with the intention of creating chaos and then building a new society on the ruins of the old.

Dostoevsky, who all his life was obsessed with the opposition between an all-powerful God and the frightening freedom of man, saw in the famous case (reported by the newspapers) an extraordinarily significant manifestation of this freedom and the incalculable uses to which it may be put in the service of the defiance of God. Dostoevsky's life passion was, Berdyaev writes, "what happens to man when, having his liberty, he turns to arbitrary self-will. Only then can the depth of human nature be seen. . . . Dostoievsky's interest begins from the moment that man sets himself up against the objective established order of the universe, cuts himself off from nature and his organic roots, and manifests his arbitrary will." [6]

What happens when man thus asserts himself absolutely, when, as Kirilov does (*The Possessed*), he declares that God and the divine laws are his own inventions? The logical answer is that he may then abolish God and invent something else in His place: most likely his, man's, own divinity. If there is no God and no immortality, then "man may well become the man-God and he may lightheartedly overstep all the barriers of the old morality of the old slave man [for] there is no law for God." [7]

Dostoevsky lived in the anxiety that such an "overstepping of all barriers" may take place any day, and he saw in the Nechaev case and in the socialist movement the initial stages of the great conspiracy.• He, too, reached back in history to the Catholic Church as the generator and exploiter of man's freedom, and did not care to make a sharp distinction between the Jesuit order and the Communist International. Prince Myshkin, in *The Idiot*, explains that both Catholics and Socialists preach equality to be attained by suppression, and warns that in the name of material progress "the friend of humanity, with his shaky moral principles, is the devourer of humanity." (p. 368.)

In *The Possessed*, which is, indeed, the story of a conspiracy (inspired by Nechaev's), the plotters freely admit that in the new order nine tenths of mankind will have to be treated like sheep—for their own happiness—by one tenth, that is, the elite. Yet, the horrible discussion is couched in rational terms and is conducted, after all, by young idealists of the Raskolnikov type. As E. Simmons writes in his book on Dostoevsky, it was the Russian novelist's growing belief that the fundamental error of socialism

---

• "Socialism . . . is above all the question of atheism, its contemporary incarnation; it is the problem of the Tower of Babel, built without God, not in order to reach heaven from the earth, but in order to debase heaven to the earth." *Les Frères Karamazov* (*N.R.F.* edition), I, 32.

was its conviction that it could organize a social system on a rational plan, that reason could take the place of human nature, of the living processes of life.• Dostoevsky, whose ideal was spiritual peace and the acknowledgement of our dependence on God, looked ahead with an undisguised shudder to the outbreak of the godless revolution; as with Nietzsche, this was no fear of the social upheaval itself: they had a rather low opinion of the institutions and civic mentality around them. But both knew that those whom Nietzsche called pejoratively "philosophasters and fraternity-visionaries," and Dostoevsky, "demons among the herd of swine," •• would not stop at the revolution but, in order to perpetuate their power would impose their rule in the name of Science and Reason. The only escape for human freedom, Dostoevsky wrote in the *Notes from Underground*, would then be in folly. Significantly, this became Nietzsche's actual solution.

The doctrine of Charles Maurras is also built on the concept of order, attacked and upset by a new mentality, Semitic and Levantine, which dismantles the classical edifice of Latin civilization and Catholic hierarchical structure. The basic inspiration of Maurras is Greco-Mediterranean: the turning point of his spiritual career was a sudden insight, gained at the Acropolis in Athens, into the essence of beauty and order—*"la belle notion du fini"*—and all his life he was to combat its opposite, the Protestant-democratic disorder in its religious, literary, and political manifestations.•••

• E. Simmons, *Dostoevsky, The Making of a Novelist*, p. 167.

This is what Dostoevsky wrote to N. Katkov, editor of the *Russian Messenger*, on April 25, 1866: "The nihilists. The doctrine wants that we shake off everything by the four corners of the tablecloth, so as to obtain a tabula rasa for action. All nihilists are socialists. Socialism (especially its Russian variety) demands that all ties be cut. They are absolutely certain that on a tabula rasa they can at once construct a paradise. Fourier was convinced that the organization of one single phalanstery would be enough for the whole world to be covered with phalansteries." *Correspondance de Dostoevsky*, III, 34.

•• In reference to the Gospel according to St. Luke. *Correspondance inédite* (Bibliothèque cosmopolite), p. 87.

••• "A lucid literary polemic led to a social and political polemic. . . . The rules of collective life and the laws of government . . . are not without relation to the principles that pre-

His horror of looseness and barbarism, of the Romantic, Rousseauistic sensibility, impelled Maurras to lead a more than half-a-century-long offensive against the penetration into France of those elements he considered noxious: Jews, Germans, Protestants, Freemasons. As he was a leading public figure, polemicist, writer, newspaper editor, and political strategist, his struggle coincided with and found expression in sixty years' French public life. Thus he had a far greater immediate impact on his contemporaries than perhaps any of the conservative thinkers of the nineteenth century, including Metternich and Disraeli, and certainly greater than Gobineau, Nietzsche, and Dostoevsky. As a French right-wing intellectual, he displayed the specifically French features of the conspiracy theory, of which he was not the sole representative in his country and in his time; shortly before his own period of influence, Edouard Drumont and Maurice Barrès, to mention only two of his older contemporaries, spoke of an immense conspiracy "to erase France from the map," a plan hatched by Freemasons, Germans, and Jews, and against whom the average run of conservatives was, in their estimation, tragically helpless.

The entire tonus of the French Right, from 1870 to this day, has been dominated by alarm and despair over the conspiracy of German-Jewish bankers, the *Dreyfusards,* the leftist unions, the progressive intellectuals. These people, these forces were, in their eyes, the microbes against which there was no counterpoison except the radical one of bloodletting (civil war).

But Maurras recognized more subtle threats than the physical presence of the *métèques.* Like Gobineau, like Nietzsche, like Dostoevsky, he lived, as it were, in a constant state of alert, expecting not the invasion of enemies, the revolt of the proletariat, or the subversion of Freemasons, but a more subtle penetration of a philosophy, a mentality. This is why he was, in reality, even more hostile to the Protestants than to the Jews: the influence of the latter, emanating from an alien group in the nation, could be better circumscribed, detected, combated; but the

---

side over the art of the poet when he reduces to order his people of ideas and words, of colors and sounds. This analogy of the two planes have given me service . . . and has helped me to render minds impassioned for the universal order less indifferent to public affairs." *Barbarie et poésie.*

Protestants, racially one with other Frenchmen, had an erroneous concept of God, the individual, and society. "The Protestant spirit, so individualistic that it borders on anarchism, dissolves society."

It was in Rousseau and in the Jacobinism derived from his ideas that Maurras detected the great conspiratorial design against the integrity of society and of civilization. Maurras was accused by his ecclesiastical critics of holding his famous thesis about the "primacy of the political phenomenon" (*politique d'abord*) over theological truth, and, later, by his Marxist critics, for whom, obviously, the political phenomenon is determined by economic realities. This is not the place for examining the merits of these charges; the fact is that Maurras saw the very concept of the State threatened by the modern anarchists whose sentimental individualism was hostile to social institutions, laws, traditions, and conventions.•

Rousseau's first premise was that "man is born free, yet everywhere he is in chains"; no, Maurras replied, man is born into a network of social relationships without which, far from being free, he would either perish or grow up as a savage. Only the institutions of society—organically linked to the traditions of the nation—and the civilized community, which exist before the individual, are capable of preparing the latter for a constructive life by channeling his individualism, his ambitions, his efforts. The individual, taken in himself, is a rather weak creature, full of defects; it is society that lends him strength, status, and role by making him a link in the great chain of civilization.

The error of the Rousseauists, according to Maurras, is, then, to build society and the political community on the

• This is what a disciple of Maurras wrote in 1942 about the reasons that he and so many other young Frenchmen had been attracted to their master: "Like many other young men of my age, at leaving college I found in Maurras, in Léon Daudet and their disciples an explanation and confirmation of many of my instinctive disgusts. On political matters I was on the side of Baudelaire and Balzac [conservative reactionaries] against Hugo and Zola [humanitarian progressives], on the side of Machiavelli's great common sense; I saw mankind as it is and I was against the divagations of continuous progress and the four winds of ideologies [*esprit*]." Lucien Rebatet, *Les Décombres*, p. 20.

weakest social phenomenon, man. The first mistake, theological and psychological, was committed by the Protestants: "If in the individual's conscience, which is by nature anarchic, we instill the conviction that he may establish direct contacts with the absolute Being, the idea of an invisible and faraway Master will weaken in him the respect he owes to his visible and immediate superiors. He will prefer to obey God rather than man." [8] So many individuals, each under the impression of receiving direct communications from the Divinity, do not form a society. This is, nevertheless, what Rousseau assumed when he saw in society a contractual, that is, *willed*, association of autonomous individuals. But, Maurras answered, society arises not from a contract of wills but from a fact of nature. If the Jacobin principle of individualism were true, we would be justified in disorganizing the army, the institutions, society itself, for the sake of one individual.• But it is a fact of nature that the individual does not choose either his father or his nation; society antedates him.

Nietzsche hoped that the Superman would bring the world a healthier awareness of the essence and destiny of man, and Dostoevsky desired to strengthen the religious spirit, the orthodox Church, the czarist State, and the Pan-Slav movement in order to fight off anarchy and socialism, imported from the West. Maurras as a practical politician and immensely influential *maître à penser* of French elites, labored to create "a clear view of patriotic necessities" and to prepare "the elite of French youth for the acceptance of a series of parallel truths in the moral, intellectual, literary and philosophical domains." [9] This he sought to achieve chiefly through the restoration and reinforcement of the two institutions he considered most crucial: monarchy and Church. Of the first, he expected a reassertion of French tradition and continuity, and the fulfilling of the arbitrator's function, so important in checking the centrifugal forces operating in a modern State. Around 1900 Maurras discovered the vital necessity of local and regional freedoms in an overcentralized country and concluded that only an undisputed head of the nation, standing above partial and contradictory interests, would be able to reconcile unity with multiplicity. Hence his militant royalism, until the end of his life.

• This was written with the Dreyfus affair in mind.

172

But it was really the Catholic Church that embodied the Maurrasian ideal. The Catholic Church, for him, was not principally the depository of Christ's message, a faith un-questioned and accepted without reticence. In fact, his thought on the matter was that the Christian religion—whose Gospels were written by "four obscure Jews"—was "anarchistic, revolutionary, and hostile to civilization";• its true representative was Protestantism not the Catholic Church. The latter was stamped far more indelibly by the wisdom of Roman statecraft than by the universality and Judaic Messianism of Christ. And this mark of Rome was what Maurras admired most, because it made of the Church the only institution surviving in the modern world that is based on hierarchy and order, and that serves as a model and inspiration for a similarly built structure, hier-archy and order in Catholic nations.•• "All my favorite ideas," Maurras wrote, "order, tradition, discipline, hier-archy, authority, continuity, unity, work, family, corpora-tion, decentralization, autonomy, organization of workers, had been preserved and perfected by Catholicism." [10]

These few examples of nineteenth-century reaction to radicalism, progressivism, and socialism present us with more than a theory (the conspiracy theory) or a mood: they contain the outlines of the critique that the majority of conservative thinkers leveled against the spirit of the age.

This critique does not have the unity of the Marxist critique of capitalist society, and much less the popular-prophetic element, which has made of Marxism—in the eyes of the masses and of intellectuals—more than a theory: at once a scientific system and a religion. The con-servative thinkers have never been popular because it follows from the nature of their thought that they must refuse to paint an image on the horizon of history, in other words, to believe, and make others believe, in a Utopia. On the contrary, if the men we are discussing have a thesis in common, it is expressed in a warning that the

• Compare with Nietzsche's views.
•• "The conviction of Maurras," wrote Vialatoux in 1927, "is not that the Church ought to become pagan, but that she is pagan . . . and that herein lies her merit. Maurras does not think of assigning a new mission to the Church; he accepts and approves her traditional mission."

human condition never really changes, and all those who tell the masses that it does are dangerous demagogues, making promises they cannot keep, but arousing dormant illusions and letting loose ferocious passions. While the doctrines issued from Hegelianism claim to have discovered the mechanism of history and the goal toward which it propels mankind, the conservative-rightist ideology seeks to reduce historical events and phenomena to a static, preordained plan, and tends to look at historical transformations as passing ripples on the ocean of permanence.

The conservative pursues the concept of order with the same amorous expectation as the progressive pursues the concept of change. It is interesting to compare the imagery of the two types of thinkers, the figures by which they represent to themselves the destiny of man. While the progressive uses variations of the symbol of the straight line (the arrow or the statistical curve), the conservative chooses in preference the circle and the rhythmic, cyclical images of recurrence. In the optimistic eighteenth and nineteenth century the history of the human race was conceived as the flight of an arrow, straight and aiming ever higher. Just before the First World War the cyclical image reappears, indicating the alarm that conservative philosophers felt about our destiny. The concept of historical cycles of Joachim de Flore and Giambattista Vico came to be studied with a perfected apparatus of research. Our civilization was declared mortal (Paul Valéry), declining (Spengler), in a state of crisis but redeemable (Toynbee).

The most influential among these cyclical doctrines was Spengler's *Decline of the West*. While we ignore the origin and cause of great cultures, Spengler taught in his own version of the conspiracy theory, once they are constituted, their nature and course are self-determined. Within each, every phenomenon has its specific stamp, from art to mathematics. The life span of each cycle leads up to identical developments, from originality to desiccated forms. Today the Nordic man becomes the slave of the machine and of the big, soulless city. This artificial growth points already to the coming ruin, to annihilation from within. Democracy defeats itself: the idealist yields to the banker who controls the votes, and to the party machinery that manipulates people; the press banishes the book, determines public opinion, and reduces individual thinking to the clichés hailed by the masses. Truth, instead of being persecuted, is passed by in silence. The way is paved for the new Caesars, whom the people, thirsting for moral leadership,· readily acclaim.

The inclination of the conservative to see the world in terms of dramatic breaks, rise and decline, conflict, defeat, and miraculous rebirth is the principal leitmotiv of his thought. Nietzsche described modern man as "rolling, since Copernicus, from the center into X . . . without goal, without an answer to his Why." • The profoundest thought of Dostoevsky was also to seek out the real foundations of man, which was not rationality as he said the West taught, but communion with God through suffering, even self-inflicted punishment. Complete self-sacrifice causes us to despise reason and to feel at peace with the divine will. His disciple, the Russian existentialist Shestov, taught that we must abandon Athens and Socratic rationality and repair to Jerusalem, the fount of true wisdom.

It is not the meek and self-immolating Slavic soul or German irrationality that speak through these thinkers. Conservative thought in England and France found the same themes, even when, as in the career of Maurras, Positivism was the initial choice. Edmund Burke expressed greater belief in the suprarational wisdom of the species (implanted by God) than in rationally conceived plans for the improvement of mankind's lot. If the world is God's design, he maintained, then we must go easy on reform and change because poverty and violence are inseparable parts of this world to which only religion may bring consolation. We should respect God's intent by studying nature and history carefully; if we recognize the necessity of change in particular instances, we must allow it to grow out of particular needs, not as a general imposition in the name of some abstraction.

It is natural that the conservative thinker thus detects a relationship between religion and society, and comes to conceive of the social order as a reflection of the divine order. If he prefers order to change, it is because from the religious standpoint change is essentially always superficial, while order expresses the deep reality of the universe.

• Compare with C. G. Jung, who wrote that modern man is "on the point of losing the life-preserving myth of the inner man which Christianity has treasured up for him."

One of the most important elements of this order is that the amount of happiness and unhappiness in the world is governed by a ratio that remains constant through the ages. "I have sometimes been in a good deal more than doubt," wrote Burke, "whether the Creator did ever really intend man for a state of happiness. He has mixed in His cup a number of natural evils, and every endeavor which the art and policy of mankind has used from the beginning of the world to this day in order to alleviate or cure them, has only served to introduce new mischiefs or to aggravate and inflame the old."

Burke was no Catholic; yet how similar his convictions are to the pronouncements of two recent popes on the matter. Leo XIII had this to say in a message dealing with the causes and remedies of economic misery: "To suffer and to endure is the lot of humanity. Let men try as they may, no strength and no artifice will ever succeed in banishing from human life the ills and troubles which beset it. If any there are who pretend differently, who hold out to a hard-pressed people freedom from pain and trouble, undisturbed repose, and constant enjoyment—they cheat the people and impose upon them, and their lying promises will only make the evil worse than before." [11] And Pius XI: "The world will never be able to rid itself of misery, sorrow and tribulation, which are the portion even of those who seem most prosperous." [12]

The philosophy embedded in these statements is admittedly a religious one; it is inspired by the Christian concept of original sin, whose social significance is that it warns man to look for the cause of his misery into himself, into his own disobedience to the divine decree. It is also a warning not to listen to those who would willfully upset the order of things. As a political force, the doctrine of original sin is profoundly antirevolutionary.•

Through the conspiracy of naïve utopians or of self-willed demagogues—the conservative concludes—tradition and the old order of society have disintegrated. Ever since the French Revolution history has been a series of betrayals, not the least decisive being the treason of the bour-

• "Whether the ideas of religion are denied or venerated, whether they are true or false, they remain the sole basis of all lasting institutions." De Maistre, *Considérations sur la France.*

176

geoisie, which in its blind pursuit of profit replaced traditional social relationships with contractual and financial
transactions. Perhaps the most dramatic picture of the
bourgeois role in the nineteenth century is painted by Bernanos, who retraces the history of bourgeois appropriation
from the land purchases under the Revolution to the alliance with Hitlerism in the twentieth century. The dominant
tone is the regret over the disappearance of the old,
agrarian society and the uprooting and proletarization of
the peasants.

Accusations similar to those made in connection with
the conspiracy theory have been sounded by conservatives since the middle of the last century. As the class
struggle was crystallizing and as its increasing vehemence
began to threaten not only the "old order" but any order
(and with it the whole Greco-Christian basis of the
Western world view), the conservatives leveled their
charges against the inferior classes and their popular tribunes, no less than against the bourgeoisie and its secular-
istic ideologues. They reproached the first, as we have
seen, for demanding and promising the pie in the sky,
thereby disrupting the measured course of society; and
they indicted the second for mismanaging the heritage
(property and power) they had wrung from the aristocracy
through the Revolution. The bourgeois-capitalist employer
was no better, and possibly worse, than the feudal landlord
used to be—the conservatives proclaimed. The latter, at
least, knew his tenants and the small gentry attached to
his household; a Duke of Saint-Simon, in the time of
Louis XIV, haughty aristocrat as he was, kept open house
in Paris for his people who came from his estate to the
capital—he lodged and fed them, provided them with
money and advice. But a Lancashire textile-mill owner,
rude and coarse and without social obligations, would ex-
ploit unmercifully his workers, men, women, and children.•
The same way in the pre-Civil-War United States: many

• Although from the opposite point of view, Marx's criticism
of the bourgeoisie sounded exactly the same: "The bourgeoisie,
wherever it has got the upper hand, has put an end to all
feudal, patriarchal, idyllic relations. It has pitilessly torn asunder
the motley feudal ties that bound man to his 'natural superiors'
and has left no other bond between man than naked self-interest, than callous cash payment." Communist Manifesto.

Southern plantation owners declared that the institution of slavery was more natural and more humane than the system of wage labor in Northern factories.

On the other hand, the bourgeois-capitalist world bred a type of politician who was no longer the broad-visioned statesman of old, but a ruthless exploiter of partial interests, either of capitalist (Whig) interests against the landowning class, or proletarian interests against the factory owners. In other words, while the bourgeois uprooted and embittered the peasant with one hand, with the other he put him in possession of democratic rights and of the ballot. In the eyes of the conservatives this was the *ne plus ultra* of mismanagement and folly, for it was obvious that the emancipated but economically inferior classes would misuse the vote, and that there would always be found dissatisfied, reckless adventurers to lead them against the bastions of order.

Thus the conservatives began to realize more and more clearly that the greatest loss they suffered in the power struggle of the nineteenth century was their loss of the laboring masses. Already the Communist Manifesto deals with the attempt of the landed aristocracy and other conservative forces to win back the proletarian workers from the clutches of modern industry, by painting an idyllic picture of the past agricultural way of life. But they were not successful in this attempt; at about the time when the Communist Manifesto appeared, Tocqueville remarked in his *Recollections* that "a hatred of the Ancien Régime and mistrust of the privileged classes remained a genuine passion among the people," although the bourgeoisie, "master of everything in a manner that no aristocracy has ever been . . . thought much more of his private business than of public affairs." [13] And Marx wrote this in the Communist Manifesto: "Owing to their historical position, it became the vocation of the aristocracies of France and England to write pamphlets against modern bourgeois society. . . . In order to arouse sympathy, the aristocracy was obliged to lose sight, apparently, of its own interests, and to formulate its indictment against the bourgeoisie in the interest of the exploited working class alone. Thus the aristocracy took its revenge by signing lampoons against its new master, and whispering in his ears sinister prophecies of coming catastrophe."

178

The conservatives, however, were even more horrified as the general industrial conditions created by capitalism were rapidly pushing the proletariat toward a class solidarity of its own, and into proletarian parties advocating the overthrow of society. For this consummation of the break the conservatives blamed capitalism, industry, and the machines more than they blamed the workers themselves. But at least it shocked them into the realization that the proletariat, however miserable its condition, could no longer be persuaded to return to the land and to be tucked away again as peasants on the fringes of society. If society was to be saved from the revolution and the Christian values from an all-out attack, the conservatives had to reorganize society, reintegrate the worker in the body of the nation, and give a new impetus to the Christian ideals. Sir William Harcourt, a politician in Gladstone's days, summed up the new mentality aptly when he declared: "We are all socialists now!" •

From the last quarter of the nineteenth century on, conservative philosophy sought to express itself in action. Two roads were open before it: one was organization on traditional lines, that is, the revival of old institutions such as guilds or the monarchy, the support given to and expected of the Church, the conscious cult of the national past, etc. The other road was the imitation of the adversaries in their political organization, social concern, mass-approach. The historical fact is that both roads were followed: some conservative thinkers elaborated the theory of a new corporatist order (supported in this by the Church), while others organized the first Catholic labor unions and study groups; some (in France at least) worked for a royalist restoration, others became sincere friends of the republican idea, watching from inside that it should not slip into excesses; there were those who expected some extrapolitical event (war, insurrection, *coup d'état*, invasion) to help them into power; others chose to co-operate with the parliamentary regimes and sought to create political parties through which they expected to reach legitimately the position of command.

• Earlier, around 1843, Louis Bonaparte, the future Emperor, wrote in *L'Extinction du pauperisme:* "Today, the reign of castes is finished; one can govern now only with the masses."

The difference between them, although perhaps more a pragmatic than a philosophical one, is that some were inside the citadel of power and others outside. This is not as frivolous a distinction as it seems, and the reasons for it are not accidental. Maurras, a par excellence representative of the conservative forces that remained "outside" of power, called his brand of nationalism "integral," and it was understood by him and by everybody else that this was to be distinguished from "old fashioned" patriotism. Indeed, nationalism, even religion, became an ideology in the mind of Maurras (and of German, Italian, Spanish, American, etc., conservatives), an ideology unable to compromise, and consequently, to reach and keep power by peaceful methods and fair play. Nationalism, religion (Catholic and Protestant), and conservative political and cultural ideas thus formed a block, and this block became the more cohesive and intransigent the longer it was denied participation and power.•

Meanwhile, the constituting elements of this ideology were further stressed and refined by excellent and sharp minds. *Nationalism* was exacerbated by the dramatic situation of minorities in the nineteenth century and by the post-Versailles revindications of the twentieth. Also, it seemed to the nationalists that the socialists leaders who, with a few exceptions, openly advocated internationalism and the supranational solidarity of the working class, were

---

• We witness a similar phenomenon in present-day United States. "The McCarthy nationalists," writes Dwight Macdonald, ". . . anxious, embittered, resentful . . . feel that the main stream of American politics since 1932 has passed them by, as indeed it has, and they have the slightly paranoiac suspiciousness of an isolated minority group. For these are men from underground, the intellectually underprivileged who feel themselves excluded from a world they believe is ruled by liberals just as the economic underdog feels alienated from society." *Memoirs of a Revolutionist,* p. 332. Whatever we think of these remarks—and I think they oversimplify the issue—they present fairly well the respective attitudes of American liberals and conservatives. As W. F. Buckley writes in *Up from Liberalism,* "the liberals' implicit premise is that inter-credal dialogues are what one has with Communists, not Conservatives, in relationship with whom normal laws of civilized discourse are suspended" (p. 23). This is the American counterpart of the French "pas d'ennemi à gauche."

squandering and deliberately ignoring the most precious capital of a nation, its loyalty to the historical memories, its natural cohesion.• They considered the socialists as disrupting elements, sentimentally uprooting the little people after the modern world had robbed them of their other roots: in the land and in an immemorial way of life.

Religion was also enrolled in the conservative-reactionary ideology. In Protestant countries it could blend relatively easily with other cults, held more basic to the deep nature of man and community: race, blood, and an almost animistic view of the soil. It became the "manifest destiny" of German merchants and military caste, of American pioneers, missionaries, and industrial barons, of British colonial officials in contact with conquered races. In Catholic countries, as we have seen in connection with Maurras and Gobineau, it was less easy to assign religion a new scope, due to Church-imposed discipline and Church-defined dogma; but it was still possible to introduce non-Christian elements into the elaboration of the religious doctrine and policy: these elements were not pagan in the Germanic sense, as in Protestant countries, but in the Greco-Roman sense, and thus more readily identifiable with certain Church attitudes and only reluctantly denounced. (As Bernanos once remarked, the success of the Maurrasian doctrine—and of Mussolini's Fascism—with French intellectuals was partly due to their humanistic education and their admiration for the Greco-Roman values.) The Catholic conservatives accepted, then, without much hesitation the efforts to bend their religion in the direction of their national interest and cultural preoccupations; they were willing, if not to

• G. D. H. Cole wrote during the First World War that "between the organized workers of the European powers there is no quarrel capable of provoking war, no national antagonism strong enough to stand against the very real sense of inter-working-class solidarity. Here then is the problem which the revolution is compelled to face. Is allegiance due first of all to the nation which includes some of all classes, or to the class which includes some of all nations? The answer to this would provide the deepest insight into war psychology, for from it at last true relations between national and class consciousness might emerge." Quoted by Anne Fremantle, op. cit., pp. 216-17.

"correct," at least to "reinterpret," certain precepts and attitudes of the Church, with the result that they played down its teaching of charity and love and emphasized a more "positive" Christianity as an instrument for the defense of the West and Western civilization.

Of the conservative *political and cultural ideas*—the third section of the "block"—it is harder to make general statements. The political reactions of conservatives, already in the nineteenth century, but increasingly in the twentieth, have been shaped by the specific situation in their respective homelands. There never was, and there never could be, a conservative "International," giving over-all directives to a party within each nation. Even less is it conceivable that individual conservatives should work out a common program on cultural matters since they are all rooted in particular traditions and instinctively fear the modern forms of bureaucratic organization, the use of gigantic abstractions, etc.

Yet certain generalizations may be made with regard to over-all conservative approach to political and cultural matters. Partly as a result of a forced and prolonged political passivity, the conservative developed a feeling of restriction. It seemed to him that the world was losing a certain quality of adventurousness, of risk, hazard, and savagery, and that, just as nature is tamed and made uniform by industrialization, so is the proud individual, the "nonconformist," by democracy, commercialism, and mass culture. In the writings of many, from Nietzsche to Ernst Juenger, in those of Bernanos, Montherlant, Evelyn Waugh, and C. S. Lewis, the tone is that of the last lonely man, engaged in a losing battle with the all-engulfing Collectivity, Party, Bureaucracy, or simply, the Modern World. The figure of the last solitary masculine specimen, hunter, warrior, and lover of women is outlined with particular clarity in the novels and plays of Juenger and Montherlant; the whole tone of conservative brooding is sensed through the mysterious, twilight atmosphere created by the German (in *The Marble Cliff*), or the last passionate, angry denunciation by the Frenchman (*Le Maître de Santiago*). M. Paul Sérant, in his book on a group of writers he calls "romantic fascists" (Drieu La Rochelle, Robert Brasillach, L. F. Céline, et al.) says that they are "characterized by a lyric quality, and their political attitude is indistinguishable from a search for a new style of collective life, for the poetization of the political and social order." [14]

The feeling of restriction, however, is only the outward sign of a very deeply felt and diagnosed ill. The conservatives have felt since the days of Chateaubriand, Burckhardt, and Lord Acton that their opponents achieved successes where they failed because they simplified the problems of society and man, presented the solutions in the name of abstractions, and restricted choice to "progress" or "backwardness." To masses dazed by modern conditions, unsophisticated in the ways of political manipulators, it was easy, the conservatives argued, to show the human being as merely an animal wishing to feed and shelter himself, make love and find entertainment. But where are the deeper yearnings of the soul and spirit, the mysterious choice between good and evil, the desire to attach oneself to leaders who embody a moral force, a charisma? The radicals and socialists seemed to ignore these problems and to laugh at the questions; at any rate, they excluded them from their platforms and programs. But how can politicians, the leaders of nations, ignore patriotism, the role of religion, the instinct to become property holder and to remain fixed in that status?—asked further the conservatives who remembered Rousseau's Calvinistic, abstract contractants, Fourier's phalansteries, Babeuf's and Proudhon's statement that "property is theft." The socialist continued to fly in the face of nationalist sentiment, make spectacular common cause with socialists of other lands, declare the proletarian homeless and an enthusiastic worker for the classless, propertyless Utopia.

The question cannot be raised here what would have happened if the conservatives' warnings had been heeded. In retrospect, anyway, it seems that socialists and democrats made two basic mistakes: having had their mouths full of the "universal man," they did not notice the vacuity of this abstraction until the men who sought desperately to re-root themselves: in the soil, in the group, in the nation, in race and in faith, attacked them with the frenzy of the frustrated. The second mistake was to imagine that the "proletarian masses" let themselves be enrolled because they dreamed of constructing a society based on collective property and collectivized existence. As the earlier-mentioned play by Mayakovsky (*The Bedbug*) shows, the individual worker did not dream of the classless society and the collectivist State, but, far more modestly, concretely, and soberly, of improving his individual lot by becoming a "bourgeois" property-owner with a reasonable hope that his son would further rise in status. Socialism could work—in a very restricted sense and coexisting with capitalism—only in the Western lands because the principle of freedom guaranteed that the worker would not be enslaved in the name of slogans advertising that the country is "his property," and that the State would not check his ambition and acquisitiveness.•

Whether more conservative influence on public and political matters would have been beneficial, cannot be decided. At any rate, in this century, and especially after the First World War, conservatism became an ideology, thus an extremist force, and the moderate conservatives no longer had a chance of making the weight of their views felt. The ultraconservatives and reactionaries were, however, their legitimate heirs insofar as their attack on contemporary society imbedded all the elements of a more than centurylong critique. What they added to it was not so much theoretical and doctrinal as practical and revolutionary.

Theory and doctrine had been supplied by a long line of distinguished nineteenth-century critics and by the continued teaching of the Catholic Church (the Papal Encyclicals, for example). Practical and revolutionary action was derived from the observation of the behavior of contemporary mass parties and their revolutionary leaders. It had long before been clear to conservatives that it behooves them to liberate the worker from the chain of leftist organizations and to reinstill in them a more realis-

---

• The Marxists noticed "somewhat late . . . that the growth of the proletariat had limits this side of a majority. First of all, the old productive classes, like the peasantry and a large section of the artisans, have mantained their positions; in the second place, a new middle class has been constituted by the intermediaries, office workers and employees, whom economic progress itself created a little bit everywhere." Henri de Man, *Au-delà du nationalisme* (Geneva: Editions du Cheval ailé, 1946), pp. 238-9.

tic world view than the one advocated by the leftist ideologues; now it dawned upon them that more was needed than an effort to direct the workers away from Marx and toward the more complete view of man as taught by the Church and advocated by conservative philosophers. The experience of study circles for workers at the close of the nineteenth century showed to the conservatives that, except for a few individual changes of heart, the mass of the workers either remained reticent at these bourgeois-sponsored courses or scorned them as attempts to detach their class from the parties and syndicates representing their real interests. A Maurras, for example, still believed that by making contact with the most intelligent among the workers, they might be persuaded to abandon socialist aspirations: from proletarian leaders in the class struggle and instigators of strikes, Maurras hoped they would become middlemen between the bourgeoisie and their fellow workers.

The conservatives gave proof of their increasing understanding of modern times the day they realized the necessity of using weapons similar to those of their opponents. These included the political party, a revolutionary doctrine, mass appeal and mass discipline, propaganda and a collective myth. The fact that this awareness took shape at the same time that Communism (Bolshevism) achieved its spectacular victory, and that it appeared as a reaction to the organization of Soviet-sponsored parties all over the world, created the impression in many observers that ultra-conservative, rightist, fascist ideology and movements were a response of reactionary bourgeois elements to the maelstrom of worker insurrection. There is, of course, an element of truth in this view, advocated, for example, by Harold Laski and, naturally, by all the Communist writers. Fascism is thus labeled as the last attempt of the proper-tied classes at fighting off the victorious advance of the proletariat.•

• There is another, quite silly, explanation of Fascism which must be mentioned on account of its easy popularity. The "psychological" explanation of Fascism is offered by second-rate thinkers who ascribe it to the "vices" of the "authoritarian mind." The authoritarian mind, coupled with frustrated sexual experiences in childhood, leads, according to this pseudo theory, to Fascist mentality. This is the thesis of one of Sartre's otherwise brilliant short stories, "L'Enfance d'un chef."

The whole truth is much more complex. It is sufficient to establish the philosophical link between nineteenth-century conservative critique of democracy, radicalism, idea of progress, on the one hand, and twentieth-century reactionary ideology on the other, to become aware of the latter's essential nature. Contemporary rightist ideology is, first of all, not anticommunist, but antidemocratic and antiprogressive. If it combats Marxism, this is not because it represents capitalist interest, but because it rejects the utopian element in Marxist doctrine. Generally speaking, contemporary reactionaries and Fascists reproach the Communists not because the latter go too far in their opposition to the bourgeois-capitalist system, but because they do not have a complete view of man to set against the one-sided, rationalist bourgeois philosophy. They attack Marxism for being a truncated, distorted system, and seek to elaborate a doctrine, anti-Marxist but also antibourgeois, in which the *homo oeconomicus* is only one part, the rest occupied by other legitimate aspirations of man.•

By these additions, however, the picture of Fascism is still far from being complete. The rightist movements of our age are, after all, not merely philosophical reactions to radical doctrines; they are mass movements, ideologically narrow like their adversaries; as revolutionary forces, they consume their own theorists and elites with the same greed as the Communist parties. A Metternich or a Burke would no more recognize in Hitler and in Mussolini their spiritual descendants than they would recognize them in Lenin or Trotsky. This means that the genuine conservatives, in their alliance with the extremist ideologues on their Right, linked themselves to people and to forces who may have put their words in their own manifestoes and on their banners, but who did not share their system of reference, universe of discourse, moral values, and ultimately, their political ideas.

In fact, if a parallel is to be found, one may safely say

• "Fascism is not Marxism, but Fascism too hates and combats the injustices against which Marxism had risen but against which it proposes its evil remedies." Robert Brasillach, *Journal d'un homme occupé*, p. 183. In a book on Fascist Italy, written in 1932, Georges Roux wondered "whether Fascism was not going to become the western form of socialism, as Bolshevism represents its oriental form." *L'Italie fasciste* (Librairie Stock, 1932), p. 113.

that the genuine conservatives have experienced similar embarrassments, conflicts, and finally, catastrophic defeats, at the hands of the extremist forces they had thought they would control, as the progressive humanists in *their* alliance with Communism. This too is an indication that these two extremes—Left and Right, Communism and Fascism —were not so far from each other as one might tend to think, not so far, at least, at a certain point of their respective evolution. "Nothing of the materialism of Liberalism and Communism is lost in Fascism and National Socialism," writes Michael Oakeshott in the Introduction to his *Social and Political Doctrines of Contemporary Europe.* "They have the advantage over Marxism because they are newer and could profit by its mistakes; but they have learnt nothing significant except that a materialistic doctrine can be made palatable in the contemporary world only by making it appear something other than it is." [15]

Perhaps the term "materialism," twice used in this quotation, is too vague to articulate the unquestionably existing differences between the doctrines of extreme Left and extreme Right. Let us note again that while far the greater section of contemporary extreme Left is channeled by the thought of Marx (and his disciples), Fascism and National Socialism had no such unified doctrine to follow; their early inspirers were practically all the nineteenth-century conservative philosophers, none of whom, not even the "racist" Gobineau, were "materialists" in the sense of Marx and his (ideological) confreres Feuerbach, Moleschott, Büchner.

Oakeshott's statement rings truer, however, when we interpret "materialism" as meaning preoccupation with class differences and the economic exploitation of the worker, the critique of the capitalist system and bourgeois morality. On these points an almost common platform may be found for Communists and Fascists.

It is, of course, a well-known fact that many leaders of the Fascist and National Socialist parties had a socialist, in many instances, Communist, background. Mussolini, Marcel Déat, Doriot, Degrelle, et al., began their political careers as leftist militants and theorists, then renounced their loyalty after failing to reform the party on a line different from orthodox Marxism, and to prevent its submission to the Russian Bolsheviks. Georges Sorel, who, toward the end of his life, observed with equal satisfaction the beginnings of both Leninist Russia and Fascist Italy, was himself a good example of the ideological similarity (but also of the confusion) between extreme Left and Right. In a very interesting way he combined the large, myth-creating inspiration of contemporary rightist movements with the leftist insistence on revolution and worker organization.

Sorel expressed the inner conviction of both Marx and the nineteenth-century conservatives when he maintained that the political thought of the Enlightenment was naïve to conceive of the complex field of human relations according to the pattern of physical sciences evolved from the time of Descartes. He indicted the thinking in "systems," which results in bitter strifes, at the end of which the victor seeks to immobilize (or to exterminate) the vanquished. Hence he distrusted those politicians, whether mandated by the socialists or by the Church, who made utopistic plans and played the role of moralist saviors of society. He believed in the legitimacy of only one sort of violence: proletarian violence, not for the expropriation of the present rulers and owners, but, in accord with Marx, for giving society and the State a new juridical frame.

Proletarian violence, in the judgment of Sorel, was not to be of vindictive nature, a war in which the defeated is executed. He answered his critics that violence would not even have to take place, but would merely serve as a myth, a lofty ideal giving a unified expression to socialist aims. The myth of syndicalism, the great event of the General Strike, was to be, in his mind, the symbol of a new, socialist cohesion to take the place of the religious idea, now discarded by society. In its name Sorel expected to see a new order arise, a new workers' elite, a new work morality.

The theme of a new "myth" runs through the entire literature and political action of contemporary rightist movements in Germany, France, Italy, and Spain. These movements needed a myth, first to counter, with its help, the one created by the French Revolution, then to put it up as a counterimage to the reality that was, after 1917, the Soviet Union. But, in a sense, the Fascist, National Socialist, phalangist parties (not to speak of the many splinter rightist parties that came into existence all over Europe—and outside—between 1919 and 1945) could partake in the general myth secreted by all workers' movements, and could look back, with some justification, to the same origin. If the giant figure of Marx had not overshadowed Proudhon, Fourier, and all the nineteenth-century utopian, corporatist, and National Socialist theorists, the leaders of twentieth-century Fascist parties would have had less difficulty identifying themselves with the common, pre-Marxian, stem.

Even so, the similarity of purpose is striking between Communism and Fascism, provided we understand that the leaders of the latter never ceased emphasizing that they represented a higher stage of socialist evolution, one which, instead of disassociating the worker from the higher values of culture, family, nationhood, and religion, sought to integrate him with the total life of society. "Fascism is a spiritualized conception," wrote Mussolini in the "Doctrine of Fascism" for the Enciclopedia Italiana (1932), "the result of the general reaction of modern times against the flabby materialistic positivism of the nineteenth century. . . . [It recognizes] the high value of culture in all its forms, art, religion, science, education." Fascism, Mussolini continued, "was opposed to Democracy which lowers the nation to the level of the majority"; the Fascist State "cannot confine itself to functions of order and supervision as [nineteenth-century] Liberalism desired. It is not simply a mechanism which limits the sphere of the supposed liberties of the individual. . . . It saturates the will as well as the intelligence . . . it is an inner form . . . it is the soul of the soul."

Mussolini expressed his belief that Fascism does not oppose but that it enriches the political thought of the last two centuries. It does not deny, he wrote, the importance of economic discoveries, but it "believes in holiness and heroism, that is, in acts in which no economic motive plays a part. . . . Fascism denies the equation of prosperity with happiness which would transform men into animals with one sole preoccupation." •

• The French Fascist writer, Robert Brasillach, speaks of the mystique and poetry of the Fascist leaders, of Mussolini "evok-

In the minds of Fascist leaders their party and their State combated Marxism because the latter offered a partial view of man and an inadequate solution for the present age of conflicts. But they always made clear their unqualified, absolute enmity to the bourgeois system and society. "In 1919," Mussolini wrote in the above-mentioned article, "Fascism was not a party, but a movement against all parties. . . . If the bourgeoisie hopes to find in us a lightning-conductor, it is mistaken. . . . We want to accustom the working classes to being under a leader, to convince them also that it is not easy to direct an industry or a commercial undertaking successfully. . . . We do not want the present political representation, but a direct representation of individual interests. . . . Return to corporations? It does not matter." The main purpose of the corporate State was, according to *The Fascist Era,* published by the Fascist Confederation of Industrialists in 1939,[16] "that of correcting and neutralizing a condition brought about by the industrial revolution of the nineteenth century, which dissociated capital and labor in industry, giving rise on the one hand, to a capitalist class of employers of labor, and on the other, to a great propertyless class, the industrial proletariat. The juxtaposition of these classes inevitably led to the clash of their opposing interests." Not a word that Marx could not have signed.

The antibourgeois tone was even more explicit in the mouths of the party-ideologues as World War II drew nearer. This is what Pavolini said at the Foreign Policy Congress in Milan, in June, 1938: "Nothing irritates us [Fascists] so much as to be taken for pillars of order. Nothing so exasperates us as the people who come to us through fear of Communism." The speaker then quoted from the review *Gerarchia,* founded by Mussolini: "Those good people [who are fearful of all social change] will have to realize, and we shall soon make them realize, that the weight of the social problem is now on our shoulders

---

ing immortal Rome and the galleys on the Mare Nostrum," of Hitler who "invents the Walpurgis night and May festivals and mixes in his songs a cyclopean romanticism," of the Rumanian Codreanu "with his legion led by Archangel Michael." Quoted by Paul Sérant, op. cit., p. 84.

and that they would be wiser to fear us than to fear Communism." •

Similar examples of kinship between Marxism and various forms of Fascism, as well as their common hatred of democracy and the bourgeois-liberal State, can be found in Germany. Two simultaneous movements may be observed there also: the middle classes, upper and lower, ruined by war, revolution, inflation, unemployment, flocked to Hitler out of fear of Bolshevization. But the nationalist-conservative elite, and especially those who sympathized with National Socialism, seemed to prefer even Communism to the weak, degenerate Weimar Republic. "Unless it were possible to re-create a form of State," wrote Ernst von Salomon, "Bolshevism must be the natural heir to the obvious and shameless dissolution of all organic strength by the ideological senselessness of the bourgeois-liberal and Social-Democrat wizards." •• Anything seemed to be better than the parliamentary system, and the preference, long before Hitler's rise to power, went to a "supra-party," speaking for all classes of the nation. People, remarked Moeller van den Bruck in the Introduction to *Das dritte Reich* (1923), "talked about freedom from parties, of a point of view above parties. . . . A complete lack of respect for Parliament . . . was very widespread."

The "myth" that could still move them was socialism in any form, and Hitler knew this well. In the words of a German exile, Reinhold Schairer, in Nazi Germany in 1935 the word "socialism" did not mean social-mindedness. "The journals and pamphlets of German youth, read by millions . . . talk of 'profit motive' and 'money bags.' . . . In the aims of National Socialism the emphasis is on the

---

• "The reactionaries think that revolutions are superfluous. But we joyously believe that they are necessary. The reactionaries are opposed to new revolutions, at least to those which would continue the preceding ones. But we see them come and they fill us with joy." Drieu La Rochelle, *Socialisme fasciste*, p. 52 (1934).

•• *Fragebogen*, p. 238.

"The temporary alliance between the elite and the mob rested largely on the genuine delight with which the former watched the latter destroy [bourgeois] respectability." H. Arendt, *The Origins of Totalitarianism*, p. 333.

second half of the title; the first is taken for granted." [17] Already in February, 1920, at the party meeting in Munich, the National Socialist theoreticians laid down, among their Twenty-Five Points, the demand for the nationalization of all business trusts and the demand that the great industries should be reorganized on a profit-sharing basis (points 13 and 14).•

In Germany, much faster and much more thoroughly than in Italy, the modern tragedy of conservatism became visible. The German conservatives wanted to preserve and strengthen the State, and with it the values of the Vaterland, which they associated with the German past, itself rooted in Christianity. It turned out, however, that their alliance with Hitler not only miscarried but was, actually, misconceived. The Nazi leaders and theoreticians were not conservative politicians and intellectuals, but tribal chiefs with a veneer of social utopianism, rendered the more dangerous as it was permeated with nostalgia and mysticism, a rather common feature of contemporary right-wing movements. They were not interested in the State as a civilized framework of society; they wanted to use it as an instrument of their dynamic ideology and world conquest. Thus they believed in a borderless State, based not on the brotherhood of men (as in the case of progressive

---

• It must be noted, however, that Hitler's personal aims and extremely strong personality managed, after various tests of force, to crush the socialist inspiration of the German National Socialist Party. After 1934 nothing remained of the radical ideas that Anton Drexler, G. Feder, Gregor and Otto Strasser, had represented, and which were embodied in the Twenty-Five Points drawn up in 1920. Hitler paid only lip service to socialistic aims, and used every means to achieve and keep power. Hence, at least before he seized power, he by no means wanted to frighten Big Industry and the Army into opposition to himself. "The capitalists have worked their way to the top through their capacity," he told his comrades in May, 1930, "and on the basis of this selection, which again only proves their higher race, they have a right to lead. Now you want an incapable Government Council or Works Council, which has no notion of anything, to have a say: no leader in economic life would tolerate it." Alan Bullock, *Hitler* (Harper & Brothers), p. 141.

utopians and socialists), but on the superiority of a master race whose nucleus was the Nazi movement.•

In addition to the State, the other, all-important instrument for world conquest was the masses. They could be enrolled in the S.A., the S.S., and other para-military organizations, and—a crucial point—they could be used to undermine the morale, the solidity and solidarity, of the army, which was a representative of the bourgeois order, historical tradition, and—in its high ranks—of the German elite. According to Hannah Arendt's analysis, whenever the Nazis could not directly destroy an organization belonging to the old order, they created an organization that duplicated the functions of the first, thereby immobilizing and neutralizing it. In the ensuing confusion, the leader's decision was what counted: a state of affairs directly contrary to the principles on which the State and society, as expressions of organized coexistence, rest.••

The leader was, of course, the incarnation of the people and the expression of their conscious and racial unanimity. Therefore no law, no freedom, no rights, were needed to protect either the individual against the community, or the latter against its leaders. The following quotation is from the *Beamten Kalendar* (1937), in which Nazi political philosophy found its best expression:

• Hermann Rauschning reports that Hitler told him on this all-important part of his ideology: "The conception of the nation has become meaningless. We have to get rid of this false conception and set in its place the conception of race. The New Order cannot be conceived in terms of the national boundaries of the peoples with an historic past, but in terms of race that transcend these boundaries. . . . I know perfectly well that in the scientific sense there is no such thing as race. But . . . as a politician, I need a conception which enables the order that has hitherto existed on an historic basis to be abolished, and an entirely new and anti-historic order enforced and given an intellectual basis." *Hitler m'a dit* (Coopération Paris, 1939), pp. 258-9.

•• "The duality of today's Italy: an old façade . . . a new edifice. . . . Each organization seems to be duplicated by a fascist organization destined to control it: the king by the Duce, the Senate by the Grand Council, the Prefects by the Commissars, the citizens by the members of the Party." Georges Roux, op. cit., p. 32.

In the National Socialist conception of the State the task is not that of protecting the individual against the State. National Socialism, on the contrary, undertakes to defend the people as a whole against the individual when his interests are not in harmony with the common weal. . . . Since there is, in the National Socialist State, no difference, let alone opposition, between the State as a separate legal structure and the totality of citizens . . . since the citizens are united by common blood and a common philosophy of life . . . it is neither necessary nor possible to define a sphere of freedom for the individual citizen as against the State. Hence, it is neither necessary nor possible to "protect" "subjective rights" . . . by means of constitutional law. . . . The supreme constitutional foundation of the Third Reich is laid down in the Party Programme . . . and the fundamental laws (purity of the race, labor service, etc.).

Once the alliance was concluded between the conservatives and what is called the extreme Right, the masses that the latter represented engulfed the conservative values. To these values lip service was still paid by party intellectuals; but the leaders and officials of the party made no serious efforts to bar the way before mass society and mass values. "I have no need to socialize the banks and big business enterprises," Hitler told Rauschning; "I socialize the human beings." The upper echelons of this society—inside and outside the party—no longer reminded one of the conservative-reactionary elite that had first encouraged the movement, just like Russia's new leading class has nothing in common with the heroes of revolutionary Bolshevism. Fascism and its kindred movements, instead of building on the existing elite, ended up by creating a new one: unsure yet cocky, unfree, artificial, corrupt. It consisted of the more reckless elements of the pre-existing capitalist cadre without definite convictions, of party officials who privately scorned the ruling ideology, and of the officers of the pretorian guard who cultivated heroic poses.

Even in countries where Fascism could not extend roots and where no unified party-ideology was elaborated or imposed, the phenomenon of gradual yielding of ground by conservative can be noted. In France and in Spain, for historical reasons we cannot go into here, Fascism was not successful in the period between 1920 and 1945, although attempts were made both to import the ideology and to develop domestic varieties. Yet, even during the short time at its disposal, the symptoms of a Fascist mentality manifested themselves: the ultraconservatives were there to encourage rebellion in the name of order, the militants were there, unhinged by the First World War and ready for a new adventure; and the ideology was there too, insisting that the gap between the working class and the rest of the nation could be and should be healed. The latter point became particularly impressive as the victory of the proletarian revolution in Soviet Russia threatened with a running fire of new revolutionary outbursts in other countries too. To the political-cultural defense line of the conservatives a new and urgent argument was added: the necessity of protecting their own respective nations from subversion by the Third International and the Komintern.

While Mussolini's shock troops were fighting Communist infiltration in the northern industrial districts, and various half-demobilized squads in Germany fought the Spartakists and the socialists of Kurt Eisner in Bavaria; in France, too, the hour seemed to have struck for the decisive battle. Bernanos describes vividly the state of mind of his fellow veterans, freshly demobilized and roaming the streets of Paris in search of work. If someone had taken the trouble of organizing them, of calling them back to discipline, Bernanos wrote later, "they would have again become an army with its leaders, its own language and inflexible comradeship, as capable of evil as of good. They would have given this army the name of a party, and Europe would have counted one more Fascism." [18]

It is with such aimless men that Hitler and Mussolini organized their movements. There were no such powerful organizers in France and Spain, and the potentiality found expression in myths, doctrines, and intellectual systems rather than in a true mass movement. The *Falange* in Spain and the various rightist formations and militias in France never became huge, cohesive, and oppressive party-organizations. The rightist program in Spain was an amalgam of the Nazi syndicalist and anticapitalist principles of Ledesma Ramos and the Maurrasian, that is, nationalist, traditionalist, and Catholic ideals of José Antonio Primo de Rivera. The two men represented two movements: the Junta ofensiva nacional-sindicalista (J.O.N.S.) and the Falange, which merged in 1934. The early death of José Antonio prevented him from assuming the post of leadership, and the Falange fell very soon under the authority of General Franco who stamped out its socialist orientation. But in the early 1930's the movement elicited the same fervor as Maurrasism in France, and its adherents promised to devote themselves to the elaboration of a new order.

The young Mateo Santos, in Gironella's great novel, is a good example of the enthusiasm thus generated by a leader and the synthesis of doctrines, sentiments, and tasks he was able to bring to confused souls. Prompted by a deep loyalty to José Antonio, Mateo Santos has joined the Falange in order to fight for social justice and the reintegration of the workers into the body of the nation. The Falange's aim was, he explained to friends, to convince the workers that they were not proletarians, but men, persons. This was to be done by persuading them that the economic aspect is not the only one, that once the material needs were taken care of, thousands of spiritual roads would open to them. Our aim, says Mateo, is to give the workers "a great collective illusion" that would keep them from starting a revolution every other day for paltry reasons. "Above all," he ended, "the Falange believes in sacrifice, it is a mystique, a total concept of life." [19]

Similar motives can be detected in the minds of those French intellectuals who, in one way or another, became involved with the cause of Fascism, National Socialism, or their domestic versions. In France, of course, the great figure of Maurras and the vastness of his doctrine had at once prepared the terrain for such sympathies and channeled it philosophically. No upstart ideologue, such as Hitler, could have notably impressed those men who proudly claimed to be disciples of Maurras. Thus the French rightists had a head start over their German, Italian, and Spanish contemporaries. In Maurras they found the full-grown, mature doctrine that the young Germans had to piece together from systems, resentments, and myths.

Yet, although they were not members of a mass party on the Nazi model, and thus did not have to make compromises with the "masses," they were unquestionably attracted by the socialist (Marx, Sorel) myth of integrating the workers with the other active elements of the nation. In this respect they were quite close ideologically to the young leftist intellectuals, and like their supposed adversaries, they despised, above all, democracy, the middle classes, bourgeois values, the profit mentality, and phony idealism.• Again Bernanos may be quoted: "From the extreme Right to the extreme Left, with the exception of a few happy mediocrities, decorated imposters, bigots, flunkeys and bureaucrats, the least one can say is that modern society finds very few who would justify and defend it." [20]

These young writers and intellectuals—Céline, Bardèche, Drieu La Rochelle, R. Brasillach, Thierry Maulnier —had chosen the Right in preference to the Left because their preoccupation with the social and moral problems of the age could not be answered by the materialism and pretentious scientism of the Marxists. The Catholic philosopher Etienne Borne recognizes in their attitude "the contempt for the trivial and the routine, the search for grandeur, the refusal of a mendacious idealism which hides a comfortable and prosperous egoism under universal morality. An effort to elaborate an idea of order by tearing it away from bourgeois compromises, finally, the certainty that there are reasons to live which are worth more than life itself." [21]

Given their background, education, Catholicism, and cultural horizon, it is not surprising that Marx repelled these young right-wing intellectuals; the fact is, however, that Maurras, with his nineteenth-century inspiration, mannerisms, and mode of fighting, could not satisfy them either. What they wanted was not only cold analysis, rational thesis, and systematic critique, but also a mystique, engagement and action. The Spanish Civil War seemed to offer such an opportunity; but even more the apocalypse whose floodgates were opened by the Second World War.

Hitler and his motorized giants represented the "new Barbarians" whom a Drieu was eager to welcome, for

---

• If the Fascist writers and intellectuals refused Communism "because they were nationalists, they refused capitalism because they were socialists." Paul Sérant, op. cit., pp. 65-6.

they were supposed to bring with them a clean and healthy vigor, shaking life into "modern man whose highest ambition and achievement was the sexual act." More than that, Fascism was to restore the rule of the elite over the "dispirited masses which have remained without spiritual guidance and moral authority." But, as we have seen, this elite fell far short of expectations; for a while the companions of Drieu continued hailing Franco, Mussolini, and Hitler as saviors of a decadent Europe, and went off to war for "Hitler's socialism," for the "international of nationalisms," in the hope for the day when "the dictators will pay homage to the resurrected Christ." (Drieu La Rochelle). But the illusion could not be kept up for long; like Von Salomon in Germany, Drieu in France expected, almost spitefully, the inevitable Russian avalanche. A disillusioned collaborator of the Germans, he wrote in 1943: "The only power capable of replacing Germany in Europe is Russia. . . . So then, in the end, it is the Russians who will cry, in a tone astonishing and perverse, seductive and crushing: 'It is we, Europe! Europe to the Europeans! Anglo-Saxons, get out!' . . . I believe that if the Russians arrived to France, the mere breath of their vitality would suffice to blow us Frenchmen away."

The movement in France ended in nihilism and despair, as it did in Germany and Italy, only under different circumstances. What had begun as a national revolution from above, built around the Maurrasian doctrine and a long, respectable conservative tradition, ended in a national catastrophe, politically and morally. The French disaster cannot, of course, be separated and separately analyzed from the Europe-wide Fascist adventure of the period between the two world wars; what happened in France from 1940 to 1945 depended, to a large extent, on the Nazi occupation of the land without which there would have been no Vichy regime even if the Third Republic had collapsed by the weight of its own impotence during or after the war. But Fascism as a Europe-wide phenomenon can be examined and judged on its own case, the more so as, to a greater degree than any other political concept, its origin, its evolution and conclusion, were circumscribed by the geographical frontiers of Continental Europe. It drew on no outside sources and was not an article of export.•

The originality of the Fascist movements consisted in adding the adjective *national* to socialism, and in creating a *mystique* to take the place of religion in the modern, industrial-democratic world. Alarmed by the disruptive force of Marxism, the leaders and theoreticians of the Fascist movements strove to reintegrate society, deny or destroy its class structure by superseding it, not, like Marx, with the concept of the "world proletariat," but with the strong national State. The strong State was to be—certainly for Mussolini and for the sincerely nationalist element among Hitler's supporters and sympathizers (Roehm, Schleicher, et al.)—the new social reality (in lieu of the workers' International and the equally international capitalism), the symbol of a new cohesion. This is what Mussolini wrote about the Fascist concept of the State in the Enciclopedia article: "Fascism is opposed to classical Liberalism which arose from the necessity of reacting against absolutism, and which brought its historical purpose to an end when the State was transformed into the conscience and will of the people." And he added: "Nothing human or spiritual exists, much less has value, outside the State."

The seeds of the disaster that was to put an end to the Fascist systems are contained in these statements, even if the circumstances created by the dictators' excesses and by the war had not destroyed them. The nationalist mystique, far from serving as a force of integration for modern man, became the source of new dissentions, ideological agitation, and civic intolerance. Instead of serving as a broader framework than Marxism could ever be, the Fascist State imposed artificial restrictions when it claimed to be its citizens' "conscience and will." In the search for a cohesion of men and a truce of ideologies, Fascism, powerless in practice, remained a myth, and as such, demanded a bloody sacrifice for its unattainable deity.

• Racism in the Union of South Africa, in the South of the United States and a few other isolated spots of the globe, has no conceptual tie with National Socialism.

6

From Ideology to Social Engineering

1. *The Failure of the Intellectuals*

In the perspective of
our analysis of three modern forms of ideology, it is now
necessary to draw up the balance sheet and answer the
central question: in exactly what sense did the intellectuals fail? But first: are we justified in identifying the
intellectual with the ideologue?

The answer to the second question may not be entirely
satisfactory, for two reasons: one is that our three categories—the Marxist, the progressive, and the reactionary
intellectual—are not completely exhaustive. The categories themselves were selected so as to be representative
and typical of contemporary intellectual attitudes, but
they are not the only ones, nor are they hermetically closed:
past and present influences, individual choices, double or
multiple loyalties rooted in background and experience,
make the borderlines necessarily blurred.

The other reason is even more important: the modern
world has been shaped by a number of very powerful
religions, philosophies, institutions. The intellectual is a
man who by definition keeps contact with the traditions
of the past and with the forces of the present, even though
he may criticize them, may be hostile to them, may even
deny their impact on him. He does not live in a social

vacuum: on the contrary, he absorbs, and reacts to, the varieties of political, social, and cultural phenomena around him far more extensively and intensively than his nonintellectual contemporaries, who are usually more preoccupied with one aspect—professional, vocational, business—of the environment. It is therefore legitimate to say that the intellectual is immersed in a climate of ideas that he is not alone to shape, but from the influence of which he is least able to free himself.

Insofar as this climate of ideas, in our Western world, is still substantially penetrated by the traditional lines of the Judaeo-Christian religion, Greek philosophy, Roman legal and political concepts, etc., the intellectual can never abandon himself completely to an ideology that either denies and belittles these bases or assigns goals in absolute contradiction to these traditions. The intellectual, in other words, can never entirely coincide with the ideologue.

But what then is the ideologue? Ideologies have been intellectual systems built around an idea that was given exclusivity or predominance over all other ideas. Hence they were bold thrusts into the world of the possible, hypotheses jealously demanding absolute recognition from history. The initial impulse was the desire to give unity to the Christian Republic, but very soon the Christian concept of spiritual supremacy was found to be unrealizable. The conflicts and contradictions of feudal society, then its clashes with the emerging world of the burghers and explorers further sharpened the tension. Yet mankind had been recognized by the Stoics of the Hellenistic period as forming one family; the Christian religion emphasized spiritual brotherhood and encouraged its reflection in the world below. Nothing was more natural than to seek new ideals for individual happiness and social cohesion, compatible to be sure with the Christian world view but holding it less and less central.

The ideologues of modern times set out on their intellectual adventures by trying to carry out the Christian ideals through their proposals, and in this they were propelled by the very dynamism and fervor of Christianity. With the passing of centuries they began to believe that they had hit upon new moral, political, and scientific instruments that would facilitate the reconstruction of society, of lost unity. However their calculations miscarried because what they proposed in view of the required unanimity and social cohesion was no longer of a transcendental nature, but a newly invented secular religion, modeled after Christianity but divinizing man and his autonomous values. Each ideology was, in fact, a new attempt to secure such a cohesion, whether the ideology of Machiavelli, Hobbes, Rousseau, Saint-Simon, or Marx, and whether its working principle was founded on absolutism, science, contractual agreement, industry, or the classless society.

From the point of view of what they wanted to relieve, none of these attempts were successful. They created new conflicts and multiplied the existing tensions. As Christianity failed to organize society here below, so did its bastard offspring, the ideologies. As the development of certain social forces during the Middle Ages exploded the framework of medieval Christian society, so the new political and social facts of the contemporary world could not be pressed onto the Procrustes bed of the ideologies. We shall review on the following pages some of the errors and failures of the three ideologies discussed in Chapters Three, Four, and Five. But it is already clear—and will be discussed in Part Two of the present chapter—that the exaggerations of the ideologies and their unsolvable conflicts had to lead to a new doctrine, a new attempt at dealing with the problems of the world, inherited and new. For lack of a better term, we shall call this new attempt *social engineering*.

In what sense did the *Marxist intellectual* fail? It is generally believed that the only preoccupation of Karl Marx was how to put an end to economic exploitation; in fact, the central thesis of Marxism is the abolition of alienation. Naturally Marx was convinced that the latter objective might only be achieved if definitive guarantees were found for the former. Even Lenin, in a letter to the physicist Philip Frank wrote that Marxism is a scientific system only insofar as economics is a science and may serve as a system of measurement for what is unmeasurable in itself: the superstructure.

Now it is obvious today to all except the willfully blind

that in Marxist societies that claim to have abolished economic exploitation,• the superstructure has been decidedly smothered, debased, and bent into the service of the Party. Economically and culturally the Soviet citizen is alienated: from the ownership of the means of production, from the fruit of his labor, from his political rights and interests, from the free pursuit of his religious, philosophical, and other aspirations. This is so true that even Togliatti, the Italian Communist leader, was led to question, after the Hungarian insurrection of 1956, the validity of Marxist *economic* doctrine (the infrastructure) in view of the fact that it creates such contradictions and oppression in the superstructure (intellectual life) that it regularly leads to violent and explosive discontent.

Whatever is right or wrong with Marxist economic doctrine, it is clear, as Fr. Perroux and others have shown, that the more the Party insists on putting it into practice, the more contradiction it creates between itself and the managers of economic life. In the eyes of the latter the discrepancy between State-directed doctrine and the actual necessities of economic realities is steadily widening, until ideology becomes, for them, a required but empty mode of expression, a means of hiding the facts. Directors and engineers thus become cynical careerists, while the idealists among them succumb to Party terror in one way or another.

What was the intellectuals' stake in the theory of alienation and superstructure? The nonalienated man was to have free access to the products of the mind, was freed, in fact, not only to enjoy and participate, but to become a creator himself; in the upper reaches of talent, a philosopher. But what is the philosopher's role according to Marxism? We have seen: to abolish philosophy—that is, the detached, critical attitude—since in the classless society, to put it bluntly, there will be nothing to criticize; the would-be philosopher-critic will coincide with the scientist (himself conceived in a simplist way): he will merely state facts.

• That this is far from true, that State ownership is the most total exploitation and even expropriation of the workers, is another decisive defeat of Marxist theory. However, its discussion does not enter into our present statement of the Marxist intellectual's failure.

Thus an immense contradiction arises: while Marxist economic life has built-in defects and abuses, the Marxist philosopher is called upon not only to approve them, but to rob the worker (all citizens are "workers" in Marxist society) of his defenses by robbing him of his critical weapons, that is, ultimately, of philosophy. The philosopher in Marxist lands may, of course, do just this from conviction, although such men must be rather rare, and the disgust for this role, expressed by refugee intellectuals—journalists, writers, artists, professors—must be very deep and very widespread. Thus it is far more likely that the Marxist intellectual, like the Marxist industrial manager, turns into a paid and prized careerist, an "engineer of the soul," as Stalin wanted him to be.

The promise of Utopia has led, in the case of the Marxist and by way of detours we tried to sketch in Chapter Three, to the corruption of the intellectuals and also of the public philosophy.• The result, as far as it may be ascertained, is lack of public confidence, a climate of cheating, blackmail, and fear, and—among intellectuals —of demoralization, listlessness, duplicity. In the resulting intellectual vacuum, the manipulation of the "superstructure" passes into the hands of Party officials who, without talent, imagination and, of course, critical aptitude, execute plans and produce quotas. The Party ideology, which must permeate all intellectual activity and creation, is too precious a weapon to be wielded by anybody save a reliable one.

The reliable ones, however, are no pure professionals who can devote themselves to their tasks with a love of the métier. There is a difference, in Communist countries, between reliability and competence. The intellectual climate is so corrupt that in high Party circles there is actually a fear of competence because the competent man calls forth the loyalty of his collaborators and creates—on no matter how small a scale—a group apart, a separateness, an intimacy that no totalitarian regime may contemplate

• In Chapter Three we found it more useful to focus on the Marxist intellectual living *outside* the Soviet orbit, because his reactions are more genuine in a free society. When the concrete results of Marxist ideology and management are discussed, it is more revealing to look at what happens *inside* Communist lands where Marxist ideology prevails unobstructed.

without suspicion. Thus the reliable manager of intellectual and cultural matters is, in most instances, a party stooge, a frustrated third-rate talent, or in more fortunate cases, an indifferent functionary doing a routine job. Such a man is the best compromise in the climate of distrust that Communism creates, because his limited horizon enables him to take for granted and represent the supposed unanimity on which the system ideologically rests. He, the bureaucrat that totalitarianism breeds and nurtures, is the expression of a supposed social consensus that he is called upon to perpetuate on his own level. In short, he is a cog in a machine, and the machine, operated from the top, is set on the single rail of history. Only the operator claims to know the track ahead, but, by Marxist definition, all share somehow in the knowledge and inspire the leaders. The goal thus being known and collectively approved, the executants, at any post, merely feed the engine; they do not set the direction.

Of the three types of ideologues the most difficult to identify correctly is the *progressive,* since his allegiance appears to be least circumscribed by a party philosophy, and since he maintains certain ties with historical humanism and with the constituted religions. Yet, philosophically, the progressive stand ought to be the clearest and easiest to locate.

We have seen that the Enlightenment *philosophes'* vague belief in progress received decisive shape and direction from the theory of evolution. Progress thus came to mean either biological or intellectual or psychosocial improvement, or even all three together; the significant thing, however, in the thinking of contemporary evolutionists is that they envisage such an evolution and improvement not so much for the individual, but for society. Father Chardin believed in a global unification of human awareness as a necessary prerequisite for any real future progress of mankind; and Julian Huxley speaks, as quoted earlier, of the "development of mankind into a single psycho-social unit with . . . a common pool of thought . . . providing the evolutionary process with the rudiments of a head."

It is clear that for these representative scientists the destiny of man coincides with that of the race; in other words, the noosphere, in their judgment and tacit hope, will be just as impersonal as the biosphere. The unit of their thinking is not the "individual beings with their plurality and essential rivalry," [1] but the race, the machine, the totality of co-operative mankind that Auguste Comte called the "Great Being."

Both Chardin and Huxley admit, the first with a trace of apprehension, the second with evident satisfaction, that in order to "progress," mankind must become an "inter-thinking group." The advantage of this is hard to see, the horror of it is much more easily grasped; but the fact remains that for all the tenants of the evolutionary theory in its broadest sense, for the Darwinists as well as for the Hegelians, the obvious and desirable end is the scientific society working with the precision of a machine. At present the progressives dream only of a total consensus among the members of society, a consensus that can be brought about, if at all, by ideological pressure only; but when this thought is projected into the future, the mechanical character of such a society is frankly discussed and accepted. In both instances the ideal is clearly revealed.

If on the level of philosophy the progressive favors the machine over man, it may be expected that on the level of public policy he is also inclined to entrust to huge, machinelike organizations the regulation of life. This inclination, which has become the major trend of our time, is manifest in all parts of life where "progressive" thinking has prevailed: nationalized economy, welfare state, the bureaucratization of human activity in general, the adoption of an industrial and commercial pattern in political and cultural enterprises. Everywhere a social machine is set up in such a way as to neutralize individual freedom and independence, and substitute the routine of social engineering with its predictable outcome.

Progressive ideology itself is emptied of significance, because it is in its nature to yield to the forms of social engineering that ultimately inspire it. For several decades the political depository of progressivism has been international socialism. Only in recent years have socialist parties been pushed in the background, a phenomenon that has now reached a stage of crisis for the parties involved. One after the other, the British, German, French, Italian, socialists have been substantially refashioning, if not their views, at least their programs, no doubt for the purpose of avoiding the now customary electoral defeats, but also because the rival parties have appropriated their theses. Thus, the eclipse of socialism is in reality a victory for their philosophy and program: it has become obsolete in proportion to the world's becoming socialist and follows the widespread predilection for collective regulation.•

The most obvious failure of the *conservative intellectual* was rooted in his inevitable alliance with reaction and Fascism. Thus, in his own way, he, too, yielded to a machine whose operators were engineers of society in their own way, that is, lightly covered with the varnish of ideology, but in reality unfree organizers.

Their case is easily a misleading one, for under Fascist regimes the State machinery itself was not dismantled, only colonized with the creatures of the movement.•• It seemed therefore that the traditional State remained in power with its civil servants; in reality, and this would have been more evident if the dynamic Fascist regimes had remained longer in power, the State was gradually yielding to a managerial class that, no longer attached to the ideology except in externals, had only one interest: to stay in power as indispensable organizers.

But even without the tragic error of twentieth-century conservative forces and classes—that of succumbing to the Fascist temptation—it was almost fatal that their thinking should lead, indirectly, to a system of social engineering. If followed to the logical conclusion, conservative philosophy encourages the status quo in the name of a refusal to tamper with what it calls the organic processes of society. Even where conservatives were obliged to adopt

• Characteristically, socialism for lack of a program turns now to the one field that has so far been more or less free of organization and State interference, the field of leisure and culture. In the 1959 elections, the trump card of the British Labour Party was a brochure devoted to the problems of education, leisure, and culture.

••In the case of both National Socialism and Fascism, as we have seen, the State was left intact, but its organs were duplicated by the corresponding echelons of the Party.

parts of the progressive program, they did so halfheartedly and made every attempt to immobilize the process of transformation as soon as it was feasible. This is quite natural, since there exists in the conservative mentality a tendency to reduce the new and changing to the old and stable; Jacob Burckhardt gives good examples of this thinking in formulas that are reminiscent of the method of La Rochefoucauld: "The greatest innovation in the world is the demand for education as a right of man; it is a disguised demand for comfort";[2] "what we regard as moral progress is the domestication of individuality";[3] "the arrogant belief in the moral superiority of the present [covers] the secret mental reservation that money making is today easier and safer than ever."[4]

Their insistence on spirituality and religion—true and necessary as it is—plays into the hands variously of bureaucrats, ideologues, and managers whose ideological conformity to their ideals suffices, in this case too, to be allowed a free hand in other essentials.

It is true, on the other hand, that conservative philosophy, as such, does not directly encourage the development of social engineering. If it does so today, this is due to the particular social and economic context in which it exists.

In summary, then, the intellectuals, attached to three main ideologies, have brought about their own decline. This means that they have encouraged and elaborated structures in society that, finally, made them superfluous, even dangerous to the new edifice.

The basic error of the intellectuals was their insistence on bringing about a universal secular society when they saw that another universal society, founded on spirituality, failed. They believed that the emancipated man, the ideal of the humanists, would be convinced—if only one appealed to his rationality—to give up enough of his freedom for the building of the good society. They believed that what the free individual voluntarily renounces, remains a kind of a free particle, out of which a collective freedom would surge. To achieve this they reached one after the other, for various scientific formulas as substitutes for

208

politics, each of them leading to a different, but equally artificial, substitute for the State.•

While one ideology—and one formula—sought to disintegrate the State and replace it with a vague "universal society" (Marxism, socialism), the other ideology—and formula—wanted to divinize the State and make it so mighty as to render it coincident with society (Fascism). In one way or the other, either by suppressing society for the sake of the State or the other way around, but mostly by mixing the two ways, the purpose was to construct a definitive society—through anarchy or discipline—and a definitive mankind, outside of which there should be nothing. All men and all their endeavors were to be subordinated to a universal system. The mirror and pattern of this universal system was the totalitarian party.

Can this be achieved? The limited human mind conceives of only two ways of achievement: one leads through a general and permanent *enthusiasm*—that is, a secular religion, decrees trying to enforce "virtues," the proclamation of high-sounding collectivistic abstractions. This road has been the greatest temptation—and deepest trap—of the ideologies, it is the one they tried to follow, inspired as they were by Christian universality and by their own inclination to favor the conquest of the *inner man*.

The other road leads through a general and permanent *organization* of the *external man*, that is, of his interests, habits, and reflexes. This is not the road the intellectuals wished to follow because it does not lead through inner consent. But this is what they had to choose after they have discredited the inner man. Impatiently pressing for the utopian goals they envisaged, they decided first to build the machine that would then persuade people and educate them in the new ways. However to run these machines—whether parties, or schools, or institutions— the intellectuals were no longer needed; in fact, their

• "The ideal of scientism," writes Hans Morgenthau, Jr., "as applied to politics is the disappearance of politics altogether. Scientism assumes that the abolition of politics can and will usher in an ideal state of society. . . . One needs only to use the right formula, to apply the right mechanical device, and the political domination of man by man and the violent clashes of human collectivities will disappear as temporary aberrations from the rule of cooperation and of reason." *Dilemmas of Politics*, p. 242.

ideology, insofar as it still reflected a transcendental image, was positively dangerous.•

This is how the *social engineer* came onto the scene.

2. The Social Engineer

Whatever the utopian dreams of intellectuals and ideologues were, they were rooted in a tradition that spoke to man of his existential richness and his freedom of choice. During the age of ideologies, science, politics, culture, were essentially free territories on which the human spirit exercised itself in its unpredictable fashion and made its breath felt in unexpected ways. Often, it is true, the intellectuals were tempted to become mandarins and impose an unnatural fixity on human affairs; but if nothing else opposed them, the tools at their disposal simply did not serve adequately such an ambition.••

• This passage from the hoped-for and enforced enthusiasm of the inner man to the conscious and "scientific" organization of the external man is well illustrated in the words of an ex-leader of Chinese Communist youth. This is what Lei, a refugee in Hongkong, told Mme Suzanne Labin, the French political writer: "The important thing is not the inside of the soul but its external expression. . . . After all, when it is said that capitalism brings about the exploitation of man by man, this does not mean that the whole person of the worker is exploited, but only his working power. The same way, if I say that communism brings about the oppression of the soul by the soul, one must understand by this that it fashions not the depth of the soul, but only the surface. The Political Bureau does not ambition that the soul of the organized man should love the soul of the organizer, but that the former should be attached to the latter as the reflection to the shining object. The Political Bureau is the lamp of China . . . and the six hundred million Chinese must become the innumerable reflections of the lamp in a mirror." *La Condition humaine en Chine communiste* (La Table ronde, 1959), pp. 259-60.

•• Nor was the repression of intellectuals by the State efficient and complete. As a liberal historian, Professor Massimo Salvadori, points out, the various despotic nations that made attempts at the suppression of the liberal movement did not constitute a universal state system. Oppression was capricious in character and greatly different on the two sides of any national borderline. *Liberal Democracy* (Doubleday, 1957).

We have seen that the intellectuals failed for two main reasons: misjudging the spiritual-transcendental nature of the Christian concept of brotherhood, they strove to bring about a new cohesion, this time secular, based on the *natural man* and emphasizing its rational features; then, science and industry placed in their hands organizational possibilities by which this cohesion could be achieved, but revealed itself hollow and artificial, or on the contrary, passionate and mindless.

But the intellectuals at least believed in a substitute religion: in a *myth* that would satisfy the irrational quest, a genuinely shared hidden treasure. Human nature is elastic enough to generate enthusiasm even for a closed system, provided the illusion of freedom is retained. Furthermore, the intellectual, as a type, was an essentially solitary explorer. He was an adventurer of the mind, blazing new paths. Even as a representative of class interests he never claimed infallibility of either goal or method, and admitted, if in no other way than by his skeptical and scrutinizing turn of mind, the probability of errors of judgment. For him, holding ideas—which he encouraged to compete freely on the market place—was compatible with a certain generosity of the mind, with a latitude within which discussion could be carried on and the opponent considered an indispensable partner in a superior kind of game.

Also, the driving force of intellectuals was derived from the Christian concept of love. It is important to note, since it is completely forgotten nowadays, that what the Christian religion teaches is spiritual, supernatural love, that is, love subordinated to the highest criterion, the adoration of God. Thus its fruits are actions that, although they discriminate between good and evil, do not become fixed in one immutable pattern. On the plane of historical and social realities this meant that, given the constant flux and change of circumstances, no social system could be conceived as being final and impose itself as leading through a unique path to a unique goal. Put differently, the duty of the individual was to save himself, but the way in which he achieved that salvation—a way of which a large section leads, at all times, through the domain of the social and political—could be multiple. Thus Saint Augustine only asked the State not to obstruct the supernatural destination of its citizens, and Saint Thomas taught that in principle Christianity is compatible with any form of government.

The intellectual ideologues, on the contrary, tried to find the *one form* of society that would insure the happiness of all, or as some of them put it, of the greatest number. Naturally, the projected Utopia could not be achieved; but at least choices were eliminated, and with the growth of science and its utilization, and through the pressure of the masses, society could finally be envisaged as a machine concerning which discussion and choice had to be more and more restricted. The rate of increase of populations, the ratio between it and the available foodstuff, the predictable growth of production, the necessities of industrializing the entire globe, the stimulation of consumption and its methods, are factors in a situation that, it is true, has been brought about independently of the intellectuals' sphere of influence and action, but it was in harmony with their over-all plans; the way to it was ideologically cleared by them.

The question that immediately arises is whether the contemporary situation does not express itself, on the intellectual level, in the form of an ideology, and whether the "social engineers" are not simply ideologues. The answer to this question is hard to give since the elements of the situation are rooted in ideologies, or were, at least, interpreted with the help of ideological concepts. The social engineers, it is true, do not act in a completely homogeneous milieu (hence opposition, debate, criticism, is not absent around them), and their activity does not remain without a residue of ideological effect. The important thing, however, is the social engineers' basic commitment: they have overcome the inhibitions that still dominated the intellectuals and have furnished their world with new objects and objectives. They have created, side by side with the world of nature, a parallel or second world, a second nature, no longer situated in the same spatiotemporal and human continuum, even if contiguous with it.

On the plane of material achievements this new world, superimposed on and sometimes integrated with the old, merely joins the existential realm: an object is an object whether it is a paleolithic utensil or a jet plane. But its psychological and ideational projection, *scientism*, considers the universe and man in it as an *environment*, whose infinite transformability is an end in itself. In this view, human consciousness is merely a (temporarily) privileged location for sizing up the rest of the universe, but neither the most perfect, nor possessing any intrinsic value. The goal is to spread this consciousness over the universe, to identify and equalize mind and matter (monism) and to set up other stations of ideation and control. Such intentions are evident in the work of scientists who reduce the activities of the human mind to the reflexes of animals, who, in their laboratories, change and dissolve emotions, endow living creatures with new instincts and strip them of their original ones. Their credo was best and most brutally expressed by Harvard professor of psychology B. F. Skinner who wrote: "As scientific explanation becomes more and more comprehensive, the contribution which may be claimed by the individual himself appears to approach zero. Man's vaunted creative powers, his achievements in art, science and morals, his capacity to choose and our right to hold him responsible for the consequences of his choice—none of these is conspicuous in the new scientific self-portrait." •

In most cases the social engineers still express their ambitions in the terms of traditional human aspirations: fear, hope, hunger, security, power, happiness. But their words are by-products of far mightier ambitions the field and scope of which is the entire universe. In this light everything is held to be a question of available knowledge and material means, because the principles of their realization are as good as granted. In the meantime, and this is the decisive point for our discussion, the smallest unit with which it is worthwhile for the social engineer to deal is society or even mankind. The two, of course, tend to coincide: it is mankind conceived as a unified society that interests him, since the plans he elaborates must be applicable to the whole field to be effective. Needless to

• Quoted by Aldous Huxley in *Brave New World Revisited* (Bantam Books), p. 95.

Professor Skinner's experiments include changing the behavior of cats and mice, making the first fearful of the second, the latter aggressive, etc.

repeat, ideological utopianism and evolutionary theory march in the same direction.

Thus, in reality, the social engineer's scope is a cosmic one: philosophically nothing ties him to the earth or to the human sphere. *Man* in his estimation is nothing but an imperfect machine, a mere tool capable of constructing better ones; hence *society* is a place of experimentation, particularly as it offers two important data: the material and the human world, which may be combined in various ways. Finally, *history* is a senseless tale of sound and fury, but not in the way the Ecclesiast meant it—which is a backhanded tribute to the Creator and His creation— but because it is the story of the unmanipulated individual and the unplanned society.

The *social engineer* is today the center of discussion of intellectual and political circles, which are alarmed by his daily expanding conquests and his apparent lack of concern for "human values." There is a frightening passage in one of Bernanos's books, in which he describes the difference between the old-fashioned soldier, handling his weapons and taking personal, bodily risks, and the modern bomber-pilot who fights by pushing buttons and whose only contact with the destruction he causes is—a few hours later—a photograph showing smoke-balls and craters. The fear expressed by Bernanos is, thus, of the technocrat who becomes an impersonal force, interested only in efficiency, that is, power, and disregarding even that tenuous but still human aspect of things that ideologies represented and respected.

Yet, in spite of Bernanos's anguished and vivid descriptions, we have no clear picture of the social engineer's significance. Not even the social engineer himself is entirely aware of his own tasks and potentialities; and his commentators and critics, like the headquarters of an army in deroute, are merely trying to guess his next move, without, in every case, recognizing the depth of his incursion.

All one can do at this point is to draw up an inventory of the means at the disposal of social engineers and of his successes. The following questions must be asked: What is the basic *view* that social engineering has of man? What *results* does it hope to achieve? By what *methods* does it try to solve its problems?

We have tried to answer the first question in this and other chapters: we have mentioned the ideological underpinning of social engineering, namely the ambition to achieve through a social machinery what the individual (on account of his imperfection but also his freedom, recalcitrance, and uncalculability) cannot be trusted to achieve, and even to want to achieve consistently; the short cuts by which the social machine may be brought within our grasp; the promise of evolution to lead us, through physical, mental, mechanical, and moral "growth," to a state of total consent.

Thus, generally stated, the social engineer desires to bring about a perfect society, that is, one in which individual actions should be powerless to impede the carrying out of collective decisions. He would not necessarily wipe out the wide range of interests, spiritual and religious life, political beliefs and moral convictions, but would try to dwarf and domesticate their meaning and impact in all areas of public life, from education to statecraft, from entertainment to literature.

In order to achieve unanimity on these matters, individual action, and thought—its regulating, rational principle —must be both brought under control and discredited; their insufficiency with regard to collective decisions must be evidenced, their isolation from the common consent stressed, their (nonscientific) vagueness and (social) irrelevance sharply brought into focus. When he explains social movements or analyzes individual motivations, the social engineer never looks for a background of mature judgments, conscious preferences, hesitations and doubts, the interplay of clear concepts within the individual mind and the willingness of others to be convinced by arguments or their freedom to refuse such; he invariably seeks psychological or sociological motives (that is, factors that are outside of the individual's sphere of consciousness or action), speaks of indoctrination and "internalization," stresses behavioral signs• and favors the techniques of an-

• In the eyes of the social engineer behavior is more important (measurable and controllable) than ideas, but even he acknowledges that ideas influence behavior; their importance must,

onymity. Hearing him, one has the uncomfortable impression that the individual is never envisaged as the locus of an internal autonomy, but rather as a chip from the block of collectivity, which possesses no other ingredient than what the block itself has in its make-up.

In the immediate, these goals are sought by reducing the complexity of man's nature to psychological and sociological data. The most influential quasi-philosophical schools today, dominating the philosophy faculties particularly in Anglo-Saxon universities, reduce all judgments to statements of *subjective approval,* plus the *request* that others approve them too. Only two questions remain to be asked: why does the subject approve, and why do others follow (or refuse to follow) him. The first issue is dealt with by psychology,• the second by sociology. Outside the two fields there is supposed to be nothing but meaningless talk.

This "black envy of philosophy to be like the physical sciences" (Berdyaev) is translated into the approach of dealing with individual and collective realities. The entire web of societal relationships becomes mechanized at the decisive junctures where the "scientific approach" is cred-

---

therefore, be decreased. If behavioral indoctrination is efficient, the subject will draw the right conclusions, namely, he will try to shape his ideas in conformity with the collectively held correct behavior. In this way, he will have purged himself and adjusted his inner life to the norms of the collectivity. The representatives of the latter: poll-takers, audience rating experts, counselors and guides, etc., discourage the formation and formulation of ideas, and eliminate them from the range of public life. They create an artificial consensus.

• "Empirical psychology, in treating of cognition, has hardly advanced beyond an inventory of acts and their associative connections. Unable to grasp the cognitive essence of consciousness, hence also the nature of the higher valuative acts, the empirical study of the psyche tends to dwell in the conditions physical, physiological, social and so forth that 'underlie' it, under the mistaken notion that these material substrata stand to the psyche as cause to effect and not as matter to form. Hence it is hardly surprising that consciousness as psychical, thus misconceived, should be 'reduced' to the physical and that its empirical study should tend to become a 'psychology without a psyche.'" H. M. Chapman, "Realism and Phenomenology," in *The Return to Reason,* edited by John Wild.

ited with infallibility. It is idle to object that the rapports between human beings remain nevertheless the same: in the family, at the place of employment, at school, in the army. This is true to a large extent and will always be true. But the engineering work should not be underestimated because it exudes its mentality at the points where social relationships meet and important decisions are made. Family love, business activity, academic achievement, determine of course the nature of human ties in the situation of the family, business transactions, colleges; but we take it increasingly for granted that at the important checking points of all these institutions mentalmechanical devices are set up to regulate social traffic and individual destiny. Psychological tests are administered in schools, business corporations, the army, and even in certain ecclesiastical orders. Whatever we think of these tests—and the overwhelming evidence shows that they are wretched but pretentious fumblings with an immeasurable reality—they restrict and mechanize responses, and perform a selection that excludes the free, the imaginative, the morally and socially rebellious. In the family, at law courts, in civil service positions, the sense of responsibility is attacked at its roots when the so-called expert is called in to weigh love, guilt, or competence by extrarational factors, that is, by a psychological and social "science" the data and conclusions of which change with every rising day. The resistance of common sense is undermined by elusive but ubiquitous persons in key positions who find it easy to shock the unsuspecting "layman" (nonspecialist) into a panicky reappraisal of all that experience, example, and tradition have taught him.

Resistance cannot be offered to these devices because they themselves confess to their present imperfection. The answer is more science, more scientific method applied to social, moral, and emotional affairs. But it is not science alone that is held responsible for working out the correct solutions: the social engineers subtly imply that for science to cover all relationships, it needs the co-operation of the whole social body, for how else could a machine operate unless all its parts are subordinated to the central purpose. In this way co-operation with expertise becomes a civic duty and a moral good; the organizational principle is imposed with a missionary zeal and accepted with that immemorial submissiveness with which man has always bowed to authority, however irrational, oppressive, or idiotic.

Thus it is not true that social engineering affects only the surface of life, that it is an indispensable but limited regulation of existence in overcrowded industrial democracies. The forever uncritical human mind no more analyzes the "scientific evidence" behind the decrees of social engineers than it analyzed the "proofs" of any ruling class in the past. The divine right of kings has simply yielded to the scientific authority of psychologists, sociologists, educators, and communication chiefs. In this lies the danger, but also the hope.•

In his Preface to a book on technocracy,[5] Father Dubarle has written that although we witness the "colonization of governments by technicians" and the "increasing determination of political transactions by . . . social techniques,"[6] the essence of the political phenomenon will remain unchanged since "its formulations are of an ethnic, linguistic and geographic nature." "Politics cannot be turned into technocracy."[7] The point Father Dubarle makes is certainly worth reflecting on; but what it omits is that the political phenomenon may be isolated from the life of society, veiled from those whom it concerns, so that, as Saint-Simon and his followers predicted, administration takes over the function of governing. The goal, said Bazard, one of the Duke's chief disciples, is "the total organization and rationalization of all human behavior within the framework of the hierarchy of the able." •• It is obvious that no government and no State is able to achieve this; but the novelty of the present situation is, precisely, that a well-indoctrinated social technique may serve as an over-all formula for all relationships in society—parental, business, civic—thereby releasing the State from interfering and enlarging its scope.

This conclusion seems to contradict the present trend

• See Chapter Eleven.
•• Bazard added that this was to be achieved without violence, through education and brotherly love. The so-called School of Saint-Simon taught that men must be placed in conditions favorable to the development of his feelings of affection, submission, love, adoration for the universal harmony. A "new tie of affection" was needed, a new faith, a new religion.

toward increased governmental interference with local matters, private initiative, etc. But the contradiction is one only in appearance. What we call the "welfare state" is not a government-imposed philosophy and policy: the proof is that even conservative governments adopt welfare methods and perpetuate them when their socialistic predecessors had initiated such measures. Rather: the welfare state is a mentality secreted by social techniques, applicable at every level and every phase of public and semipublic life. "What is new today," writes Peter Drucker, "is that we are becoming capable of doing systematically what before has usually been a streak of lightning, and that we can organize ordinary mortals to do what before could usually be done only by the rare genius." [8]

The last statement is, of course, an exaggeration; but what is not is that the invention or idea of the genius may be immediately applied in a mechanical fashion, that important scientific and organizational discoveries may be made by the rapid reviewing of all possibilities which, as formulable data, had been fed to a machine. Everything from medical discoveries to the adoption of the best war strategy may be obtained through such methods. Naturally, it is true that the factor of decision remains a human one: the machine may only review the alternatives among which it is a human responsibility to choose. But such decision-making has always been done at the top of the social hierarchy; the significant thing is that below that level the same model is followed: the individual is replaced or dis-placed, and the web of society is ordered by the mechanistic principle of the best pattern found. "The true power of the machine," wrote R. Seidenberg in a closely reasoned, but unfortunately little-noticed, book, "in its effects upon the standards of society [is] that . . . following an inherent principle of organization, it will demand an ever greater degree of integration and coordination in the social aspects of life commensurate with its own perfection." [9] And then: "The efficient functioning of organization depends upon the unhampered orderliness, the exact and predictable course not only of all elements within the related whole, but equally of all contiguous elements. Thus organization, by virtue of its inherent morphological relationships . . . exerts always an implicit pressure in favor of further organization." [10]

But, one may argue, if society is, in this fashion, drawn ever closer, then the accumulated knowledge will serve the individual exactly as much as the collectivity, in fact, the equilibrium, if anything, will be firmer than in the past when societies were top-heavy, with competence and authority concentrated at certain power-points and leaving the individual exposed through his ignorance and weakness. We have seen, however, that this is not the most probable line of development: the evolutionists speak of a collective mind, of a rudimentary head toward which the human race evolves in its biopsychological mutations. The same evolutionists, and other scientists or social engineers, are of the opinion that the intermediary steps between our own "anarchic" individuality and the faraway time when the race will coalesce into one superbeing, are those institutions that express today mankind's unity on the international level.• The already-quoted Father Dubarle admits that we are at "the social confluence of the world and the very first emergence of institutions, under the form of 'high authorities' which will preside the organizations generated by this confluence." [11]

The social engineers predict that such intellectual concentrations will be beneficial to mankind as a whole and to each individual as well. The idea advanced by Julian Huxley of a "thought bank" is considered by them in all seriousness. To an inquiry of *The New York Times* in 1958, one of the scientists consulted about the socio-intellectual aspects of the year 2000, Professor John Weir of the California Institute of Technology, answered that there will be no conflict among the thinking of individuals because "a common Thought Bank will be established from which all will receive instructions [through electronic means—this was not clearly explained in the article written for laymen] and to which all may repair in case of doubt." Less "scientific" but equally enthusiastic for a society that will have eliminated "divisiveness," are the recommendations of Professor Robert C. Angell. In *Free Society and Moral Crisis*,[12] the author identifies what he calls the "moral web" with socialized attitudes, and "moral crisis" with deviant behavior. It is incidental to our present argument that Mr. Angell never tells us how one distinguishes whether a "deviant" group is *good*

• See Chapters Seven and Eight.

or *bad*—how one tells a saint from a delinquent, a gang from the twelve apostles—when both disrupt the social fabric and neither behaves according to "the common values of their culture." What is, however, relevant here is that the remedies he suggests for "social and moral integration" are all collectivistic measures, reached through public discussions in high schools, television panels, Boy Scout and YMCA programs, group therapy, prisoner rehabilitation, and so on.

Mr. Angell is, of course, only one of the many social engineers who insist on strengthening social cohesion and the competence and authority of the collectivity over against the individual. None of them declares himself openly against the latter: on the contrary, as said before, they imply that the individual will be the ultimate beneficiary of the collective knowledge and power. Yet, basically, they all mistrust the individual; not, let us hasten to add, from the point of view of the individual's evil penchants as taught by religions; but because the individual is free when, from the vantage point where they stand they see in him all the potentialities of a machine and of parts of a machine.

This freedom, this incalculability, is the great stumbling block for the social engineer in his cosmic-social design. If man cannot be directly persuaded to renounce it, and if he persists in rebelling against all forms—brutal or subtle—of oppression, only one road remains, that of treating him as a *sick man*, held in bondage by a tragic misconception. This is, of course, just another way of discrediting his uniqueness as are the many attempts at underplaying his rationality, loyalty to ideas, power of abstraction, or fervor to commit himself to causes.

In a letter to Frau von Stein (1787), Goethe wrote: "I think it is true that humanity will triumph eventually, only I fear that at the same time the world will become a large hospital and each will become the other's humane nurse." While one may question the desirability of a "triumph" obtained through permanent habitation in a hospital, one must admit that Goethe's premonition was superb. Indeed, Professor Lawrence K. Frank, in his article "Psychology and Order in Society" • writes that "an

• *Esprit*, Jan., 1959. This text was part of a symposium on the state of social sciences in America today.

advanced industrial civilization cannot function according to the un-motivated choices and decisions of un-informed individuals," but that it needs increasingly "the services of counseling and orientation." Actually, he compares the desirable relationship between these "counselors" and the rest of the population to the one between doctor and patient. In order to persuade the latter that this relationship is in his own interest, Mr. Frank suggests that in "our democratic societies" such far-reaching changes in societal relationships and decision-making that he advocates can only be achieved through "education and persuasion." But then what is the task of the schools, which are "the institutional pivots where the transformation of the social order" will take place? In other words, what are education and persuasion? "Education," anwers the professor, "has now, apparently for the first time, the difficult duty to help students to un-learn—that is, to liberate them of the traditional and outmoded folklore, beliefs and postulates."

Thus we see that the natural tendency of social engineering is to weaken the individual, first his grip on matters of public interest, then his competence in issues concerning his closest circle and even himself. This is to be accomplished in various ways, some of which we have discussed, but which are worth repeating: the unlearning of the past—habits and knowledge—so as to unfasten one of the most substantial of human links; the discreditation of ideas and of conceptual thinking generally, thus shaking the individual's confidence in his judgment and critical ability; the confusion of the private and the public spheres in situations where social motivation must take precedence: the techniques of "group thinking," "collective decision-making" are the means to achieve this goal, and also testing, which persuades the individual that only collective (statistical) and scientific criteria are relevant in judging and categorizing him.• Finally, when all the roots of "divisiveness" have been extirpated and the individual, stripped of his individuality, has put on the mental uniform of a hospital patient, the social engineer is ready to infuse into him the benevolent directives of the "thought

---

• To belong to a given category of I.Q. measurement has today almost the same determining significance as that of belonging to a caste in India. One category is hardly more "scientific" than the other.

bank." This is how R. Seidenberg describes this process:
"As mankind establishes an ever larger bank account of
small accretions, the individual finds himself on the edge
of an ever wider circle of knowledge, inherited experience,
etc. The individual as such might thus remain stationary
in his mental capacities and endowments while society
continues to evolve; indeed, the mechanism of the process
must inevitably reduce the individual to a more or less
limited, vicarious and partial share in the ever widening
panorama of social enterprises. . . . We may advance socially while remaining stationary as individuals." [13]

Was Karl Jaspers not justified when he wrote some
twenty-five years ago that "freedom may have been only
a passing moment between two immeasurably long periods
of sleep"? The first was the emergence of man amid other
biological forms; the second may coincide with the benevolent despotism of the social engineer.

7

Planetary Coexistence

It is only natural that the trend toward social engineering appears, first, within national communities, and among them, in the technically and socially most advanced ones. Ideologies have had their greatest impacts on individual nations because the conflict of classes that these ideologies accompanied was, primarily, a national, not an international, phenomenon. Moreover, the "age of ideologies" coincided with the "age of nationalism" in which every nation tried to keep out foreign ideological influence and was even willing to go to war to extirpate or block the source of such ideologies.

Within the national communities of the Western world —and under different conditions in the Soviet orbit too— the concept of the welfare state has spread rapidly and victoriously, and the welfare state, based on social peace and ideological consensus, engenders and encourages the techniques we have identified as social engineering.

Thus the second half of the twentieth century witnesses a curious inconsistency in its general situation and outlook: while the individual nations gradually eliminate social strife within their borders, they maintain, in their relationships with each other, a "state of nature," that is, conditions leading to sharp conflicts, armed readiness, local and general wars, and stiff economic and ideological, even cultural, competition.

From the point of view of intellectuals, we witness, accordingly, an increased interest—roughly since the end of the First World War—in the field of international relations where the characteristic traits for which the intellectuals have been known may be given a larger scope than within the national community. There seems to be a greater challenge in a situation where the means and ends are far from settled than in the wide and straight avenues of the welfare state; and goals that the intellectuals could not accomplish within their own society—tradition, the memory of previous conflicts, the very narrowness of the field of action, have been the main obstacles—they may recast so as to fit an incomparably larger one where practically nothing of the sort has been tried yet.

In fact, it is easy for the disappointed intellectual—both in the West and in the East—to persuade himself that things as he had conceived them could really not work within the limited framework of a given nation, but only within a "world community," and with gigantic forces supporting them. He may think in this way, first of all, because he is usually far less well acquainted with the problems of this "world community" than with those existing in his own country: while he evaluates the latter with some accuracy, and thus weighs its various factors by their real importance, he tends to fill the gaps in his knowledge of faraway circumstances with the abstractions of his ideology. In the second place, this same ideology, conceived and shaped with the universalist design of the nineteenth century, seems always to be more relevant, more applicable, to global problems than the local, particular ones. The intellectual believes that he is consistent with his ideological commitment when he transfers his interest and activity to the general condition of the planet and helps direct the destiny of mankind from which that of his own class or nation will also ultimately depend.

However, there is nothing surprising in the fact that the intellectual is accompanied in this planetary excursion by the social engineer. Precisely because the sphere of international life has been only so sketchily charted, the latter finds an even greater challenge, and in a sense, less obstruction to his work. True, the international land-scape is dotted with jealous sovereignties that present exasperating hurdles to general designs; but where the ideologue is not allowed to pass, the technician may be a welcome advisor since his action is considered by definition neutral, and subject to verification and control.

In fact, many important *technical* problems must be solved before any *intellectual* network may be spread over the earth. It would be impossible to distinguish clearly where the work of the social engineer ends and that of the intellectual begins, since any advance in this terra incognita provokes side problems of all sorts. For example, the exploitation of oil among a primitive population must take into account a series of factors, ranging from anthropological and linguistic ones to those posed by the resettlement or the stabilization of nomadic tribes.

Thus the laying of the foundations for an international community—or as I prefer more prudently to call it, for a *planetary coexistence*—involves experiences from the national past of the participants *and* entirely new experiences, which have never before appeared in the lives of men. The question will be, in this chapter and the next: what is the possibility that the rules securing a planetary coexistence will favor the techniques of social engineering over the ideologies and other specific activities of intellectuals?

Let us first turn our attention to the largely technical and sociological preconditions of planetary coexistence. Several factors facilitate, indeed, render inevitable, the emergence of a world-wide mentality.

(1) The increasingly planet-wide *communication system* has a multiplicity of aspects and effects. News coverage by radio, television, newsreels, and newspapers not only delivers an instantaneous impression, but even the format and "packaging" of these impressions tend to be uniform. The costs involved in maintaining such networks are such that by necessity only a small number of agencies may fulfill the task, and these agencies learn from each other the most efficient methods or they must disappear from the competition. These methods, on account of the speed of reporting and news carrying, teach that *compression* is an

indispensable way of presenting news, with the result that the public receives stereotyped images, comments, and conclusions, always couched in the same vocabulary.•

Also to the field of communication belongs the extraordinary flourishing of international trips, visits, tourism, student exchange, cultural exchange—no longer restricted to the economically privileged sections of the population, but increasingly to all classes. Or, at the other pole of the use of rapid communication and traveling, military assistance may now be dispatched with the speed of the decision itself. Not to mention the combat readiness of bomber planes, it is enough to compare the speed of naval intervention of the Russian fleet in the war against Japan in 1905 and that of the United States Sixth Fleet in Lebanon, in the summer of 1958.

(2) In a different order of things, but one not without some rapport with the spread and speed of communications, we witness the rise of a general awareness that conditions and environments can be changed by human means. Different regions of the earth formerly believed to be unchangeable and in a sense sacred are shedding their particularistic ways and adopting—largely through the imitation of other areas—new methods, aims, outlooks, and norms. Industrialization, to mention only one example, must follow the same pattern in Outer Mongolia and Central Africa, partly because of the inherent pattern of industry as a structure of dealing with materials and men, partly because they imitate a small number of focal areas that supply them with technicians and information.

One may, of course, argue that after a while these regions will have assimilated even their industries and adapted them to the national, racial, or civilizational modes of thinking and acting. And it may be true that a factory or a network of super highways will be differently conceived and managed in a Mediterranean country than in

• Michael Clark, one-time correspondent of *The New York Times* in North Africa, writes that one of the most experienced American reporters suggested to his younger colleagues to write only about what the public "back home" is interested in hearing and with the bias that is theirs: in that particular territory these items were: the scandals involving U.S. air bases and the bad treatment of their colonial population by the French.

and around Birmingham or Detroit; the working rhythm of the employees, their work mentality, the place work occupies in their life and the way it influences it, may all vary from one place, climate, and tradition to the other. But the factors favoring similarity seem to be more decisive; in the Soviet orbit ideology and party discipline impose the same pattern of industrialization from Prague to Peking. The iron conformism of Party-management goes to ridiculous exaggerations in its imitation of Russian experience, regardless of local conditions and even at the expense of efficiency.• In the Western world the United States serves as a model, not so much in what it produces, but in its organization of production, the public relations policy of its industries, the methods of industrial research and development firms. And in spite of ideological and other differences, Soviet leaders make no secret of their admiration for the American methods they seek to transplant to their country, as they have done ever since the twenties, with the help of American and German engineers.

(3) A third factor is the increasing similarity of conditions and of psychology in modern mass societies. This does not mean that a certain social differentiation is not taking place under our eyes; new sets of leaders are emerging who try, even more desperately than in the past, to differentiate themselves from the masses either in certain conspicuous ways or by the secret knowledge that they are the ones who pull the wires that set their fellow men into motion.

Yet, even these leaders—and they are difficult to locate in modern society—are tied to the communities in which they occupy important posts by the innumerable controls to which they are subject and by the satisfactions they must provide lest, if not the masses of men, other individuals and groups evince them. Since they have no status to protect them and surround them with an aura of respectability even after their fall from office, the power struggle that locks them with other contestants may be extremely

• A ball-bearing plant started in Hungary in the early 1950's had to be built at the same distance from Budapest as its model was built from Moscow. This was carried out in spite of the fact that the spot happened to be a sandy area, unsuitable for the precision work required.

sharp. But this has relatively little effect on the people at large, who are protected by institutional safeguards against any serious jolts.

Below the level of this very elastic and very mobile leadership, the modern mass society counts mainly by the weight of its number. Money-economy, capitalist methods and mentality, an uprooted proletariat, easier communication, etc., created, in the course of the nineteenth century, a social amalgam of statusless individuals fending for themselves and atomized, yet, for this very reason, increasingly dependent on mass organizations representing them. The statusless individual, although he was encouraged by the democratic-liberal slogans about equality, equal opportunities, and the equal worth of each human being, discovered very soon that individual effort, even ruthlessness, was the best way to fight for a place under the sun. Most people, however, are unable to furnish this effort and generally refuse, or are frightened by, the risks involved. As Henri de Man wrote, "freedom counts above all for a minority privileged by a long, hereditary security; the popular masses, driven by the fear of unemployment, bankruptcy, and misery, seek the political and economic protection of the State." • Nobody wants real competition today, asserts also a student of American business corporations; "fundamentally," writes Adolf A. Berle, "they all want, not a perpetual struggle, but a steady job—the job of producing goods at a roughly predictable cost, under roughly predictable conditions, so that goods can be sold in the market at a roughly predictable price." [1]

The consequence is that everybody prefers to band together in pressure groups, not so much for securing a privileged treatment, but for insuring themselves that progress and benefits will not bypass them. These individuals, whether workers, businessmen, white collar people, or employees of any sort, hardly differ from one group to another, and the groups themselves, whether corporations,

• *Au delà du Nationalisme,* p. 85.

The relationship between the need for security and the much lesser need for freedom is the topic of Hilaire Belloc's *The Servile State,* written in 1912. "Though all nowadays contrast slavery with freedom to the advantage of the latter, yet men then accepted slavery freely as an alternative to indigence." (Henry Holt, 1946), p. 35.

unions, or other interest groups, display very similar structures also. The only difference is that which follows from the nature of the democratic society: these groups do not advance simultaneously, but, due to retarding maneuvers, to sudden pressures and emergencies, or to the rhythm of the legislative procedure, they enter the main avenues of progress one by one, at a predictable speed and following an almost pre-established pattern.

But there is more than just the elementary desire to protect one's economic interests. The modern faceless individual, blending into the crowd with his fellows, needs a mode of self-identification far more than in prerevolutionary times when man was defined by the place of his birth and condition assigned to him. Increasing equality, itself the cause and effect of universal education, universal draft system, and similar living and working conditions in urban centers and in suburbia, provide few means by which the individual may distinguish himself socially, while he lives, politically and intellectually, in a world that speaks to him of his rights, his individuality, his uniqueness. The result is that he clings desperately to signs of self-differentiation, on the one hand, and, on the other, to associations that require his loyalty more meaningfully than the impersonal State and an abstract mankind.

At the peak of the bourgeois era, *individual competence* served as a means of differentiation and distinction. Setting the industrial and democratic apparatuses into motion, not to speak of other growing mechanisms of the time, was a task worthy of pioneers and often of titans. Explorers, industrial barons, barricade fighters, even the bureaucrats of the modern State, could feel the strain in their physical and mental muscles, in their tasks of organization, reform, or production-increase. In many respects the nineteenth century resembled the Renaissance: it had its maecenases, its *condottieri*, its adventurers, its risks, its style.

At the decline of the bourgeois era, when, as Gunnar Myrdal wrote, "the fighters of the earlier age have obtained all they had set out to win," crushed by industrial empires, powerful unions, mass parties, ideological uniformity, mass production and mass affluence, the individual has more difficulty distinguishing himself from the mass, and the mass has fewer and less articulate examples in which to

230

observe and admire excellence. Society, its agencies and organizations, have, in fact, real hardship in devising ever faster new methods by which the indispensable social process of *identification* may be secured, while, ever faster also, democratization and uniformization render these methods obsolete. For example, an academic degree is hardly identified as a symbol of achievement, when its obtention is facilitated for such a number of people that its distinction-value disappears.•

We witness, in these years, the *personality factor* as a new means of social detection. The identification of individuals, a criterion of categorization as well as a new measuring rod of excellence, is processed by such means as questionnaires and tests, which try to find out, with the crude and simplified instruments of a popularized "psychology," what meaningful correlation may be established between individuals, groups, functions, and social requirements. This very method reveals that we live in a classless society dissatisfied with its own lack of differentiation but unable to fight it because it is ideologically committed to it. On the other hand, however, the classless society in which traditional ties—religious, paternalistic, and moral—snap under an impossible strain, stimulates the creation of new myths, of a secular code of behavior, and of techniques of social adjustment. Uniformity of conduct is thus secured together with ideological consensus; the danger of ideological deviation and unorthodox behavior is thus drowned in the sea of psychological manipulation by publicity and propaganda, the condition of an orderly circulation through the avenues of the classless society. Thus the democratic mass structure of modern Western societies is, for more than one reason, a powerful factor in elaborating a global pattern of organization. Domestic

•Quite recently, letters of recommendation by faculty members have appeared as requirements almost more important than grades and diplomas. The latter have become so easy and automatic to obtain that without a good set of solid recommendation their value is questioned. But now we witness the beginning of a trend to write one standard letter, which the departmental office then retypes as often as is necessary. In other words, letters of recommendation, too, are becoming easy to obtain, and the day may be near when some other form of believable guarantee will have to be supplied.

stability releases a considerable interest and energy for external action which, for reasons discussed above, pours into the channels feeding the network of international coexistence and planning. Also, domestic order successfully established in "pilot societies" is imitated in more backward ones where, as in ex-colonial nations, the institutional foundations for it had been implanted generations earlier.

In spite of what has been said in the above-outlined three points, it would be naïve to expect all present factors to work for international peace, even for international co-operation. I have deliberately chosen the more neutral term, "coexistence," taking into consideration the fact that underneath the trends discussed, or parallel to them, there is the will of nations to secure advantages for themselves, to spread their own beliefs and methods, and to go to war for their interests if necessary. The term "planetary coexistence" does not exclude any of these choices and actions.

In this and the next chapter I want merely to outline a new sphere of activity and accompanying mental attitude in which social engineering finds a tremendously important outlet for its bent for organization and uniformization. There is more than a remote analogy between, on the one hand, the inner disunity and conflicts of Western societies, the resulting ideological strifes and the triumph of the social engineers, and, on the other hand, the fierce competition and wars of the "planetary society," its ideological conflicts and the increasing authority of technical solutions. Influential individuals and groups are pressing for global economic co-operation, global taxes to support the backward territories, a global army and a world government, even for a world-wide moral consciousness. Whatever the future prospects of these recommendations, there is no doubt that they are important elements in our century; there is even less doubt that the tactics, the methods, the announced aims, fall under the category of social engineering as we have defined it.

There seem to be two main issues the solution of which is credited with influencing in a decisive way the emergence of a world-wide *feeling* of unity and community of *interests*. The more immediate issue, to many observers, appears to be the reconciliation of the United States and the Soviet Union towards a larger synthesis of efforts directed to the global improvement of mankind. The second issue, more remote but more fundamental, is the total reconciliation of economic and social interests within each national community, the introduction of complete economic democracy and democratic way of life.

In the first issue several arguments are involved. One is the very spectacular but, I think, least important one of nuclear threat, which is said to endanger the future of mankind. Those who brandish the issue use it as a campaign slogan in domestic and international politics; those who listen to them lack the political sophistication to know that any issue would fulfill the same purpose, that is, of indicating the sharpness of the American-Soviet conflict of interests.

A second argument is aimed at the desirability of general disarmament for the economic benefit of mankind. The sixty to seventy billion dollars spent yearly on the armament race by the two super powers only, is twice the amount that according to the economists, would be necessary annually to aid substantially the underdeveloped areas of the world. The partisans of disarmament forget, of course, that even if such sums were liberated, there is no indication that they would be redirected to help the needy areas. In fact, American-Soviet rivalry, armed and otherwise, may turn out to be more beneficial for the economically backward nations, for whose friendship each competes, than a peaceful world in which the natural selfishness of nations might favor a greater degree of economic isolation.

The third argument is more realistic than the first two. It has to do with the increasing similarity that industrialization and its accompanying phenomena impose on both societies, American and Soviet. The first has, naturally, a great advance over the second; but as the Harvard economist W. W. Rostow indicated in a series of articles in *The Economist*,[2] the fact is that over the past century the economic development of Russia has been "remarkably similar to that of the United States, with a lag of about thirty-five years in the level of industrial output, and of about fifty-five years in industrial output per head." The French economist Fr. Perroux has reached the same conclusion by observing, as we have mentioned in Chapter Three, the increasingly clear outcome of the battle waged in the Soviet Union between the Party and the managerial class. As a consequence, the two Empires (Perroux includes under each the less important powers grouped around the two nuclei) are becoming similar insofar as the United States has adopted many measures of economic planification, while planning in the Soviet Union is subject to important practical modifications resulting from managerial resistance. This is natural in view of the fact that both systems "must maintain themselves on the technical and economic level reached by the other; hence, there are numerous ways, open or hidden, official or semi-official, which permit the exchange of economic innovations." ³

The second condition of planetary coexistence is the previous and underlying stability within the individual nations, at least the most important ones among them.•

It is a well-known statement of Thorstein Veblen that all relationships in modern society tend to conform to the pattern of business relationships. "The mechanical concatenation of industrial processes makes for solidarity in the administration of any group of related industries, and more remotely, it makes for solidarity in the management of the entire industrial traffic of the community." ⁴ This is the conclusion of Peter Drucker too, who points out that big business has become, in the last thirty years, a social institution, and that management plays today a central social function through its multiple preoccupation with the employees' various interests.

Beyond the sphere of even the largest corporation there is the State with its welfare policy and bureaucratic management. Max Weber saw this as the natural consequence of modern historical evolution: in his judgment, after the expropriation of the feudal estates and the "nationalization" of arms and armies, the State had to "socialize" inevitably economic life also. In the words of Karl Mannheim, "the Western democracies . . . are transforming the

• This idea was already emphasized by Condorcet and by those who followed him: the two conditions of progress were the development of equality among individuals within one nation and the destruction of inequality among these nations themselves.

liberal conception of government into a social one. This is chiefly because the State no longer confines its attention to the three spheres of legislation, administration and jurisdiction, but is changing into a social service State." [5]

Under State Sponsorship and modern fiscal policy, the working classes have improved immeasurably their economic and social status. The skilled workers, foremen and work supervisors, the manager and the union official have joined the middle class and have helped the promotion of the masses of workers underneath them, knowing well that their own prosperity depended on the continued advance of the productive forces. The advance of the productive forces, however, meant not only the consolidation of gains for the workers and the guarantee of continued profit for capital; it also meant concessions on both sides, which may be summed up in one sentence: the workers accepted democratic capitalism and capitalism came to terms with the welfare state. If it had followed Marx and Lenin, the working class could have turned into a revolutionary movement, not contented until bourgeois society has been swept away. (Precisely because this did not happen, Lenin, in his pamphlet *What is to be done?* [1902], urged the Communist Party to become the driving force in the name of the proletariat.) Instead, the worker found satisfaction in a "fairly regular progress and showed himself willing to fight for what he wanted within the rules of political democracy. He chose to identify himself with his national society rather than with the abstract world of allegedly down-trodden industrial workers everywhere." [6]

Capitalist ownership, in its turn, also made considerable concessions. They may be measured not only by the general well-being of workers in Western societies, but also by the structural changes that have affected, in the last decade, industrial production. More and more, the workers are associated with the enterprise, so that they may envisage today, in the words of André Philip, "not the mere increase of their nominal wages, but a right of intervention in the policy of price-fixing, investments, and, generally, in the real decisions concerning economic and social life." [7]

Now this outstanding success in the elimination of class antagonism has a considerable impact on the unsolved problems of international coexistence as well. Let us sum up the reasoning involved.

Those who think of the planet as the dwelling place

of the "family of man," are struck by the potential historical similarity of individual societies and mankind. They have analyzed the history of class conflicts and have concluded that the present relative social peace has been accomplished mainly by the gradual concessions of the upper classes: nobility, monarchy, capitalists, etc.

Now the present international conflicts are not sharper and more irremediable than the class conflicts of the past; in fact, the argument runs, the main causes behind both have largely been of an economic nature: from a planetary point of view the "upper classes," the "rich," are those nations that have accumulated wealth (productive capacity, capital goods, colonies, easy access to raw materials and a dominating voice in fixing their prices), while the poor and underprivileged are the have-not peoples that until now have been in a colonial or semicolonial status, nonindustrial, raw-material producing (often of only one product, thus more vulnerable to price fluctuations), and nonexistent as conscious, national entities.

It is in the interest of both sides to come to terms: the former group can only maintain its level of prosperity and its rate of progress if it contributes to the betterment of the latter; otherwise violence will be sooner or later unavoidable, in the form of a general uprising of the backward against the advanced. On the other hand, the powerful productive system of the wealthy nations would not be able to continue, much less to expand, if it did not find a market of immense proportions in the now underdeveloped areas. A peaceful settlement, the more near equalization of conditions all over the globe, is thus the first imperative of this century.

The argument thus outlined is, at present, adopted by a number of influential statesmen and economists. It is also the conclusion of a recent debate between Pierre Mendès-France, Aneurin Bevan, and Pietro Nenni; • it enjoys the

• "The political transformation we witness is similar to the one which took place inside the modern countries in the nineteenth century and which is known as class struggle. . . . The same situation appears now on an international plane where a kind of class struggle has started. . . . It is impossible that, in the long run, there might coexist certain islands of prosperity and a mass whose situation would become increasingly backward, miserable and on the brink of starvation." *Rencontres—Nenni, Bevan, Mendès-France* (Julliard, 1959), pp. 163-4.

236

support of important newspapers like *The Manchester Guardian* and *Le Monde*. The already-quoted Rostow articles, to which *The Economist* gave prominence, provide it with further justification within what the author calls the "theory of growth": the conflicts of the last one hundred years or so, Rostow argues, originated in the fact that various countries reached the successive stages of economic development at different times. When all will be on the same step of the ladder, a more harmonious relationship will ensue; at that point "the arena of power is likely to become truly global for the first time; and within it, power will be progressively diffused. The image of a bi-polar world, already inaccurate, will become more and more inaccurate. The image of Eurasian hegemony, fearful and enticing, will lose its reality, and world domination will become an increasingly unrealistic objective. This is the setting in which the problem of peace will present itself." •

As many other economic theories, Rostow's too wears the blinders of specialism: it does not explain, for example, why do only certain nations and not others display a tremendous ideological force at given phases of economic development. Thus it is insufficient to explain conflicts by the discrepancy of growth alone, and, consequently, the peace and harmony that Rostow foresees may not be achieved by the equalization of economic conditions—a typically American feature in Rostow's thinking.

Let us, however, examine the arguments of some others concerning the rise in economic level and living standard of underdeveloped nations, a rise of which so much is

---

• Rostow, loc. cit.

A similar conviction underlies the writings of Tibor Mende, a Hungarian economist now living in France. He believes that every great power chooses, at the initial stages of its industrialization, one of two roads: either imperialistic self-affirmation, or general comfort for its masses of consumers. But they all end up, according to Mende, with the second choice; Russia is in that period now, and China will be there twenty-five years hence, "provided mankind will push it towards the way of peace" ("Dix ans de communisme en Chine," *Le Monde*, weekly edition, 29 Oct.–4 Nov., 1959). Mende seems to neglect the ideological aspect of Russia's and China's "period of growth," their aggressive expansionism, and Marxist-Leninist approach to world politics.

expected: the elimination of wars, the establishment of world government, and the unity of mankind.

Although it is unlikely that power will ever be equally diffused over the surface of the earth, it seems that evolution points in the direction of a new pattern of power-concentration: the commonwealth pattern. Several factors favor this development.

One is, of course, the tie—institutions, language, culture, economic interests, technical assistance—that still links the ex-colonial territories to the ex-colonizing nations. No matter how violent the break between them may be, it will be found, when the aroused passions calm down in both camps, that both profit by their association. The newly emerging nations must push industrialization if they are not to sink back to a new colonial status, veiled by slogans. They are generally raw-material producing territories, and as Pierre Moussa analyzed it in *Les Nations prolétaires*, [8] such countries must live by a precarious budget since the world market prices depend on the law of supply and demand.• In such a situation the industrially developed nation to which they are economically attached may fill in the gap and subsidize the current or projected works of modernization.

Secondly, it is also evident that the general conditions in most of these new nations are not such that they would encourage individual investment. The individual investor may not mind taking certain risks, especially if he finds compensation in lower wages, hence in lower production costs, but modern industrial plants need more than just their own equipment: they need a good transportation system, roads, electric power supply, adequate housing for their employees, etc. In underdeveloped areas these preconditions for industrialization must be created first; it is natural that, rather than foreign investors and

• An example: a few years ago when a lag developed in American car production, the Bolivian tin mines were forced to shut down. International agreements to consolidate world prices of raw materials are usually opposed by American businessmen, who insist on applying in their purchases the law of supply and demand. In the few cases when such agreements could be reached, they were torpedoed by the Russians whose main concern is to maintain the proletarian nations in a revolutionary frame of mind.

foreign powers, those will have an immediate advantage who are more familiar with the situation, that is, the ex-mother country.

Thirdly, whether it is accomplished with the help of the ex-colonial power or with that of another industrially developed nation, the modernization of the backward areas must be conducted on such a large scale that State investment will be favored over private investment. And this State aid will not be directed to individual entre-preneurs in the recipient nation—where there are few such entrepreneurs—but to the respective governments. Thus over-all negotiations can be conducted, saving much dispersion of efforts, and planning may be applied which is favored not only by the nature of the tasks, but also by the usually socialist background of the new nations' leaders.

Even on the basis of these probable lines of evolution it would for the moment be hazardous to predict how many commonwealths or international communities will emerge during the next decades. Four such systems seem to exist today, with a large, more or less uncommitted sector: the British Commonwealth, the French *Commun-auté*, the Soviet orbit (with China), and the United States (with Latin America). All four are, however, in a state of transformation, with nations leaving or joining them, while the sponsoring powers try to extend their sphere of economic and political influence.

Instead of analyzing the particular patterns emerging within these four power-concentrations, it is sufficient for our purpose to look at the two larger patterns that are developing on the two sides of the Iron Curtain, the Western and the Soviet system, or as Fr. Perroux calls them, the American and Soviet Empires.

It is undeniable that one important form of contest between these systems is to carve out from the uncom-mitted and underdeveloped lands as much as possible for their respective spheres of power and influence. The efforts of each, however, are determined by one end-product: raising the standard of living of the populations and integrating them into the current of international co-existence. Thus, if we disregard, for the moment, the respective ideological driving power, the two "empires" differ more in the means they employ than in the end they pursue. In fact, many statesmen, international journalists, and economists are convinced that ideology in this instance is only a *phase,* necessary to supply the energy with which primitive populations must be whipped into activity; the end is inevitable industrialization and modernization.

From the point of view of sheer economic development the suffering of millions is a passing contingency. In one way or another, constraint and political imposition are used even in those countries that actual Communist power has not reached, but whose leaders believe that the cohesion vital for effective nationhood may only be obtained through the strong methods inspired by Marxism. In Africa's new States the centrifugal force of the tribal structure must be overcome and the sparse population assembled for various works to be carried out; in Asia the innumerable millions present a still greater imperative to be harnessed for productive enterprises; and South America also seems to discard its liberal governments in favor of mass movements and socialistic methods.

Thus whether under American or Soviet sponsorship, or in the few examples of mixed systems (socialistic *and* private enterprise) like in India or Israel, similar tasks encourage the use of similar ways. Even if in the end there will be no combined world investment into backward areas, a world government, if not in name then in its interests and activities, is the likely outcome.

This does not mean that great and aggressive ideologies, or their residual movements, will not divide the globe among themselves; it only means that they will not differ in their essential aspects. If one or another country chooses a particular method and a particular ideology, the choice might be dictated not by clear-cut differences, but by factors such as past experience with imperialism, degree of development, success or failure in coming to terms with the erstwhile mother country.

It is then the methodological, technical aspect that is likeliest to bring about the rapprochement of nations and blocks. The same techniques used in industries and armies,• the same methods adopted by the institutional

• "The cost of combat material has now increased so greatly that a country of forty millions can no longer afford to pay for

and educational structures, the same solutions devised for urban settlements and the leisure time of working millions, point in the direction of a world-wide approach to basic problems, even if on another plane ideologies still retain a divisive influence. This tendency toward homogeneity is the most significant phenomenon of the age on the threshold of which we find ourselves at present.

---

a complete panoply. Fifty years ago the armed forces of a small country reproduced on a microscopic scale those of a large country. . . . Today, nothing of the sort is possible. . . . A coalition now results in the integration, not the juxtaposition of national armies." Raymond Aron, *The Century of Total War,* p. 301.

8

Planetary Ideology

In his *Considérations sur la France*, Joseph de Maistre wrote this: "It seems to me that every true philosopher must choose between two hypotheses: either that a new religion will come to birth, or that Christianity will renew its youth in some extraordinary manner."

We have seen that at least from the Renaissance on this has been the main preoccupation of the intellectuals and also that this ideological but somewhat abstract, concern —a religion or a substitute religion, myth, force of cohesion—turned into an urgent problem in the first decades of the nineteenth century, when it became apparent that industrialization would at once sharpen hitherto existing antagonisms and spread the material preconditions of these antagonisms over large surfaces of the globe. A unified world view, adapted to the anticipated and desired homogeneity of the material infrastructure, was seen now as an absolute necessity, both as an organizational principle and an inspiration for new effort. Saint-Simon, author, among other books, of *Le Nouveau Christianisme*, expressed this thought with his accustomed clarity: "People have thought that the whole religious system would disappear because they have succeeded in showing the decadence of the Catholic system. They are mistaken: religion cannot disappear from the face of the earth; it can only be transformed." [1]

This religious character of the coming world system, naturally a religion without faith in a transcendental, personal God,• was seen by the most clearsighted observers of the age: Tocqueville understood that the popular revolutions that were wrecking the existing order were "not only a question of the triumph of a party; the aim was to establish a social science, a philosophy, I might almost say, a religion, fit to be learned and followed by all mankind." [2] Lacordaire, having attended a lecture given by one of Saint-Simon's disciples, declared that "it was, perhaps, not merely a philosophical system [that he heard expounded] . . . but one that could contain the destinies of mankind."

This religion, or philosophy, or social science, by whatever name the contemporaries of Saint-Simon called it, was to retain some of the paraphernalia of the Christian religion, it even expressed itself in Christian terms, but was to order its dogmas so as to serve this-worldly, secular ends and, ultimately, the organization of industrial work-discipline. Dogmatism was required by Auguste Comte as "the normal state of human intelligence"; as all dogmas, the newly elaborated ones were also to be interpreted by "competent authority." •• The latter's power, however, was not based on belief and divine ordinance, but on progress and

• "Like the Saint-Simonians, Renan wished that the highest spiritual preoccupations should be integrated with life, that artists, men of knowledge and faith should be the guides . . . should create enthusiasm and inspire virtue. Renan and the Saint-Simonians wanted things to be permeated with poetry, and that these things, analyzed and understood, should bring about a philosophy which is truly religious because it is human. As they conceive Him, God is only the new name for society or for reason on their way to perfection, that is, the sum of knowledge, art, and morality, elevated to their highest expression." Maxime Leroy, *Histoire des idées sociales en France*, II, 353.

•• Comte expected a resurgence of morality through the creation of an elite living from the work of others. It is not the institution of property which maintains the workers in an immoral dependence, but the absence of a religious link between them and the employers. Comte meant the religion of positivism.

on work for the general interest of the people. "Blessed be the yoke," wrote Enfantin, Saint-Simon's elected successor, "imposed by the conviction which satisfies all sentiments; blessed be the power which drives men on to progress."

In spite of this pagan turn of the religious spirit, De Maistre was not alone in imagining that the Christian religion, too, may "renew itself." About a hundred years after Saint-Simon, *religious socialism* came to join as a full-fledged doctrine the *socialist religion*. The ideal of Martin Buber, of Paul Tillich, was to introduce religion in the workaday world in order to sanctify the latter. The question was, however, whether, by that time socialism was not a more vigorous, attention-commanding ideal than religion. The religious socialists thought they might circumvent this danger by purifying religion, which would then become a more exalted *terrain d'entente*: "dogma and ritual," wrote Buber, "are secondary to real reciprocal relation with the mystery of God and to the reciprocal relation with the mystery of man." But relationship with the mystery of God is an individual affair (as Tillich emphasizes it in his theology), and the "relationship with men" is less often and less importantly stamped with the recognition of human solidarity than it is organized by "dogma and ritual." In other words, if religion retreats into the unorganizable sphere where the religious socialists try to quarantine it—the sphere of the dialogue between God and the individual—or when it is reduced to a stark affirmation of "human fellowship," then a substitute religion will step in to organize human rapports, but to organize them in the name of some secular dogma.

But it is a mistake to imagine that secular dogma can only be one or another of the presently so aggressive ideologies: communism, socialism, fascism, progressivism. If there is any truth in our description of social engineering, then it is clear that it, too, is perfectly capable of secreting an ideology, unidentifiable by means of known and now popular political concepts, yet fulfilling the conditions of a system of belief. The modern world, as we have argued, is gradually de-politicized; and effective, ideologically neutral organization and technique take over the role of political ideas. Again Saint-Simon, who predicted this turning of politics into an exact science, can be quoted:

244

"Politics no longer works in the midst of vague conjectures: it is no longer exposed to the caprice of circumstances; its fate is no longer attached to a regime or a ruler: its domain is known, its methods are understood; from now on the science of societies has a principle, and it becomes finally a positive science." [3]

Let us add, lest a serious misconception arises, that the "political principle" will remain intact as long as men confront men, in any way, on this earth.• But Saint-Simon was right in assuming that scientific knowledge would absorb a considerable sector of what had been before the domain of political regimes and of the ideas that inspired them.

Returning to our discussion, we should realize that social engineering, seeking to stabilize and equalize conditions, to co-ordinate interests at various junctures, to adjust people to their work, their abilities and leisure opportunities, conforms to the basic aspirations expressed by the ideologies. What the latter were unable to achieve, for lack of material preconditions and adequate organization, social engineering, corresponding to a higher level of productivity and more efficient communications, attempts to accomplish.

This is done on two levels to which social engineering claims to reduce the problem of the individual and society in the contemporary world: the levels of *work* and *leisure*. These two, as intellectual problems demanding a continuous solution, correspond to the two most important phenomena with which social engineering ultimately deals: the problem of *production* (hence: standard of living, distribution, consumption, hygiene) and of *free time* (hence: selective consumption, mental hygiene, distribution of information and knowledge, education, culture).

It is obvious that the two axes of this system of coordinates cannot be separately envisaged today: the problems within the spheres of production and of free time have numerous points in common, actually they often coincide. The consequence is that we may speak of a *continuum* of work and leisure, since the avowed goal of social engineering is to integrate the two aspects of human activity, that is, to render work culturally (intellectually) significant and rewarding, and to render leisure worklike,

• See Chapter Eleven.

purposeful, "educational," and finally, an ancilla of universal understanding and peace.

Let us examine then the three aspects of the emerging planetary ideology, the problems of *depolitization*, of *work*, and of *leisure*.

(1) The increasingly uniform features of societies in various parts of the world, discussed in the previous chapter, provide, of course, many of the common beliefs, impressions, and opinions; also, much of the external behavior, style, appearance, that serves as a precondition to the formation of planetary thought-patterns. In the chapter on the social engineer we showed that in important sectors of life, human relations become mechanized by the interposition of crudely fabricated formulas, which guarantee a degree of social peace but destroy the immediacy of human rapports: in such enormous mass organizations as business corporations, political parties, labor unions, and schools, and by the extension of the methods practiced therein, also in family life and small groups, a certain mechanization prevails by which the individual is increasingly isolated, discouraged in his natural, spontaneous reactions, and forced into using channels of communication that are artificial, impersonal, and remote. The speedy and efficient manipulation of these channels creates the impression that more attention than ever is paid to the individual: his needs, his interests, his opinions; but in fact those who have access to these channels generally take a calculated guess concerning the average reaction and must neglect the extent to which the individual recognizes in the compound result his own thinking, his own aspirations, his own personality. Yet, he is bound to accept the average reaction as the legitimate expression of his fellow men, for he has no means of proving the contrary.

The individual is thus left to himself, with the alternative of either becoming his own guide in the maze of modern life, or of submitting to the orientation by the new landmarks of social existence. Most of the traditional, clearly visible landmarks have been chopped off; the new ones have not yet grown to full size and are, anyway, covered with the posters of democracy, equality and freedom. But, as Professor Ferrater-Mora, speaking of Caesarian Roman society, remarked, "leveling is not always equivalent to equality and still less to fraternity; men do not become brothers merely by becoming equal; what happens is that the center of power becomes progressively less localizable and hence less responsible." [4]

Since there is very little by which the members of the new society may distinguish each other, since they tend toward uniformity, or at least, interchangeability, in dress, manners, and speech, since their names tell increasingly less of the former deeds and reputation of a family, a clan, or a class, they become recognizable and identifiable by a series of new social tags and tools, such as questionnaires and *curricula vitae*. In theory, nothing prevents this procedure from being effective; but it is obvious that by certain of its features it may easily become technical: the questions are mass-produced, the answers, after some practice, tend to become stereotyped. As cards and forms are increasingly processed by machines or by machinelike and indifferent bureaucrats, it is in the interest of candidates, interviewees, job-solicitors, army recruits, to produce the expected reaction since nobody will take the time to pay special attention to the deep, the different, the complex, the genuinely human. Thus a further screen is lowered between one human being and the organization, one man and the next.•

Under these conditions can we speak of a planetary mentality, of a planetary ideology? There is no contradiction here; the individual has been cut off from the roots he had in small units—the family, the small town, the local tradition, the friends of youthful years. The groups and associations to which he may attach himself are far removed from his immediate understanding and loyalty, but they do command his interests at a level the significance of which he cannot grasp well. Political parties, workmen's unions, bureaucratic groups, etc., are such new power-concentrations, veritable feudalities that are able to protect the individual from the impact of the

• In the preindustrial past the individual was paid even less attention by the organizations recruiting him. But his inner life and reactions were not scrutinized, were not forcbly integrated with his tasks and activities. Modern organizations demand, however, not only loyalty but conformity as well. They restrict the area of inner life.

terrific forces operating in modern society but are unable to do more for him, to be his home, to treat him as an individual. Indeed, they themselves derive their power from the *number* of people they protect, and they must count in units instead of in human beings.

These power groups, however, are not significantly different from each other. Their organizational principle is similar, they imitate each other's methods, and use hardly different slogans. As it was hard to tell one feudal fortress and its armored lord from another fortress and another lord, it is equally hard to distinguish the headquarters of General Motors from that of the AFL-CIO, and Mr. Charles Wilson from Mr. George Meany.•

The same thing may be said of the modern political party. Ignazio Silone has called attention to the phenomenon that parties that used to be centers of political opinion now discard their ideological coloration and become shelters for masses of people: artisans and businessmen, workers and intellectuals, who need protection vis-à-vis the State or, on the contrary, wish to have access to benefits and positions that only the State can dispense. This is true today not only of the American parties which openly grant their protection, patronage, and remuneration to a wide variety of people, but increasingly also of parties in western and central Europe. There, for lack or scarcity of those private associations for limited purposes which abound in the United States, the political party provides even more than a protective cushion in an increasingly government-run existence: youth groups, sport clubs, women's organizations, etc.

In proportion as the traditional parties neglect their ideological origin and are depoliticized, the hard core, the bureaucratic party apparatus (machine) takes over the manipulation of the mass of adherents, using the same

• "Like other labor organizations, the I.L.G.W.U. was ruled by a hierarchy. Elections and conventions were a formality of merely ritual significance. The same officers were elected and reelected, usually without even token opposition. . . . The union was operated like a well-run business, and like many corporations it had its charities, both private and public. . . . Most of the union's activities were benevolent, though paternalistic." Ralph de Toledano, *Lament for a Generation* (Farrar, Straus & Cudahy, 1960), pp. 93-4.

techniques as the other giant organizations. All that the ordinary member does is to sell his vote, become the vassal of the party; he is then assured of certain compensations. Hence, it is less and less necessary to *persuade* him: it suffices to send him the directives of the party, as it is enough to regulate parliamentary life also by directives to the party's voting members. The latter cannot very well appeal to the mass of voters above the head of the party machine, for however attractive they may make themselves, they will not be elected unless the party approves. As Bertrand de Jouvenel remarks, the result is that "sovereignty passes from parliament to the victorious machine, and elections are no more than a plebiscite by which a whole people puts itself in the power of a small gang." • This is totalitarianism that promises security and destroys liberty, unites the spiritual and the temporal powers. Society is returning "to the form of cohesion which is that of the primitive tribe." Since in such instances Party and State have coalesced, the individual, insofar as he is not actually crushed, has only one authority to turn to for life, safety, and livelihood, for education, leisure, and source of information, and for protection against the accidents of existence.

(2) In spite of the similarities to which Professor Ferrater-Mora, for example, calls our attention between the decaying Roman Empire and our own time, there is at least one essential difference: the fantastically proliferating bureaucracy in fourth- and fifth-century Rome was a cause and symptom of material misery; today, at least where this bureaucracy is free of absolutistic State control and ideological pressure, its ubiquitousness and hidden power are compatible with prosperity and material progress. The reason may be that today, bureaucracy is not

• *On Power*, p. 275.

This is true, in a smoother, softer way of democratic regimes also where, as Walter Lippmann wrote, "the powers which were ceded by the executive [after World War I] passed through the representative assemblies . . . to the mass of voters who, though unable to exercise them, passed them on to the party bosses, the agents of pressure groups, and the magnates of the new media of mass communication." *The Public Philosophy*, p. 13.

the feature of State administration exclusively; other large formations have their own bureaucratic apparatuses, and between them and the State numerous frictions may exist. At any rate, modern mass organization, whether the State, corporations, parties, or syndicates, seems to promote, not hinder, the well-being on which society rests.

But organization itself is not sufficient. Earlier in the industrial era, up to and including the first decades of this century, it was believed that production was a relatively simple goal to attain, provided the hours of work were long enough, the workers' motions rationalized, and some physical preconditions observed. Only recently have other aspects of productivity been studied and found to be perhaps even more important: the moral and psychological condition of the worker, his ideological *encadrement*, his motivation, his relationship to the management and to the other workers.

This interest in *work* as a complex phenomenon is not new; it is the fruit of the two hundred years during which it was the central preoccupation of economists, industrialists, social reformers, etc., whose texts abound in urgent recommendations that all members of society should produce and none should remain a parasite. Adam Smith and Ricardo founded their theory of value on *work,* the Saint-Simonians saw in it the one sacred road to social emancipation and universal peace, and Marx regarded it as the action by which not only nature but the entire alienated human condition will be transformed. In his own witty fashion, G. B. Shaw wrote in one of the earliest Fabian tracts that "Socialism means nothing less than the compulsion of all members of the upper class, without regard to sex or condition, to work for their living." [5]

Josef Schumpeter has pointed out that worker discipline in the capitalist era was an inheritance from the age of feudalism; the worker, as his peasant ancestor, knew that only by hard work and obedience might he gain the approval and material compensation he needed for his security and sustenance. The age of democracy and syndicalism has put an end to this quasi-feudal relationship. The worker, a free citizen and voter, protected by the union and by the party, must be differently "motivated" if one expects him to produce and thereby to supply the material conditions to an abundant peace time consumption, or the policy of full employment, military preparedness, etc.

In the Soviet orbit this problem is solved, ultimately, by coercion; but to satisfy the myth of the workers' State, even there the Party officials and managers seek to provide an added stimulation by frenzied production campaigns, by "Stakhanovism" and "Gaganovism," • by a system of bonuses, and by abundant publicity, on posters and newspapers, for the "heroes of production" (while also publicly dishonoring the slack, the lazy, the latecomer, the absentee).

Where no such State-devised "incentives" exist, the problem is more complicated. No matter how many inventions are said to relieve the drudgery of work, the production methods make the worker bored and detached from the process as well as from the product. More than that, and against the claims made in the name of "intellectualized" work, he is equally indifferent to the social significance of production, whether this is done for the "building of socialism," "emancipation from the yoke of colonialism," or for the simple democratic reason of "prosperity for all." Simone Weil understood this when she wrote, after a year of hard physical work at the Renault plants: "It is not only necessary that the worker should know the meaning of what he does, but, if possible, that he should understand its use, and should be aware that he is transforming a part of nature. It would be good that for each worker his own work were also an object of contemplation."

There have been, in the Western world, various attempts to bring into a closer contact the worker and his work, to integrate his ambitions as a human being with the daily task of earning his bread. The solution has been sought at several levels: financial benefits, participation in management, co-gestion, a voice in price fixing (and the related issue of real wages), organization of work, shareholding, etc. One can say, generally, that in Anglo-Saxon countries some form of union intervention prevails, while in Latin countries, where the unions are more concerned

---

• Gaganova is the woman worker who, after fulfilling her own quota, helps others fulfill theirs. Thus she represents the idea of solidarity with the spirit of competition.

with over-all political aims than with industrial aims, there is practically no worker participation in management.•

In Soviet-sponsored regimes there is, of course, nominally, and in Yugoslavia actually, a degree of worker determination, although, by its natural limitations, this cannot influence such decisions—made by the State—as what happens to the product, how much of it is reinvested, how much is turned over for the upkeep of bureaucracy. But from the experience of free countries and free unions, the conclusion may be drawn that worker satisfaction does not depend on the ownership of the enterprise—which would bring with it responsibility where it cannot fully exist—but on such factors as better interpersonal rapports, work conditions, and informal consultation and briefing. What is thus attempted, as in the studies of Kurt Lewin and of Jacques Van Bockstaele, is to create cohesion (*esprit de corps*) in smaller groups by acquainting the members with the structure of the performance and its relationship to the task of each.

(3) In all these attempts and experiments there is a great deal of effort spent on persuading the worker that he is an individual on whose shoulders a considerable responsibility rests. One may discuss the extent of this responsibility, that is, the extent to which a man may be made actually to feel responsible for occurrences taking place in his proper sphere of action or outside. I do not think it is quite clear to most people dealing with this problem whether the feeling of interest, concern, and responsibility is coextensive with the present state of world-wide news communication. In other words, I contend that hearing and learning about distant events, even feeling their impact on our life, does not necessarily entail any serious intellectual penetration and emotional sympathy. In yet other words, in order to create a planetary ideology, the leaders of opinion and the idea-men must work out slo-

---

• Germany seems to have adopted an intermediate position. There is "Mitbestimmung" in the coal and steel industry. In most other industries worker-delegates limit themselves to the protection of employees in their places of work. Considerable attention is paid, in the large plants, that industrial profits should not go into financing political parties.

gans sufficiently inclusive and general to bridge the inevitable gap between the individual who experiences his increasing insignificance and absorption in the group and a wider community which is potentially mankind.

One thing then is clear: the improvement of the conditions of work, the incentives and rewards of production, the rise of workers to a solid middle-class status, while not sufficient to integrate people's mentality, have undeniably established a "society of producers" (the old Saint-Simonian dream). This, in turn, has created a physical, mental, and social climate in which all may be reached, persuaded, experimented upon. The same language, that of the mass media, adjusted for the special persuasion of this or that group, may be applied to convey information, express opinion, poll responses, and infuse basic ideas. A vaguely felt but general disappointment with religions and ideologies favors the spread of this language (and the mentality it inevitably represents), which speaks in the name of a secular code of morality and behavior. As it at least imitates the language of science, it conveys the tacit assumption that man's destiny is no longer problematic, that he holds it in the palm of his hand. While it is true, as said before, that man lacks the faculty of feeling responsible for distant occurrences, this language, these media of communication, create a substitute feeling, a mixture of sentimentalism, humanitarianism, and preformed, superficial information; many take it for the crude beginnings of a planetary mentality.•

The best single form under which these "larger ideas" may be approached is the new concept of *leisure*. Leisure is not the same as the rest period we traditionally associate with time spent away from work, the dissolution of physical fatigue. In the new notion several components must be distinguished.

As the nature and significance of *work* change, so do the nature and significance of leisure. We have stated above that work is still "boring," tiresome, exposed to all kinds

• B. de Jouvenel, no sentimentalist and no ideologue, speaks of the "new spirit of stewardship of the earth." "Now that we have reached the limits of the Earth, we understand: this is the land of promise, the land beyond Jordan, a land of milk and honey, to be enjoyed and cherished and tended." "A Place to Live In," *Modern Age,* Winter 1959-60.

of vexations; in fact, while Marx attacked only industrial work as deadening for the intellectual faculties and alienating the worker from his human qualities, today the workers in the administrative sectors and various services and service industries may make the same complaint. In other words, what is called intellectualized working conditions are not a serious improvement except, of course, physically; the "mental" world is no more open to a modern white-collar worker than it was a hundred years ago.

Yet, his *impression* is different, because he is integrated into a larger continuum, which he shares with other categories of people. The environment of his work has become very similar to the other environments he knows: the office, the airfield lobby, the bank, even the factory workshop, have been adjusted to the appearance of the home, the school, the church gathering, and the restaurant. Modern furniture with its wide possibilities of adaptability, the design and fabric of curtains and rugs, the ubiquitous radio and other sound devices, all are planned to create not so much a uniform as a continuous ambience in which the "worker" moves. In a sense, increasingly fewer objects and gadgets remind him that he goes from home to the office, to the train, to the meeting, to a lecture: he finds the same comfort, the same efficiency, the same smile on the almost uniformly dressed people he meets and with whom he conducts his business or engages in recreation.

Add to this picture another trait of similarity between work and leisure: the fact that both are integrated in the circuit of production and consumption. The material products must be bought and consumed in order to make place for new ones: as leisure time increases, industry invades the leisure market and applies the same iron law of appetite-stimulation and obsolescence, excitement for novelty through various sales techniques and packaging. To the extent that the place of work is socialized and made receptive to a nonwork atmosphere, the leisure industry discovers it as a market possibility just as it has discovered the home, the school, etc.

Naturally, the home also adopts features that are characteristic of the place of work. A recent Jacques Tati film ingeniously stressed the similarity between a push-button "modern home" and the push-button (automated) modern factory. In order to achieve the desired comical effect, the people in both were depicted as slaves of the machine, with their awkwardness in adjusting their human bodies and normal rhythms to those required by the mechanisms. But this is only the indignant social critic's view: today's industrial worker no longer faces the seriocomical horrors of the early Chaplin movies; and Jacques Tati's serio-comical husband and wife seem to enjoy their mechani-cally efficient dwelling place, as is evidenced in almost every New Year's issue of *Life* magazine, which describes the mechanical wonders of the soon-to-come American dream home.

Finally, the third aspect of the modern concept of leisure connects it with the concept of culture. Simply stated, the problem is this: how will modern man spend his increasing "time-off" so as to absorb the "cultural values" that relieve his monotonous existence, and yet be protected against his own violent inclinations when relieved from work-discipline?

The second point here is as important as the first: the more lucid students of modern life see a connection be-tween the uniformity, sentimental philanthropy, and hos-pital atmosphere of the welfare state and the incredibly violent outbursts of juvenile delinquency in such "pro-gressive" countries as the United States and Sweden. In other words, while the modern conditions of prosperity and social peace and ideological stagnation provide ma-terial satisfaction and security, they do not answer, in fact, they suppress and deny, the existence of deeper drives, which nevertheless want to assert themselves. If they cannot find outlets in war, in fights for a cause, in political commitment, or simply, in loyalty to a man and to an ideal, they are bound to explode through some form of cynical indifference to suffering, through vice, gratuitous violence, and destruction.

This undeniable fact, however, conflicts with the inter-pretation of culture, prevalent today, as a leisure activity, therapeutic in its effects—that is, releasing the destructive energy by sublimating it—and domesticable for social uses. The result is an extraordinary restriction of the meaning of "culture" and "cultural value," until they become the equivalent of "play," while the cultured man turns into a part-time *homo ludens.*

But we are not concerned now with the dangerous shortcomings of the present definition of culture—although this definition is constantly translated into reality by the cultural policies of governments, foundations, schools, and museums. The important point for us is that leisure itself has become, from a personal, individual affair, a collective concern, a sort of discipline and mentality, corresponding to and supplementing work discipline and work mentality in the life of modern man. As work is supposed to create a rapprochement among people—for the purposes of teamwork, interdependence of all phases of work, interdependence of various industries, etc.—so leisure is intended to establish, above the level of work, a rapprochement of mentalities, a community of concerns, a realization of human solidarity.

The earlier pointed-out continuity of the fields of work and leisure has, already in itself, a domesticating effect on leisure as the basis for a planetary ideology: in former times leisure had to be very different from work, it had to be, indeed, its exact opposite: at fairs and inns, at balls and festivities, the no-work, no-discipline, no-worry elements were stressed; gaiety, physical and moral abandonment, were tolerated as natural. In our world, work conditions are "clean": the corresponding leisure does not have to be a complete break with it, only a different dosage of work and leisure: more of the latter, but even so, as pointed out earlier, "constructive," "informative," "educational," promoting "worthy" (humanitarian) causes. In other words, as the term admirably describes it, not leisure but *leisure activity.*•

• In his article "A Shorter Work Week?" Sidney Lens, a Chicago trade-unionist, raises some of the issues with which we are dealing here. His text is a perfect illustration of the "global" ideological approach to the problem of leisure. He recommends continuing the forty-hour week, but with five to fifteen hours of it devoted to education, that inevitable fetish of the social engineer. "The factory of the future," Lens writes, "might reward a worker not only for what he produces in the way of goods, but for what he does to enlarge his own personality. He might be given good marks or poor marks. . . .

Several aspects of modern leisure do not interest us here: they are subjected to investigation from many quarters and their relevance is studied from the point of view of entertainment media, the success of the do-it-yourself industries, the fact that much of leisure time is reconverted by the beneficiaries into time for a second job.

From the angle that occupies our attention the following phenomena are significant: leisure is conceived as the opportunity of the "worker" to be educated at once for personal satisfaction and for the tasks that are supposed to lie ahead of mankind. Personal satisfaction is the relatively unimportant part, as it is unmeasurable, despite the efforts of play therapists, recreation experts, and cultural idea-men to "understand" and direct it. At any rate, personal satisfaction is expected to be the by-product of the successful pursuit of and participation in the collective goal since this goal—planetary coexistence—is expected to permeate the consciousness of all individuals. In other words, the mere fact that work as well as play are performed in the light of the successful organization of the planet for shared happiness, gives a direction to both these activities. Nobody denies the individual's right to leisure and enjoyment; but it is hoped that the liberated energies for leisure activity and enjoyment will be channeled toward the construction of a still better world, with still more leisure, enjoyment, and constructiveness.•

Gradually, education and work become part of an integral process." These recommendations, we are told, are predicated on whether "the values of society, labor unions, and the rank and file of workingmen make a fundamental turn in the direction of humanism. . . . Indeed, no difficulty need be overpowering once there is a reorientation of our value system." *Commonweal*, April 29, 1960.

• A current idea in many American school districts is that we learn the works of foreign literatures in order to promote international understanding and good will. When asked why they would like to travel abroad, many students answer that they want to spread friendship, work for a better relationship among the nations of the world, etc. Education departments, in particular, are exponents of the "planetary point of view," insist on their students' "international mindedness" and on the re-evaluation of their attitudes so as to fit in with the coming "one world."

"Normally and logically, leisure ought to incite people to take a more active part in public life under all its forms. Leisure is a necessary condition of the democratic man . . . we ought to encourage this awareness of social relations so that leisure should be an opportunity to develop voluntary cooperation among people." [6] Indeed, the nature of work and the tasks assigned to production impose an inevitable differentiation: there are many degrees of talent, knowledge, skill, and responsibility involved in the universe of work; work cannot be made equalitarian, it demands a division of labor, a hierarchization of roles in spite of recent efforts by industrial psychologists to establish harmonious social relations in plants, department stores, and offices. The engineer and the laborer may fraternize at picnics or Christmas parties, but both know well that back in the workshop the former's power and responsibility will immediately climb back to the required degree and will include the right of commanding, demoting, and dismissing the latter.

No such limitations exist in the sphere of leisure, in which everybody may take an equal part, and where superiority and inferiority of status have no economic or social consequences. Leisure specialists point out that there are today no privileged forms of leisure, and that worker and executive may both indulge in every previously "aristocratic" pastime such as theatrical performances, hunting, or golf. In leisure activities, social equality may be complete, the consciousness of all participants bathing in the same atmosphere.

Thus when the shapers of a planetary ideology speak of education for leisure they mean the encouragement of the working population to demand more leisure time, and the availability of all recreational facilities for general use. But they also mean thereby to awaken the consciousness of all classes to their rights, not only the right of work, but also that of leisure and pleasure. It will be remembered that before the 1959 British elections both Conservative and Labour Party, embarrassed by a lack of serious issues in a prosperous country, concentrated on demands for more and better organized leisure. The pamphlets that both parties issued were not so much concerned with the traditional cry to reduce the working hours, but with the problems of filling the time of leisure, and with the desirable degree of State support and intervention in this field.

As in other respects—*political life* and *work—leisure* is increasingly organized on a giant scale, by governments, the leisure industries, the entertainment media, and foundations. By the mere weight of its being organized and by the similar techniques used by the organizers, leisure becomes directed and oriented. Even without any ideological purpose involved, the nature of contemporary organizational methods would impose on leisure a collectivist stamp, or at least, would offer a strong temptation to whoever—the State, the Party, an educational monopoly—might want to channel it in certain directions. Even if the immense power and prestige of such institutions as UNESCO were never utilized for ideological purposes, the mere existence of such a body—the availability of resources, the influence and techniques it commands—creates the vehicles for a unifying or uniform approach, modus operandi, and goals pursued.

In this purely formal treatment of the developing planetary ideology, we tried to abstain from discussing the probable content of such a global unanimity. Much could be said and predicted about it, about the forces that promote it, and the speed with which it penetrates our lives, institutions, and thinking. But my goal here is rather to suggest organizational trends, leading to uniform blocks of belief, method, and way of life; this is sufficient in itself to indicate what sort of ideological content, under the present circumstances, is likely to fill the molds and channels thus prepared.

One last word on this subject. Planetary ideology, as I have said at the beginning of this chapter, cannot be defined and formulated with our accustomed political concepts. I have used the term "ideology" to describe it because it answers, across the centuries, the great design of ideologues and intellectuals who wanted to give mankind a system, a principle of cohesion, a secular religion by which to live. From our previous discussion it is evident why the social engineer and not the declining ideologue-intellectual gives shape to this system today. But, let us not forget, the social engineer took over from the intellectual when the latter demonstrably failed, by dispersing people's loyalties instead of organizing them centripetally. Thus the social engineer, in a sense, fulfills the task left undone, and occupies a place left vacant: his goal is ideological in nature, only he approaches his work from the opposite end, as it were. His goal, too, is to answer man's immemorial desire for *peace, prosperity,* and *unity,* aims that have been the stumbling blocks for the intellectuals. The picture we have outlined in the last two chapters contains the same goals, even if on the new roads of society and under new names, they are at first sight difficult to recognize.

Planetary ideology is the last attempt to secure universal peace through the *depolitization* of the individual and the nature of his allegiance; to secure prosperity through *work* and a new *work-motivation;* and unity through (directed) *leisure* and culture.

9

The American Intellectual

"It is for America," wrote Hegel in *The Philosophy of History*, "to abandon the ground on which hitherto the History of the World has developed itself." [1] The new ground was to represent, indeed, a break in the historical continuity of the ages, a settlement and a community as close to a utopian state of affairs as it was feasible for men to establish. We have seen in Chapter Two that the anarchistic-democratic ideas of seventeenth-century England could not flourish in their country of origin, and that they were carried across the ocean in the messianic imagination of the nonconformist sects. "If there was ever a people," wrote Daniel J. Boorstin of this migration, "whose intellectual baggage equipped them for a journey into Utopia, it was the New England Puritans. In their Bible they had a blueprint for a Good Society; their costly expedition to America gave them a vested interest in believing it possible to build Zion on this earth." [2]

It is important to note in Professor Boorstin's judicious phrase this juxtaposition of Zion and Utopia. We have indicated earlier that the intellectual-ideological history of modern times may be written as a search for a substitute for the *Respublica Christiana*, for the Zion that David and Solomon, blessed by God, so gloriously united and ruled. On the soil of the old continent, labored by the steel plow of History, such a Utopia could not be erected; but the virgin lands of America offered an unprecedented opportunity to do just that: "the history of the New England pulpit," Mr. Boorstin continues, "is an unbroken chronicle of the attempt of leaders in the New World to bring their community steadily closer to the Christian model." [3] The New Englanders, writes Professor Herbert Schneider, identified themselves with the Israelites "driven from their homes into a wilderness not out of punishment, but for the sake of building a promised land." [4]

Thus the American intellectual, from the beginning, was of the conviction that the material as well as spiritual preconditions for a harmonious society were given, and that success or failure would ensue depending on the correct application of the blueprint, of the formula. As Mr. Boorstin further remarks, "the New England meeting-house, like the synagogue on which it was consciously modeled, was primarily a place of instruction"; not of *debate*, but of *instruction;* the New England elders were not tolerant of other views and did not think of setting up institutions by which opposition could have been gradually expressed, as was the case, around the same time, in Europe. They excluded from government the subversive elements, since life in the wilderness favored not the discussion of subtleties but the unity of efforts in combatting a hostile nature.

The overcoming of external obstacles and, to achieve this goal, the guaranteeing of internal cohesion, became the double task and everyday experience of all Americans. This attitude was stamped on the mind of America's intellectuals as well: "In the United States," Karl Mannheim noted, "the elite have been absorbed in problems of organization, and this has determined, to a very large extent, the intellectual outlook of the whole nation." [5]

As has been said before, the American, intellectual or member of any other category of the population, thought of himself as possessing a *formula* by which his tasks, individual or collective, might best be carried out. In fact this belief in formulas is the most important single characteristic of the American mentality, one which explains American efficiency and optimism, but also intellectual insecurity and poverty of imagination.

It is the heritage of Calvinism that sees in a certain behavior not the cause but the sign of salvation, of being among the elect. The Zion of the early immigrant and the Calvinistic conception of life of his puritanic mentality developed in Americans a conviction that they live on the land of the elect—"God's own country"—and that adjustment to this ideal community is the expression of being worthy of it. Although the religious concept properly called has been drained off from American life, the basic conviction has remained unaltered, only the contours of the belief and the behavioral conformity to it survived. Thus even the radical movements in the United States, especially those outside of the political context (a strong preserve, to this day, of the Anglo-Saxon mentality and historical tradition) such as cultural, artistic, intellectual, and educational trends, carry in themselves the fear of originality and the secret, unconfessed preference for the comfort of formulas. Even the so-called progressive movements try their best to prescribe the attitude of progressivism, to formulate—not conceptually, which is an indispensable way for an idea and its partisans to identify themselves—in terms of *behavior* what is expected of members, joiners, followers. This is, perhaps, what authorizes Mr. Boorstin to write elsewhere that "American history could be described as 'closed' at both ends: both origin and destination appear fixed." [6]

This search for the formula is manifest in spheres as distant from each other as leadership and spontaneity. The leader is one who knows the rules, who can demand, without self-affirmation and controversy, without scandal or bad feeling, that the followers absorb and assimilate the rules. He is at the point of junction of various interests and embodies the consensus which, without deciding the merits of the respective viewpoints and without arbitrating among them, is virtuous on account of its neutrality.•

The same way with spontaneity which, when encouraged, is at once surrounded, not by conditions that would strengthen and challenge it, but by formulas that turn it

• In Europe it is the medieval-feudal structure—not to go back farther—that established the meaning of leadership. Its structure is pyramidal; its source authority; its cement the feeling of respect (what Bagehot called the "deferential society").

into orthodoxies. Whether the debate concerns the teaching of gifted children,• the love of parents for their offspring, the search for popularity or for genuine ideas or new forms of creation, the Calvinistic terror of nature and instinct immediately stifles whatever would strive to be original, and substitutes for it meaningless slogans, pleasing but empty abstractions, and some—inevitable—blueprint. One sad result is that, not being allowed to be truly spontaneous, children, parents, and artists indulge then in a formless and extreme license, putting on a garb of nonconformity, violence, and nihilism. The "beatniks" are a good example of this oft-repeated abortive rebellion against the fetish of formulas.••

The above considerations have not been irrelevant to our subject. They indicate, to a certain extent, why the intellectual in America is looked upon, and accepts himself as, essentially, the *organizer*, the formulator of the rules, the specialist, the expert. The goals and tasks to be organized are, of course, given, and are considered as data of nature, or at least, the data of the ideal community of human beings. While the European intellectual's historical memory speaks to him of regimes the foundation and principles of which contradicted one another within the history of any single nation, his American counterpart is able to look back upon one continuous regime, with one fundamental philosophy and one basic document, the Constitution.

What does American history tell him? First of all that "the settlement of America was a selective process. . . . It appealed not necessarily to the ablest or the strongest, but usually to the most enterprising. In a sense it may be said that America was from the beginning a state of

---

• Innumerable studies are conducted to probe the "emotional disturbance" and "social insecurity" of gifted children and students, whom even the schools consider rather embarrassing to have. However, it is reassuring that their intellectual endowments cannot be denied and that they do not "compensate" their excellence by acting according to the standards of mediocrity.

•• The present vogue of psychology must be explained, in my opinion, by the fact that it supplies sex and emotional life with the respectability of science and scientific formulas, without which the puritanic mentality could not accept them.

mind and not merely a place." [7] The American nation has no history fading into a mythical past, American political parties and institutions cannot have a mystique; the entire "American experiment" has been conducted in broad daylight, and the forces that shaped the country were either subjected to rational control or identified in terms of this or that human group: immigrants, Founding Fathers, industrial barons, New Deal brain trusters.

In the second place, the history of America is one of fast population growth through the immigration of foreign elements. But, however resigned the immigrants were to turn their back forever on their native countries, to them "America seemed unstable; it lacked the orderly elements of existence. Without security of status or the recognition of rank, no man, no family had a proper place in the social order. Only money talked." [8] "Family, dignity counted for nothing here. He merited consideration who had acquired a secure existence and had shown thereby his capacity to deal with the New World." [9]

This initial rootlessness was responsible for the fact that Americans never knew exactly where they "fitted" in, and that they had to rely on external signs of wealth, success, and even of a degree of adjustment to indicate their status. This was not only the immigrant's experience: with every wave moving *westward* to fill the continent, a new immigration took place, and when this was finished, a just as intensive and aggressive *upward* movement started to climb the ladder of wealth and respectability. The newly arrived, and even his children, were thus rootless in the new environment; they were obliged to imitate the people they saw around themselves, to accept, without criticism, their standards and behavior, and to hold on to the acquired status, knowing that without a tradition-sanctioned name or title the accumulation of material success was their best guarantee and social *carte de visite.*•

• This attitude is, of course, changing. According to E. Digby Baltzell, the United States is developing an upper class like the European aristocracy. The signs of membership in it are high social status, wealth, Anglo-Saxon origin, Episcopalian church-affiliation, ivy-league education, club membership. This class, according to Mr. Baltzell, emphasizes Protestant ethics and is suspicious of leisure; it is hard-working and responsible in its exercise of power.

Thus, thirdly, Henry B. Parkes is right when he says that "to a much greater degree than elsewhere, society in America was based on the natural man rather than on man as molded by social rituals and restraints." [10] This is true, in the first place, of the immigrants in the seventeenth as well as in the nineteenth century, who deliberately left their homes and the ancestral traditions, ready or obliged to start again by their natural capabilities only; it is true, furthermore, in the eighteenth-century sense of the word, according to the Encyclopedists' vision of man as a being endowed by the natural light of reason, and only hampered by environmental restraints, traditional mores, religion, and superstition; and it is true in yet another sense, the American dream of an unfettered existence, not receiving the law from anybody, an outlaw, cowboy, pioneer. From the tales of Leatherstocking to those of the Superman, a considerable trend in American imagination (and fiction) speaks of the will and belief that there is always an escape from civilization toward the frontier where one may build a Utopia of anarchism and outlawry.

"No facts are to me sacred," wrote Emerson, "none are profane; I simply experiment, an endless seeker with no Past at my back." [11] The American writer has adopted, by and large, this attitude, or, when he felt the need for an artistic tradition, he became an expatriate. With Emerson (and Melville and Mark Twain) began that strange line of writers who no longer had the specific New World optimism of Franklin and Jefferson, but, knowing that there was no return (to Europe) either, set up their tents in the no man's land of loneliness, cynicism, and masochistic acceptance of defeat.

But the American intellectual has little in common with the writer, in contradistinction to the European intellectual who is of a definitely literary-philosophical bent, and who has a style, an esthetic dimension. While the American *writer*—Melville, Thoreau, Mark Twain, Dreiser, Henry James, Scott Fitzgerald, Nathanael West, Steinbeck, Upton Sinclair, Sinclair Lewis, Arthur Miller, J. D. Salinger—is critical, dissatisfied, despairing, the American *intellectual* has accepted his society, the role he plays in it, and the tasks assigned by it. The reason is that the writer, in no matter which society, probes the human condition, and thus, in America, he becomes conscious of the absence of roots—in history, environment, nature, and society—of the plight of the "natural man," the insecure, the lonely man. He describes the contradictions of the "American dream" and reality, denounces the false situations created by an aggressive and ubiquitous business civilization, and satirizes the sugar-coating that, instead of veiling, shows up the harshness of life in cruder colors. The intellectual, on the contrary, has dreams of power and influence, and considers the manipulation of society his legitimate reserve. Not without partners, of course; unlike the European intellectual, he does not seek power for the sake of prestige, exalted position, and charismatic leadership; he is aware that the nation was built by a different type of human being, the rugged pioneer, the crafty, but equally rugged, businessman, and lately, the bureaucrat, the pioneer of the welfare state. But precisely: he thinks that with the last-mentioned, his own hour has also struck, and he claims now to occupy a respectable position in the rank of the builders of society.

The intellectual in America has, thus, no major quarrel with the powers that be, and he dreams of no revolution or violent change by which he would take the place of the powerful. A manifestation to the contrary, that is, a bitter denunciation of the powerful (discounting the attacks on "capitalism" and "warmongering" by the Communists) like that of C. Wright Mills's *Power Elite* is most rare, and is met, both by fellow intellectuals and the popular press, with incredulity, uneasiness, and bad temper. Thus when Mills's book was published, *Time* magazine deplored its content and tone, using the characteristic American argument: what will foreigners think of us if they read of the nasty rule of power in the United States?

Mills's attack being the exception, the normal attitude is that the American intellectual admires and adopts the techniques of the dominant mentality, because he too wants to achieve the success he sees firmly established in other camps. The result is a wholesale commercialization and industrialization of most intellectual endeavors, education, entertainment, art, press, and various other cultural institutions. What are the immediate consequences? The adoption of business slogans and attitudes creates among

American intellectuals a basic service mentality. Since *qua* intellectuals: professors, idea-men, entertainers, journalists, critics, publishers, foundation staff-members, etc., they do not expect profit in the business sense, nor is their contribution to the nation's well-being, prosperity, security, measurable in concrete terms as is that of the business world (and of which the business world never ceases reminding the public), they do everything in their power to compensate society for the apparently "useless" activity in which they indulge. They constantly seek to justify themselves by proclaiming their sincere efforts to work for the common good at whatever, very often hypothetical, level the common good chooses to make its claims. Thus it is interesting to watch (here I may speak from a long experience of personal observation) the utter humility with which the teacher and professor submit to the pupil and student (the youth of America is, of course, considered as the most precious part of the common good!), the servile attitude they adopt regarding the youngster's wishes and whims, real or imagined interests.

It follows from the service mentality of the American intellectual that he becomes a kind of glorified public-utilities man. The democratic distrust of excellence and the narrow interpretation of the common good accumulate obstacles in the path of talent. The man who furnishes proof of his exceptional qualities is soon absorbed by administrative duties, assigned to him in the belief that his talents as an individual may be put to what seems to be an even better use in the direct service of the collectivity. From business corporations to schools, from the entertainment world to political life, committee work is not only an essential part of everybody's active hours, but one which leads more surely to rewards, remuneration, and prestige than does genuine creation. This is not only the game co-natural to democracy; it is also a version of the Calvinistic distrust of spontaneity and independence of thought, the *committee* being the living *formula* that helps domesticate (more often: extirpate) originality.

Finally, the service mentality leads to the rather unfortunate situation in which partial groups and minorities —ideological, racial, national, religious—conceive of themselves as by definition handicapped because "divisive," eventually even "un-American." A Catholic sociologist,

Thomas O'Dea, calls attention, for example, to the phenomenon that Catholic intellectuals, by desperately trying to adjust to both Society and the Church, became timid, passive, unproductive, and unoriginal.[12] More important than creation, then, is the "dialogue" by which opposition, or mere differences of views, might be bridged. In many instances, however, this is impossible as when differences of dogma or ideology stand in the way of agreement. What happens then is that the core of the debate is carefully avoided and only surface discord is mentioned; in this way a formula of reconciliation may, indeed, be worked out, but at the expense of having left the essential problem untouched.

The consequences of all this is that the American intellectual feels himself on more secure grounds—and may expect a greater recognition and remuneration—when he absorbs himself in organizational tasks. There seem to be two main reasons for this:

(1) The first is that society in America had to be built not organically, but by successive additions. There was, for example, no continuity of classes, the industrial workers did not grow out of a pre-existing peasant class, and the new capitalists of the nineteenth and twentieth century did not originate from an earlier aristocracy, nor did they intermarry with one. The indentured peasant or semi-peasant immigrants were free, after a number of years of service, to set out on their own and become independent farmers or artisans; later immigrants, if they managed to save enough as workers of a construction team or otherwise, were also free to try their fortune elsewhere, without the hindrance of the past; and fortunes were amassed outside the traditionally well-to-do classes, often overshadowing the latter.

The ensuing chaos and economic jungle soon created problems to which, in the European societies, solutions would have been either indefinitely postponed, or found through revolutions. America could neither postpone their solution, nor wait for violent outbreaks: the American ideal was one of equality of opportunity, and no class thought of itself as entitled to keep others out of prosperity for long; and the lessons of European history showed the unwisdom of letting grievances accumulate until an outburst may no longer be checked.

Theodore Roosevelt understood this when, at the beginning of this century, he warned the capitalist class that a reform of the abuses was the price to pay in order to be saved from a socialist revolution. The reform-minded intellectuals thus considered it a patriotic as well as a philosophical task to devote their energies to the transformation of society where concrete, *ad-hoc* problems were waiting for them, arising from the pluralistic nature of that society. Unlike the European intellectuals, they did not have a quasi-mystical national history, studded with heroes and saints and fabulous battles, the image of which they could have set against new social movements; on the contrary, they had to point to the totality of the institutional and socioeconomic achievements, a kind of argument of which there could never be enough and which had value only insofar as such achievements continued to grow and multiply. This is how, with men like Beard, Dewey, Veblen, and Holmes, "American history and philosophy became concerned with the Negro problem, imperialism, trusts, the labor movement. To these problems the band of new scholars hoped to apply the scientific method." [13]

Thus, what the historical and philosophical argument was for the European intellectual, the scientific and social argument became for the American. Thus every institution which in Europe was destined to be a depository of past wisdom and a brake on new trends became in America a laboratory of social service for the present and of further experimentation for the future. This is true of the law courts, the schools, museums, cultural foundations, political parties, etc.

The reverse of the medal is that the American intellectual is so absorbed in his direct organizational tasks that he does not possess the detachment and the broad vision necessary for truly great accomplishments. Also, as an organizer and social engineer, he has the nostalgia of the real man of action that he himself cannot be, and remains with a sense of inferiority when he compares his own impact on the environment with that of the pioneer, the businessman, and the specialist, the labor leader and the politician.

Hence a systematic denigration of the intellectual values and standard he is supposed to represent. What is even worse, he casts suspicion on the individual himself and clearly extolls the communal mentality and methods as if this were a solved dilemma between good and evil. "The mere absorption of facts and truths," wrote Dewey, "is so exclusively individual an affair that it tends very naturally to pass into selfishness. There is no obvious social motive for the acquisition of mere learning, there is no clear social gain in success thereat." •

The obsession with "social motivation," with the need to justify individual action, thought, and originality by a preferably close-at-hand communal benefit is the major characteristic of the American intellectual. This mentality is stamped not only on political and economic issues, but even on such endeavors as philosophy, theology, and art; in each of these fields it is not the authority of geniuses, but society as such that is trusted to bring about improvement and progress, which are, in turn, measured in terms of benefit to society.••

The popular philosophies are all involved with semantic and linguistic analysis and discourage the existentialist trends; the latter's escape from what Heidegger calls the sphere of public opinion and into search for self-identification is considered a rather obscene enterprise, whereas the former may serve as an instrument for establishing a common conceptual pattern among the groups of a pluralistic society, and for putting the "scientific" language in the place of those which express a variety of value systems. Similarly in theology. While European Protestant schools (Barth) emphasize the unique authority of the Bible, American theology looks at society and evolution, and under the influence of James and Whitehead, sees

• *The School and Society* (1899), p. 28.

"Veblen's interpretation of the study of classics, correct spelling, elegant diction, syntax and prosody as conspicuous waste was intimately related to Dewey's views of the traditional school as uselessly formal and symbolic." Morton White, *Social Thought in America: The Revolt against Formalism,* p. 100.

•• As Mr. Peter Drucker writes with the pomposity of the "new, modern business outlook," "today's organization builds a collective, that is a genuine social whole, on the individual acting as an individual and committing himself as an individual." In spite of the threefold repetition of the word "individual," no one can mistake where the emphasis lies.

God as a *process* that produces in time a better world. The same way, Europeans stress the unique value of Jesus' mercy on the Day of Judgment, whereas the Americans stress the democratic processes of society as propelling mankind closer to the ideal.[14]

(2) The second reason that the American intellectual feels at home in his role as an organizer, co-ordinator, and engineer of society is that he thus conforms to the American genius of building the society of the future, Utopia. For Americans, and not for the intellectuals alone, organizations and institutions are goals in themselves, insofar as they are all destined to be mirrors of society, small replicas of the community. The American who distrusts individual theory and tends to weaken its impact on society by subjecting it to various screening processes (the *committees* serve this purpose, among other things) favors the setting up of miniature communities within which the ideas will be first tested by the behavior of the members. This is true of schools and even classes no less than of the gigantic business corporations.

The same is true of the entire American society where the historical consciousness is provided less by the *continuity* and continuous deepening of traditions and memories, than by the successive *layers* of an evolving society, the latest always better than the one before it and thus alone deserving recognition. The past is forgotten because its being "dated" shows it up almost manifestly as a failure. On the contrary, the present state, and the always just-emerging future deserve all the attention and glamorizing effort: those who busy themselves around it, who are in the spotlight, have the power to turn toward themselves the admiration of their fellow citizens.

But the "present" and the "future" are not the only time categories having weight and meaning; "Utopia" is a third category, one that captures the American imagination at least as powerfully as the other two—even more so, since while "present" and "future" are organizable and manipulable, "Utopia" is always just a little "beyond." In fact, it is no exaggeration to say that utopianism is the idealism of the American whose practical-mindedness would not allow him to indulge in making images that have no chance of becoming concrete.

But, let us not forget, Utopia is not a form of individual

salvation, not even one of individual contentment: it is a collective goal that can be reached only by an ever-increasing collective effort and higher degree of cohesion. In America, however, it is also a release of pent-up longings and secret satisfactions that the puritanic modes of feeling have restrained. Thus Utopia in America means at once a higher form of social organization *and* a dream of lawlessness; insistence on adjustment *and* hope of anarchy. Many observers of the American scene have called attention, in one way or another, to the fact that in the American mind the Calvinist and the anarchist are forever fighting it out. While the European revolts against a known order that he senses both in the universe and within his soul, an order whose existence he acknowledges and whose dogmas and restrictions he admires, the American does not know against what he revolts, that is, he considers norms and standards man-made conventions, unjust and stupid, to be overpowered by will and action. Since, however, evil—as his ideology inherited from the eighteenth-century Enlightenment tells him—is not a permanent feature of things in his eyes, he persuades himself that it is merely a passing problem, subject to some solution.

The American intellectual is thus by definition a "progressive" and a "utopian," one who likes to believe that what is wrong can be righted by human action, and that the accumulated constructive actions lead, in a rather straight line, to organized well-being and freedom. But it is precisely this belief—and the premises on which it rests (and some of which we have enumerated)—that poses the intellectual dilemma so characteristic of this century; the faster and more complete the progress, the greater the general indifference, the more numerous the "dead souls," the more acute the social disintegration. Yet the American intellectual can no more abandon his optimism than can any other ideologue. This society has been forged by the successful solution of a number of tremendous problems, partly with the help of an ideology that emerged stronger from each successful test. The solutions were always "liberal": the absorption of immigrants, the vote and education extended to all, the abolition of slavery, the association of workers to the conduct of business in a prosperous nation. The American intellectual has no other model—historical, political, or social—before him to imitate. He is enclosed in a trend and in a role from which he neither can nor wants to free himself.

In a recent study, Professor Seymour M. Lipset has come to the conclusion that the American intellectuals are, in an overwhelming number of cases, "leftists," affiliated with the Democratic rather than the Republican Party, and rather with the left-wing (A.D.A.) than the right-wing of the former. "Perhaps even more conclusive evidence that the intellectual is attracted to the ideological left is the fact that the relatively small leftist third parties, both Socialist and Communist, seem to have secured more support from intellectuals than from any other stratum of the population." [15] The author himself points out that the essential feature of the leftist ideology, egalitarianism, is stamped on the American intellectual's consciousness by the Declaration of Independence and by the American creed. Among other things, this is what explains the fact that any foreign leftist import, European radicalism in the nineteenth century and Russian Communism in the twentieth, elicits an immediate echo in his heart.•

Is there an alternative for him? In the last decade or so, conservatism or neoliberalism has tried to acquire respectability both as a philosophical position and an encouragement for practical politicians to oppose the welfare state. It is no coincidence that the vogue of conservatism has run parallel to the appearance of a deadly enemy at the gate, Soviet Communism and imperialism, which attracts the nation's attention, for the first time in a protracted manner, to the world outside it. The first real threat to American security and well-being, the first alarm at the vulnerability of Utopia has brought a shock to the American consciousness that has not yet been dissipated. The very duration of the cold war creates an atmosphere intolerable to this consciousness, which likes to believe that

---

• It is true, on the other hand, that as Leon Samson, quoted by Lipset, argues, the principal cause for the failure of the socialist movement in America is the fact that the proclaimed goals of socialism are so closely identical with those of "Americanism" that Americans feel no need to adopt a "foreign" version of their own creed.

all problems have a solution—furthered by reasonable talk, underlying fellowship and common interests, contractual agreement—and which is unable to envisage that an evil situation should be lasting. If Soviet Communism is evil, the American seems to ask, why is it that God does not strike it off the surface of the earth? •

Under these conditions, conservatives, as we have seen in Chapter Five, tend always to indict a conspiracy that prevents this act of God or, at least, weakens the government's determination to deal with the anomalous situation. While such a conspiracy cannot be proved to exist, the conservatives are justified in suspecting many individuals and groups who, given the general "progressive" mentality of most American intellectuals, bureaucrats, and government experts, may be actually inclined to accuse the "capitalists" of their own country of all imaginable sin, and correspondingly exonerate the Communists who parade with the same slogans as they themselves.

On the domestic scene proper, the conservatives have a far more difficult problem to face. Let us repeat: the *nature* of American society and government is progressive, and the progressive forces, from the age of Jackson to that of the Supreme Court decision on desegregation, have won every single issue and in a remarkably short time. Thus, historically, the conservative has no solid ground to stand on and easily incurs the accusation of either being in the pay of "reactionary capital," or of merely being slow and indolent, reluctant to go along with betterment at the required speed. It is obvious that this *depaysement* of the

• The American myth, writes Professor Hans Morgenthau, Jr., speaks about a golden age of past foreign policy in which no power, cruelty, and will to dominate was used, and of a golden future in which the world will happily coexist in a federation modeled according to the United States. In the meantime, the present is evil because Russia thwarts the American-sponsored organization of world harmony. This character description by Professor Morgenthau is confirmed by General de Gaulle, who in his wartime conversations with Roosevelt understood the President as believing, and working for, a world system of peaceful American hegemony, after the evils of British, French, Dutch, colonialism, world-wide misery would be replaced by a peaceful co-operation of democratic peoples, including Soviet Russia.

conservative has been made even more acute since the "age of Roosevelt," which has institutionalized much of the progressive blueprint and has injected a considerable amount of utopianism into the conduct of foreign affairs.

Faced with this situation, the American intellectual is reluctant to call himself a conservative because the elements that constitute his intimate conviction simply do not make sense in the context of American history, society, and expectations. Thus he is forced to use the terminology of European conservatism (or classical European liberalism), by which he then definitely bars any chance of a fruitful conversation with his fellow Americans. When he looks at the two political parties, or at the policies and statements of American institutions in general—welfare agencies, higher courts, schools, artistic institutes—nowhere does he find words and programs other than such as are informed by the spirit of progressivist ideology and utopianism. Thus the scope for debate and controversy is singularly narrowed, unlike in European countries where progressive forces, even when victorious, must come to terms with ideologies and terminologies clearly opposed to theirs, and where these progressive movements themselves have a historical tradition—and therefore a dimension—of their own. "Europe," Professor Morgenthau writes, "in contrast to America, has known classes, determined by heredity or otherwise sharply and permanently defined in composition and social status, which have had a stake in defending the present status quo or restoring an actual or fictitious status quo of the past. But for the defense or restoration of what status quo could the U.S. conservative fight? For private power, states' rights, the abolition of the income tax, exclusive male suffrage, slavery, or perhaps, the British monarchy? The absurdity of this rhetorical question illustrates the absurdity of the conservative position in terms of purposes within the context of American politics." [16]

The religion of progress and Utopia, however, has consequences beyond the *political* attitude and outlook. "The dream of a millenial existence," writes an intelligent observer, Henry B. Parkes, "free from sin and evil, has continued to inspire radicals, whether they follow the teachings of John Calvin or those of Karl Marx. And from the times of the Puritans who hoped to achieve 'a new heaven and a new earth' in Massachusetts, down to the present day, this dream has been particularly associated with the American continent. The belief that America has a peculiar mission to establish a new and higher way of life has, in fact, become a part of the American character, even though few Americans have been prepared to interpret it in any very radical fashion." •

Not in a radical fashion, perhaps, when measured by contemporary standards, yet in a manner that is stamped with the spirit of the American experiment. The dream of a "millenial existence" concerns a society of equals. In order to promote it, democracy is utilized as an ideology, that is, not as a method restricted to the political sphere, but as a universal formula to be applied to every endeavor. This is how mediocrity is produced (and consciously pursued) in a society where so many channels are open to individuality and excellence.

Here again, the popular denunciations by culture-critics are directed at the commercialization of the American scene. And, as we have remarked, it is true that the American intellectual is irresistibly attracted by the successful methods of the business world. But the roots of the situation lie deeper. Parallel to general commercialization there is in the United States a general *intellectualization* of the public the effects of which have not been sufficiently explored. The culture-critics usually remain on a superficial level when they indict the anti-values, the artificiality, the phony sentimentalism, of the businessman; hence the cry that the American people and its leaders are "antiintellectualist" is misleading, and does more harm than good to the important issue of clarifying the nature of American civilization. The heart of the matter is just the opposite: the excessive intellectualization of American society.

John Dewey, in 1927, saw the problem of progress as the "intellectualization of the public at large." In the al-

• *The American Experience*, pp. 81-2.

The eighteenth-century view of man and society is obvious in such statements as that of Jefferson, who referred to the United States as a "universal nation, pursuing universally valid ideas," and John Adams, who declared that "our pure, virtuous, public spirited federative republic will . . . govern the globe and introduce the perfection of man."

ready-quoted study by Professor Seymour Lipset, it is pointed out that there are proportionately more "intellectuals" in the United States than in any other Western country, and that, contrary to the American intellectual's "self-image as one of low status . . . academic and other intellectual occupations in the United States are high in social prestige." [17] Any observer of the American scene will testify that in no other country are there so many committees, panels, journals and broadcasts of popular culture, adult education courses, lecture bureaus, "intellectualized" advertisements, and "artistic" posters as in the United States. Practically any man or woman with a college degree may call himself an intellectual, not because of his culture or competence, which is most often amazingly low, but because of some urbane contact with the world of sophistication: art, science, education, philanthropic support of general intellectual improvement or cultural institutions. The work-leisure-culture continuum of which we have spoken in the preceding chapter is already a *fact* in American society where the democratic ideology cannot tolerate the idea of excluding anybody from material, social, or cultural benefits.

The result is the absence of selective processes, or the establishment of a misplaced, mechanized selection; the irresistible attraction of and drive toward mediocrity; and the confusion of authentic and artificial, of superior and well-packaged, of depth and popularity. This is natural: culture, education, information, considered as rights, not achievements requiring extra effort, must, by necessity, reflect back on the sources that dispense them as fringe benefits of citizenship. Instead of rising, mediocrity brings down to its own level whatever comes in contact with it. Thus the American intellectual is practically anybody, Joe and Jane College. They serve the "dream of millennial existence" as well as their own interest when they militate for the diffusion rather than the concentration of intellectual activity and cultural values. The structure of society facilitates their activity: decentralization of churches and school boards, the cultural and educational endeavors of associations, groups, women's clubs, the entertainment world, local committees, etc., require an intellectualized personnel which, however, is not supposed to be out of touch with the limited ambitions of these varied employ-

ers and think beyond the average level of the membership. Thus the quality and nature of this intellectual-cul-
tural activity expresses that famous "common denomina-
tor" which, in America, is an ambiguous term: ideologically
desirable, but damnable from the point of view of genuine
intellectual effort.

It is the ideological viewpoint that wins out; as a collective body, the American intellectuals are committed to the
intellectualization of the public, even though the best
ones know that this is a flagrant contradiction to human
nature, to the law of large numbers, and to the possibilities of any society. Thus while the intellectual, as we have
seen earlier in this chapter, is called upon to perform the
function of mediation between the groups of the pluralistic
society, he is also enjoined to *justify* the existing or emerging mass values. It is essential to realize that these mass
values are not necessarily welcomed by the intellectuals
as cultural manifestations; in fact, each time these intellectuals congregate—formally in committees and meetings,
informally at cocktail parties or among friends—the main
topic is the denunciation of mass values, mass culture, and
mass mentality, in terms that would put to shame any
group of European aristocrats. But they are never denounced ultimately and irrevocably since they are signs and
symbols of *social cohesion,* of the efficacy of the democratic machinery of education, press, and mass communication.

The justification (not necessarily the defense) of mass
values is, in a sense, the protection of a social class, the
fluid but ubiquitous and permanent mass-middle class so
characteristic of the United States and practically coinciding with the nation. In the absence of a one-party
ideology and centrally guided political behavior, in America it is the democratic credo, reinforced by the business
mentality, that sets the pace for public thinking. This is
not the socialist realism that rules over the minds of
Soviet writers and artists; it is its counterpart: *democratic
illusionism,* expressed in all the manifestations of mass
culture. Since the United States is a free land, there exist,
side by side with mass culture, and criticizing it, any
number of genuine creators of theories, works of art, intellectual movements, erudite accomplishments, plays,
novels, etc. But the play of social and business factors

safely circumscribes the spread and effectiveness of these creations: the center of the stage is occupied by those illusion-fabricating mechanisms which cater to the taste of the "American public," a prosperous, dynamic, and satisfied middle class representing the near-totality of the population.

It follows not from the mere existence of this middle class, but from its priviledged position vis-à-vis the intellectual, that *its* taste is the dominant one, *its* endless thirst for illusion and entertainment sets the pace for American life. It is relatively immaterial whether this privileged position or the illusion-and-entertainment industry should take first responsibility. In the July-August, 1952, issue of *Partisan Review*, C. Wright Mills, participating in a symposium, wrote: "I would impute the leveling and the frenzy effects of mass culture in this country not to 'democracy' but to capitalist commercialism which manipulates people into standardized tastes and then exploits these tastes and 'personal touches' as marketable brands." But we have stated that democracy, when applied *as an ideology* to all forms of life and to institutions, necessarily leads to the pursuit of mediocrity—which, then, spreads an ideal climate for uniformity of thinking, taste, and behavior, easily exploited by "capitalist commercialism" denounced by Mills. Moreover, as we have also stated, the mentality of commercialism (I would prefer to call it the mentality favoring mediocrity) pervades even those circles and enterprises that are free from the so-called scourge of capitalism and profit-mindedness.

But Mills's above-quoted view is held, generally, by most of his fellow intellectuals and also by many artists and writers. In other words, it is not democracy as an ideology they denounce, but an evil manipulation of democracy by the capitalist profiteer, vulgar because he shares the public's bad taste, and evil because he perpetuates it. This is the reason that the intellectuals' revolt in America starts on the Left, that socialism is extolled as capable of substituting profiteering by disinterestedness, a listless anonymous public by a purposeful community of cultured individuals.

The writers and artists who, as a rule, are less political-minded, join in denouncing capitalism for the shallowness of the cultural landscape. Malcolm Cowley, writing about the artists of the 1920's and 1930's, remarked, "their function as a class was to be the guardians of intellectual things, and yet they were acting as propagandists for a way of life in which the intellect played a minor part. They were selling their talents and yet they did not know what to do with the money they received, except spend it for automobiles and gin and the house beautiful, exactly like the gulled public for which they were writing and drawing." [18] The situation described by Cowley has not changed essentially in the 1950's; the American writer and artist still ambition to live up to middle-class standards, except that these standards have become different: participation in—and scorn (with a tinge of remorse) for mass-media glibness; the combination of Madison Avenue style with Greenwich Village affectation of stylelessness; the tight pants and pullover of the beatnik, which then yields, when its owner has arrived, to the gray flannel suit of the foundation official. But inside it is the same spiritual vacuum and moral misery for not having "guts."

For this, as for most other things, society is blamed, and the blame is dressed in the terminology of leftist denunciations. But, as Seymour Lipset implies in his study, the American intellectual's dilemma is that while he is well compensated in money, influence, power, and in a way, even in social prestige, the inherent egalitarianism of the American-brand democracy secretly disturbs him. He resorts, as we have explained above, to European concepts in his laments, but he and his audience are visibly uncomfortable with the obligation to use an alien vocabulary. Hence, as soon as he sets out to denounce American civilization systematically, the American intellectual is necessarily misunderstood, since he puts himself *outside* the accustomed frame of reference. This happens, incidentally, whether he uses the classical European "leftist" or "rightist" terminology.

We have seen what misunderstandings are caused when the "rightist" terminology is used, as by neoconservatives. But, although Marxism in the 1930's and 1940's was incomparably more successful among the American intelligentsia, it, too, remained a definitely alien doctrine. By the 1950's, when Senator Joseph McCarthy made his memorable denunciations, it was truly a cast-off garb, and these denunciations affected mostly ex-Communists who since their youth had turned "respectable."

This does not mean that fifteen to thirty years ago American liberals and progressives were not powerfully tempted by the prestige of ideologues. Leon Samson, as quoted by Seymour Lipset, argued that "the principal cause for the failure of the socialist movement in America has been the fact that the symbolic goals of socialism are so closely identical with those of Americanism that Americans feel no need to adopt a 'foreign' version of Americanism." Yet, at the time it was felt that "Americanism" was more truly expressed by Russian-style socialism than even by the New Deal, considered a halfway house toward the truly good society. "Liberalism or progressivism," writes Ralph de Toledano of the 1930's and 1940's, "put aside the minimalist socialism of its childish days. . . . The Soviet underground . . . made full use of these socialist-cum-Keynesian-cum-Communist idealists. They packed the Party fronts, they opened their hearts and their pockets, they created an intellectual climate." [19]

These considerations lead us to the core of the American intellectual's plight and dilemma. Briefly: he brings about, organizes, and cautions a civilization he both admires and finds tragically lacking in genuine values. This dual reaction, hiding a more deep-seated ambiguity, sets the tone of his usual public attitude: "objectivity," which characterizes his books, speeches, lectures, and panel discussions; he makes an honest effort to balance one fact with another, this disapproval with that praise. But, except in rare morbid moments, he ends up, like Max Lerner in his recent bulky study, by singing a "patriotic paean to American growth." [20]

Looking at it from the angle of vision of our study, it may be stated that the American intellectual's problem arises from the fact that he must sacrifice his values as an intellectual to his role and function as a social engineer. This statement needs to be qualified.

Social engineering as an ideology is the pursuit of an idea to its logical end: the idea is Utopia on earth. But attachment to Utopia, utopian thinking, is also an American mode of thinking, an outgrowth of the American experiment. In this sense it cannot be called Utopia since as part of the American nation's mental baggage, it has *roots*, it is a *tradition*. More than that, utopianism is the ultimate form of the American search for identity, a search that can have no ideally happy conclusion except with the good society, the Zion, the final *justification* for the immigrant, for the government by, for, and of the people, for the definitive—that is, American—way of life. This impatient and nervous need for justification of the very existence of American society is perhaps the most powerful driving force propelling this country forward—to good and to evil. As James Burnham remarked, "The American nation is not a super-being on whose altar the subject is ready to sacrifice blood, treasure and life, but a mere practical convenience, the only justification for which is its ability to serve the interests of private citizens. . . . Few of the nations most ambitious and able citizens have gone into political or military life. It has been business in particular, and to a lesser extent the civil professions that have attracted those equipped with talent, intelligence, creative imagination and even the will to power." [21]

Gertrude Stein said that "it is difficult for America to prove itself American, a difficulty no other nation has ever had." Indeed, from the beginning of American history the problem arose how to fit new and contradictory national experiences (the Mexican War, "manifest destiny," the institution of slavery, Civil War, the Industrial Age, imperialistic interests, the world wars, depression) into the framework of a previously formed image of the American man, virtuous and natural, and of the American nation, happy, isolated, outside and above history. The eighteenth-century philosophy and the Puritan background provided a rather limited framework, because they expressed, once and for all, a certain view of man and society, and excluded others. Consequently, as Richard Hofstadter has put it: "it has been our fate as a nation not to have ideologies but to be one."

In the course of the nineteenth century, from Bancroft and Whitman to Theodore Roosevelt and Wilson, there has been a continuing quest for further elucidation and self-identification, accompanied by subsequent repudiations of the various images of what constitutes America and Americanism. New experiences, conflicting with the hard block of the ideology mentioned by Hofstadter and Hans Kohn, have not been fully assimilated, thus always leaving the door wide open for the coming of the Good Society—sometimes in vulgar, at other times in idealistic, forms. Thus the series of nineteenth-century shocks continues; it is, in fact, amplified and made more dramatic. The resurgence of the Negro question in a nation adulating equality; the appearance of an American Empire, military and economic, for a nation isolationist deep in its heart; the irrestible surge of the welfare state in a nation priding itself on economic individualism and private initiative; the bomb of Hiroshima for the conscience of a nation believing itself good, innocent, and moral—all these experiences prevent the process of self-identification, confuse the public philosophy, and enervate intelligent citizenship.•

For all these reasons, then, the American intellectual's commitment to Utopia is extremely strong. The organization-mindedness, the social engineering implied in the balancing of views and interests among the groups of a pluralistic society, the belief in magic formulas, which at once harness the "evil" in nature and make the latter productive, the continued effort to justify American society in terms of success—are the main elements which show up the intellectual as a social engineer. It must be added immediately, however, that as we have seen, two distinctly American factors modulate the definition of the intellectual in the United States as a social engineer. The first is that the country itself was built on a utopistic view of nature, history, society, and the individual (a vincible nature, an ahistoric idea of history, the good society, the perfectible individual); the second is that from the beginning the intellectuals were either integrated in the pursuit of social goals, or else ignored and excluded; at no point did they have the spiritual-intellectual-social authority of

• What is one to make, for example, of the statement by Peter Drucker, an apologist for big corporations and their new-style "management philosophy": "Society needs a return to spiritual values—not to offset the material but to make it fully productive." A British reviewer aptly called this phrase, and the entire last chapter of Mr. Drucker's *The Landmarks of Tomorrow*, "the theology of General Motors" (John Caxton, in *The Manchester Guardian Weekly*, June 11, 1959).

their European counterparts. In other words, they did not make the Danaean gift of ideology to their nation, they found that ideology imbedded in the nation's fabric. The choice was not theirs.

Such recent studies as those of David Riesman, William H. Whyte, C. Wright Mills, Walter Lippmann, indicate fairly accurately the growing trend toward social engineering. Two facts hamper their analyses and prevent them from being deep and exhaustive: one is that they show social engineering as a *new* phenomenon in American life, in fact, as a break with the past: other-directed versus inner-directed man, corporation ethics versus protestant ethics. The other mode of approach that necessarily obscures the issue is that these authors, and others, identify the whole trend with the general technological mentality that pervades the world today. In either instance a specifically American phenomenon, or the American features of a world-wide phenomenon, are not examined in their particular setting.

What then are the features of America's intellectuals as social engineers? Only a few can be mentioned here, those which are usually listed by the critics of American civilization as the "manipulation" of life, opinion, and taste. This is, after all, the theme elaborated by Riesman, Whyte, Mills, Lippmann, and also by Russell Kirk, Paul Tillich, and many others.

For most other parts of the world a feudal or quasi-feudal system has traditionally articulated the power rapports among men and their social groups or classes. Obedience, respect, authority, etc., are the natural feelings that various institutions embodied and enforced, and continued to nurture in people's souls. When power and authority coincide, they may represent an awesome force, but all those who find themselves within its sphere of influence at no matter what level, possess, at least, an instrument of measuring their own position in society and in the power-system surrounding them.

The existence and self-assertiveness of authority is not at all a negative, oppressive force, although it may, of course, be corrupted like any other institution. In fact, man's inner life is mutilated when it is deprived of submission to authority, which orientates him and releases him of an impossible total responsibility and self-reliance.

The great French actor, Jean-Louis Barralt, recounts that in his apprentice years he felt such an awe for his teacher, Charles Dullin, that one night, meeting him unexpectedly on the street, he backed into the gutter, unable to face the admired and adored master. Yet, he reports, Dullin more often berated than praised him, was an extremely stern mentor, and demanded perfection from him as from his other pupils.

Now the egalitarian ideology of America generally deprives people of the experience of awe and respect. Foreign and native child psychologists usually conclude from their contact with American youth that their much-discussed and advertised "psychological unbalance and insecurity" stems from the fact that they never confront authority: father and mother remain blurred images of permissiveness, the teacher is known to have no power over the disorderly, and the advertising system specializes in flattering the whims of teen-age and sub-teen-age groups. For the adolescent or the college student the atmosphere is further preserved when the American ideology is brought to bear fully upon him, providing him with the first adult manipulative devices by which genuine differences between individuals may be glossed over, sugar-coated, eroded, or outright denied.

Nevertheless, authority exists and society would fall apart without it. But as C. Wright Mills notes, "authority is power that is explicit and more or less voluntarily obeyed; manipulation is the secret exercise of power, unknown to those who are influenced," • or, we might correct, *known* to them yet voluntarily veiled by common social habit and consensus. It is this "hidden persuasion" that, developed into a web of hardly different manipulative relationships, forms the climate of "other-directedness," described by

• *The Power Elite,* p. 317. The text continues: "Manipulation becomes a problem wherever men have power that is concentrated and willful but do not have authority, or when, for any reason, they do not wish to use their power openly. . . . Small circles of men are making decisions which they need to have at least authorized by indifferent or recalcitrant people over whom they do not exercise explicit authority. So the small circle tries to manipulate these people into willing acceptance or cheerful support of their decisions—or at least to the rejection of possible counter-opinions."

David Riesman. "The other-directed person is trained to respond not so much to overt authority as to subtle but nonetheless constricting interpersonal expectations." [22] Riesman points out that this training in manipulation and acceptance of being manipulated appears in the early years: "The other-directed child is taught at school to take his place in a society where the concern of the group is less with what it produces than with its internal group relations, its morale." [23]

As Vance Packard's popular book *The Hidden Persuaders* shows, it is widely believed that veiled manipulation is a method of American business and advertising, which introduced it into American life in general. The truth is, rather, that these practices are only an application of a deeper trend, imposed by the democratic structure of society. It seems, indeed, that the utopian, apolitical nature of the American ideology, reinforced by economic prosperity, favors the depolitization of life, which, in turn, facilitates manipulation. "One might agree," wrote David Reisman, "that American life can be sufficiently satisfying, even for many in lower income ranks, to justify indifference to political efforts at improvement. . . . They are rich and comfortable enough to afford more food, more telephones, more trips than most people, in their security they can afford more political indifference." [24] This was also the general thesis of Samuel Lubell in two of his books, *The Revolt of the Moderates* and *The Future of American Politics*.

Its critics charge, then, that the American society allows itself to drift toward a state of affairs in which hidden groups will increasingly manipulate it but still in the name of the principles and values to which it has learned to respond favorably and which it would not think of openly repudiating. Walter Lippmann speaks, for example, of a "pseudo-environment of inaccurate news," which the communication media spread over the heads of people and which is the precondition of successful manipulation.

The other precondition is even more characteristic of the American scene. It is believed by most Americans, it is indeed an essential thesis of the public philosophy, that private, voluntary associations should do the job of conducting public and semipublic transactions wherever government and established institutions would tread too heavily. This is also the classical tenet of English liberalism, from Locke to J. S. Mill, and it was a most salutary concept as long as it could be practiced, that is, in the age of weak and narrowly conceived governments. But today, in the age of an ubiquitous and coercive government, when it would be even more vitally important, it is less and less feasible because the mass vote in favor of increased government intervention is used to thwart the function of voluntary private associations; the latter's rights survive as token rights, with only the shadow of power to influence the public weal. Historically, these associations were excellent substitutes for central action; today they tend to become façades behind which the public is lulled by a semblance of action into a state that may be called *passivity by participation.*•

Under such circumstances private groups are reduced to impotence, although externally their role and activity appears important. The original "political space" occupied by them is, however, invaded by government and bureaucracy, or by pressure groups that enjoy governmental support. These groups still parade as private associations and claim, when needed, the privileges that a democracy habitually extends to minorities; but, in fact, they secure the monopoly of manipulation in important fields and bar any further movement and dissent in those areas. Smaller groups are reduced either to impotence or to the necessity of using the same language as the big pressure organization and governmental bureaucracy from which it is practically indistinguishable. The result is that up and down the scale of private and semiprivate associations there develops a semblance of activity—a pseudo-participation as the credo of democracy demands it—without any new ideas or unorthodox action being generated. Terms like "dynamism," "brainstorm," "bold and imaginative think-

• "One may wonder whether the profusion of information followed by debate does not create a substitute for action in all domains. The development of the pleasure of conversation in free time should not be interpreted as a preparation or completion of active participation in the life of society, but a substitute for such participation. The inflation of the information received, given and exchanged, may create the illusion that we *do* much for society; in reality we only *chat* about it." Riesman, in *Esprit* symposium on American social science, Jan., 1959.

ing," serve, often in good faith, as veils for inaction, conformism of ideas, fear of originality. The manipulator knows, of course, that in reality very few people take an interest in public affairs, and that even fewer are competent to do so; but this, in the United States, is ideologically inadmissible. The "intellectualized" public is credited with a healthy interest in civic and general affairs, whether this is borne out by the votes, the results of statistics, polls, or not. One consequence is a constant artificial whipping up of interest and participation; the other is the claim—in politics, business, cultural life—that important decisions are arrived at on the basis of popular consultation, mass taste, audience rating. Occasionally the vacuity of such claims becomes suddenly apparent: in 1959 when the Soviet "ultimatum" focused attention on Berlin, *The New York Times*'s pollsters, touring the country, found that about forty per cent of the population lacked any knowledge of the Berlin situation.

As we have seen, it is impossible to diagnose the failures and lacunae of the American intellectuals as symptoms of a newly contracted disease. We have noted, on the contrary, the organic development of social engineering in America from the traditional role of these intellectuals, a role they have always accepted. They have become social engineers because society recognized them only as "experts" and specialists, and never asked of them leadership and guidance.

The significant thing is precisely that the American intellectuals have accepted these tasks and this role, as they have accepted other tasks throughout the history of the nation. From simple "organizers" they became, when the need was felt, "social reconstructionists" (Dewey, Holmes) at the turn of the century, and fifty years later, caterers to mass society and formulators of the new, civic morality of the socialized man. In this sense their condition, their goal and conceptual world, foreshadows the general condition of tomorrow's intellectual. It is in the light of their experience that intellectuals in many other parts of the world are beginning to study their societies and their own position within them.

10

The European Intellectual

It is not a bad vantage point for the study of the European intellectual to begin with certain comparisons to his American counterpart. Ever since the end of the eighteenth century the United States became for Europeans a kind of mirror and a temptation, which at once attracted and repelled them. They saw in the American conditions and in American society a Utopia, but not such a distant one as to be unimaginable on European soil, in fact, a logical conclusion of many theories by European thinkers.

When, in the twentieth century, the United States further developed some of the features that Europeans found disturbing: materialism, commercialized culture, mass democracy, the victory of scientism over the tragic sense of life, the intellectuals of the old continent understood that in looking at America they were contemplating their own future.[1] From that time on, that is, since the end of the First World War, the question became *how long* can Europe withstand "Americanization"; and even this question had to be rephrased after the Second World War: *in what ways* will "Americanization" affect Europe?

Now the term "Americanization" is not to be taken as signifying only the influence of the United States on Europe, the impact of the G.I.'s and of the American Way of Life. Under this word, which is in itself a formula, many preoccupations find a comfortable shelter: the relationship of elites and masses, the extension of the democratic concept to cultural policies, the techniques of depersonalization, the obsession with science, the shallow uses of leisure, and finally the whole network of social rapports which derives from values accepted and taught.

But the end of the Second World War saw an unexpected complication of the problem of "Americanization." Indeed, by the middle of the century it became clear to European intellectuals that the question was not only one of choosing or rejecting the American influence, but of understanding that the future pointed inexorably toward mass societies and mass values. In other words, it had to be realized that America was not the only extra-European "invader," but that Europe was assailed by the Soviet Union too, another power that by its philosophy and its values, its aims and techniques, was alien to the Continent although geographically on the same map with it. Prior to the Second World War and due to hostility to Fascism, the intellectuals of Europe were simply not aware that on the Eastern borders a mass society was abuilding; for them the Soviet Union was still the Russia of Gogol and Dostoevsky, combined with that of Lenin, Trotsky, Lunacharsky, Tchicherin, that is, of Westernized gentlemen and scholars, the more intriguing on account of their revolutionary ideas.

But around 1950 it became suddenly clear that it was no accident that the world—and Europe—came to be divided between two superpowers, both very different in their history and development, yet resembling each other in many disturbing ways. Statements by Tocqueville, Marx, Disraeli, Danilevsky, were quoted, predicting the emergence of the United States and Russia as arbiters of the world,• and new remarks were added that tried to clarify the ideological nature of both. It slowly became recognized

• "The future of the world is between these two great empires [the United States and Russia]," said Adolphe Thiers more than one hundred years ago. "One day they will clash and people will witness a struggle of which the past cannot give any idea, at least with regards to the masses involved and the physical impact. But the time of great moral phenomena has passed." Quoted by Sainte-Beuve in his *Cahiers,* Dec. 19, 1847.

that beyond the obvious labels—"Captalism" for one, "Communism" for the other—the two giants had a common optimism in the future of mankind as a universal society, a common belief in the perfectibility of men through education, social enlightenment, and communitarian mentality, and an equally great confidence that a scientific public philosophy is most conducive to progress and co-operation.

In order to reach these conclusions, the more lucid European intellectuals had to discard their prejudices favorable to Marxism and hostile to capitalism, and establish on new foundations their criticism of mass society in general. Having had no direct experience with mass civilization and mass democracy, they had to learn from travels, vicarious experiences, cultural contacts, and political events that beyond the old terms—capitalism, communism, socialism—the overwhelming reality of the century is the mass society, the mentality it exudes, the techniques it encourages. Whether mass society was conceived in freedom or slavery, made, of course, an enormous difference; from the guarantee of civil rights to the ruthless totalitarianization of society the distance must be measured in light-years. But for the European intellectual, who knew neither the United States nor Soviet Russia intimately, only such features of both tended to stand out which indicated a common attitude to life: uniformization through a ubiquitous party or ubiquitous business interests; official enthusiasm for the communist man or the common man; emphasis on material achievements; discouragement of inner life; the use of stultifying slogans; etc.

In 1954, André Malraux, a representative European intellectual, recognized in an interview that the influence of the United States is not the great question facing Europe. What is important, he said, is that the civilization in formation is bound up with the entire world. In the opinion of Malraux, for Europe the problem presented itself as an "integration of the new with ever living molds." And when pressed to define the nature of this mold, the specifically European value, he concluded, apologizing for the simplification yet quite firmly, that this value, best expressed by Michelangelo, is the "will to transcendence," creation with a "heroic and tragic resonance."

However, another European writer-intellectual, Aldous Huxley—who, significantly, has had a direct and long experience in the United States—had come to the disturbing conclusion that culture, that is, the inner man, cannot survive without tragedy, that is, outside traditional society, where human rapports and not scientific organization, prevail. This is the disillusioned statement of the World Comptroller in the *Brave New World* from which everything incalculable, the last ounce of freedom and hence the restlessness accompanying creative work, had been eliminated. Huxley expressed here the secret thought, the tragic *déchirement* in the consciousness of the European intellectual at mid-century when he rejects both the American and the Soviet solutions, but feels irresistibly pushed in the direction of the mass society they represent.

"In recent years," Professor Seymour Lipset wrote in *The New York Times* (1958), "as Europe has become more like America in its economic and class structure, many European intellectuals have been in despair at the rapid increase of similar popular patterns of culture in their own countries. Perhaps the growth of mass culture in Europe is a result of the fact that for the first time the lower classes have enough money and time to make their own demands in the culture market felt." Indeed, innumerable symptoms of "Americanization" thus understood could be arranged into an imposing array of proofs. In various polls French workers are quoted who prefer American novels to French ones "because they are written so that the simple people may understand them"; an ex-German emigré, Frederick Morton, quotes a young German writer who told him: "There is no longer a society to write about. In former years you knew where you stood: the peasants read the Bible; the bourgeoisie read Goethe; the maniacs read *Mein Kampf.* Now people no longer have any opinions; they have refrigerators. Instead of illusions we have television, instead of tradition, the Volkswagen. The only way to catch the spirit of the times is to write a handbook on home appliances." In England, behind the façade of a "deferential society" (as Bagehot called it), in which the higher classes set the external forms of life, mass culture is making deep inroads, submerging the belt of housing projects around the big cities. Sensationalist press and vulgar television programs are the daily fare of millions of Englishmen, while the book-reading public has been constantly diminishing in number since the war and as a result of postwar fiscal measures.

Raymond Aron observed that in postwar Europe problems of production, better distribution of wealth, and social status preoccupy people more than do ideologies. Both Left and Right evoke the specter of the *technocrat* (another "American" image), the depoliticized efficiency expert who sacrifices or outright ignores the values embodied in a long cultural heritage. His very presence indicates deep structural changes to come, not the least of which would be the placing of European economy on a continental basis, encouraging mass production and jeopardizing the cultural diversity hitherto the treasure and self-image of Europe. The loss of empires (by England, France, Holland, Belgium, Italy) and of the eastern European hinterland (source of raw materials as well as a market for finished products) equally oblige the western European nations to constitute larger economic units and to strengthen them with various political measures designed to bring about, ultimately, a kind of federation.

The Marshall Plan had opened the European market for American industry, but also for development firms, methods of production, and patterns of merchandizing and advertising. At first the Marshall Plan seemed to be an *ad hoc* solution, an experiment with limited scope; Raymond Aron could write a few years ago that the American industrial techniques belong to an age with which European industry has not yet caught up. "Workers and intellectuals," he wrote, "are suspicious of concentration on productivity: the first suspect a subtle form of exploitation, the second fear for the survival of cultural values."

The emergence of the Common Market changed this situation almost overnight. The six-nation "little Europe" began to adopt the suspected American techniques, and to feel, at the same time, stronger vis-à-vis the formidable rich uncle. What is more, its stability and relatively low wage policy have made it a desirable ground for American industrial investment; entire production plants are moving across the ocean from the United States to Europe, escaping the high wages imposed by American labor policy and finding a new market for their products. To mention only one example but one that will have a far-reaching impact on the entire way of life of Europe, IBM plants have been set up in Milan, West Berlin, Stuttgart, and France, designed to satisfy the new consumer demand for, among other things, electronic card systems used in administration, business, schools, etc.

The consequence will be twofold: American labor will finally find it necessary to pressure the labor force of Europe into demanding higher wages, and thereby "Americanize" its standard of living. Since American plants are not likely to leave a freshly conquered market, this eventual wage rise will not affect the influx of American capital. But it will result in a new industrial pattern: instead of the Americanization of Europe, we will then speak of an "Atlantization" of both continents. Once again we may quote Malraux, who said that a culture is never taken over as a whole; "the new culture is not the sum-total of those that preceded it, but their metamorphosis."

In the face of this developing new civilization the European intellectual is possessed with contradictory feelings. Generally speaking, he is inclined to think that the values embedded in the fabric of European life will remain there indefinitely. His historical memory and the vicissitudes of his own time tell him that only the surface changes, that there are constants in the human condition that shape the life of individuals and societies. Outside of his own frame of reference he notes the existence of two other societies—both European in origin but uprooted and in a sense still unsure of themselves—where the intellectuals assert that they have created at least the image of the coming man, the ideal man, and for the concretization of which they work single-mindedly and with the purposefulness of fanatics. In contrast to them, the European intellectual has no clear purpose, no exclusive image of man, because his consciousness is constituted by layers of historical images superimposed, of many types equally valuable, unique, and irreconcilable. He envisages all his aspirations as tending—but only *tending*—toward a Platonic ideal, never reaching it but keeping faith that it exists. The incurable wound in all his meditations is the knowledge that failure exists and that it is human; his only advantage over the others is that he is not afraid of failure and does not try to eliminate it.

His knowledge that failure exists teaches him that

civilizations are mortal, and also that their inner equilibrium depends on certain elements of divinity and humanity within. Thus the problem of *diversity* arises as a
condition of freedom, and conditioned, in turn, by it. The
great warning of Ortega y Gasset was against the absorption of civilizational values by mass uniformity; and he
understood the weakening of the numinal element in the
West manifest in the dehumanization of art which no
longer finds nourishment in a universe deprived of passions
and emotions; a world of objects with which no human
intercourse is possible.• A "brave new world."

Is Europe then condemned to anarchy, to the impossible
love of contradictory types and aspirations? Christopher
Dawson has written that "European culture can tolerate a
much greater degree of internal tension than can other
civilizations, without losing its sense of continuity and
community. This is largely due to the fact that in the past
the opposing religions and ideologies of the West possessed
a common origin and shared certain common principles
and beliefs." Denis de Rougemont expressed a similar
view when he wrote that in the Europe of tomorrow the
diversities and local varieties "should neither remain isolated nor intermingle, but remain in tension. The health
of Europe requires that it navigate between the Scylla of
particularisms and the Charybdis of leveling centralism."

Thus eminent thinkers recognize that the essence of
Europe is a *state of tension,* not a common ideology. Tension exists in the continent's historical past, between its
philosophical roots in Plato versus Aristotle, the Greek and
Roman genius, the barbaric element and the maturity of
civilization. Christianity itself carried this tension in its
bosom when it assigned to the human being unattainable
ideals of angelic goodness, while it permitted that he be
assailed by the temptations of his freedom. Chastity, honor,
sacrifice, charisma; Saint Bernard, Don Quixote, Michelangelo, Goethe, all represent a tremendous effort to come
to grips with the human material and subdue it, at the
price of detaching themselves from the human community.

• In the modern novel "se trata de pintar un hombre que se
parezca lo menos posible a un hombre." *La Deshumanizacion
del Arte,* p. 20. "Asistimos al drama real de unas ideas como
tales, de unos fantasmas subjetivos que gesticulan en la mente
de un autor." p. 36.

Yet this very detachment usually took communal, though exclusive, forms. Transcendance achieved longed-for fraternity, and distinction naturally sought the solace of order, code, and privilege. The whole structure of society encouraged this process of elite-formation, partly because it found in it a justification of inequality.

The crisis set in when *inequality* itself began to be questioned. The intellectual class of Europe, long engrossed in the preparation of a Promethean revolt, was nevertheless taken by surprise when it realized that the new reality, the emerging society, was ready to overflow the molds of the old categories. Historical experience and wisdom were ordained by a hierarchy of values in which the individual stood apart and above the community, entering into a dialectical relationship with it. It is through him that values became accessible to the community; his mind was the inevitable receptacle and clearing house.

The new societies that developed outside Europe were based, as we have seen, on different premises. America represented equality and prosperity; Soviet Russia was to become the home of the communist man who transforms every idea into a new form of reality (just as, in Lenin's phrase, he was to use his gold as tiles for the lavatory floors). The instrument of transformation in both societies was science and technology, made indispensable for the subjection of vast spaces, the exploitation and production of wealth, the presence of millions as workers and consumers.

Prosperity, science, technology, the natural man. None of them is alien to the European continent, but they can be said to have existed there as temptations rather than realities. The transformations of the last decades, however, the closer contact with American society and Soviet system, the defeat suffered by European intellectual ideas and the consequent feeling of inferiority, finally the "revolt" of the European masses, have brought the so-far latent conflicts into the open.

One important condition of this was that the European intellectuals should gain a new social vision. After the war, and while armies from other continents were stationed on their soil, they were forced to break out of their national isolation and recognize a new, Europe-wide dimension. They had to discover Europe in a new light, the light in which Americans, Russians, Canadians, looked at it. The result was a *continental consciousness,* an awareness of similarity in the place of local preoccupations and differences.

A second condition was that, for the first time in Europe, the problem of the collectivity versus the individual should be posed in nonpolitical, let us say, cultural, terms. Throughout political, military, and social upheavals the primacy of the educated over the noneducated was never questioned. Today Europe is inundated by a new middle class, that is, from the intellectuals' point of view, a new public, more school children, and more people to be informed and entertained. Cultural life, so far the preserve of restricted groups, must be opened to large numbers.

The intellectuals of Europe are determined to keep the initiative in their own hands, but this is a difficult task for two reasons:

For the first time in hundreds of years (since the Arab renaissance of the early Middle Ages, to be exact), Europe finds itself, in important respects, in the role of pupil rather than teacher. Whatever its cultural pride, from the United States and also from Soviet Russia, a new cultural policy aimed at millions and adjusted to their level, new techniques of dealing with masses and mass problems, are penetrating the old continent. The advantage of this is that Europe is able to select, adopt and discard, and try to work out a *European* solution. Yet, their hands are no longer completely free because—and here we come to the second reason why the task is difficult—the new leisure breeds its own world, its specialists, manipulators, and taste. Sooner or later the European intellectuals will have to discover that the new classes—or the ubiquitous middle class on the American model—may not be satisfied with the extension of traditional cultural benefits, but will demand a new concept and a new approach.

Judging again by the American example (and by the production fever manifest in the speeches of Soviet officials), this new concept is very likely to be that of mass culture. So far, only scattered instances may be noticed of this, since what makes the essence of mass culture, *obsession with objects* (corresponding to spiritual vacuity), could not develop on a truly large scale. But it may be assumed that this has had only technical obstacles, to be soon overcome. At that moment, the consumers and possessors of those objects will be in a position to dictate their preferences and their values, and the latter, in turn, will be subject to manipulation by the new class of social engineers.

Thus the European intellectual is in the process of experiencing the conflict between technology-bred prosperity on the one hand, and the values of hierarchy and culture on the other. But this experience is not so obvious as it seems, not so obvious as it is, for example, for some American critics of mass society. The European intellectual is used to an unquestioned spiritual and intellectual leadership. He inherited the benefit of the reverence owed to the priestly caste in traditional societies and that of the more modern respect due to the formulators and systematizers of class ideologies. It is sufficient, even today, to compare his position and prestige—as professor, writer, artist, thinker, journalist, party-ideologue—with those of his American counterpart to understand his views of society and its future. He is conscious that he is still wedded to the ideal of individual achievement and excellence, whereas the American intellectual opens himself to commercialization and team-mindedness, the Soviet intellectual to complete subordination to Party directives.

But the European intellectual's exalted position bars his understanding of the coming mass society. With some simplification we may say that he tends to evaluate social forces as ideological movements, that is, primarily agitations of the mind. Again, in contrast to the American intellectual who is inclined to consider and judge the motions of history by observing the *material substratum,* the European thinker feels that he dominates them when he grasps their *philosophical refraction.* While the American intellectual contents himself with moderate action and minor roles on the immense chessboard of society and seeks the mimicri of bureaucracy and committee work in order to remain inconspicuous, the European intellectual elaborates systems, in advance and above the level of actual social transformations, and waits at the next corner for reality to catch up with them.

Hence the ambiguous feeling with which he looks forward to change: *apprehension* in the face of transformations, and *impatience* when they do not occur as expected.

In the meantime, those who would like to slow down the rhythm of history (traditionalists, political rightists) and those in whom expectation overcomes fear (progressives, political leftists) engage in verbal battle, condemning or justifying changes that have not even taken place. This battle is not futile: however esoteric and theoretical it may seem, it contributes to the conceptual clarification of anticipated events, indeed to keeping alive the "ever-living molds" of which Malraux said that they must channel the new.

In order to describe the problematics of the European intellectual, we first have to understand the situation in which he finds himself. Around him the characteristic features of a mass society develop more fully every day with an increasing assertiveness. The conditions of mass industry and mass entertainment are laid; the institutional consecration of these economic and social realities cannot be postponed indefinitely; in fact, they are already outlined in the founding documents of the Common Market and other co-operative organizations like Euratom, Eurovision, and O.E.C.E.

But we have noted in the chapters dealing with social engineering, planetary coexistence and ideology that these realities and institutions are the natural fruit of a developing collectivistic ideology, and that in turn they contribute their share to the strengthening and articulation of this ideology. And although we have said above that the "essence of Europe is a state of tension, not a common ideology," the question facing Europeans today is whether the advantages of social cohesion do not overwhelmingly favor collectivistic solutions.

Of the latter, Europeans have had ample experience in the recent past. They therefore reject the totalitarian principle, as do the eastern European nations which, in spite of years of oppression and indoctrination and the constant threat of Soviet arms, continue a sort of passive resistance, showed in production lag, the permanently acute agricultural problem, and, in an atmosphere of *"homo homini lupus,"* general indifference toward collective welfare. But, for reasons enumerated earlier in this chapter, the European intellectual realizes that the world has entered upon an era of mass organization and corresponding mass ideology. His efforts, at present, aim at mastering the factors at work, reconciling them with traditional values, and warning where this seems impossible.

There seem to be three intellectual reactions before the problems of the present, and each displays these factors. They are the *humanization of technology, existential humanism,* and *religious humanism.* In the center of each the basic preoccupation is that held up by Malraux in a discourse before an audience at UNESCO: "The problem we face today is to know whether on this old continent man is dead or alive."

(1) In the eyes of many, perhaps most, European intellectuals the crisis of our time is expressed in Goethe's poem, *Der Zauberlehrling.* The physical forces liberated by the successive scientific and industrial revolutions have become, in this view, unmanageable: the *individual* sees the texture of his existence radically changed by the intrusion of technology between himself as a human person and the world of nature and the world of his fellow men; the *collectivity* sees itself regrouped in view of more efficient production, and, losing its roots, is the more easily exploited by people who have a better command of the machines and the rapports of production they establish.

Moreover, the liberation of physical forces and the domination of technology have altered the *psychological* awareness of the individual and the psychological rapports among members of society as well. The world of the machines and the technological mentality have introduced an element of artificiality into human existence, the consequence of which is a certain loss of equilibrium, a false consciousness. If the Marxist intuition is followed and modern civilization is conceived as the epiphenomenon of industrial production, then the worker becomes, as Marx said, "the living limb of a dead mechanism."

Under these conditions, psychology itself becomes mechanistic and helps establish the technological discipline that further alienates man from his normal functions. "Watch out!" cried Bernanos in one of his prophetic works, "among all the techniques there is a technique of discipline for which the mere obedience of the past is not satisfactory. Obedience used to be obtained by all kinds of empirical methods, so that we may say that it was less a discipline than a moderate disorder. Technique, on the other hand, will sooner or later insist on forming its own collaborators who will belong to it body and soul, who will accept without discussion the technical concept of order, life and the reason for living. In a world entirely devoted to Efficiency and Production, it is imperative that each citizen, from his birth, should be consecrated to the same gods. Technique cannot be called into question since the solutions it imposes are by definition the most practical." [2]

It is understandable that in Europe, where technology has been a *temptation* since the Greeks, and where, once it materialized through industry, it clashed with the traditional ways, it represents a challenge to thinking men, a total challenge that requires a total response. It is also understandable that only the present generation has achieved sufficient involvement in the technological phenomenon—through war, unemployment, and stepped-up industrialization—to grasp some of its perplexing implications. Both Gabriel Marcel and Romano Guardini note that in the nineteenth century the birth of technology had been assisted by midwives who were never possessed of the technological mentality themselves. Only in our age have technology and the mechano-human manipulative devices entered into an alliance in which the line of separation between the human being and his tools is no longer clearly distinguishable.

We have seen in Chapter Three how this phenomenon had been built by Marx into the core of his system, and how he denounced—and thought to remedy—alienation not only under capitalism but of the entire human condition once and for all. Marx's ideas on the subject were so influential that they are found inevitably at the basis of all modern theories that indict technology, the system of production, and the structure of society for the dehumanization of man. But the problem, even without the Marxist comments, is a genuine one, and it absorbs the attention of many a first-rate thinker.

Technological humanism is an expression in which both terms are equally stressed. The European intellectual is convinced today that technological civilization and the modern world it penetrates so as to be inseparable from it are realities with which man must come to terms, which he must master. The "humanization" of the machine and the machine-created conditions seem to him the supreme task, since the absence of such efforts would only facilitate the conquest by the nonideological technologue and the power-hungry technocrat—the European name for the "social engineer."

This project finds its natural place in the wider philosophical ambition of reconciling the *subject* and the *object* in a higher synthesis. Hence Husserlian phenomenology has constituted itself as the speculative justification of the enterprise, the guarantee that the human being may look with sympathy at the world of objects, whether created by nature or by the hands of men. The Husserlian echo is heard in the words of Em. Mounier when he maintains that the human person is both natural (immersed in the physical world) and transcendental. But man preserves his independence vis-à-vis the natural world: "Man's exploitation of nature is not destined to erect upon the web of natural determinism another network of conditioned reflexes"; yet he respects the objects that surround him: "to be made merely instrumental to profit, deprives the things themselves of the intrinsic dignity which poets, for example, see in them." [3] And he adds that when we degrade the objects, we end up by degrading human relations as well since on a certain important level objects express and symbolize these relations.

However, machines are no mere objects; for one thing, they represent a phase once removed from the world of creation and are themselves supremely clever manipulators of that world; for another thing, they mechanize even the human rapports, subjecting the workers to a nonhuman contact with one another. Mounier went so far as to say that "the development of the machine has called into question the entire human condition." [4] But then he also added that a systematic "anti-machinism" is a bourgeois invention.

Indeed, it has been maintained, rightly or wrongly, that there is a basic distinction between the middle class and the socialist mentality in their respective denunciation of the machine and of industrial civilization. The political Left, in Europe, following Marx, has concentrated its attack on the capitalist use of the machine, that is, private ownership, the enforcement of production quotas and work-rules from above, the chaotic, un-co-ordinated system of production for profit and for the free market. The political Right, on the other hand, denounces the machine as the symbol of materialist preoccupations, economic greed, and Mammon worship. "Man must be made to execrate the machine," wrote Bernanos, "that is a life oriented by the notion of production, efficiency, and profit." [5]

Thus the classical Right would put the machine in a sort of social quarantine as something unclean with which contact should be minimal, because no political system is immune from its corruptive power. "Capitalism, democracy, fascism, all of them may be destroyed from within by the technological mentality," wrote F. W. Juenger. The classical Left, on the contrary, has seen in the machine the means by which the contradiction between capital and labor becomes unbearably sharp and thus the instrument of working-class conquest of the entire society.

Technological humanism has undeniably profited from both views; from the Left it has taken the idea that the worker who fashions the material and handles the tools must be reconciled with both; from the Right it has learned to distrust the technological mentality even in a society where improved material conditions prevail. It displayed a certain originality in understanding that the world of the machines and that of men are in a close relationship, so that the term "industrial civilization" indicates a necessary unity, not a separation, a contradiction.

In Europe, according to the technological humanists, "culture" has come to denote a system in opposition to that of "technology." It is presented, writes Jean Lacroix, "as a system for the defense of man, implying that the technical objects do not contain a human reality." But, he remarks, "if culture remains simply what it has been traditionally, it is false because it no longer fashions man's attitudes in modern civilization. . . . The new philosophy is bound, therefore, to reintegrate the *technical* into an enlarged notion of the *cultural*. . . . No culture can exist if our concern shies away from our objective accomplishment."

Simone Weil too, in whose person the highest intellectual preoccupations so beautifully harmonized with the effort to understand the life of workers, expected to put an end to alienation-through-work by a "re-rooting" (ré-enracinement) in the world of objects. She spoke of man who "comes to grips with nature and asserts himself as the only

free being in the created universe." "What marvelous full-
ness life could reach through a civilization where work
would constitute the par excellence human act!" [6]

The main preoccupation of the humanists of work is to
bring about a society without distinctions of class, wealth,
or education, based on the primacy, on the "nobility," of
work in its rehabilitated forms. In other words, technological humanism ends up by speaking the language of
Utopia (and, more often than not, the language of Marx)
since, to mention only one point that weakens its arguments, at present, under the impact of new technological
inventions, work is becoming more, rather than less, differentiated.

The technological humanists have many lofty ideals on
their program: they speak of the machine endowed with
a "soul," of the reconciliation of specialties through the
unity of science, of eliminating the distinction between intellectual and manual labor, between servile and noble
tasks. Also, they are nostalgic for the pre-industrial, pre-
capitalist age when artisanal knowledge was compatible
with personal dignity and pride of accomplishment, and
work was not fragmented by excessive division of labor.
They expect a technological-humanist era to usher in true
democracy in which a "functional elite" would keep in close
touch with the masses and would constantly renew itself
through recruitment at this source.•

Thus the theses of the technological humanists do not
differ essentially from the subjects discussed in the chapters on Marxism and on the planetary ideology. They, too,
are predicated on the intellectualization of the masses and

• The fear of the Left that the technocrats will not form such
an elite is clear in the following passage of *Le Socialisme trahi*
by André Philip: "The directors of corporations possess the
sense of public interest and recognize the necessity of economic
organization; they represent the most progressive element of
economic life; among them are a large number of those who
inspire and work for Europe-wide institutions. The danger is
that, proud of their value, persuaded that a profound economic
transformation is necessary, they are working *for* the people but
without the people, and contribute to the formation of a techno-
cratic directorate which demands a strong discipline, a powerful executive, and a government with authoritarian tendencies."
p. 22-3.

the humanization of technology. "In a truly humanistic (non-capitalistic) state of culture, the things of the world would be proportioned to man," wrote Maritain, considered the mentor of many technological humanists.[7] And Jean Lacroix carried this belief one step closer to Marxism when he assigned to philosophy the task of "granting freedom to all that man alienates from himself." It is obvious that the technological humanists treat machine civilization as if it were a mental category whose fate depends on our awareness of the machine's functions and our love for it. In other words, they are seduced, beyond Marxism, by the alleged state of equilibrium that existed between contemplation and *techné* in the Greek mind. What they overlook is that whatever the nature of that equilibrium may have been, in our world it is definitely upset since *techné* has become the enormous universe of technology.•

(2) After having been extolled as the representative philosophy of the century, existentialism has been lately degraded to the status of a passing mood in a war-torn Europe whose somber horizon is said to have expressed itself in a correspondingly pessimistic view of life. Existentialism is, of course, a great deal more than a mood; but we may ask, in this connection, Why did it become, in postwar Europe, a constituent of intellectual consciousness, an inspirer of artistic and literary form?

The answer is that existentialism was an attempt to explain the nihilism of the prewar generation and to reconcile the latter's immorality and despair with the possibility of an ethical system.•• In other words, human action, degraded and discredited, needed a kind of rehabilitation as the sick man needs some encouraging words before he may again try to walk. E. M. Cioran has felicitously captured the spirit of European intellectuals waiting for just such an encouragement: "Skepticism has lived, and the intellectual,

• According to Henri Marrou, himself rather sympathetic to the objectives of a technological humanism in which he sees the only way of saving the humanistic values from being engulfed by "other forms of culture," the Greek choice of the *contemplative* in preference to the *technical* was a conscious one. (In *A History of Education in Antiquity*.)

•• In his prologue to *Actuelles II*, Camus wrote in 1953: "We begin to emerge from a state of nihilism. . . . Once again a morality has become possible."

frustrated by his doubts, is searching for the compensations of a dogma. Arrived at the frontiers of analysis, taken aback before the abyss he finds there, he retraces his steps and grasps the first certitude he encounters." [8] But Cioran saw clearly that the intellectual abandons his skepticism with a considerable reluctance, and that he becomes a "fanatic without convictions," a "hybrid thinker," attached to the old "through the form of his intelligence, and to the new through the ideas he defends."

And it is very true that the thinkers and writers whom we link with existentialism seem to defend certain ideas, but without conviction, without the warmth of commitment. It is, perhaps, for this reason that they have consecrated the term "involvement" (*engagement*) in which they really do not believe in any except a formal way. Sartre understood this flaw of the system when he wrote that, all told, existentialist humanism is not attacked for its pessimism, but for its *hard optimism* (*dureté optimiste*).

The main concern of this trend is then the rehabilitation of action—and of man who acts—in a world without meaning whose conceptual and political framework is, however, still rationalistic. The moral imperative of this world was expressed by the young André Gide in 1894: "The wise man lives without morality, according to his wisdom. We must try to reach this level of superior immorality." [9] But it is obvious that this ethical system was a failure, and Simone de Beauvoir, indeed, drew a different conclusion from the nonexistence of God: "Far from authorizing all license, the absence of God, that is, the loneliness of man in this world, turns his actions into final, absolute commitments. He is responsible for a world which is not the product of an alien power, but of himself. . . . A God may grant pardon, erase sins and compensate the righteous; but if God does not exist, the faults of men are inexpiable."•

• *Pour une morale de l'ambiguité*, p. 23.

The same problem beset Nietzsche whose obsession was, as Walter Kaufmann writes, "to escape nihilism which seems involved both in asserting the existence of God and thus robbing this world of ultimate significance, and also in denying God and thus robbing everything of meaning and value." *Nietzsche, Philosopher, Psychologist, Antichrist*, p. 86.

In what way and in the name of what value is man responsible for anything outside of the satisfaction of his own needs—biological, or as Gide insisted, "superior," that is, esthetic? How is the human being justified in establishing rapports with others; what is the nature of friendship, love, generosity, charity? These questions are philosophical ones, but it must be understood that in the contemporary climate of Europe they have been "existential" problems; answers to them were expected to be, above all, lucid and stark in the face of old philosophical and political illusions. Ultimately they were to be not only answers to individuals, but also solutions on a collective level. In a sense, the survival of civilized society depended on them since what is the social order if not a web of human actions for a meaningful purpose?

An important text of existentialist humanism is Jean-Paul Sartre's essay in which he justifies the rapport between these terms.[10] It is significant that the author wrote this text in answer to charges that existentialism (or, at least, his own version of it) is quietistic, pessimistic, and discourages action (Marxist reproach), or that it displays the sordidness of the human animal (Catholic reproach).

Sartre argues that by putting on man the heavy burden of *defining himself* and of inventing the values by which he lives, existentialism endows him with a high degree of personal responsibility, thus placing him on a noble pedestal. What is more, man makes his choices in full knowledge that they might be imitated by others• and thus, theoretically, raised to the dignity of categorical imperatives. His humanity is further emphasized by the fact that he knows he must pay a high price both for being free and for assuming responsibility for others: "Man is condemned to be free," writes Sartre in a passage that has become famous, "condemned because he has not created himself . . . and free because once thrown into this world, he is responsible for all he does." [11] And then: "Who proves that I am called upon (*désigné*) to impose my concept of man and my choice on mankind? . . . Every man must tell himself: am I one who has the right to act in

---

• In the Sartrian language: "en se choisissant, il choisit tous les hommes."

such a way that mankind might model its actions on my own?" [12]

It follows from an examination of this and other texts that humanism as conceived by Sartre means, as he himself asserts, man's transcending himself in goals, accomplishments, self-enrichment—through action. Sartre is even eager to call existentialism a "doctrine of action," that is, one by which action is rehabilitated, justified. In his case, as well as in that of other, kindred thinkers, the seduction of Marx is obvious in that they cannot consider as legitimate a philosophical system which is not, at the same time, an invitation to action.

The same is true of Camus and Malraux. Although their thought is less systematic, they can be said to be even more illustrative of existentialist humanism, because they grasp and express its underlying motivations with the artist's intuition and through the personal experience of very sensitive men receptive to the influences of the contemporary European milieu.

They too are obsessed with the justification of man's activity—elementary as well as exceptional. The words of Karl Reinhardt concerning the existentialist view of philosophy apply to them also: "Existentialism calls attention to the fact that philosophy is a truly human discipline precisely because it always includes venture and risk, and reflects in both its sublimity and frailty the ambivalence of human existence." [13]

"Venture and risk" are well-observed obsessions of this humanism, which seeks the dignity of man in action, but in an action that must be the more dramatic as it remains without an echo in an indifferent universe. This is why Malraux celebrates T. E. Lawrence, the lonely man who "wanted to mark history with his presence"; why he invites "the thousands of human beings to unite in revolutionary hope and action so that they might not be masses but fellow-men";[14] why, in his biographer's words, he points to the work of art as a "mirage of eternity." [15]

While André Malraux's world, devoid of love and sentimentality, celebrates exceptional action—revolution, artistic creation, historic involvements—Albert Camus, a more alive, warm, and "Mediterranean" writer, represents the other facet of action worship: the justification of everyday concern, of the Sisyphean tasks, which confer on man dignity through the servitudes of an average existence. To be sure, he, too, spoke of the artist as a rebel trying to "ravish from history its elusive values" and of the revolutionist who awakens to his humanity through the solidarity of common suffering; but, *in fine,* Camus accepts the wisdom of Cineas[16] that "between the atom and the universe the task of man is to live and to persevere." "In our quality as artists," he wrote in *Actuelles II,* "we do not have to participate in the agitations of the world."

Sartre was right when he pointed out that existentialism preached the validity of action by repudiating determinism. "Choice," "project," "freedom" are frequent terms of existentialist literature, and, in the words of Henri Peyre, the over-all effect of the Sartrian texts is a divorce of *human* from *material* reality.[17] Camus himself manages to overcome the temptation of suicide (the supreme logical act in an absurd universe) only by using action as an "antidote to despair." In other words, existentialist humanism has abandoned the concept of a rational history in which "disorder" was considered merely an accident. It has discovered that disorder was the very core of man's existence and thus of history as well.

There is no way of "stepping out" of this predicament since "man is condemned to be free." But precisely: his freedom can be best proved in and by action. Action is not a consequence of certain recognized values that give it a divine guarantee; on the contrary, action, that is, man's self-projection, is a creator of values. As P.-H. Simon remarked, the existentialists want "to drive out from history the obsession of the absolute . . . [because] only free man is capable of making his own history." [18]

The question is not so much whether they succeed in expelling the "obsession of the absolute" from history—as this: did they elaborate a valid, acceptable view of action and of man who acts?

Three such "views" may be said to have competed in the minds of Europe's intellectuals in the past several decades: the Marxist doctrine of social transformation, variations of Georges Sorel's "myth" for a workers' society (the National-Socialist and Fascist doctrines were its tributaries), and the "humanisms" like the ones we are discussing, which attempt to "save" action in the philosophical sense, although they recognize the porous nature of the agent, man.•

Much has been written about the Marxist choice by which most prominent existentialist thinkers have alienated their freedom. In spite of the clear-sighted warning that Sartre launched in his essay "Matérialisme et Révolution" (1946) concerning the incompatibility of existentialism (a philosophy of freedom) and Marxism (the philosophy of historical determinism), he himself gave the example of yielding to what appeared to be the invincible attraction of Communism. Others, like Camus, opted for less intransigent forms of Marxism, sometimes very personal forms of libertarian socialism, unorthodox Communism, etc. But although Sartre himself admitted that Marxism had a decisive impact on his generation••—which we may interpret as implying that the Marxist solution does not logically follow from the previous existentialist choice—the truth is that postwar existentialism was unable to bridge the gap it had discovered between man and the world, between man and his activity, among the members of human society. Briefly, existentialism defined man's freedom altogether negatively, as a bold but desperate projection of nothingness into the world of compactly packed objects.

Thus both Sartre and Camus, the most representative figures of the postwar philosophico-literary ambience, while setting out to rehabilitate man, succeeded only in designing such an ambiguous image of him—floating between despair and exaltation—as to discourage any real solution in the philosophical order. This is so because their existentialism emphasizes that aspect of man by which he is a totally "other," unrecognizable to his fellow's eyes, and thus an

---

• *Porous* is used here in the sense in which Sartre calls man the flaw in the universe who "negates" (*néantiser*) the world.
•• "The men of my age know it well: more even than the two world wars, the great event in their life has been to face constantly the working class and its ideology, which gave them an irrefutable vision of the world and of themselves. For us Marxism is more than a philosophy: it is a climate of our ideas, the soil which nourishes us, the true movement of what Hegel called the Objective Spirit." "Le Réformisme et les fétiches," *Les Temps Modernes,* Feb., 1956.

object for him. Between the burdensome freedom of *existence,* which manifests itself in doubt, guilt feeling, sensation of absence, and suspension of judgment (*epoché*); and the compactness of *essence,* man and the world can come to terms only in the processes of history and its dialectical windings. Thus the solution, once more, is projected into Utopia.

(3) As an individual (*pour-soi*) man is guilty in the sense that he is committed to the hopeless project of becoming complete (*pour-soi-en-soi*), that is, divine. This is, however, a "useless passion," Sartre tells us, yet one that stamps our humanity with the basically somber outlook that Sartre himself called, as we remember, a hard optimism.

Present-day European religious humanism grew out of, among other sources, the realization that *man* must be saved at the same time as his *action,* for otherwise the latter is either a Sisyphean act or the instrument of the will to power. Of the three intellectual movements, then, only the third understands that in order for action to have meaning, the human being himself must be considered an intelligible agent, and that this, in turn, is predicated on his transcendance toward God. In other words, man is not a useless passion, but a being responsive to a Being higher than himself. Man is the shepherd of Being, as Heidegger puts it.

Naturally, religious humanism bases its teaching on the individual as such, that is, on the *person,* not on the individual who emerged as a consciousness only in contact with the collectivity, the conditions of his work, his social class, or with history. "The person whom Marx strives to liberate," Maritain writes, "is conceived as purely immanent in the group. Hence the only emancipation which Communism could achieve would be that of the collective man, not of the individual person." [19] This distinction is made by all great religious thinkers of the last hundred years, beginning with Kierkegaard who, according to his manner, underlined it very heavily: "The immorality of the [nineteenth] century . . . consists . . . in an extravagant contempt for the private individual. . . . People today have existence in horror . . . because . . . they dare live only in a mass, leaving no elbow room among each other so as to feel that they exist. . . . The task of the subjective thinker is to express . . . what is human in existence." [20]

For Kierkegaard the truth that his contemporaries were thirsting after (a thirst caused by the ultrarationalism of the Hegelian world system) was not of a cognitive nature. In his conclusion to the *Unscientific Postscript* he wrote: "The philosophy of pure thought is for an existing individual a chimera, if the truth that is sought is something to exist in." Only existence does not have to be *thought* in order for it to be real, and he who chooses to live in it remakes himself through every new choice since he arrives at them outside of the rational, logical sequence. The *tour de force* in the Kierkegaardian philosophy is, of course, the fundamental choice (belief in a rationally unguaranteed God), itself ungrounded, but from which all subsequent choices follow.

After the Protestant (Lutheran) Kierkegaard, the Orthodox Leo Shestov, too, wagered on God. He called attention to the paradox not noticed by the classical rationalists —Spinoza, Leibniz, Kant—that man, in search of freedom, should accept an impersonal necessity (universal laws, science, determinism), and even subject God to it; the fault of man, Shestov writes, the original sin of Adam, is to consider it terrible "to abandon oneself in the hands of the living God, but accept lightheartedly the submission to a system of necessary laws." [21] Man should think according to the "categories of life" that bring out the ever-renewing marvel of God "for whom nothing is impossible," not even to erase what *is*, such as when Christ abolished the sins of men. The goal that religious philosophy pursues is to recover the freedom of Adam, the trust that God is all-powerful.

Kierkegaard and Shestov represent the extreme wing of modern religious speculation. Their merit was to combat an equally extreme rationalism which, when it finally broke down, left in its wake a disoriented human being desperately searching for new moorings. Also, they contributed strongly to the rehabilitation of philosophy as a discipline attached to the study of *being*, not merely to that of scientific investigation (epistemology, logical positivism). Thus a platform was erected for a new humanism. As Berdyaev has written: "The chief characteristic which distinguishes philosophic from scientific knowledge is that philosophy knows being in and through man, and finds in man the solution of the problem of meaning, while science knows being as it were apart from man and outside him."

But while on the fringes of the Continent the Protestant and Slavic soul—for different reasons—sought the dissociation of man and reason, Catholic and Jewish thought, in central and western Europe, pursued their reconciliation. This meant also the effort to bring into a synthesis the spiritual and material world, the individual and society. We have noted the insistence of Em. Mounier, following in this his master, Maritain, that the world of objects should be respected in the fashion of poets and artists. This thought received a far more significant expression in the writings of Simone Weil, who saw the entire history of the West—its science, art, and statecraft—illumined by the spirit of religion that crowns it. She found that "Greek geometry and the Christian faith flow from the same source," [22] and saw in the recognition of this unity a condition of changing our outlook on life; since, as she noted in *L'Enracinement* too, the modern world suffers gravely from the belief that science belongs exclusively to the world of nature, while, in truth, science "is only a reflection of the world's beauty."

The Platonism of Simone Weil, by which she sought to reintegrate science and the world of things into philosophy through a concept of the cosmos, could not ignore the human being; in fact, it raised man to the highest level by subordinating him to God. As Father J. M. Perrin and the philosopher Gustave Thibon write about her in their book of reminiscences, everything in her early training, especially her contact with the thought of Spinoza, "predisposed her to see the religious sentiment as the highest manifestation of human life. . . . But an altogether different fact imposed itself on her mind: the light descends from above; she received the certitude that not man, but God is the measure of things"; that man is able to transcend himself, this is what she called faith and supernatural love.[23]

His transcendance does not contradict man's longing for being in society. The question is only whether he will be lost in the impersonality of the mass, or will bring to society his own personality as a factor of articulation. Man may be *bundled* with the crowd like a stick in a bundle, wrote Martin Buber, carried by movements extraneous to him; or he may be *bound* to the community as the body politic, and then his condition implies "the confrontation of each movement carefully." The individual must work at the transfiguration of the crowd, the mass into a community, otherwise the person becomes derivatory and is excused a personal response in every realm that joins him to the whole. For his own sake and for that of the collectivity he must preserve himself as a person because "the collectivity cannot enter, instead of the person, into the dialogue of the ages which the Godhead conducts with mankind." [24]

The central concern of the religious humanists is, then, to oppose the modern confusion of the two realms: individual and collectivity; they achieve this not by setting up a dichotomy, a jealous separation, but by emphasizing man's dual nature as an inhabitant of both. Bernanos expressed this thought with great clarity when he reminded the collectivists of their exaggerations: "Man is not made to live alone, and the strayed members of the flock invariably end by coming back to it. Whereas if man one day sacrifices the rights of the Person to some collectivity, he will never find them again, for that collectivity will ceaselessly grow in power and efficiency." [25]

Not having to justify the condition and even the existence of man as the technological and existentialist humanists deem it necessary, the religious humanists are in no obligation to exalt *work* above man's other aspirations. For the first two categories of thinkers labor represents the only tie (if we discount revolutions) linking men together who are otherwise bound up in their egoism like the monads of Leibniz in their windowless existence. The impact of Marx on them further explains why work is so crucial since it determines man's contact with nature and its organization is responsible for the internal rapports of society. For the religious humanist man is a far richer creature, linked to the natural and to the transcendental world by an infinite number of ties. This is why Josef Pieper can afford (in *Leisure, the Basis of Culture*) to speak of counteracting the cult of work with the cult of divine worship, and of contemplation as the real purpose of leisure.

Summarizing the situation of the intellectuals in Europe, one may say that their central preoccupation is to secure for the Continent a smooth transition from what is still a largely traditional society to an industrial community of nations. The problem is, of course, singularly dramatized by the fact that the modern concept of a technological society, the modern forms of mass culture, and the modern forms of social cohesion and ideological consensus are exemplified, in their eyes, by the two superpowers, the United States and the Soviet Union. In this way, the intellectuals are able to crystallize in their minds the *processes* that point to a probable future, and the *results* they want to work for or avoid.

However, it is one thing to possess the intellectual equipment with which to face a potential situation, and another to cope with it when it becomes a reality. By and large, the European intellectual is convinced that he can grasp and command all the forces of the new age, and that with his long historical experience he can even set an example to younger civilizations. But when everything is said and done, it seems that he is far more capable of drawing the ultimate philosophical-political conclusions about the coming era of social engineering (and of translating these conclusions into vibrant pieces of literature and art) than of preparing original forms of protection and adaptation. For example, in the cadre of what one might call a "literature of warning," three European writers have expressed the very essence of the fear that grips the world before the rise of utopian-totalitarian society: Kafka, Huxley, and Orwell have explored all the circles of the hell into which mankind may be descending. Yet, there has been no corresponding concrete achievement to present the alternative. Or again: a very large number of European thinkers, Ortega y Gasset, Toynbee, Jaspers, Heidegger, G. Marcel, R. Guardini, and others have analyzed with extraordinary lucidity the contemporary concepts of mass mind, decline of civilizations, the inroads of mechanization, etc.; but their conclusions are vitiated by either the world-historical perspective they take, or by the fact that their image of the new age is influenced by their contact with its political-ideological representatives only. In short, they are not directly acquainted with the social engineer and the mass society he represents, but rather with the (Western) Marxist ideologue, the technician, the enthusiast of progress, who have not managed to create, so far, the social context necessary to their activities. This abstract treatment may be seen from the example of the various "humanisms" we have discussed that try to instill human values into man's relationship with the machine, but only succeed in recommending some watered-down version of the Marxist world view and enclose the human being into a deceptive self-exaltation.

Having but an abstract schema and conceptual grasp of technology and seeing it as the ideological residue of the machine, the European intellectual speaks of it as of an *idea,* an *entity* that can be accepted, rejected, administered in doses, integrated in the culture, or subordinated to spiritual values. This metaphysical approach, however, does not go to the heart of the issue: technology is more than the "mentality" that the machine exudes, it is an adjunct and a precondition of social engineering insofar as it facilitates the *gathering and serializing of data* (social calculus, testing, planning, etc.), and offers social *solutions* that appear obvious, scientific, and testable.

For these reasons, social engineering cannot be restricted to the world of material objects; it infiltrates the human rapports as well, which it tries to shape and interpret according to methods derived from technical problems and accomplishments: law of averages, collective efficiency, the needs to formulate and mechanize human reactions.•

It follows from the consideration of technology as an entity that can be circumscribed and, as it were, exorcised by the philosophical treatment, also limited and dominated, that the European intellectual tries to entrust an *elite* with its manipulation. Depending on whether we speak to a socialist, a technocrat, a conservative, a Catholic, or a Communist, each will conceive of this elite in a different way, but each will also take it for granted that technology

• Much of contemporary social engineering originated in military science, the movements of large numbers of men under arms, the problems of dealing with supply, logistics, battle morale. The French ideologues of the early nineteenth century, and many Saint-Simonists, were graduates of the Ecole Polytechnique, founded by Napoleon for the study of military problems, engineering, etc.

must be "mastered" by one. Denis de Rougemont told me a few years ago that since the present formula of Western democracy is no longer valid, the function of governing must be entrusted to a new elite, whose historical task might be to preside over the destinies of a federated Europe. This statement sums up the present concern of European intellectuals at least in one important direction; they have believed, from Plato to Mosca and Toynbee, that everything is a question of elites and that elites construct the molds for the rest of society. What the European intellectual has failed to see, at least so far, is that the depolitization of life and the equalization of classes may throw the intellectuals off their balancing function, and unseat them from their position as an elite.

So far, the intellectuals have known only political-ideological elites, that is, products of the postmedieval fragmentation of the political-religious community. Therefore they tend to see the now emerging elite of social engineers in a similar light, and are convinced that the future will develop according to the mentality that the new elite adopts. What is so hard for them to understand is that this new elite will not be the depository and articulator of values that then shape the public philosophy; the public philosophy will flow from unidentifiable sources, partly as the reverberation of ephemeral demands by a ubiquitous "public," partly from the quasi-scientific interpretation of these demands and needs by an equally ubiquitous bureaucracy. Both public demand and bureaucratic interpretation *bypass* the screening process of ideas and ideologies, thus eliminating the traditional function of intellectual elites. Such elite groups will continue to exist, of course, but without appreciable influence on the public. As Leo Strauss has written, "when the authoritative type is the common man, everything has to justify itself before the tribunal of the common man; everything that cannot be justified before that tribunal becomes, at best, merely tolerated, if not despised and suspect. And even those who do not recognize that tribunal are, willy-nilly, molded by its verdicts." [26]

Now, unless we play on words, we must agree that the common man cannot form an elite except in the demagogic vocabulary of the social engineers themselves. Yet, as Professor Strauss has perceived, the common man may shape the values of a society precisely by his ephemeral demands, his impatience with subtlety and depth, his forcing open the shells in which values are slowly maturing. That in these processes he is assisted by the social engineer is a truism. But it would be inexact to conclude that the social engineers play the role of an elite; in fact, it would be more accurate to say that there exists a logical and inevitable co-operation between him and the common man, that they form the double phenomenon of mass civilization. The advance of one represents the progress of the other.

11

Intellectual and Philosopher

1.

"The position of intellectuals," wrote Karl Mannheim, "presented no problem as long as their intellectual and spiritual interests were congruous with those of the class that was struggling for social supremacy. They experienced and knew the world from the same utopian perspective as that of the group or social stratum with whose interest they identified themselves. This applies as well to Thomas Münzer as to the bourgeois fighters of the French Revolution, to Hegel as well as to Marx. . . . Their [the intellectuals'] situation becomes questionable, however, when the group with which they identify themselves arrives at a position of power, and when, as a result of this attainment of power, the utopia is released from politics." [1]

If the intellectuals bore allegiance to "intellectual and spiritual interests" and could conclude alliances with classes "struggling for social supremacy," then obviously these classes were also carriers of some ideals, compatible with the values held by the intellectuals. And it is true that social classes, in their forward drive to a place under the political sun were instruments of progress. But is this the progress that the intellectuals themselves envisaged? In other words, how is one to understand the use of the term "utopia" in the above-quoted text? It turned out that the struggle of social classes, no matter how antagonistic their interests were, resulted in a social harmony in which the rights achieved by one ultimately benefited the others too. For example, the emergence of the working class as consumers has been found to contribute decisively to the general prosperity, stability, and security of the whole society. In this sense, the preconditions of Utopia have been reached, as is illustrated by the present success of social engineering, which builds on the values of the generalized middle class which includes now almost everywhere the workers too.

Also in this sense, "utopia has been released from politics," that is, the search for a peaceful and prosperous world, insofar as the search is channeled by ideologies. Mannheim states correctly that intellectuals are no longer needed for the final consolidation of power. But he does not say that this is only because for the next phase in the development of the classless society, ideologies will be useless; he takes one more decisive step.

Karl Popper, in his *Poverty of Historicism*, devotes an interesting chapter to the "holistic or Utopian social engineering," which aims at "remodelling the whole of society in accordance with a definite plan or blueprint" (p. 67). Popper argues that, in reality, social engineering defeats its own purpose because "the greater the holistic changes attempted, the greater are their unintended and largely unexpected repercussions, forcing upon the holistic engineer the expedient of piecemeal improvisation" (p. 68). From defeat to defeat, the holistic social engineer will be led "to extend his programme so as to embrace not only the transformation of society . . . but also the transformation of man" (p. 70). And, in fact, this is what Karl Mannheim, quoted by Popper, actually envisaged: "The political problem," he wrote, "is to organize human impulses in such a way that they will direct their energy to the right strategic points, and steer the total process of development in the desired direction." [2] This is why, in Mannheim's description, ideologies will be useless in the stage of consolidation of the new, "reconstructed" society.

As Karl Popper rightly points out, this program "substitutes for the demand that we build a new society fit for men and women to live in, the demand that we *mould* [my italics] these men and women to fit into this new society." ³ In other words, according to Popper, the manipulation that Mannheim foresees would no longer have human beings for its objects, but mechanized robots. The game would thus be tricked. But, after all, Karl Popper, as an eminent logician, analyzes this text for its consistency, and thus misses the utopian drive it contains. Mannheim's demand should be interpreted as meaning that the reconstruction of society will involve action on two levels: the creation of an institutional framework *and*, since this is not sufficient, the molding—scientific direction, economic planning, vocational orientation, psychological counseling, and social conditioning—of the future citizen.

At any rate Popper correctly diagnoses this proposal as a call for social engineering. When Mannheim speaks of the organization of "human impulses," he clearly does not mean ideas and concepts, or even passions and interests, but that area of personality and group mentality with which the psychiatrist, the motivational researcher, the personality tester, seek to interfere, which they try to manipulate.

The emotional, and even more, the behavioral, terminology of social engineering indicates the area in which this manipulation takes place: leadership, co-operation, unanimity, team spirit, "togetherness," adjustment, organization-man, other-direction, are based on uncontrollable, non-rational impulses or indoctrinated behavior about which practically any statement may have some ephemeral *hic-et-nunc* validity, but which cannot be proved or disproved. Since these areas are not subject to rational discourse, they become privileged fields of social engineering: those who are thus manipulated have no way of resisting because they cannot even band together for lack of a common level, a consensus of impulses, so to speak.

But if the concern with *politics* has shifted to the *organization of human impulses*, then clearly the intellectual, who by definition cannot accompany the social engineer all the way, has become a displaced person—through his own fault. To be charitable to him, we may say that he did not become aware of where the logic of his ideologies was leading until what he had undertaken fell to the lot of the social engineer. At that point his ideas begin to exist in a social-intellectual vacuum and cannot compete with the verbal tools of social engineering, which affect the public mind in a more impressive way since they are made up of nonrational slogans and platitudes, translated into the language of gestures and controlled behavior.

The main reason for which the intellectual has had to abdicate is his monistic philosophical position. As we have said in other chapters, since his conviction is that the goal and meaning of history is to build the good society, the basic commitment of the intellectual is to secure a collective salvation for mankind. It is this false aim that vitiates his view of the human being and of the nature of politics: he tries to mold man according to a model of angelic perfection, trusting that he might alter the nature of politics so as to make of it a religion, the final and exalted unanimity of co-operating units. *Units*, since we cannot designate as *men* human beings deprived of individuality, self-interest, incalculable choice, briefly, of freedom.

Thus, in the last analysis, the failure of the intellectual —and his decline—is due to his philosophy built on errors. This is why he and his legitimate heir, the social engineer, believe that man can be frozen into a machinelike being, and his transactions, that is, politics, can be summed up and directed by a set of mechanical formulas. They do not understand, as Hans Morgenthau, Jr., writes, that "political problems cannot be solved by the invention of a mechanical formula which will allow mankind to forget about them. . . . Being projections of human nature into society, they cannot be solved at all. They can only be restated, manipulated, and transformed, and each epoch has to come to terms with them anew. . . . The moral problem of politics is but a peculiar instance of the moral problem which man encounters whenever he acts with reference to his fellow-man." [4]

In the second part of this chapter we shall outline the only course that intellectuals may follow in the future if they want to regain not so much their influence, but much more important, their integrity. We will discuss, in other words, not ideologies, but philosophy and the road that might lead the *intellectual* back to the status of *philosopher*. At present let us discuss the three consequences of the philosophical error we just denounced, consequences that are like stations on the intellectuals' road to Calvary: one-world, unitary ideology, and history as god.

(1) In a sense the failure of the intellectuals has been the failure of Western humanism and liberalism based on the Greek pattern of thought. What Leo Shestov called the drama of choice between Athens and Jerusalem has also been at the root of the intellectuals' errors and of their timidity. They, whether humanists, ideologues, liberals, or Marxists, and their enemies who moved in the same universe of discourse, denounced at once the various versions of the society based on classes and the "obstacles" that stood in the way of man's emancipation sponsored by reason alone. Thus the critique of society and its institutions went parallel with the ultrarationalistic view of man as a Saint George defeating the dragons of darkness, irrationality, particular interests, and superstitions.

The development of the Western concept of liberal society is thus historically linked to the humanistic view of the individual, himself conceived as the arbiter of easily harmonizable forces within. To the benevolent republic, ruling peaceably over the various enlightened interests, there corresponded the image of the open-minded and reasonable individual ready to improve himself further as more education brought him more reasonableness and peaceful intentions. "In the liberal world," wrote R. Niebuhr, "the evils in human nature and history were ascribed to social institutions or to ignorance or to some other manageable defect in human nature or environment." [5]

But, as Niebuhr points out, and as we have seen in the chapter on the progressive intellectual, the Marxist doctrine was always one up on the liberal world view. Where the latter ascribed the evil in history to social institutions in general, Marxism put the responsibility squarely on the institution of property; whereas liberalism hoped to enlighten people's self-interest through education and the scientific planning of society, the Communist dogma was more specific: the abolition of individual property will lead, in Engel's phrase, to a state of innocence with "no soldiers, no gendarmes, no policemen, prefects or judges, no prisons, laws or lawsuits" and, in Lenin's and Bukharin's statement, to eternal peace since wars are exclusively the products of capitalism and its built-in predatory imperialism. While the liberal view sought to bring about social harmony through economic manipulation: graduated taxation, educational measures, compulsory schooling, etc., Marxism believed that only one class, the proletariat, had the vocation of abolishing class conflicts in general: by conquering society and making its own values universal.

Thus on every point vital in the management of society, liberal and Marxist thinking, the first gradually and experimentally, the second with a radical determination, have been preparing a state of affairs in which it was believed that interests can be harmonized, conflicts eliminated, power abolished, the global community established. Engels' just-quoted phrase, if projected from the national context to the world scene, should be translated as the ultimate annulment of all that has made up a political community at any time of history. And with our awareness that the political concepts of an age or of an ideology are always in close relationship with its image of man, we may say that for Engels's ideal to materialize, purely "political" instruments, such as institutions, constitutions, and legal systems, are not sufficient; as implied by Mannheim, the human being himself must be transformed.

We witness, in other words, a novel version of gnosticism, rooted, as Eric Voegelin points out, in the profound dissatisfaction with the world as *it is*, a total rejection of history, a passionate and aggressive insistence that both should be radically transformed. But while the Gnostics and Manicheans were dreaming in a world where neither global organization nor an elite controlling it was possible, their present-day fellow ideologues potentially possess the organizational means to impose at least the external framework of "total regeneration." This is, of course, the guiding line of Marxism, which claims that the proletariat is the self-conscious movement of the majority of men and thus acts for the entire mankind; and, as Niebuhr writes, "liberal culture" is based on the same impatience "with the seeming limitations of human wisdom in discerning the total pattern of destiny and with the failure of human power to bring the total pattern under the dominion of the human will." [6]

Taking for granted that there is between the liberal-progressive and the Marxist ideologue only a difference of degree, we may conclude that for both the process of *dis-*

alienation of man cannot be achieved without disalienating history itself. The transformations in the modes of production and in the ownership of its means are but the conditio sine qua non of a more general transformation, at the end of which history itself is to be salvaged and lifted "from the realm of necessity into the realm of freedom." In other words, what has been so far is not considered history but a kind of blind groping among tyrannical institutions, evil plots against the freedom and happiness of mankind; history will only come into its own with the establishment of a universal society, a secular New Jerusalem.

It is true that this final phase will be preceded by destruction. Intellectuals today throw up their hands in horror before destructiveness in which they are incapable of discerning the twin sister of creativity since they are informed by a one-sided humanism and consequently a limited imagination. Yet they are ready to attack with the utmost ruthlessness the structure and institutions of the present world which, in their view, hinder the gestation and birth of "true society" and the "new man." As Gerhart Niemeyer writes of the Communists, "they do not merely want to rule the world; they mean to destroy it. To them, the present-day world is false, corrupt, wholly devoid of any good, deserving total rejection. Its institutions, ideas, emotional patterns, must be utterly eradicated. . . . The 'true' society will emerge from this vale of struggle once all remnants of the present-day 'false' society have been removed." [7]

It stands to reason that these utopian expectations are based not on love of mankind as it is matter-of-factly but, in truth, demagogically claimed, but on hatred of it since it spells an incurable dissatisfaction with, and contempt for, human nature. At the same time they are based on the ultrarationalistic claim that there is no mystery either in man, in history, or in the universe that we could not fathom, examine in our scientific laboratories, social experiment stations, and psychoanalytic couches—and learn to manipulate and control. But how would we profit—it is asked—by remedying social, psychological, and historical evils if we were not able, at the same time, to guarantee a new existence for the new mankind *in toto,* if, in other words, we allowed the seeds of new dissentions to be sowed among men? Indeed, numerous statements by contemporary scientists imply that the gain would not be worth the trouble if we could not organize society the same way as we can now organize matter and the material world. What is more, the latter directly depends on the former, for the benefits of science can only be enjoyed by all and secured for all if mankind evolves into a coexisting unity, a universal society, and is untaught the earlier distinctions, differences, competitive spirit, desire for individual excellence, etc. Simultaneously, as we have seen in previous chapters, *politics*, which always assumes *the other* as a partly unknown entity—and thus organizes defense, attack, alliance of compatible interests—would be replaced by *social technique*, which assumes the other to be a mere mechanism to be completely known, or reduces the other to a state of mechanical simplicity in order to achieve its manipulation.

Manipulation is, naturally, domination. Thus the universal collectivity, the one-world proposed by the utopian, would have to be either ruthlessly dominated and repressed by an elite, or its members reduced to a state of unfree mechanisms and controlled as such. Yet this is the solution toward which the ideologues are now pushing, partly with unthinking and naïve enthusiasm, partly with some reluctance but propelled by the earlier acquired momentum, built up through the centuries. And not only the ideologues and social engineers: our decades seem to be the historical point at which the ideological drive and the amorphous but violent aspirations of large masses meet. Today it is easier than ever to persuade these masses, by word and example, that the ideologues, far from being motivated by a hatred of existence and freedom, express the idealism with which men look at the future. At a time when the two large empires, the United States and the Soviet Union, embody two ideologies the ultimate concern and justification of which is the universal society they compete to organize, much of the international spirit is suffused with similar dreams; a climate of ideas is established in which any delay of the one-world is considered anomalous, anachronistic, the conspiracy of evil men and obscene forces.

Social engineering stands in the same relationship to the one-world collectivity as ideologies stood to social classes.

By definition, however, the social engineer has no adversary except another social engineer who develops still better means of control. Thus the earlier discussed depolitization, the "release of Utopia from politics" introduces a phase in man's history characterized, in the words of Max Weber, by "a mechanized petrifaction, varnished by a kind of convulsive sense of self-importance."

Thus the very structure of a universal society would inhibit that faculty of man by which progress is accomplished, a progress interpreted not in a mechanistic restrictive sense but as that which results from the ever-novel inventiveness of associations of free individuals. The French ethnologist Claude Lévy-Strauss writes that progress is, after all, imitation of other groups—provided these groups remain reasonably apart. Once they coalesce and lose their identity, the interchange becomes superficial, emulation is extinguished, and contact corruptive rather than stimulating.• The same phenomenon is analyzed by Leo Strauss on the level of advanced civilizations:

An open or all-comprehensive society would consist of many societies which are on vastly different levels of political maturity, and the chances are overwhelming that the lower societies would drag down the higher ones.

An open society will exist on a lower level of humanity than a closed society which, through generations, has made a supreme effort toward human perfection. The prospects for the existence of a good society are therefore greater if there is a multitude of independent societies

• "Voici, devant moi, le cercle infranchissable: moins les cultures humaines étaient en mesure de communiquer entre elles et donc de se corrompre par leur contact, moins aussi leurs émissaires respectifs étaient capables de percevoir la richesse et la signification de cette diversité." *Tristes tropiques,* p. 33. This observation calls for an explanatory remark: the emissaries of a culture need not perceive the "richness and significance" of another in order to imitate it, react to it, assimilate certain parts of it. The invading Spaniards in Mexico and Peru very likely did not perceive the significance of the Aztec and Inca cultures, or they did not care, or they even despised them as inferior by the standards of Christian values. This is true also the other way around: for the American autochthons the Spaniards were simply godlike beings. Yet, this lack of comprehension did not prevent the development of a distinctive Spanish-American civilization.

than if there is only one independent society. If the society in which man can reach the perfection of his nature is necessarily a closed society, the distinction of the human race into a number of independent groups is according to nature.[8]

The one-world, then, appears on the horizon of possibilities not as the continuation of the historical process, but as its end, and the fate of mankind resembling, as Bergson warned, that of the Lepidoptera. As we have said before, the universal society would be apolitical, which means forcibly held together, as totalitarian organizations are. Its *individual* members would be, in Jung's phrase, "depotentiated," deprived of ambition, creativity, and with neutralized inner stimulation. Perhaps they would not be more destructive than the juvenile delinquents roaming our streets, but the very unimaginativeness and sullen nihilism of the latter shows that even their instincts would be cowed and reduced to powerless animalism. The *groups* of such a world-regime would be equally depotentiated, they would turn into pseudo groups, that is, not free associations with a creative scope, but listless and frivolous playthings, authorized, as Niebuhr remarks, by the sociologist and psychologist who stand by the throne of the universal despot, the scientist king.•

These groups would be pseudo groups because every meaningful activity would be removed from their sphere of preoccupations. The universal State would not (and could not) accept leaving any important concern in the hands of private and local organizations, but would have to gather all material on and about which decisions are made under its own experimentation, expertise, and jurisdiction. In the perfected world apparatus, writes Karl Jaspers, "there would be a purposive economy wherein, by compulsory social service, the needs of all would be supplied. No further decisions would have to be made. In the cycle of the recurring generations everything would go

• "Committees of psychologists will argue with committees of moralists and committees of theologians until the citizen's every last indefeasible right will be warranted by half a score of governmental offices, open daily from 9 to 5, excepting, of course, for Sundays and holidays." Georges Bernanos, *Lettre aux Anglais*, p. 183.

on unchanged. Without struggle and without the spice of hazard, the joys of life would be provided for all in un-alterable allotments, with the expenditure of little labor and with ample scope for pastime." [9]

This coincides with our own earlier conclusion that *leisure* will be the one basic problem of the future society, but a leisure that will be the principal area of indoctrina-tion and regimentation. We have seen that those theories which represent, as it were, transitional forms between ideologies and social engineering, such as the study of leisure, economic (or technological) humanism, and the disalienated "joyous individual" of the Marxists, conceive of individual autonomy as expressing itself through leisure. The error of their thesis is obvious and we have denounced it before: to imagine that with everything else being centrally, universally organized, *culture* may still be left in individual and creative hands is a paradox that life would refute in no time. But it is today a widely held paradox: ideologues and social engineers are indeed per-suaded that "culture" is a separate entity, the free area in an otherwise organized social system. Politics, eco-nomics, institutions, the State, law, and property are evil; culture is the exclusive point at which man may com-municate with a "higher life." This idea, incidentally, follows logically from Marxist and liberal detestation of the world, and reveals the fragmentary character of their system, its inherent Manicheism. But even if we accept their separation of the sphere of politics and the sphere of culture, we must show it as an impossibility that the latter alone might miraculously escape world-wide manipu-lation, central direction. In the field of leisure and culture, as in everything else, the world-state is fated to draw all interests into its own orbit, and would leave to individuals and associations not the substance but the shadow.•

(2) Not even the utopian mentality can afford to live and labor in a vacuum; while, generally, it represents the most powerful drive in the history of the modern world,

• "We see the gradual spreading of the idea of a universal re-public, based on the principle of the absolute equality of men and the community of goods; a republic from which all dis-tinction of nationality would be banished. . . . Put into prac-tice, these theories are bound to unchain a regime of inimagin-able terror." Benedict XV, on July 25, 1920.

utopianism feeds on particular events, which it interprets according to its own doctrinal needs. We have mentioned the utopian's impatience with the present world, which in his view merely prepares the accession of mankind to the level of organized perfection; it is evident that he sees in every historical phenomenon of some importance a sign, a portent of millennium, a decisive turn of events introducing something totally different from what has existed.

It must be added that this *ideological sensationalism* is nourished by the present conditions of mass civilization and its communication network. Walter Lippmann observes that with the accession of large masses to a position of power, i.e., to a position in which, although real power is denied to them, the compensation of "being informed," entertained, and polled is not, national, international, cultural, moral, political issues, must be presented in simplistic terms, calling for purely positive or purely negative reactions, based on emotion rather than reason. In this context every occurrence is dramatized, described in quasi-apocalyptic terms, introduced and discussed in a manner reminiscent of circus managers who vaunt their spectacle at the fair.

It is less surprising, then, that even the more responsible people: professionals, specialists, publicists, philosophers, prefer to issue manifestoes, announce grave events, and call attention to coming cataclysms. It would be unfair, however, to accuse them of merely wanting to attract attention; rather, they are yielding to the drive inherent in their utopian mentality which commands a view of the world informed by the Messianic spirit.

Many examples may be cited to show that the world tomorrow is expected to be totally different from the world of today; not only in its outward appearance; new urban-rural centers of habitation, unheard-of technological realizations, interplanetary travels, revolutionary conquests in hygiene, food supply, and news-carrying, but also in its political forms of human coexistence, moral and religious values, psychological changes, cultural appetites, emotional responses. An examination of newspaper and magazine articles, books, public debates, shows that many thinkers, among them quite serious and respectable ones, habitually consider that any one or all of the following phenomena might fundamentally transform the human condition and the fabric of history: world wars, the existence of nuclear energy, the so-called population explosion, the new ratio between work and leisure, the appearance of under-developed countries on the world scene, and so on. A tremendous expectation surrounds these changes and in-ventions, so that it is considered quite admissible to speak of radical revolutions each time a numerical increase or a new chemical formula results in an alteration of power-rapports, degree of comfort, or form of conflict.

The significant thing about these comments accom-panying the changes is that they express admirably the utopian mentality in its quest for a proof of the malleability of human nature and for an ideology that makes room for this malleability. The sad fact (for the utopian) is that in spite of political revolutions, technical inventions, etc., the stability of human nature has obstinately refuted the utopian's fondest hopes for a universal society, a true and effective social science, the ideological uniformization of men. Hence the utopian, obliged to keep postponing his final reform, seizes every opportunity to announce the Great Transformation: in the name of free inquiry, but in fact in the hope of elaborating the ultimate, irrefutable ideology, he demands a re-examination of good and evil necessitated by the atomic bomb; of the institution of marriage, so as birth control may be institutionalized and the "population explosion" arrested; of national sovereignty and nations in general, in order to abolish the "institution" of war; of the human "psyche," so as to instill in people—and preferably in infants—generosity, love of mankind, social concern. One can truly say of the utopians, with Chesterton's phrase, that "because we may possibly grow wings, they cut off their legs."

The one great concern in the back of these radical renovations of politics, morality, religion, emotions, and way of life is to facilitate the gestation period of the uni-versal collectivity. The utopian feels that he is the veritable pioneer of the one-world society, preparing a rather smooth transition provided his counsel is listened to. Otherwise, as he makes it amply and repeatedly clear, the same tre-mendous changes will take place nevertheless, only they will be accompanied by cataclysmic upheavals. All he proposes is to adjust ourselves morally, etc., to the coming world-state and its technological and organizational instruments.

The expected result, the utopian's image of the coming —and final—world is, however, only one aspect of this mentality. The other, equally important side of his convictions is reflected in the *techniques* he believes to be in conformity with the true nature of the post-utopian society. We have seen that the utopian has politics in horror, condemns power unequivocally as a devilish invention and an anomaly in a world approaching a millennial existence; he intends to substitute for it a unanimity based on the, to him, only acceptable concordance of interests. He rightly envisages that power is like a liquid, naturally flowing from higher to lower altitudes, but he believes that through the necessary leveling the liquid would evenly distribute itself, that is, in practice, power and discord would be abolished.

This belief is directly responsible for the utopian's favorable view of the State as the central and neutral locus of power, and of the universal State as an all-benevolent organization. The State, once it ceases to be the instrument of one class, resumes its original destination as the expression of the totality of men, no longer subdivided into classes and thus in various relationships with it. The State is, then, the ideally even distribution of power, the liquid spread over the unobstructed social vista.

We have said, in the above passages, that the utopian thinker looks at the general course of contemporary developments as the precursor of the transformations he anticipates. His concept of the universal State as an essentially *good* because, from the point of view of power, *neutral* (all-embracing) entity, is then a working hypothesis, a guiding line for action. Since politics, morality, religion, even human emotions, are supposed to adapt themselves to the conditions posed by the universal State, the latter's coercive methods will be indistinguishable from its citizens' interests, problematics, and value system. Unanimity thus taken for granted, it is of little significance whether the techniques used for the promotion of social goals are imposed by an elite, or proposed by the "public," or again worked out by special teams of experts; coming from the "upper" or the "lower" strata of the universal collectivity, these measures are recognized as the only possible ones; as they are held to transcend partial interests, any question concerning their origin, their proponents and manner of imposition is obtuse. This explains the candor with which collectivistic theorists, from the Levellers and Rousseau to Marx and the social engineers, make room in their systems for elites: they seriously believe that these are *not* elites, but any group through which the social evidence makes itself transparent and articulate.

This political "innocence" of the new elite is manifest in its solemn renunciation of *force* as an instrument of government and of human transactions in general. Since force is considered evil, flowing from inequality among individuals and groups, the universal collectivity of equals can have no use for it; it is replaced by *ethical* relationships, which are introduced into the community by exhortations, public oaths, protestations of innocence. A few months before he fell from power, at the height of the Reign of Terror, Robespierre declared: "We wish to substitute in our country: morality for selfishness, honesty for sense of honor, duty for good manners, reason for fashion, contempt of vice for contempt of misery, generosity for vanity, love of glory for love of money, truth for fame, the greatness of men for the meanness of the noble class." [10]

As we have noted before, these virtues cannot be controlled, defined, enforced, discussed; particularly when applied to entire communities, they become empty slogans and can never be validly stated. In fact, the only consequence of any attempt to enforce them is that they become cheap, objects of cynicism and ridicule; if they have any effect on the behavior of individuals and groups, it is to discourage their practice. Ironically, only *force,* namely unctuous, hypocritic force, is able to impose virtue on society, a make-believe virtue, a collective self-mystification. Thus it is better to recognize, as Niebuhr does, that "the relations between groups must always be predominantly political rather than ethical, that is, they will be determined by the proportion of power which each group possesses at least as much as by any rational and moral appraisal of the comparative needs and claims of each group." [11]

Any attempt at a transvaluation of the values that normally govern political life and human existence in general is fated to fail when the enterprise is approached from a purely rational angle; the chief instrument of political activity, under these circumstances, must be sheer power, the more ruthless as it must veil its frustrations in the face of an impossible and inhuman task. Changes in history are the results of genuine ethical visions, but not even they can alter basic rapports and the nature of power; they can only introduce new factors into a situation. Underlying these visions there are not rational systems or the preaching of good will, but profound experiences. "The social mutations which have enlarged our freedom of choice have nearly always been the jump in the dark of an outstanding genius or a new, dynamic social group—acts of will, despite the observed social laws." [12] But geniuses cannot be produced at will, and social groups become dynamic only when a sudden insight, carried precisely by a genius, explodes in their midst. The world collectivity, if anything, is the logical denial of such groups and such dynamism. Its planned society and loudly proclaimed virtuousness hide rather than eliminate the power struggle. Thus, like power-groups in modern Communist regimes, the factions of a world government while sharing a unitary ideology, would still fight each other; the occupancy by any one faction of the center of power would mean not the renunciation of force, but a further refinement of its uses.

(3) As we have said above, the utopian's ultimate concern is to salvage history, to establish on earth the dominion of freedom, unselfishness and permanent peace. In order to achieve this end, he means to annul all that he considers evil, so that the end result might be no mere improvement of man's lot, but actually a society based on virtue; not the history of human beings, but the chronicle of divinity.

This "divinity" is not God, for the utopian, even when he is religious, does not imagine Utopia as ushered in by a Day of Judgment and as a continued presence of God among His flock, now reconciled with Him. "Divinity" means, instead, the adoption by men on earth of those teachings which are generally attributed to some sort of natural religion. In fact, these teachings are often stated as merely the opposite of what we denounce in our individual fellow men and in those who have power over us: the simplistic picture that even brilliant men like Rousseau, Fourier, Marx, Lenin, not to mention contemporary thinkers like Bertrand Russell and John Dewey, do not hesitate to paint of the Perfect Society and the one-world indicates the extent of naïveté in which one may indulge once the philosopher or the historian "install themselves at the end of time." [13] From the imaginary vantage point it is easy to develop a godlike overview and build a system of exhaustive historical explanation, a kind of meta-history dealing with history, which virtually ends once we have rationally "understood" it; from then on, as Marx proposed, we may assign for ourselves the task of changing it in accordance with the infallible insights we have gained. The only remaining problem is to draw up the blueprint, eliminate the obstacles—material and human—and carry it out.

Thus the utopian, even while he is among us, situates himself *beyond* history, at the precise point where history becomes, according to him, universal society. This is because, in Maritain's words, he pursues his ends absolutely, while the Christian knows that "this world will never be reconciled fully with Christ within history." [14] The same distinction was made by Saint Augustine, who knew the Manicheistic bent of thought intimately for having been seduced by it in his youth. His answer to utopianism is as valid today as it was in the fourth century A.D. He denounced as a "ridiculous fable" the expectation that a Second Coming would transfigure the structure of history; there will be no Paradise on earth and the tension between the two kingdoms will remain permanent. "There will be no divinization of society beyond the presence of Christ in his Church."

Considering history as God, has, of course, a number of consequences. Those prophets who speak in the name of this deity have a social view of transcendence, i.e., they envisage the ideal as embodying itself in a perfect form of society, made permanent by enforced unanimity. Moreover, they exclude individual betterment, or rather, view it as a corollary of collective interest and accomplishment: society is no longer judged by them in terms of securing freedom and genuine development for the individual, but, on the contrary, they weigh the individual's value according to his contribution and submission to society.

Another consequence of divinizing history is that not only the individual, but the collectivity too, is oppressed and deflected from its real destination. Man wants his god to be perfect, and even on the divine throne history must perform in conformity with this expectation. "History," wrote R. Niebuhr, "is a long tale of abortive efforts toward the desired end of social cohesion and justice in which failure was usually due either to the effort to eliminate the factor of force entirely or to an undue reliance upon it." [15] No matter which way history is "directed" in an effort to extract Utopia out of its womb, whether we adopt the techniques of nonresistance to evil and do not check power with power, or strive to gather all controlling elements in our hands, the collectivity is bound to suffer from our excesses. The structure of the earthly order, that of human existence and society, is such that while its constituting elements remain the same, they must be learned, interpreted, and utilized in every age anew and by every generation.

2.

In the course of our discussion in this chapter and others we have seen mainly two concepts of man confront each other, and the intellectuals progressively identified with one of them. This was so because they wanted to succeed with thought-systems where religions had failed, because they subordinated the philosophical search to ideological expediencies, and because, with the help of the scientific method and science-inspired pride, they insisted on transsubstantiating the human condition.

We have seen that as a result the intellectuals experienced a twofold failure: one was the *liberal trauma* of seeing the factors by which more freedom was to be achieved become the very tools of a new obscurantism. To mention only one example, State power, which the intellectuals sought to build up into a coercive instrument for assisting the masses, has become a silencer of criticism. And, not learning from the lesson, the same intellectuals try to deprive the State of its normal attributes of power in the international order (which is still in a "state of nature") by persuading it to make a gift of its sovereignty to a world government without realizing that the larger unit would be even more oppressive; it would no longer be subject to a moral code which stood, at least in the conscience of men, above the nation-state.

The other failure of the intellectuals consists in the conceptual preparation of an *ethico-social surreality* intended to take the place of reality itself. In other words, the intellectuals used their association with class interests not merely and not so much to fight for justice, but to give shape to an abstraction, to the curse of Utopia in their thinking. I have quoted Karl Mannheim at the beginning of this chapter that Utopia is released from politics when the political goal of a class is reached; but more than that has happened: not only is the intellectual dismissed with the general depolitization of the classless society; he is obliged to witness the degeneration of his own ideals at the hands of the social engineer. The latter no longer respects the image of God in man, but proceeds to adjust his inner life—personality, privacy, sense of mystery and freedom—to a purely external goal: the ideal community of manipulated robots.

The social engineer, in his turn, profits also by the ambiguities of the intellectual heritage. The reason that even among lucid men the danger of social engineering is only rarely understood, let alone denounced, is that several centuries' intellectual-ideological activity has obscured its essence, has made it appear desirable philosophically and inevitable historically. First, we have become used to taking it for granted that speculation about political and social matters should be heavily weighted on the side of the collectivity, and should all but ignore the individual; in the second place, we have come to accept that our thinking is determined by our social position, ideological commitment, and theories about the predictable evolution of history. The result is that our discussion has lost sight of the roots of society *in* the individual, and considers its only serious concern *which* form of development society, as an independent, self-sustaining entity, should take.

This is the exact reverse of medieval preoccupations— and incidentally, it is thereby explained why there were no intellectuals as such in the Middle Ages; for the medieval man, as we have shown in Chapter One, society and its structure were once and for all given, namely as a reflection of the divine order, analogous in heaven and on earth. It was the individual who, through his participation in the mystical body of Christ and through his membership in the Church, was important in the eyes of God, not the community; it was the individual whose fate, sins, repentance, and salvation were the important matter; his submission to or defiance of the social order were not weighed in terms of benefit or loss to the latter, but in terms of whether he did or did not follow the divine decree. All in all, theoretically at least, the community was considered an *instrument* helping or hindering the individual's earthly course, not a goal in itself, but a testing ground for individual virtue or weakness.

It should be understood that I am not arguing for the superiority of the medieval concept, but merely pointing out that ours is almost diametrically opposed to it. Without pursuing the comparison, I want to point out that if we hesitate to denounce the goals and methods of social engineering, it is because our intellectual ancestors committed themselves to the idea that the community had an altogether independent life from that of its members, and that the requirements of the community must be unquestionably accepted by them. To put it briefly, most authors say today, without even paying attention to the enormity of this *idée reçue*, that various over-all community goals—world government, ideological consensus, perfect society, permanent peace,—are ideal solutions to our "problems," but that they either are still in the distant future, or might actually never materialize. Very few dare say unequivocally that these goals are unrealistic to strive for, impossible of realization, and monstrous as conceived.

The intellectual, indeed, must be purged of much of his heritage if he is to confront this controversy in a less ideological and more philosophical way. In other words, as long as he accepts that ideology should determine his philosophical outlook, not only will his speculation remain vacuous, but he will not be master of the process that translates ideas into realities. The ideology-inspired goals to which he adheres are of such a nature that social engineering alone is able to envisage their concrete materialization—at the cost of an enormous sacrifice, that of humanity and freedom.

The detestation of the world *as it is* and the hope for Utopia are, indeed, the ties that join together ideologue-intellectual and social engineer. The difference between them is not a philosophical one, and if, nevertheless, we distinguish between them, it is because the pace of historical development has separated *in time* the respective social-political-cultural context in which they were active and made them emphasize two apparently different things. The intellectual was concerned with the world as it was and wanted to change it; but not only his activity, even his imagination, was necessarily limited, and thus could not have a clear picture of what he was actually working for. The social engineer, on the other hand, possesses the instruments of change and may, as a result, engage in the construction of Utopia.

However, there is no serious philosophical disagreement between the two: both plan to lift human destiny out of the hands of chance and make it secure and scientific.[16] We have seen that this is no mere matter of choice; the social engineers are not a group of plotters who waylay society and rob it of its freedom. The social, national, and colonial upheavals of the nineteenth and twentieth centuries have created a favorable intellectual climate for the search for global solutions and formulas, and so have the technical inventions in the fields of communication and military science. The need for a "planetary coexistence," as we have called it, is not the result but the cause of the sudden authority of social engineering; the latter has been a possibility and a temptation that gradually has become irresistible as more traditional solutions failed, or simply, were impatiently and uncritically rejected.

The basic question that social engineering asks is: how to deal with *masses* and *numbers?* The immediate problems it faces and formulates are, of course, in the material order; but coextensively with the material order and with the solutions attempted therein, there are problems of another kind—organizational, psychological, educational, moral—which also demand attention, and often turn out to be more important. Social engineering thus persuades itself that the scientific approach may be applied to these areas; and the scientific approach means a marshaling of *facts* in the light of a *theory*, and the elaboration of a *method* by which the data will be understood, handled, experimented upon, and finally, brought under control.

Of the terms used in this definition of the scientific approach, *theory* is, of course, the decisive one, since there is no science, not even a beginning of investigation without a hypothesis, which then thickens into a theory. This theory is precisely the philosophical core of utopianism, namely that mankind must reach a state of perfection, i.e., it must be put in complete control of its destiny. We have seen what this aim implies from an organizational angle: increasing centralization, the reduction of the individual to the status of robot functioning in a prescribed way at work and leisure, and the existence of a directing bureaucracy made ubiquitous through perfected communication techniques. But these "reforms," securing mankind against all external accidents and primarily against the "old Adam," this social hygiene reminiscent of the world turning into a huge hospital as Goethe predicted, presupposes a concept of man which, in turn, may be expressed in the language of philosophy.

Let us remember that modern science, as Nietzsche said, ejected man from the center of creation toward the peripheries. Ever since, the many philosophical-ideological systems have attempted to explain his new and desperate position to this exile and to supply him with "reasons" why he should accept his new, and from now on final, straight-lined destiny. The utopianism embodied in social engineering is the last explanation offered to man removed from his confidence in creation, an explanation coming at the end of the series, and in a sense, including, affirming, and negating all the previous ones: affirming, because it promises what they had promised; negating, because the condition it sets to delivery is renunciation of freedom.

Renunciation of freedom implies that the collectivity will be endowed with all that the individual gives up as too burdensome, risky, incalculable. The bargain is an alluring one, since man is always strongly tempted to discard freedom in favor of security and material benefits. The "elites" too would find their advantage since, whether on the Left or on the Right, they no longer believe in democracy but only in a paternalistic directorate, be it called managers, experts, planners, world government, ubiquitous agencies, or any other network. Their condition would be just as permanent as the order of world-society itself.

Now an extremely significant consequence follows from the renunciation of individual freedom: the collectivity must assume an augmented version of all those mental and spiritual activities that have informed individuals and their complex rapports with each other and with society. Accordingly, we nowadays hear talk of vastly increased *intelligence* necessary to cope with global problems; of a new *ethical* consciousness and heightened sense of responsibility; of improved *education* to face these responsibilities intelligently; of the citizen's need to be better *informed* since he must make more important decisions than ever. In other words, the requirements that are advertised transcend the capacities, natural abilities, normal sphere of interest, ethical concern, intellectual limitations, etc., of the individual and address themselves to an imaginary human being. As such a human being is not available, gigantic organizations and institutions—veritable superindividuals—must be endowed with the required characteristics.

But by leaving behind the individual as inadequate for the tasks we propose, we only transfer his inherent limitations to the group. There are, of course, problems of organization in which the group as group is far more efficient than the individual, although it is ultimately the latter who carries the burden of decision-making, timing, and courage; but as soon as we leave the domain of purely practical action and carrying-out of individually made decisions, intelligence, moral consciousness, educability, self-commitment, have their natural limits, even in groups, and these limits coincide exactly with the intelligence and other traits of the individual. We must accept as axiomatic that the moral consciousness, intelligence, educability, self-commitment of a collectivity, cannot be greater than that of the individual. The collectivity carries with it the dimensions of individual qualities, it does not qualitatively increase them; in fact, it is a fortunate case when it preserves intact the qualities with which an individual may be endowed, and does not increase, by its sheer number and force, the latter's weaknesses and vices. "The extension of human sympathies [toward ever-larger communities]," R. Niebuhr remarked, "has resulted in the creation of larger units of conflict without abolishing conflict. So civilization has become a device for delegating the vices of individuals to larger and larger communities." [17]

It would be quite easy to show the impossibility of making substantial steps toward the "improvement" of the above-mentioned qualities and virtues (intelligence, moral consciousness, etc.) and even easier to prove that such progress, once achieved, would, as Niebuhr implies, only *displace, not abolish,* the area of conflict. The same elements would be demonstrably present, but, as on an enlarged photograph, they would display different dimensions from the original. *Intelligence* cannot be increased because it always confronts problems of its own creation in the light of new data. If by its progress we mean the pooling of intelligence available to a group, a nation, the entire world, we abandon the sphere of intelligence itself and enter the ethical domain where choices, decisions, norms, and interests are involved, with, as a possible result, the conflict of intelligently formulated alternatives. This is the reason, incidentally, that the utopians envisage a state in which intelligence is no longer an individual talent but appears as the collective mind of a collective body: thereby the element of conflict could be eliminated and mankind's unique and unified intelligence applied scientifically to all the problems before it.•

Similarly, what does *more information* mean other than the effort of a few individuals to understand the nature of political, social, and other kinds of phenomena and enable themselves, without much hope of communicating their insight, to see behind the struggles, movements, and conflicts of the world scene? As with intelligence, any substantial increase in the amount of the information received and digested, whether in the area of diplomacy or

• This goal is, knowingly or not, pursued by such philosophical schools as logical positivism and the Vienna Circle. They strive to achieve a kind of scientific status for intersubjectivity, by which the always new and unpredictable reactions among men would be replaced by the exact science of language signifying in every case an exact and constant meaning, referring to exactly described objects or events (*Erlebnisse*). The social engineer could not dream of better tools than such a scientific language in social relationships.

business, would correspondingly strengthen the very devices by which it is disseminated, make them more adroit, competitive, and manipulative, but not more factual, truthful, stimulative of intelligent search. Furthermore, the nature of politics being what it is, that is, feeding on differences, unilateral advantages, positions better than that of the adversary, a "more informed" public would become merely a new element in the complex of the information-world. *Information* is not an end, but an instrument; as soon as public opinion became a force in the modern world, a power-factor in political life, various interests have seized upon it as they had seized upon other power-factors in the past. But the proportion, in number, power, and influence, of the decision-makers to the information-seekers has remained constant.

Mutatis mutandis, the same statements may be made about the spread of *education*, the abolition of *war*, the increase of the *sense of responsibility*, the advancement of *equality* among people or nations. In these areas too, even if we accept, in a certain restricted sense, that progress is possible, we must admit that the dimensions of new problems will, by definition, surpass the available resources in morality, intelligence, education, which must catch up with the new problems, thereby creating still others. To take social and economic *equality* as a last example: is it not obvious that as soon as a level, no matter how high, is secured by large numbers, the talented and the shrewd ones wish to measure their own outstanding ability and skill by reaching a yet higher level, above their fellow men? Their new and superior position creates, in turn, power and prestige around them, they become focuses of authority, thereby further increasing the distance between themselves and those in lower positions. It has been said, and with good reason, that in order to establish equality, coercion must be used, that is, a measure of freedom must be given up; but even in a society of equals, who would coerce people if not a set of superiors who, for proclaiming themselves "more equal" than the rest, have no less recourse to force.•

• E. von Kuehnelt-Leddihn remarks that "psychologically, rule stemming from a person considered superior is less oppressive than coercion exercised by equals—not to mention that exercised by those felt to be inferior." *Equality vs. Liberty*, p. 88.

All this would not have to be brought up if the claims made today about the natural capacities of individuals and the moral and organizational possibilities of society were not so exaggerated. The ensuing failure and disappointment are used then as a justification for the social engineers to demand more efficient organizations and more superhuman virtues. These miracle cures are taken for granted in a mass age, and belief in them is spread by the intellectuals and their heirs. Hence the impatience with anything but total liberation (from alienation), total peace (against the threat of war), total unity (abolishing all conflicts). The sentimentality of the social prophets obscures, as Niebuhr notes, "the fact that there can never be a perfect mutuality of interest between individuals who perform different functions in society. . . . Man will always be imaginative enough to enlarge his needs beyond minimum requirements and selfish enough to feel the pressure of his needs more than the needs of others." [18]

These truths are overlooked because the utopians conceive and judge the problems of *politics* in terms of *history*, and history in terms of *religion*. In this light the present appears cursed with all the characteristics of a valley of tears, compensated for not in an afterlife and through a drama whose performer, hero or victim, is the individual, but in Utopia into which mankind as a whole may march.•

Now, it is futile to tell men that this is the "best of all possible worlds," that all effort to improve it is a waste of time, and that virtue consists in submitting to its conditions. This is, by the way, the temptation of the "reactionary" whose mistaken belief is, in Chesterton's words, that "if you leave things alone, you leave them as they are. But you do not. If you leave a thing alone you leave it to a torrent of change." [19] If the "liberal" mentality is prone to take flights into Utopia, the "reactionary" is guilty of sensing plots in every human enterprise involving hope, enthusiasm, and will to change. The correct attitude in the

---

• Even the great Protestant theologian Karl Barth is guilty of utopian thinking when he dismisses politics as irrelevant in the light of religious truth. Perceiving no difference between the political destinies of people under Communism and under the Western systems of government, he advises Christians to submit to Soviet rule, however despotic.

face of this conflict must stem, as I have said before, from a rediscovery of philosophy which has enough courage to free itself of the historical-ideological-utopian perspective. Briefly put, this philosophy must re-emphasize man versus the collective body (with its envisaged collectivized mind), freedom versus the mechanization of inner and social life, common sense versus faith in science.

This does not seem a spectacular program, yet it is from efforts at philosophical clarity that mankind has always profited most. In fact, this is not a "program" the outcome of which would be yet another version of Utopia. Utopian systems have among their motive forces the acquisition of power for a small group for the purpose of making human destiny "secure," "scientific." This type of thinking has so permeated the minds of our intellectuals that even when they oppose an artificial rigidification of history, all they can propose is—another Utopia. A few years ago Mr. Lewis Mumford published a book entitled *The Transformations of Man*,[20] in which he recommended, in view of spreading "world culture" among "posthistoric men," denationalized governments, detheologized religions, and world-citizens turned policemen to extirpate what he calls "outbreaks of private and collective criminality." Aldous Huxley, author of the pioneering and symbolic antiutopian *Brave New World*, has lately contradicted his earlier position in an astonishing fashion: in a series of lectures sponsored by the University of California, he advocated the strengthening of love among people by suggesting that mothers all over the world, while suckling their babes should rub them against other people and animals saying "nice-nice, good-good," and should point at everybody around repeating some incantatory formula like "this is a good man, we must love him." Mr. George Lichtheim in an article on "The Role of the Intellectuals" [21] waxes enthusiastic over the perspective that the intellectuals may become the universal brain that will organize and think for the coming closely knit world-society. (Mr. Lichtheim makes ample use of Father Chardin's predictions of such a final stage in the evolution of man.)

The return to philosophy would be, at the same time, a return to *man*, with the result that collective goals would no longer be glorified as if they were moral substitutes and religious objectives. The present utopian thinking has completely confused the most important issue political philosophy knows: the relationship between the individual and the community. Even as acute an observer of human affairs as R. Niebuhr—quoted several times on these pages —labors under the illusion of a dichotomy between "moral man" and "immoral society"—as he struggles against his own secret bent to see society become one day as "moral" as some individuals may be in exceptional instances. The utopians, on the contrary, hope in their simple-mindedness that the potential goodness of the well-organized society will eventually rub off on the rebellious individual, curbing his instincts and enlightening his irrationality.

The truth of the matter is that while some individuals may actually reach near-perfection, men and women in this sublunar world are forever imperfect—but not more nor less than society itself. The latter bears, after all, the myriad imprints of individual acts, motivations, suspicions, and generosity; it cannot transcend, except like the individual, occasionally, the limitations of human nature. It is the philosopher's duty to interpret this truth as signifying the permanence of human nature and thus to restore man to his central position in our speculation and therefore in the universe as it interests us. This demand is bound to meet the horrified cries of the utopian, the social scientist, and the thinker who has made his philosophy subservient to ideological considerations. But it is the only realistic one. If we face the problem of man honestly, we must admit that the discovery of interstellar space, the exploration of depth psychology, the conquests of physical sciences, and the socioeconomic upheavals of the last century or two have not shifted, contrary to appearances, the interest *away from man*, the center and permanent object of our preoccupations. Criticizing the utopian trends of fifty years ago, Chesterton remarks: "The size of the scientific universe gave one no novelty, no relief. The cosmos went on forever, but not in its wildest constellation could there be anything really interesting . . . such as forgiveness or free will. The grandeur or infinity of the secret of its cosmos added nothing to it. It was like telling a prisoner in Reading gaol that he would be glad to hear that the gaol now covered half the country." [22]

Camus may call human destiny absurd, Freud may predict the "end of an illusion," Russian physicists may declare that the Sputniks have not met God in space, and the biochemists may break open the secret of the proto- plasm; man always comes back to himself, his vital reflec- tions discard the explanations of science and the philoso- phers' systems: he asks the same questions as at the beginning of time. "Men in general are neither very good nor very bad, but mediocre," wrote Tocqueville to a friend. "Man with his vices, his weaknesses, his virtues, this con- fused medley of good and ill, high and low, goodness and depravity, is yet, take him all in all, the object on earth most worthy of study, of interest, of pity, of attachment and of admiration. And since we haven't got angels, we can attach ourselves to nothing greater and more worthy of our devotion than our own kind." [23]

Thus, to philosophize is always to rehabilitate the essen- tial importance of the human dimension, and hence the dignity of man. This was the meaning of the Socratic quest, and also the meaning of Pascal's anguish at the threshold of the Cartesian revolution of science. In this respect, Pascal is an even more significant figure of philoso- phy than Socrates: his was the first brutal reaction to the claim of science to remove man from his position as a privileged being in creation; nobody has so far been able to improve upon his demonstration why science is un- satisfactory to give man meaning and to fill his heart with joy.

This point must be well understood. Pascal was no obscurantist, but he measured how far science (*esprit de géometrie*) may go and become irrelevant to the prob- lematics of human destiny. The achievements of science are not denied by this stand, nor are they dismissed as the ostrich with its head burrowed in sand dismisses reality. What is asserted is that our original endowments as they reflect on the data of experience, are, with all their limita- tions and imperfections, the only necessary and indis- pensable means by which we confront existence, the only weapon commensurate with our struggle.•

• "In so far as we are individuals, each of us is a fragment of a species, a part of this universe, a single dot in the immense network of forces and influences, cosmic, ethnic, historic, whose laws we obey. We are subject to the determination of the phys- ical world. But each man is also a person, he is not subject to the stars and atoms; for he subsists entirely with the very sub-

Does this mean that philosophy coincides with the right use, the critical use, of common sense? It does. "The philosopher can reflect," Father Coppleston writes of Thomas Aquinas, "on the ordinary man's awareness of attaining truth, but he has not at his disposal some extraordinary and special means of proving that we can know truth or that 'knowledge' is knowledge. . . . Aquinas would say that the sort of proof [some philosophers] are looking for is inherently useless and indeed impossible, but that it does not follow that we cannot both attain truth and also know we can attain it. We do not need any further guarantee of our ability to attain truth than our awareness or recognition of the fact that we do in fact attain it." •

This position, I say, is valid with regard to epistemology; but its validity is even more evident when one reflects on the political sphere, our present concern. Again, it is not a blueprint for resignation and passivity; we should, however, interpret it as a philosophy, a system of organized observations. And observation teaches us that the moral nature of man—from which his political existence derives —limits him to the acceptance of the structure of the world as it is, which is at the same time the richest and most varied thing he can imagine. Thus utopian thinking is not merely futile, it is also profoundly immoral since it contradicts the structure of man's thought and action in its applicability to the world. Since it misleads man, it is an ultimately irresponsible doctrine.

---

sistence of his spiritual soul, and the latter is in him a principle of creative unity, of independence and of freedom." J. Maritain, *Scholasticism and Politics*, p. 66.

• *Aquinas*, p. 48.

The contrary position, i.e., the demand that knowledge supply its own proof, was brilliantly attacked by Chesterton: "It is idle to talk always of the alternative of reason and faith. Reason is itself a matter of faith. It is an act of faith to assert that our thoughts have any relation to reality at all. . . . In so far as religion is gone, reason is going. For they are both of the same primary and authoritative kind. They are both methods of proof which cannot themselves be proved. And in the act of destroying the idea of Divine authority we have largely destroyed the idea of that human authority by which we do a long-division sum." *Orthodoxy*, pp. 58-60.

The philosopher does not deny that history is the story of change and struggle, and that we, who are embarked on its waters, should use reason, intelligence, and moral direction to steer safely. However, he denies that *good* may be so increased as to obscure *evil*, that man may be substantially changed, and that society may take upon itself the qualities denied to individual man and thus secure happiness for the latter.

In fact, all utopians follow a pattern of thought that leads to the exact opposite of what they envisage in their sentimental reasoning. Utopia is a way of making men good who otherwise refuse to be good. The utopian is then obliged to build a community that would exhibit all the qualities that are either not found in the individual, or are counterbalanced in him by other traits. The expected result is that the community will be "good" instead of the recalcitrant individual, who must then only be cooperative. "If we cannot produce virtuous individuals," the utopian says, "let us produce a virtuous society; instead of individual virtues, we shall have social virtues."

In this way, the utopian always confuses the individual and the social and favors the one that seems to him more docile. We have indeed anarchists and totalitarians in the utopian camp, but far from being opposite types, they represent two aspects of the same basic orientation. The orientation is to build a social body, a mankind that thinks and acts as *one*, that is both persuaded and organized in view of becoming "perfect."

The social body of the utopian is thus an immensely enlarged individual, endowed with the ultimate in intellectual powers, moral consciousness, universal concern, information, culture, and kindness. But, after all, is the Big Individual not a sign of admission that the ordinary man could not be cajoled, forced, educated, informed, sensitized into what he is not? Is it not a symbol of the ideologue's failure to intensify virtue, to perfect the individual, to be the superman not even to a new mankind, but, indeed, a god in a new race of gods? •

• "According to Mrs. Besant the universal Church is simply the universal self. It is the doctrine that we are really all one person; that there are no real walls of individuality between man and man. If I may put it so, she does not tell us to love

Hence the striking intellectual failure of the ideologue, fruit of his profound immorality. In all truthfulness, his is the sin of pride, the sin that requires the greatest stupidity. It is ironical that he who is committed to a rational-scientific world view, should be the real simple-minded one, the poor in the soul. Will it be forgiven him?

---

our neighbours; she tells us to be our neighbours. . . . The intellectual abyss between Buddhism and Christianity is that for the Buddhist or Theosophist personality is the fall of man, for the Christian it is the purpose of God, the whole point of his cosmic idea." Chesterton, op. cit., pp. 244-5.

Notes

ONE: THE EMERGENCE OF THE INTELLECTUAL

1. Otto Gierke, *Political Theories of the Middle Ages* (Boston: Beacon Press, 1958), p. 9.
2. Marcel Pacaut, *La Théocratie* (Aubier, 1957), p. 15.
3. Ernst Cassirer, *The Myth of the State* (Garden City, N.Y.: Doubleday Anchor Books, 1955), p. 132.
4. Gierke, op. cit., p. 86.
5. Ibid., p. 87.
6. Cassirer, op. cit., p. 172.
7. *Le Concept de classes sociales de Marx à nos jours* (Centre de Documentation Universitaire, 1953-4), p. 133.
8. George H. Sabine, *A History of Political Theory* (New York: H. Holt, 1937), p. 403.
9. *Leviathan*, i, 14.
10. Hannah Arendt, *The Origins of Totalitarianism* (New York: Meridian Books, 1958), p. 146.
11. Charles Morazé, *La France bourgeoise* (B. Colin, 1946), p. 121.
12. Basil Willey, *The Seventeenth Century Background* (Garden City, N.Y.: Doubleday Anchor Books, 1953), p. 40.
13. A. M. Wilson, *Diderot: The Testing Years* (New York: Oxford University Press, 1957), p. 133.
14. Ibid., p. 149.
15. *Montesquieu par lui-même* (Editions Ecrivains de Toujours), p. 38.
16. *Correspondance littéraire*, V, 389.
17. *Confessions* (1756), IX.
18. Condorcet, *Sketch for a Historical Picture of the Progress of the Human Mind* (New York: The Noonday Press, 1955), pp. 201-2 and p. 192.

TWO: THE SHAPING OF IDEOLOGIES

1. Lord Percy of Newcastle, *The Heresy of Democracy* (Chicago: Henry Regnery, 1955), p. 40.
2. Condorcet, *Sketch for a Historical Picture of the Progress of the Human Mind* (New York: The Noonday Press, 1955), p. 127.
3. Ibid., p. 9.
4. Ibid., p. 192.
5. Hannah Arendt, *The Origins of Totalitarianism* (New York: Meridian Books, 1958), p. 126.
6. Quoted by Walter M. Simon, in "Saint-Simon and the Idea of Progress," *Journal of the History of General Ideas*, June, 1956.
7. *La Droite en France* (Aubier, 1954), p. 30.
8. *Contrat social* (Edition Beaulavon), p. 164.
9. *Reflections on the Revolution of Our Time* (New York: Viking Press, 1943), p. 364.
10. *Social Statics*, pp. 79-80.
11. *The Challenge of Facts and Other Essays*, p. 90.
12. Ibid., p. 57.
13. Tocqueville, *The European Revolution and Correspondence with Gobineau*, Jòhn A. Lukacs, ed. (Garden City, N.Y.: Doubleday Anchor Books, 1959), pp. 193-4.

THREE: THE INTELLECTUAL AS A MARXIST

1. In a letter to Theodor Cuno, Jan. 24, 1872.
2. Martin Buber, *Paths in Utopia* (Boston: Beacon Press, 1958), p. 133
3. Hannah Arendt, *The Origins of Totalitarianism* (New York: Meridian Books, 1958), p. 469.
4. "On Historical Materialism," 1892.
5. "Retour à Marx," in *Cahiers Internationaux de Sociologie*, 1958.
6. Ibid.
7. Georg Lukács, *La Destruction de la raison* (Paris: L'Arche Editeur, 1958), I.
8. Henri Lefèbvre, *La Somme et le reste* (Paris: La Nef de Paris, 1959), II, 659.
9. Ibid., p. 524.
10. Ibid., I, 39-40.
11. *Literatur und Klassbewustsein, Existentialisme ou Marxisme?*, *La Destruction de la raison*.
12. Lefèbvre, op. cit., I, 158.
13. Ibid., p. 221.
14. Harold J. Laski, *Reflections on the Revolution of Our Time* (New York: Viking Press, 1943), p. 5.
15. Max Adler, *La Pensée de Marx*, p. 108.
16. P. Naville, *De l'aliénation à la jouissance* (Librairie Marcel Rivière, 1957).
17. Lefèbvre, op. cit., II, 401-2.
18. *Contrat social* (Editions Sociales), p. 99.

19. In *La Nation Française*, May 29, 1959.
20. Gooch, *English Democratic Ideas in the Seventeenth Century* (New York: Cambridge University Press, 1954; third edition), p. 179.
21. Ibid., p. 43.
22. Librairie Marcel Rivière, 1959.
23. P. 397.
24. *Entretiens sur la politique avec Sartre, Rousset, etc.*, p. 99.
25. *The New Science of Politics* (Chicago: University of Chicago Press, 1952), p. 125.
26. *Trotsky's Diary in Exile—1935* (Cambridge, Mass.: Harvard University Press, 1958).
27. "Mao, Marx and Moscow," *Foreign Affairs*, July, 1959, p. 564.
28. Presses Universitaires de France, 1959.
29. Ibid., p. 115.
30. Ibid., pp. 143-4.

FOUR: THE INTELLECTUAL AS A PROGRESSIVE

1. *Contemporary Capitalism* (New York: Random House, 1956), p. 217.
2. *Scholasticism and Politics* (Garden City, N.Y.: Doubleday Image Books; first published in 1940), p. 97.
3. *The Phenomenon of Man* (New York: Harper & Brothers, 1959), p. 112.
4. Ibid., p. 20.
5. *Nature and Functions of Authority* (1940), p. 52.
6. *Communication, Organization and Science* (Indian Hills, Colo.: The Falcon's Wing Press, 1958).
7. Camus, *Remarque sur la Révolte*, p. 22.
8. Ibid., p. 12.
9. Camus, *L'Homme révolté*, p. 36.
10. *Remarque sur la Révolte*, p. 19.
11. *L'Homme révolté*, pp. 306-7.
12. Ibid., p. 232.
13. Ibid., pp. 280 ff.
14. Sidney Hook, *John Dewey, His Philosophy of Education and Its Critics* (New York: Tamiment Institute, 1959), pp. 21-2.
15. *My Life*, p. 560.
16. Sidney Kaplan, "Social Engineers and Saviors: Effects of World War I on some American Liberals," *Journal of the History of Ideas*, June, 1956.
17. *Social Thought in America*, pp. 243-4.
18. Ibid., pp. 244-5.
19. *My Life*, p. 474.
20. *The Russian Revolution*, p. 314. My italics.
21. *Humanisme et terreur*, p. 165.
22. *Memoirs of a Revolutionist*, p. 293.
23. Ibid., p. 295.
24. Ibid., p. 296.
25. *The Religious Situation*, p. 112.

354

26. Ibid., p. 116.
27. Ibid., p. 112.
28. Quoted by Pierre-Henri Simon, *L'Esprit et l'histoire*, p. 121.
29. *Le Cloître de la rue d'Ulm*, p. 203.
30. "La Démocratie est une idée neuve," *Esprit*, Sept., 1959, p. 180.
31. *Les Noyers de l'Altenburg*, p. 98.
32. *Le Mythe de Sisyphe*, p. 154.
33. Quoted in André Breton, *La Clé des Champs*, p. 37.
34. Merleau-Ponty in his discourse at the Geneva Encounters in 1951.

FIVE: THE INTELLECTUAL AS A REACTIONARY

1. Tocqueville, *The European Revolution and Correspondence with Gobineau*, John A. Lukacs, ed. (Garden City, N.Y.: Doubleday Anchor Books, 1959), p. 203.
2. Ibid., p. 285.
3. Modern Library edition, p. 624.
4. *Beyond Good and Evil* (Modern Library), pp. 578-9.
5. Ibid., pp. 494-5.
6. Berdyaev, *Dostoevsky*, p. 45.
7. *The Brothers Karamazov* (Modern Library), p. 789.
8. "Trois idées politiques," in *Oeuvres capitales*, II, 88.
9. Henri Massis, *Maurras et son temps*, I, 68.
10. Quoted by Jacques Julliard, "La Politique religieuse de Charles Maurras." *Esprit*, March, 1958.
11. From the encyclical *Rerum Novarum*, Sec. 14 (1891).
12. From the encyclical *Atheistic Communism*, Sec. 15 (1935).
13. *The Recollections of Alexis de Tocqueville*, J. P. Mayer, ed., p. 224 and p. 3.
14. Paul Sérant, *Le Romantisme fasciste* (Fasquelle, 1960), p. 10.
15. P. xxiii (New York: Cambridge University Press, 1939).
16. Quoted by Hannah Arendt, *The Origins of Totalitarianism* (New York: Meridian Books, 1958), p. 258.
17. *Not, Kampf, Ziel*, quoted by Lord Percy of Newcastle, *The Heresy of Democracy* (Chicago: Henry Regnery, 1955), p. 105.
18. *La France contre les Robots*, p. 112.
19. *The Cypresses Believe in God*, pp. 446, 456.
20. *Les Enfants humiliés*, p. 71.
21. Quoted by Henri Massis, *Maurras et son temps*, II, 116.

SIX: FROM IDEOLOGY TO SOCIAL ENGINEERING

1. *The Phenomenon of Man*, p. 112.
2. *Force and Freedom*, p. 152.
3. Ibid., p. 149.
4. Ibid., p. 150.
5. Jean-Louis Cottier, *La Technocratie, nouveau pouvoir* (Paris, 1959).
6. Ibid., p. 26.

7. Ibid., p. 28.
8. *Landmarks of Tomorrow*, p. 32.
9. R. Seidenberg, *Posthistoric Man*, p. 133.
10. Ibid., pp. 104-5.
11. Preface to Cottier, op. cit., p. 28.
12. Ann Arbor: University of Michigan Press, 1958. Preface by Reinhold Niebuhr.
13. Seidenberg, op. cit., p. 190.

SEVEN: PLANETARY COEXISTENCE

1. *The Twentieth Century Capitalist Revolution*, pp. 51-2.
2. Aug. 15 and 22, 1959.
3. *La Coexistence pacifique*, p. 15.
4. *Theory of Business Enterprise*, p. 17.
5. *Man and Society in an Age of Reconstruction*, p. 336.
6. Rostow, loc. cit.
7. *Le Socialisme trahi*, p. 211.
8. Presses Universitaires de France, 1959.

EIGHT: PLANETARY IDEOLOGY

1. *Oeuvres complètes*, I, 121.
2. *Recollections*, p. 75.
3. *Industrie*, XVIII, 189.
4. *Man at the Crossroads* (Boston: Beacon Press), p. 76.
5. Quoted by Anne Fremantle, *This Little Band of Prophets: The British Fabians*, p. 10.
6. From the article of Louis Raillon, June, 1959.

NINE: THE AMERICAN INTELLECTUAL

1. P. 87.
2. "The Puritan Tradition," *Commentary*, Aug. 1958.
3. Ibid.
4. *The Puritan Mind* (Ann Arbor: University of Michigan Press, 1958), p. 26.
5. *Man and Society in an Age of Reconstruction*, p. 84.
6. *America and the Image of Europe* (New York: Meridian Books, 1960), p. 174.
7. Henry B. Parkes, *The American Experience*, p. 7.
8. Oscar Handlin, *The Uprooted*, p. 115.
9. Ibid., p. 191.
10. Op. cit., p. 10.
11. *Essays*, I, 297.
12. *American Catholic Dilemma*.
13. Morton White, *Social Thought in America: The Revolt against Formalism*, p. 46.
14. D. Williams, *What Present-day Theologians Are Thinking* (New York: Harper & Brothers, 1952).
15. "American Intellectuals: Their Politics and Status," *Daedalus*, Summer 1959.
16. *Dilemmas of Politics*, p. 286.

356

17. P. 469.
18. *Exile's Return*, p. 209.
19. *Lament for a Generation*, p. 162.
20. *America as a Civilization* (1957).
21. *Congress and the American Tradition*, p. 89.
22. *The Lonely Crowd*, p. 288.
23. Ibid., p. 85.
24. Ibid., p. 197.

TEN: THE EUROPEAN INTELLECTUAL

1. See Georges Duhamel, *Scènes de la vie future*.
2. *La France contre les Robots*, pp. 194-5.
3. *Personalism*, p. 12.
4. Symposium on Industrialization and Technocracy, Paris, 1949.
5. *La France contre les Robots*, p. 140.
6. *Oppression et liberté*.
7. *Humanisme intégral*, pp. 204-5.
8. "Sur une civilisation essoufflée," *Nouvelle Nouvelle Revue Française*, May, 1956.
9. *Journal*, p. 55.
10. *L'Existentialisme est un humanisme* (1946).
11. Ibid., p. 37.
12. Ibid., p. 31.
13. *The Existentialist Revolt*, p. 17.
14. *Les Voix du Silence*, pp. 513-14.
15. Gaëtan Picon, *Malraux par lui-même*.
16. Simone de Beauvoir, *Pyrrhus et Cinéas* (1944).
17. "Existentialism: A Literature of Despair?", *Yale French Studies*, Spring-Summer 1948.
18. *L'Esprit et l'histoire*, p. 77.
19. Maritain, *The Person and the Common Good*, p. 83.
20. "Fragments du post-scriptum," *Nouvelle Revue Française*, March 1939.
21. *Athens and Jerusalem*.
22. *Intuitions pré-chrétiennes*.
23. *Simone Weil, telle que nous l'avons connue*.
24. *Between Man and Man*, p. 80.
25. *Plea for Liberty*, p. 262.
26. *Natural Right and History*, p. 137.

ELEVEN: INTELLECTUAL AND PHILOSOPHER

1. *Ideology and Utopia*, p. 258.
2. *Man and Society in an Age of Reconstruction*, p. 199.
3. *The Poverty of Historicism*, p. 70.
4. *Dilemmas of Politics*, p. 241 and p. 272.
5. *The Irony of American History*, p. 4.
6. Ibid., p. 67.
7. "Risk or Betrayal? The Crossroads of Western Policy," *Modern Age*, Spring 1960.
8. *Natural Right and History*, pp. 131-2.

9. *Man in the Modern Age*, p. 70.
10. February 5, 1794. Quoted by Bernard Faÿ, *La Grande Révolution*, p. 434.
11. *Moral Man and Immoral Society*, p. xxiii.
12. R. Crossman, "Explaining the Revolution of Our Time. Can Social Science Predict Its Course?"
13. Jacques Maritain, *On the Philosophy of History*, p. 162.
14. Ibid., p. 155.
15. *Moral Man and Immoral Society*, p. 20.
16. H. Belloc, *The Servile State*, p. 127.
17. *Moral Man and Immoral Society*, p. 49.
18. Ibid., pp. 195-6.
19. G. K. Chesterton, *Orthodoxy*, p. 212.
20. New York: Harper & Brothers, 1956.
21. *Commentary*, April, 1960.
22. Chesterton, op. cit., pp. 111-12.
23. Letter to Eugène Stoffels, Jan. 3, 1843.

Index

Abélard, 8
Acte gratuit, 154
Acton, Lord, 182
Actuelles II, 305n., 309
Adams, Henry, 161n.
Adams, John, 276n.
Agrippa, Menenius, 17
Ahrendt, Hannah, 24, 49, 76, 190n., 192
Alembert, Jean Le Rond d', 28, 46
alienation, 37, 54, 76, 78ff., 83f., 98, 107, 139, 150
American Experience, The, 276n.
Anabaptists, 63n., 103
Angell, Robert C., 219f.
Anti-Dühring, 91
Aragon, Louis, 156
Aristotle, 41, 295
Aron, Raymond, 240n., 293
Au-delà du nationalisme, 183n., 228n.
Auden, W. H., 156

Augustine, St., 12n., 37, 210, 335
Augustus, 13
Avenir de la science, L', 47n., 57, 61n., 123n.

Babeuf, François-Emile, 63n., 182
Bacon, Francis, 45, 77
Bacon, Roger, 8
Bagehot, Walter, 262n., 292
Bakunin, Michael, 73
Baltzell, E. Digby, 264n.
Balzac, Honoré de, 160, 170n.
Bancroft, George, 282
Barbarie et poésie, 169n.
Barber, Eleanor, 31n.
Bardèche, Maurice, 196
Barrault, Jean-Louis, 285
Barrès, Maurice, 7, 169
Barth, Karl, 270, 344n.
Barzun, Jacques, 137n.
Baudelaire, Charles, 161, 170n.

Bazard, Armand, 217
Beamten Kalendar, 192
Beard, Charles, 269
Beauvoir, Simone de, 102, 128, 306
Bebel, August, 93
Becker, Carl, 29
Bedbug, The, 109, 110, 183
Belloc, Hilaire, 228n.
Benda, Julien, 7, 80n.
Benedict XV, 329n.
Bentham, Jeremy, 62
Berdyaev, Nicholas, 106n., 148, 166, 215, 312
Bergson, Henri, 80n., 82, 91, 123, 328
Berle, Adolf A., 228
Berlin, Isaiah, 160n.
Bernanos, Georges, 71n., 176, 180f., 194, 196, 213, 300, 303, 314, 328n.
Bernard, St., 8, 295
Besant, Annie, 349n.
Bevan, Aneurin, 235
Beyond Good and Evil, 165n.
Bismarck, Otto von, 65, 69
Bockstaele, Jacques van, 251
Bodin, Jean, 23
Bolingbroke, 31
Bonald, Louis de, 161
Boniface VIII, 5
Boorstin, Daniel J., 135, 260ff.
Borne, Etienne, 196
Boucher, Maurice, 164
Bourgeoisie in Eighteenth Century France, 31n.
Bourne, Randolph, 141f.
Boutang, Pierre, 158
Brasillach, Robert, 181, 185n., 188n., 196
Brave New World, 292, 345
Brave New World Revisited, 212n.
Brecht, Bertold, 156
Breton, André, 155f.
Brothers Karamazov, The, 166f.
Browne, Sir Thomas, 27

Brownites, 103
Bruno, Giordano, 18
Buber, Martin, 49, 74, 243, 314
Büchner, Friedrich, 122, 186
Buckley, Jr., William F., 179n.
Bukharin, Nicolai, 323
Bullock, Alan, 191n.
Burckhardt, Jacob, 58n., 182, 207
Burke, Edmund, 72, 162n., 174f., 185
Burnham, James, 21n., 282
Byron, Lord, 59, 153

Cabet, Etienne, 49
Cahiers des doléances, 35
Calvin, John, 275
Campanella, Tomasso, 27
Camus, Albert, 99f., 128ff., 154, 305, 308ff., 346
Captive Mind, The, 147
Captivity of Avignon, 13
Carlyle, Thomas, 62n.
Cassirer, Ernst, 16, 18f.
Castries, Marquis de, 26
Catroux, Georges, 66n.
Céline, Louis-Ferdinand, 181, 196
Century of Total War, The, 240n.
Chambers, Whittaker, 101
Chaplin, Charles, 254
Chapman, H. M., 215n.
Chardin, P. Teilhard de, 123ff., 127, 145f., 153n., 204f., 345
Charlemagne, 5
Chastellus, 33
Chateaubriand, François-Rene de, 58, 152, 161, 182
checks and balances, 15
Chesterton, Gilbert Keith, 331, 344, 346, 348n., 350n.
Cioran, E. M., 305f.
Civil War in France, The, 86
Civitas Dei, 11

Civitas Solis, 27
Civitas Terrana, 11, 118
Clark, Michael, 226n.
Codreanu, Zelea, 189n.
Coexistence pacifique, La, 111
Cole, G. D. H., 180n.
Colet, Louise, 161
Comité National des Ecrivains, 102
Commune, 70, 82, 86, 101
Communist Manifesto, 5, 176f.
Comte, Auguste, 46, 49, 64, 205, 242
conciliar power, 16
conciliar supremacy, 15
Condillac, E. Bonnot de, 122, 126
Condition humaine en Chine communiste, La, 209n.
Condorcet, Antoine-Nicolas de, 29, 32n., 34f., 37, 44ff., 60, 69, 77, 233n.
Conscience malheureuse, La, 98
Conscience mystifiée, La, 84
Conservative Mind, The, 61
Considérations sur la France, 175, 241
Constant, Benjamin, 39, 44
Contemporary Capitalism, 51
contract theory of society, 15, 32n., 40
Contrat social, 34, 37n., 41, 50
Contre-un 41n.
Contribution to the Critique of Political Economy, A, 78
Copernicus, Nicolas, 174
Coppleston, F. C., 348
Correspondance de Dostoevsky, 168n.
Correspondance inédite de Dostoevsky, 168n.
Cortes, Donoso, 161
Counterrevolution of Science, 48n., 58n.
Cournot, Antoine-Augustin, 59
Cowley, Malcolm, 279f.
Crime and Punishment, 166

Critique of the Gotha Program, 85f., 93
Croly, Herbert, 141
Cultural Foundations of Industrial Civilization, 53n.

Danilevsky, Grigori, 43, 290
Dante, Alighieri, 14f.
Darwin, Charles, 67, 124, 160n.
Daudet, Léon, 170n.
Dawson, Christopher, 295
Déat, Marcel, 186
Declaration of Independence, 135
Decline of the West, 173
Décombres, Les, 170n.
De la Félicité publique, 33
Defensor Pacis, 14f., 30
De Gaulle, Charles, 274n.
Degrelle, Leon, 186
Descartes, René, 39, 187
Deshumanizacion del arte, La, 295n.
Dewey, John, 121, 130, 141ff., 269f., 276, 288, 335
dialectical materialism, 43, 141
Dialectique du vingtième siècle, 21n.
Dialogues Concerning Two New Sciences, 18
Dictionnaire philosophique, 46
Diderot, Denis, 26, 28, 38, 46, 122
Dilemmas of Politics, 65n., 140n., 208n.
Ding an sich, 91
Discours sur l'origine de l'inégalite parmi les hommes, 33, 35, 40
Discourses, The, 17f.
Disraeli, Benjamin, 169, 290
Djilas, Milovan, 101, 149
doctrine of the two swords, 11
Domenach, Jean-Marie, 101f., 146
Dominic, St., 8

362

Doriot, Jacques, 186
Dos Passos, John, 156
Dostoevsky, Fedor, 166ff., 171, 174, 290
Dostoevsky, The Making of a Novelist, 168n.
Dreiser, Theodore, 265
Drexler, Anton, 191n.
Dreyfus, Alfred, 69
Dreyfus case, 7, 69
Dritte Reich, Das, 190
Drucker, Peter, 218, 233, 270n., 283n.
Drumont, Eduard, 169
Dubarle, Dominique, 217, 219
Dullin, Charles, 288
Duplessis-Mornay, 23

Eastman, Max, 143
Ecole Polytechnique, 58, 316n.
economic determinism, 43
economic liberalism, 46
Einstein, Albert, 110, 137
Eisner, Kurt, 194
Eluard, Paul, 156
Emerson, Ralph Waldo, 62n., 256
Encyclopédie, 28, 46, 63, 77, 122, 126
End of the Modern World, The, 10n.
Enfantin, Barthélemy-Prosper, 243
Engels, Friedrich, 49, 63f., 73, 77f., 81ff., 87f., 91, 93, 103, 323f.
English Democratic Ideas in the Seventeenth Century, 31n.
English Restoration, 25
English Revolution, 32n., 63n.
Enlightenment, 30f., 33, 42, 45, 62f., 77, 117, 122, 187, 272
Enracinement, L', 313
Equality vs. Liberty, 343n.
Erasmus, Desiderius, 20

Erasmus of Rotterdam, 20n.
Esprit des lois, L', 29
"Etat de guerre, L'," 33
European Revolution and Correspondence with Gobineau, 61n., 70
existentialism, 306ff.
Extinction du pauperisme, L', 178n.

Fabian Society, 69, 120n.
Fadeev, Aleksandr, 106n.
Falange, 194f.
Fascism, 92, 157, 180, 184ff., 188ff., 193ff., 206, 208, 290
Fast, Howard, 94n., 101
Fathers and Sons, 138
Faust, 46
Feder, G., 191n.
Federalism, Socialism, Antitheologism, 73n.
Ferrater-Mora, José, 245, 248
Feuerbach, Ludwig, 77, 105, 122, 186
Fitzgerald, Scott, 265
Flaubert, Gustave, 161
Fondane, Benjamin, 98
Force and Freedom, 58n.
Fougeyrollas, Pierre, 107
Fourier, Charles, 49, 62, 69, 168n., 182, 188, 335
Fragebogen, 190n.
Franco, Francisco, 195, 197
Frank, Lawrence K., 220f.
Frank, Philip, 201
Franklin, Benjamin, 265
Frederick the Great, 44
Freemasonry, 116
Free Society and Moral Crisis, The, 219
Fremantle, Anne, 120n., 180n.
French Revolution, 34ff., 44f., 47n. 55, 63n., 65n., 67, 76, 158f., 162n., 187, 319
Freud, Sigmund, 346
Furstenberg, Jean, 21n.

Future of American Politics, The, 286

Gaganova, 250n.
Galbraith, John Kenneth, 120n.
Galileo, Galilei, 18, 26f., 29, 39n.
Gandhi, 137
Garibaldi, Giuseppe, 55
Genealogy of Morals, 165
General Will, 34, 37, 43, 65n., 119
George III, 135
German Ideology, 83
Gide, André, 98, 126, 306f.
Gierke, Otto, 13, 16f.
Gironella, José Maria, 195
Gladstone, William Ewart, 178
Gobineau, Joseph-Arthur de, 61n., 69, 162ff., 166, 169, 180, 186
Goethe, Johann-Wolfgang von, 46, 59, 220, 292, 295, 300, 340
Gogol, Nicolai, 290
Gooch, G. P., 23, 31n., 32n., 99
Gregory VII, 12
Grimm, Frederic-Melchior, 33
Grotius, Hugo, 30
Guardini, Romano, 10n., 21, 301, 315
Guérin, Daniel, 100ff., 108
Guests, The, 110
Guizot, François, 49, 64
Gurvitch, Georges, 20f.

Harcourt, Sir William, 178
Hayek, F. A., 47n., 48n., 58n.
Hazard, Paul, 29
Hedgehog and the Fox, The, 160n.
Hegel, Georg Wilhelm Friedrich, 37, 43, 62, 66, 78ff., 97f., 162, 164, 260, 310n., 319

Heidegger, Martin, 98, 126, 128, 270, 311, 315
Helvétius, Claude-Adrien, 28
Henri IV, 23
Heraclitus, 125n.
Hervé, Pierre, 90n., 101
Herzen, Alexander, 114n.
Hidden Persuaders, The, 286
Highway, The, 114
Histoire des idées sociales en France, 242n.
History of Education in Antiquity, A, 305n.
Hitler, 191n.
Hitler, Adolf, 92, 129, 144, 185, 189ff.
Hitler m'a dit., 192n.
Hobbes, Thomas, 24, 30, 33, 36, 63, 201
Hofstadter, Richard, 282f.
Holbach, Paul-Henri d', 31
Holmes, Oliver Wendell, 269, 288
Homme révolté, L', 99n., 100
Hook, Sidney, 130f., 143
House of Intellect, 137n.
Hudson, G. F., 111
Hugo, Victor, 59, 160, 170n.
Huizinga, Johan, 20n.
Hume, David, 62
Hus, Jan, 9
Huxley, Aldous, 212n., 291f., 315, 345
Huxley, Sir Julian, 123ff., 127, 146, 204f., 219

Icaria, 50
Idiot, The, 166f.
Ilenkov, V., 114
Industrial Revolution, 36, 43, 54,
Industrie Littéraire et Scientifique, 47
intermediate bodies, 16, 35
investiture, 11, 13
Italie fasciste, L', 185

Jacobinism, 52, 158, 170
Jacqueries, 10

James, Henry, 265
James, William, 270
Jaspers, Karl, 222, 315, 328
Jeanson, Francis, 100
Jefferson, Thomas, 265, 276n.
Jesuits, 27
Jeunesse du socialisme libertaire, 100
Joachim de Flore, 173
José Antonio, 194f.
Journal d'un homme occupé, 185n.
Jouvenel, Bertrand de, 248, 252n.
Juenger, Ernst, 181
Juenger, F. W., 303
Jung, Carl Gustav, 174n., 328

Kafka, Franz, 315
Kant, Immanuel, 312
Kapital, Das, 81
Katkov, Nicolai, 186n.
Kaufmann, Walter, 306n.
Kepler, Johannes, 26
Kerensky, Alexander, 140
Khrushchev, Nikita, 101, 108, 111, 113
kibbutz, 74
Kierkegaard, Søren, 98, 311f.
Kirk, Russell, 8, 61f., 284
Koestler, Arthur, 101
Kohn, Hans, 283
Kolnai, Aurel, 75n.
Komintern, 194
Kossuth, Louis, 55
Kuehnelt-Leddihn, Erik von, 343n.

Labin, Suzanne, 209n.
La Boétie, Etienne de, 41n.
Lacordaire, Jean-Baptiste-Henri, 242
Lacroix, Jean, 146, 303, 305
Lament for a Generation, 247n.
La Mettrie, Julien de, 122, 126
Landauer, Gustav, 74

Landmarks of Tomorrow, The, 283n.
Languet, 23
La Rochefoucauld, François de, 207
La Rochelle, Pierre Drieu de, 181, 190n., 196f.
Laski, Harold, 31n., 65, 94, 140n., 184
Lassalle, Ferdinand, 58
Lawrence, T. E., 308
League of Nations, 133
Lefèbvre, Henri, 80f., 83f., 89, 92, 96
Leibniz, G. W. von, 312, 314
Leisure, the Basis of Culture, 314
Lenin, Vladimir Ilich, 43, 49, 64n., 85ff., 91, 97f., 103, 108, 143f., 185, 201, 234, 290, 296, 323, 335
Lens, Sidney, 255n.
Leo XIII, 175
Lerner, Max, 281
Leroy, Maxime, 242n.
Letronne, Jean-Antoine, 58
Letter on Humanism, 126
Lettre à ses commettants, 35n.
Lettre aux Anglais, 328n.
Levellers, 23, 63n., 99, 103, 159, 333
Leviathan, 24f., 30
Lévy-Strauss, Claude, 327
Lewin, Kurt, 251
Lewis, C. S., 181
Lewis, Sinclair, 265
Lex Rex, 23
Liberal Democracy, 209
libertines, 39
Lichtheim, George, 345
life-adjustment education, 116
Light Shining in Buckinghamshire, 32n.
Lippman, Walter, 248n., 284, 286, 330
Lipset, Seymour, 273, 277, 280f., 292
Locke, John, 30ff., 36, 43, 287

Index 365

Louis XIV, 25, 32n., 176
Louis XVI, 25
Lubell, Samuel, 286
Lucretius, 153, 155
Lukács, G., 82, 88, 90f., 103
Lukacs, John A., 61n.
Lunacharsky, Anatoli, 290

McCarthy, Joseph, 135, 179n., 280
Macdonald, Dwight, 114n., 144f., 179n.
Machiavelli, Niccolo, 16ff., 30, 201
Machiavellism, 16, 106
Maistre, Joseph de, 33n., 160n., 175, 241, 243
Maître de Santiago, Le, 181
Mallarmé, Stéphane, 68
Malraux, André, 7, 128, 154ff., 291, 294, 299f., 308
Man, Henri de, 183n., 228
Managerial Revolution, The, 21n.
Mandouze, André, 146
Manichaeism, 12, 329
Mannheim, Karl, 233, 261, 319ff., 324, 337
Mao Tse-tung, 108
Marble Cliff, The, 181
Marcel, Gabriel, 301, 315
Maritain, Jacques, 119, 126n., 132, 305, 311, 313, 335, 348n.
Marrou, Henri-Irénée, 305n.
Marshall Plan, 293
Marsilius of Padua, 13ff., 30
Marx, Karl, 37, 42f., 50f., 58, 62, 64n., 66, 69, 73, 77ff., 90, 92ff., 97ff., 103ff., 109, 125n., 142, 162, 176f., 184, 186ff., 196, 198, 201, 234, 249, 253, 275, 290, 300ff., 304, 308, 311, 314, 319, 333, 335
Marxism, 4, 52, 76f., 82, 89, 94ff.., 98, 101, 105, 108, 113f., 117f., 122, 139f.,

144ff., 148, 159f., 172, 185f., 189f., 198, 201f., 208, 239, 280, 291, 304f., 310, 323f.
Marxism and the Linguistic Question, 113
Marxisme en question, Le, 107
Materialism and Empirio-Criticism, 91
"Matérialisme et Révolution," 310
Maulnier, Thierry, 196
Maurras, Charles, 69, 168ff., 174, 179f., 184, 195f.
Mayakovsky, Vladimir, 109f., 149, 183
Meany, George, 247
Mehring, Franz, 88
Mein Kampf, 292
Melville, Herman, 265
Mémoires d'outre-tombe, 58, 161
Mémoires d'un Révolution-naire, 110n.
Memoirs of a Revolutionist, 114n., 179n.
Mende, Tibor, 236n.
Mendès-France, Pierre, 141, 235
Merleau-Ponty, Maurice, 144, 149
Mersenne, Marin, 39n.
Messner, Johannes, 120
Metternich, Klement, 161, 169, 185
Meung, Jean de, 10n.
Michelangelo, 291, 295
Michelet, Jules, 56
Mill, John Stuart, 36, 69, 73, 287
Miller, Arthur, 265
Mills, C. Wright, 266, 279, 284f.
Milosz, Czeslav, 147
Misery of Philosophy, The, 82
Moleschott, Jacob, 186
Moeller van den Bruck, 190
Molière, 132

Montaigne, 126
Montesquieu, 29f., 45, 77
Montherlant, Henri de, 181
Montuclard, Abbé, 146f.
Morazé, Charles, 25
More, Sir Thomas, 27n.
Morgenthau, Jr., Hans, 65n., 136, 140n., 208n., 274f., 322
Morin, Edgar, 83, 98f.
Morton, Frederick, 292
Mosca, Gaetano, 317
Mounier, Emmanuel, 302, 313
Moussa, Pierre, 237
Mumford, Lewis, 345
Münzer, Thomas, 63n., 319
Mussolini, Benito, 180, 185f., 188f., 194, 197f.
Myrdal, Gunnar, 229
Mysticism and Logic, 153n.

Napoleon, 55, 316n.
Napoleon III, 178n.
National Socialism, 186, 190, 193, 195, 198, 206
Nations prolétaires, Les, 237
Naville, Pierre, 95
Nechaev, 166f.
Nef, John U., 53n.
Nenni, Pietro, 141, 235
neoconservatism, 8
Newton, Sir Isaac, 26, 29, 31, 110
Niebuhr, Reinhold, 323f., 328, 333, 336, 342, 344, 346
Niemeyer, Gerhart, 325
Nietzsche, Friedrich, 68, 82, 163ff., 168f., 171f., 174, 181, 306n.
Nietzsche, Philosopher, Psychologist, Antichrist, 306n.
nihilism (aesthetic, moral, philosophical), 71, 153, 156, 263
Notes from the Underground, 168
Nouveau Christianisme, Le, 241

Oakeshott, Michael, 186
O'Dea, Thomas, 268
On Power, 248n.
Origin of the Family, Private Property and the State, The, 87
Origin of Russian Communism, The, 106n.
Origins of Totalitarianism, The, 190n.
Ortega y Gasset, José, 295, 315
Orthodoxy, 348n.
Orwell, George, 315
Owen, Robert, 47n., 49, 62, 69

Pacaut, Marcel, 12n.
Packard, Vance, 286
Parabole, 49n.
Parkes, Henry B., 265, 275
Parmenides, 161
Pascal, Blaise, 105, 347
Pasternak, Boris, 96
Paul, St., 37
Pavolini, Alessandro, 189
Percy, Lord of Newcastle, 41f., 95
Périer, Casimir, 70
Perrin, J. M., 313
Perroux, François, 111ff., 202, 232, 238
Peyre, Henri, 309
Phenomenon of Man, The, 123, 153n.
Philip, André, 121n., 234, 304n.
philosophes, 25, 29f., 33, 35, 44, 46, 62, 162n., 204
Philosophy of History, The, 260
Philosophy of John Dewey, The, 142
physiocrats, 48
Picasso, Pablo, 156
Pieper, Josef, 314
Pius XI, 175
Plato, 7, 22n., 162, 295, 317

Plekhanov, Georgi, 88
Plotinus, 162
Political Concepts of Richard Wagner, The, 164
Pope, John, 31
Popper, Karl, 302f.
positivism, 62
Possessed, The, 166f.
Pour une morale de l'ambiguité, 306n.
Power Elite, The, 266, 285n.
Praz, Mario, 161
Prévert, Jacques, 156
Prince, The, 18n.
Principles of Sociology, 51
progressivism, 70, 117f.
Proudhon, Pierre-Joseph, 42n., 82, 93, 182, 188
Public Philosophy, The, 248n.
Pushkin, Alexander, 114n.

Quesnay, François, 46
Quinet, Edgar, 56

Ramos, Ledesma, 194
Randall, Jr., J. H., 142
Rauschning, Herman, 192f.
Rebatet, Lucien, 170n.
Recollections, 177
Reformation, 13, 19f., 22f., 63f., 158
"Réformisme et les fétiches, Le," 310n.
Reinhardt, Karl, 308
Remarque sur la révolte, 99n.
Rémond, René, 59
Renaissance, pre-, post-, 19ff., 63, 66, 68, 118, 126, 152, 229
Renan, Ernest, 47n., 57, 61n., 123n., 242n.
Rencontres—Nenni, Bevan, Mendès-France, 151, 235n.
Republic, The, 21
Respublica Christiana, 11, 14, 21, 260
Retour de l'URSS, 98
Return to Reason, The, 215n.

revocation of the Edict of Nantes, 32n.
Revolt of the Moderates, The, 286
Ricardo, David, 249
Riesman, David, 284, 286f.
Road to Serfdom, The, 47n.
Robespierre, Maximilien de, 34f., 43, 56, 99, 120, 333
Roehm, Ernest, 198
Rohan, Duc de, 38
Rolland, Romain, 57, 148
Roman de la Rose, 10n.
Romantisme fasciste, Le, 181
Roosevelt, Eleanor, 137
Roosevelt, Franklin Delano, 274n.
Roosevelt, Theodore, 269, 282
Rostow, W. W., 52, 54, 232, 236
Rothstein, Jerome, 127
Rougemont, Denis de, 125, 295, 317
Rousseau, Jean-Jacques, 26, 30ff., 40ff., 50, 56, 58, 62, 64ff., 69, 97, 117, 119, 149, 159, 170f., 182, 201, 333, 335
Rousset, David, 150
Roux, Georges, 185n., 192n.
Royalists, 59
Russell, Bertrand, 68, 137, 153n., 155, 335
Russian Revolution, The, 87n.

Sade, Marquis de, 129
Saint-Just, Louis de, 99
Saint-Simon, Claude-Henri de, 44ff., 57ff., 62, 64, 66, 74, 117, 201, 217, 241ff.
Saint-Simon, Louis de, 176
Sainte-Beuve, Charles-Augustin, 290n.
Salinger, J. D., 265
Salomon, Ernst von, 190, 197
Salvadori, Massimo, 209n.
Samson, Leon, 273n., 281
Sand, George, 56

368

Sartre, Jean-Paul, 8, 100, 102f., 106n., 128, 148, 184n., 307ff.

Schairer, Reinhold, 190

Schiller, Friedrich von, 59

Schilpp, P. A., 142

Schleicher, General Kurt von, 198

Schneider, Herbert, 261

Scholasticism and Politics, 126n., 348n.

School and Society, The, 270n.

Schopenhauer, Arthur, 131, 136

Schumpeter, Josef, 249

Schweitzer, Albert, 137

Scott, Sir Walter, 59

Second Sex, The, 128

Seidenberg, R., 218, 222

Semaine sainte, La, 156n.

Sérant, Paul, 181, 189n., 196

Serge, Victor, 110n.

Servan - Schreiber, Jean - Jacques, 151

Servile State, The, 228n.

Shaw, George Bernard, 249

Shestov, Leo, 98, 174, 312, 323

Sieyès, Abbé, 35f.

Silone, Ignazio, 101, 156, 247

Simmel, Georg, 53

Simmons, Ernest, 167f.

Simon, Pierre-Henri, 309

Simon, Yves, 125

Simon de Bisignano, 13f.

Sinclair, Upton, 265

Sketch for a Historical Picture of the Progress of the Human Mind, 32n., 34

Skinner, B. F., 212

Smith, Adam, 249

Social and Political Doctrines of Contemporary Europe, 186

Social Thought in America: The Revolt Against Formalism, 270n.

Socialism: Utopian and Scientific, 63n., 84

Socialisme trahi, Le, 121n.

socialist realism, 113f.

Socrates, 347

Soirées de Saint-Petersbourg, Les, 33n.

Somme et le reste, La, 89

Sorel, Georges, 69, 187, 196, 309

Spartakists, 194

Spencer, Herbert, 50f., 67

Spender, Stephen, 156

Spengler, Oswald, 4, 173

Spinoza, Baruch, 312f.

Spirit of History, 62

Stalin, Joseph, 83, 92, 95n., 105n., 113, 129, 144, 147, 203

Stalin-Hitler Pact, 88

Starobinski, Jean, 29, 45

States-General, 35

Stein, Frau von, 220

Stein, Gertrude, 282

Steinbeck, John, 265

Stirner, Max, 83

stoicism, 5

Strachey, John, 51, 119f.

Strasser, Gregor, 191n.

Strasser, Otto, 191n.

Strauss, Leo, 317, 327

Sumner, W. G., 67

surrealism, 156

Swift, Jonathan, 31

Synge, John Millington, 156

Tableau philosophique successif de l'esprit humain, 46

Talmon, J. L., 33f.

Tati, Jacques, 253f.

Tchaadayev, Peter, 114n.

Tchicherin, Gregory, 290

Théocratie, La, 12n.

Thibon, Gustave, 313

Thiers, Adolphe, 290n.

Third International, 194

This Little Band of Prophets: The British Fabians, 120n.

Thomas Aquinas, 8, 37, 211, 348

Thoreau, Henry David, 265

Thorez, Maurice, 156n.

Tillich, Paul, 145f., 243, 284

Tito (Josip Broz), 108

Togliatti, Palmiro, 202

Toledano, Ralph de, 247n., 281

Tolstoi, Leo, 160n.

Toqueville, Alexis de, 61n., 69f., 72, 162, 177, 242, 290, 347

totalitarian democracy, 15, 34

Toward the Critique of Hegel's Philosophy of Right, 90

Toynbee, Arnold, 4, 173, 315, 317

Transformations of Man, The, 345

Trilling, Lionel, 154

Tristes tropiques, 327n.

Trotsky, Leon, 87n., 103, 108, 110n., 141, 143, 155f., 185, 290

Turgenev, Ivan, 185

Turgot, Jacques, 25, 28, 36, 46

Twain, Mark, 265

unanimity, 33f., 41f., 56f., 85n., 118, 332

Union of Soviet Writers, 113

United Nations, 133, 136

Unscientific Postscript, 312

Up from Liberalism, 179n.

utilitarianism, 59, 62

Utopia, 20, 36, 43, 62, 69, 75, 87n., 97, 109, 111, 134ff., 151, 156, 159, 172, 182, 203, 211, 260f., 265, 271, 273, 275, 281ff., 289, 320, 327, 334, 336f., 339, 344f., 349

Utopia, 27n.

Valéry, Paul, 68, 173

Vercors, 103

Veblen, Thorstein, 233, 269f.

Vialatoux, Joseph, 172n.

Vico, Giambattista, 173

Vienna Circle, 342n.

Viereck, Peter, 7

Vigny, Alfred de, 59

Vindiciae contra tyrannos, 23

Vishinsky, Andrei, 66n.

Voegelin, Eric, 105, 324

Voltaire, 25f., 28f., 31, 38, 46

Wagner, Richard, 164f.

Waugh, Evelyn, 181

Webb, Sidney and Beatrice, 120n.

Weber, Max, 233, 327

Weil, Eric, 147

Weil, Simone, 250, 303, 313

Weir, John, 219

West, Nathanael, 265

What is to be done?, 85n., 234

White, Morton, 142, 270n.

Whitehead, Alfred North, 68, 270

Whitman, Walt, 282

Whyte, William H., 284

Wild, John, 215n.

William of Occam, 9, 13, 15, 17

William III, 32n.

Wilson, A. M., 28, 126

Wilson, Charles, 247

Wilson, Woodrow, 282

Wolfe, Bertram, 79n.

worker-priests, 147

Worker-State, Thermidor and Bonapartism, 108

Wycliffe, John, 9

Yoffe, A. I., 110n.

Yugow, A., 144

Zinoviev, Grigori, 110n.

Zola, Emile, 170n.

Zorza, Victor, 112

Zorin, 110

THOMAS MOLNAR

Thomas Molnar was born in Budapest on June 26, 1921. He took degrees in French literature and philosophy at the University of Brussels and a doctorate at Columbia University and is now Professor of French and World Literature at Brooklyn College. Mr. Molnar is the author of two other books, *Bernanos: His Political Thought and Prophecy* and *The Future of Education,* and of numerous articles in American, French, Belgian, and German journals.

MERIDIAN BOOKS

published by The World Publishing Company
2231 West 110 Street, Cleveland 2, Ohio

M1	ABINGER HARVEST *by E. M. Forster*
M3	ROUSSEAU AND ROMANTICISM *by Irving Babbitt*
M4	IMPERIALISM AND SOCIAL CLASSES *by Joseph Schumpeter*
M5	WAYWARD YOUTH *by August Aichhorn*
M6	THE PLAYWRIGHT AS THINKER *by Eric Bentley*
M7	THE PHILOSOPHY OF MODERN ART *by Herbert Read*
M8	CREATIVE INTUITION IN ART AND POETRY *by Jacques Maritain*
M9	OUTLINES OF THE HISTORY OF GREEK PHILOSOPHY *by Eduard Zeller*
M10	LANGUAGE AND THOUGHT OF THE CHILD *by Jean Piaget*
M11	SEVEN TYPES OF AMBIGUITY *by William Empson*
M12	ESSAYS ON FREEDOM AND POWER *by Lord Acton*
M13	THE MAN OF LETTERS IN THE MODERN WORLD *by Allen Tate*
M14	THE ORDEAL OF MARK TWAIN *by Van Wyck Brooks*
M15	SEX AND REPRESSION IN SAVAGE SOCIETY *by Branslaw Malinowski*
M16	PRAGMATISM *by William James*
M17	HISTORY AS THE STORY OF LIBERTY *by Benedetto Croce*
M18	NEW DIRECTIONS 15: INTERNATIONAL ISSUE
M19	MATTHEW ARNOLD *by Lionel Trilling*
M20	SHAKESPEAREAN TRAGEDY *by A. C. Bradley*
M21	THE DEVIL'S SHARE *by Denis de Rougemont*
M22	THE HERO WITH A THOUSAND FACES *by Joseph Campbell*
M23	BYZANTINE CIVILIZATION *by Steven Runciman*
M24	ESSAYS AND SKETCHES IN BIOGRAPHY *by John Maynard Keynes*
M25	NIETZSCHE *by Walter Kaufmann*
M26	THE MIND AND HEART OF LOVE *by M. C. D'Arcy*
M27	CONGRESSIONAL GOVERNMENT *by Woodrow Wilson*
M28	TWO ESSAYS ON ANALYTICAL PSYCHOLOGY *by C. G. Jung*
M29	THE WRITINGS OF MARTIN BUBER *edited by Will Herberg*
M30	BERLIOZ AND HIS CENTURY *by Jacques Barzun*
M31	FREEDOM, EDUCATION, AND THE FUND *by Robert M. Hutchins*
M32	A PREFACE TO LOGIC *by Morris R. Cohen*
M33	VISION AND DESIGN *by Roger Fry*
M34	FREUD OR JUNG? *by Edward Glover*
M35	THE MAKING OF EUROPE *by Christopher Dawson*
M36	THE FORMS OF MUSIC *by Donald Francis Tovey*
M37	THE VARIETIES OF HISTORY *edited by Fritz Stern*
M38	THE ESSENCE OF LAUGHTER *by Charles Baudelaire*
M39	EXISTENTIALISM FROM DOSTOEVSKY TO SARTRE *edited by Walter Kaufmann*
M40	ITALIAN PAINTERS OF THE RENAISSANCE *by Bernard Berenson*
M41	SIGHTS AND SPECTACLES *by Mary McCarthy*
M42	MOHAMMED AND CHARLEMAGNE *by Henri Pirenne*

M43 THE WHEEL OF FIRE *by G. Wilson Knight*

M44 GOTHIC ARCHITECTURE AND SCHOLASTICISM *by Erwin Panofsky*

M45 FREUD AND THE 20TH CENTURY *edited by Benjamin Nelson*

M46 POLITICS AND THE NOVEL *by Irving Howe*

M47 A SHORTER HISTORY OF SCIENCE *by William Cecil Dampier*

M48 A GUIDE TO CONTEMPORARY FRENCH LITERATURE *by Wallace Fowlie*

M49 THE RENAISSANCE OF THE 12TH CENTURY *by C. H. Haskins*

M50 NEW POETS OF ENGLAND AND AMERICA *selected by Hall, Pack, and Simpson*

M51 ST. AUGUSTINE: HIS AGE, LIFE, AND THOUGHT

M52 CIVILIZATION ON TRIAL *and* THE WORLD AND THE WEST *by Arnold Toynbee*

M53 RELIGION AND CULTURE *by Christopher Dawson*

M54 PROUST: A BIOGRAPHY *by André Maurois*

M55 ST. THOMAS AQUINAS *by Jacques Maritain*

M56 MEMOIRS OF A REVOLUTIONIST *by Dwight Macdonald*

M57 DEBATES WITH HISTORIANS *by Pieter Geyl*

M58 POLITICS: WHO GETS WHAT, WHEN, HOW *by Harold Lasswell*

M59 GODS AND HEROES OF THE GREEKS *by H. J. Rose*

M60 RELIGION IN AMERICA *edited by John Cogley*

M61 MEN AND IDEAS *by Johan Huizinga*

M62 WITCHCRAFT *by Charles Williams*

M63 SCENES FROM THE DRAMA OF EUROPEAN LITERATURE *by Erich Auerbach*

M64 THE HUMAN MEANING OF THE SOCIAL SCIENCES *edited by Daniel Lerner*

M65 ARISTOTLE *by W. D. Ross*

M66 THE DISINHERITED MIND *by Erich Heller*

M67 THE BOOK OF JAZZ *by Leonard Feather*

M68 THE WORLD OF ODYSSEUS *by M. I. Finley*

M69 THE SCROLLS FROM THE DEAD SEA *by Edmund Wilson*

M70 GREY EMINENCE *by Aldous Huxley*

M71 THE LOGIC OF THE SCIENCES AND THE HUMANITIES *by F. S. C. Northrop*

M72 HISTORY 1

M73 ON MODERN POETS *by Yvor Winters*

M74 THE MAIN STREAM OF MUSIC AND OTHER ESSAYS *by Donald Francis Tovey*

M75 JONATHAN EDWARDS *by Perry Miller*

M76 THE CONFEDERACY *edited by Albert D. Kirwan*

M77 TALENTS AND GENIUSES *by Gilbert Highet*

M78 APES, ANGELS, AND VICTORIANS *by William Irvine*

M79 PAINTING AND REALITY *by Etienne Gilson*

M80 MOZART'S LIBRETTOS *translated by Robert Pack and Marjorie Lelash*

M81 PHILOSOPHY IN THE MIDDLE AGES *by Paul Vignaux*

M82 THE RECOLLECTIONS OF ALEXIS DE TOCQUEVILLE *edited by J. P. Mayer*

M83 HISTORY 2
M84 ON LOVE *by José Ortega y Gasset*
M85 THE ROMANTIC ENLIGHTENMENT *by Geoffrey Clive*
M86 ANSWER TO JOB *by C. G. Jung*
M87 NEWMAN *by Louis Bouyer*
M88 THE NOBLE SAVAGE 1 *edited by Saul Bellow, Keith Botsford, and Jack Ludwig*
M89 AMERICA AND THE IMAGE OF EUROPE *by Daniel J. Boorstin*
M90 PHILOSOPHY OF SCIENCE *edited by Arthur Danto and Sidney Morgenbesser*
M91 AMERICAN FOREIGN POLICY *edited by Robert A. Divine*
M92 DIONYSUS IN PARIS: A GUIDE TO CONTEMPORARY FRENCH THEATER *by Wallace Fowlie*
M93 THE KING AND THE CORPSE *by Heinrich Zimmer*
M94 THE BEDBUG AND SELECTED POETRY *by Vladimir Mayakovsky*
M95 HISTORY 3
M96 GOD AND THE WAYS OF KNOWING *by Jean Daniélou*
M97 AN OUTLINE OF PHILOSOPHY *by Bertrand Russell*
M98 SENATOR JOE MC CARTHY *by Richard H. Rovere*
M99 ON ART AND ARTISTS *by Aldous Huxley*
M100 I REMEMBER *by Boris Pasternak*
M101 A HISTORY OF THE UNITED STATES: FROM THE AGE OF EXPLORATION TO 1865 *edited by Hugh T. Lefler*
M102 THE NOBLE SAVAGE 2 *edited by Saul Bellow, Keith Botsford, and Jack Ludwig*
M103 THE IDEAL READER *by Jacques Rivière*
M104 THE PERSIAN LETTERS *by Montesquieu*
M105 THE AMERICAN PRAGMATISTS *edited by Milton R. Konvitz and Gail Kennedy*
M106 JERUSALEM AND ROME: THE WRITINGS OF JOSEPHUS *edited by Nahum N. Glatzer*
M107 LORD WEARY'S CASTLE *and* THE MILLS OF THE KAVANAUGHS *by Robert Lowell*
M108 THE GRASS ROOTS OF ART *by Herbert Read*
M109 LECTURES ON MODERN HISTORY *by Lord Acton*
M110 THE MEANING AND MATTTER OF HISTORY *by M. C. D'Arcy*
M111 THE AUTOBIOGRAPHY OF EDWARD GIBBON *edited by Dero A. Saunders*
M112 AESTHETICS TODAY *edited by Morris Philipson*
M113 THE NOBLE SAVAGE 3 *edited by Saul Bellow and Keith Botsford*
M114 ENCOUNTERS IN HISTORY *by Pieter Geyl*
M115 A HISTORY OF THE UNITED STATES: FROM 1865 TO THE PRESENT *edited by Frank W. Klingberg*
M116 THE NAZIS: A DOCUMENTARY HISTORY *edited by Walther Hofer*
M117 HISTORY 4
M118 THOMAS MANN: THE IRONIC GERMAN *by Erich Heller*
M119 OUTLINES OF CLASSICAL LITERATURE *by H. J. Rose*

M120 GOD AND THE UNCONSCIOUS *by Victor White*

M121 HELLENISTIC CIVILIZATION *by W. W. Tarn*

M122 A GUIDE TO CONTEMPORARY ITALIAN LITERATURE *by Sergio Pacifici*

M123 THE SUPREME COURT OF THE UNITED STATES *by Paul A. Freund*

M124 THE RENAISSANCE *by Walter Pater*

M125 THE NOBLE SAVAGE 4 *edited by Saul Bellow and Keith Botsford*

M126 THE MERIDIAN COMPACT ATLAS OF THE WORLD

M127 AMERICA IN THE WORLD *edited by Oscar Theodore Barck, Jr.*

M128 THE DECLINE OF THE INTELLECTUAL *by Thomas Molnar*

M129 YEARS OF CONSCIENCE: THE MUCKRAKERS *edited by Harvey Swados*

M130 ESSAYS ON FAITH AND MORALS *by William James*

M131 STEPHEN CRANE *by John Berryman*

M132 THE ROMANTICS *edited by Geoffrey Grigson*

M133 ANARCHISM: A HISTORY OF LIBERTARIAN IDEAS AND MOVEMENTS *by George Woodcock*

M134 HEREDITARY GENIUS *by Francis Galton*

M135 NEW POETS OF ENGLAND AND AMERICA: SECOND SELECTION *edited by Donald Hall and Robert Pack*

M136 THE NOBLE SAVAGE 5 *edited by Saul Bellow and Keith Botsford*

M137 IN PRAISE OF ENLIGHTENMENT *by Albert Salomon*

M138 THE DEATH OF SOCRATES *by Romano Guardini*

484

THE DECLINE OF THE INTELLECTUAL
Thomas Molnar

". . . one of the most important works of ideas of the past years. The author's knowledge of French and European thought from Montaigne and even before, to Sartre is astounding . . . I admired without reservation the penetrating nature of his insights."

Henri Peyre

"I find this book so absorbing, and I am impressed with the author's erudition, intelligence and lucid style, that I am moved to express my admiration."

Eugene Lyons

"The author's intransigently personalist Catholic-European scale of values and cultural background are responsible for this book's fascination . . . The author's classical and medieval learning and his prodigious reading in modern Western literature, philosophy, and political theory give richness and depth to his writing."

Alger Hiss, *The Village Voice*

". . . Thomas Molnar's book is not only true; it is intellectually exciting and it will remain a necessary handbook for anyone interested in the decisive problem of the 20th century."

Frank S. Meyer, *Modern Age*

"I submit my opinion that serious-minded readers and students of the social sciences will be amply rewarded by a careful study of this supremely well-organized and well-written book by one who proves himself to be a thinker of deep wisdom and authority."

Clark Kinnaird, *Parade of Books*

"In a saner age Thomas Molnar's *The Decline of the Intellectual* would become a political classic overnight . . . The truly breathtaking aspect of Molnar's book is the sharp observation of the way the three kinds of ideologues, the Marxist, the Progressive, and the Reactionary are at work around us."

Garry Wills, *National Review*

Meridian Books are published by
The World Publishing Company • Cleveland and New York

Date Due